Voices from the Italian Renaissance

The Italian Renaissance was a period of intense cultural transformations when the ancient world was being rediscovered and a New World had been literally discovered. Between the thirteenth and the seventeenth centuries, traditional beliefs were being challenged as people across the Italian Peninsula explored new ways of thinking about religion, politics, and society and introduced startling innovations in the arts.

This book contains more than a hundred selections of primary sources—the historian's raw material in the form of memoirs, letters, treatises, sermons, stories, poems, drawings, paintings, and sculpture. Here are eyewitness accounts of cold-blooded murders, lavish court pageants, the Sack of Rome, and the Black Death; first views of Michelangelo's Sistine frescoes and glimpses of the surface of the Moon through Galileo's telescope. These sources bring the reader into direct contact with the creators of the great Renaissance works of art, literature, philosophy, and science, as well as lesser-known people, who in their own words express emotions of love, loss, and spiritual yearning.

Selected to accompany and supplement *A Short History of Renaissance Italy*, the primary sources in this book make it an ideal course reader for students of history or art history. Yet this volume can be read just as well on its own; each selection is clearly introduced, annotated, and provided with references for further reading. These sources reach out to an audience beyond the classroom—the general reader or the traveler to Italy—anyone curious to learn more about the Italian Renaissance will find themselves swept into conversation with these vibrant voices from the past.

Lisa Kaborycha holds a Ph.D. in medieval and early modern European history from the University of California, Berkeley and has been the recipient of a Fulbright Fellowship, a National Endowment for the Humanities Fellowship with the Medici Archive Project, and Harvard's Villa I Tatti Fellowship in Italian Renaissance Studies. In addition to *A Short History of Renaissance Italy* (2023), she is the author of *A Corresponding Renaissance: Letters Written by Italian Women, 1375–1650* (2016). For years, Kaborycha taught courses in Renaissance history for the University of California and currently works as adjunct professor at the University of New Haven Tuscany Campus and lecturer at the British Institute of Florence.

Voices from the Italian Renaissance

A Sourcebook

Lisa Kaborycha

Routledge
Taylor & Francis Group
LONDON AND NEW YORK

Designed cover credit: Andrea del Sarto, Portrait of a Young Man, c.1517–18, National Gallery, London

First published 2024
by Routledge
4 Park Square, Milton Park, Abingdon, Oxon OX14 4RN

and by Routledge
605 Third Avenue, New York, NY 10158

Routledge is an imprint of the Taylor & Francis Group, an informa business

British Library Cataloguing-in-Publication Data
A catalogue record for this book is available from the British Library

ISBN: 978-1-032-25627-6 (hbk)
ISBN: 978-1-032-25630-6 (pbk)
ISBN: 978-1-003-28428-4 (ebk)

DOI: 10.4324/9781003284284

Typeset in Sabon
by Apex CoVantage, LLC

Contents

Figures

Preface

The young man sitting and reading his book has just become aware that someone has entered the room behind him. He swivels his head over his shoulder to see who has interrupted him, and he catches our eye. We do not know who this young man in Andrea del Sarto's striking portrait is, what his profession might be, or what his intense gaze is attempting to convey. And yet he seems poised to speak to us.

This book in your hands is a collection of primary sources from the Italian Renaissance that "speak" to us. Here you will find selections of stories, poems, letters, memos, historical accounts, tax records, travel guides, biographies, diaries, sermons, plays, government statutes, as well as treatises on art, science, philosophy, love, politics, and etiquette, many in dialogue form. There are also primary sources in the form of sculpture, architecture, drawings, and paintings, like the one by Andrea del Sarto on the cover. What all of these have in common is that they were created by men and women who lived in Italy between 1200 and 1650. Whether written in Italian or Latin, painted in tempera or oils, created by an individual, a community, a single artist, or a workshop, these sources reveal to us the realities of those people's lives. They give voice to their passions, concerns, and their understanding of the world they inhabited.

There's that word—it's in the title of this book—why "voices"? Arguably, if there's something we definitely lack from the Renaissance, it's the actual voices. Human history, prior to the advent of sound recording in the mid-nineteenth century, has been passed down in silence. Nevertheless, in a sense, primary sources do "speak" to us, and it can be electrifying when across time we feel them connect with us simply and directly. However, the process of making them speak is neither simple nor direct. Such documentary evidence, the raw material of the historian, is rarely transparent. To access their content there is a need for the mediation of an expert who takes the full historical context into consideration. When you read a historical work written today, you are reading a secondary source, that is, you are reading a historian's interpretation of the past.

Someone will have located the work, often in an archive or other repository of documents, handwritten in an old script that needs to be deciphered.

If written in a foreign language, the document will have to be translated, and the language will be an archaic version, unlike the one used today. Then, along with study of other primary sources and a vast array of scholarly secondary sources accumulated over decades or centuries, the historian takes the document and attempts to fit the piece into the larger puzzle of a long-ago world, to tell its story. When you read that history, the voice speaking from those pages will be authoritative, hopefully it is engaging and vibrant, but it is always the voice of the modern historian.

In this volume, I have provided readers with the primary sources to interpret for themselves. I have tried to present these sources in a form as close as possible to the original centuries-old documents. The English translations I have chosen are a mix of recent ones—many are my own—as well as much older ones. Some of these translations are old enough to be considered primary sources in their own right, such as an Elizabethan translation of Contarini's treatise on government (**#57**), which shows how closely English contemporaries observed the Venetians. In the case of these older translations, I have sometimes had to make slight adjustments to language and spelling to make them more readable. For translations of Italian verse—aside from a weak attempt to catch the flavor of rough sixteenth-century doggerel (**#20**)—in the interests of clarity I have generally opted for free verse or prose.

Each primary source, or cluster of sources, is introduced by an explanation of the context. Some of these introductions are lengthy, others are briefer, especially when the material is covered more fully in my textbook, *A Short History of Renaissance Italy* (Taylor & Francis, 2nd edition, 2023). I designed this sourcebook as its companion; whenever a broader historical context is needed, it can be useful to consult the textbook. By thumbing through the textbook's index, it is easy to locate information about historical people, places, events, and works of art mentioned here. I also provide supplementary material on my website: www.lisakaborycha.com. That said, *Voices from the Italian Renaissance* can be read on its own, without reference to outside material. To that end, I have included footnotes where necessary to clarify a passage, and there are references at the end of each section that can guide the reader toward further reading.

The primary sources here are grouped loosely within eight thematic parts. However, individual selections do not always fit neatly within a particular group; there is plenty of overlap. To give just two examples: Catherine of Siena's letter to the pope (**#27**) is in Part III on the interrelation of sacred and secular, but it could just as well be included in Part VI on politics; Lorenzo Valla's critique of the *Donation of Constantine* (**#13**) is in Part II on humanism, but could easily fit just as well in Part III or in Part VI. I invite the reader to cross over these somewhat arbitrary boundaries and draw their own connections between the various sources.

Ideally, this collection will achieve a kaleidoscopic effect: although the individual sources at times produce fragmentary insights, when combined, the many sources hopefully evoke the complex cultural, political, and spiritual forces at work in Renaissance Italy. Returning to the metaphor suggested by the title of this volume, all the voices included here do not sing in unison; some are in direct counterpoint, others are not even harmonious, but entirely discordant. And sometimes, when least expected, two will sing together, across centuries—St. Francis of Assisi (#1) and freethinker Giordano Bruno (#10) both invoke the splendor of the Sun in similar terms; two contemporaries—Girolamo Savonarola (#54) and Niccolò Machiavelli (#19), men with radically different worldviews—express themselves in strikingly similar terms. And how does Vasari's story of Leonardo da Vinci's dragon (#7) connect with the naturalist Ulisse Aldrovandi's (#79) similarly fabricated creature?

I could go on and on listing the many correspondences and contradictions between these primary sources, but I leave it for readers to discover these on their own, and each will draw their own conclusions. For it must also be said that there is rarely a single, definitive answer to a question about the past. Look closely at the portrait by Andrea del Sarto, the book in the young man's hands, as well as the hands themselves. Are they unfinished, or perhaps blurred by an inept restorer? There is so much that is unresolved and left open to interpretation in the study of history. Like that blurry book, the effect can be unsettling and profoundly unsatisfying for anyone who seeks certainties about the past. But when you do connect with a person from the past and manage to hear their voice even fleetingly, the study of history can be not only rewarding but also exhilarating.

Part I

The natural world

Figure 1.1 Leonardo da Vinci/Andrea del Verrocchio, *Lilium candidum*, Royal Collection, Windsor.

1 Expressing reverence for all of creation

Francis of Assisi, *Canticle of the Creatures*, 1225

Thomas of Celano, *The First Life of St. Francis*, 1228

The son of a wealthy cloth merchant, the child born in the Umbrian town of Assisi was baptized by the name of Giovanni while his father was away on business in France. On his return, Pietro called the boy Francesco, or "Frenchy" after the country that played such a large part in the family's fortune. It stuck, and Francis of Assisi (Francesco di Pietro di Bernardone, *c.*1181–1226) would give his name to one of the most influential Christian movements in history, the Franciscan order. Though he eventually rejected his father's mercantile way of life, the French culture with which Francis had been raised—especially Provençal troubadour lyric verse—stayed with him. After his mystical conversion, he often spoke or sang in French, sometimes dancing as he preached, and his companions were sometimes called *ioculatores domini*, (minstrels of the Lord). Francis attracted numerous followers among the laypeople of his day through the direct, poetic language he used to express himself and the simplicity of his spiritual message, which was inspired as much by the natural world as by the example of Christ and the apostles. Like Jesus in the *Sermon on the Mount*, who admonished his followers to "behold the fowls of the air" and to "consider the lilies of the field," trusting that the Lord would provide for them as he did for his other creatures, Francis and the members of the Order of Friars Minor that he founded rejected worldly possessions and embraced religious poverty. Already during his lifetime Francis was revered, considered an *alter christus* (another Christ) by some, and he was canonized less than two years after his death. Weakened after years of fasting and other physical hardships, he wrote the *Canticle of the Creatures* while suffering his final, excruciating illness,[1] though one would never know from the freshness, lyricism, and pure joy radiating from these verses. Francis wrote this poem in his native Umbrian dialect, in everyday vernacular, rather than high church Latin, and it is often considered the first masterpiece of Italian literature. One of the followers of Francis, Thomas of Celano (d.1260), the saint's earliest biographer, wrote his first *Life of St.*

DOI: 10.4324/9781003284284-2

Francis at the request of the pope two years after Francis died. Thomas's account, in which he describes Francis's attitudes toward the natural world, beautifully echoes the sentiments expressed in the *Canticle of the Creatures*.

Francis of Assisi, *Canticle of the Creatures*, 1225

Most High, all-powerful, good Lord,
Yours are the praises, the glory, and the honor, and all blessing.

To You alone, Most High, do they belong,
and no human is worthy to mention Your name.

Praised be You, my Lord, with all Your creatures,
especially Sir Brother Sun,
Who is the day and through whom You give us light.

And he is beautiful and radiant with great splendor;
and bears a likeness of You, Most High One.

Praised be You, my Lord, through Sister Moon and the stars,
in heaven You formed them clear and precious and beautiful.

Praised be You, my Lord, through Brother Wind,
and through the air, cloudy and serene, and every kind of weather,
through whom You give sustenance to Your creatures.

Praised be You, my Lord, through Sister Water,
who is very useful and humble and precious and chaste.

Praised be You, my Lord, through Brother Fire,
through whom You light the night,
and he is beautiful and playful and robust and strong.

Praised be You, my Lord, through our Sister Mother Earth,
who sustains and governs us,
and who produces various fruit with colored flowers and herbs.

Praised be You, my Lord, through those who give pardon for Your love, and bear infirmity and tribulation.

Blessed are those who endure in peace
for by You, Most High, shall they be crowned.

Praised be You, my Lord, through our Sister Bodily Death,
from whom no one living can escape.

Woe to those who die in mortal sin.
Blessed are those whom death will find in Your most holy will,
for the second death shall do them no harm.

Praise and bless my Lord and give Him thanks
and serve Him with great humility.

Thomas of Celano, *First Life of St. Francis*, 1228

Chapter XXI preaching to the birds and the obedience of the creatures

While many were joining the brothers, as already related, the blessed father Francis was travelling through the Spoleto valley. He reached a place near Bevagna, in which a great multitude of birds of different types gathered, including doves, crows, and others commonly called *monaclae*.[2] When Francis, the most blessed servant of God, saw them, he ran swiftly toward them, leaving his companions on the road. He was a man of great fervor, feeling much sweetness and tenderness even toward lesser, irrational creatures. When he was already very close, seeing that they awaited him, he greeted them in his usual way.[3] He was quite surprised, however, because the birds did not take flight, as they usually do. Filled with great joy, he humbly requested that they listen to the word of God.

Among many other things, he said to them: "My brother birds, you should greatly praise your Creator, and love Him always. He gave you feathers to wear, wings to fly, and whatever you need. God made you noble among His creatures and gave you a home in the purity of the air, so that, though you neither *sow nor reap*, [Luke 12:24] He nevertheless protects and governs you without your least care." He himself, and those brothers who were with him, used to say that, at these words, the birds rejoiced in a wonderful way according to their nature. They stretched their necks, spread their wings, opened their beaks and looked at him. He *passed through their midst*, [Luke 4:30] coming and going, touching their heads and bodies with his tunic. Then he blessed them, and having made the sign of the cross, gave them permission to fly off to another place. The blessed father, however, went with his companions along their way rejoicing and giving thanks to God, Whom all creatures revere by their devout confession.

He was already simple by grace, not by nature. After the birds had listened so reverently to the word of God, he began to accuse himself of negligence because he had not preached to them before. From that day on, he carefully exhorted all birds, all animals, all reptiles, and also insensible creatures, to praise and love the Creator, because daily, invoking the name of the Savior, he observed their obedience in his own experience.

Chapter XXIX the love that he had toward all creatures for the sake of the creator

To enumerate and recount all the things our glorious father Francis did and taught while living in the flesh would be a lengthy or an even impossible task. Who could ever express the deep affection he bore for all things that belong to God? Or who would be able to tell of the sweet tenderness he enjoyed while contemplating in creatures the wisdom, power, and goodness of the Creator? From this reflection he often overflowed with amazing, unspeakable joy as he looked at the Sun, gazed at the Moon, or observed the stars in the sky. What simple piety! What pious simplicity! Even for worms he had a warm love, since he had read this text about the Savior: "I am a worm and not a man." [Ps 22:7] That is why he used to pick them up from the road and put them in a safe place so that they would not be crushed by the footsteps of passersby.

What shall I say about the other lesser creatures? In the winter he had honey or the best wine put out for the bees so that they would not perish from the cold. He used to extol the artistry of their work and their remarkable ingenuity, giving glory to the Lord. With such an outpouring, he often used up an entire day or more in praise of them and other creatures.

Notes

1 The circumstances surrounding the composition of this work are recorded in the so-called "Assisi Compilation" in *Francis of Assisi: Early Documents*, Vol. 2, 120–1; 184–8.
2 Jackdaws.
3 With the phrase "The Lord give you peace."

Sources

Francis of Assisi, *Canticle of the Creatures*, in *Francis of Assisi: Early Documents*, ed. Regis J. Armstrong, J.A. Wayne Hellmann and William J. Short. New City Press, 1999–2001, Vol. 1, pp. 113–14.

Thomas of Celano, *First Life of St. Francis*, in *Francis of Assisi: Early Documents*, ed. Regis J. Armstrong, J.A. Wayne Hellmann and William J. Short. New City Press, 1999–2001, Vol. 1, pp. 234; 250.

References

Moloney, Brian. *Francis of Assisi and His "Canticle of Brother Sun" Reassessed*, Palgrave Macmillan, 2013.

Robson, Michael J.P. ed. *The Cambridge Companion to Francis of Assisi*, Cambridge UP, 2012.

Thomas of Celano. *St. Francis of Assisi: First and Second Life of St. Francis with Selections from Treatise on the Miracles of Blessed Francis*, trans. Placid Hermann, Franciscan Herald Press, 1988.

Thompson, Augustine. *Francis of Assisi: A New Biography*, Cornell UP, 2012.

2 Giotto and the birth of "modern" art

Dante Alighieri, *Purgatory* XI, *c.*1314

Giovanni Boccaccio, *Decameron* VI, *c.*1350

Cennino Cennini, *Craftsman's Handbook*, *c.*1398

Filippo Villani, *On Florence and Her Famous Citizens*, *c.*1400

Lorenzo Ghiberti, *Commentaries*, *c.*1542

Giorgio Vasari, *Lives of the Artists*, 1568

Figure 1.2 Carmine Madonna Master, *Madonna del Popolo*, *c.*1260, Brancacci Chapel, Santa Maria del Carmine, Florence.

Figure 1.3 Giotto di Bondone, *Ognissanti Madonna* (*Maestà*), *c.*1310, Uffizi

Giotto di Bondone (1267–1337) was a celebrity in his own lifetime. He painted for the papal court, the king of Naples, as well as for the wealthiest, most powerful men in Florence, Assisi, Padua, and Milan. Giotto's contemporary, Dante commented on the painter's fame, as did generations of Renaissance Italians after him. All of them marvelled at how Giotto entirely changed the course of art and they remarked on the extraordinary "modern" innovations

DOI: 10.4324/9781003284284-3

he introduced. When, by the mid-sixteenth century, Giorgio Vasari came to write his influential *Lives of the Artists*, Giotto's place as founder of the new style of painting was well-established. But what was this new or "modern" style that Vasari and the others refer to? A key component was the artist's ability to faithfully reproduce the natural world. This included imparting a sense of cubic space, volume, and spatial depth to his compositions. A century before Brunelleschi's discovery of the mathematical rules for representing linear perspective, Giotto achieved an effect of spatial realism that, though imprecise, was revolutionary. Moreover, his use of light and dark shadowing and soft modeling of human forms contrasted with the older Greek style. The so-called "Byzantine" school of painting represented Christ, the Virgin Mary, and saints in an elegant, stylized, and static manner, iconic images to be adored and worshipped from afar. Even when Giotto represents Mary with the Christ Child seated on a throne like royalty as they were often represented, in his *Maestà* (in English "majesty"), he brings these holy figures down to Earth and imbues them with expressive gestures and human warmth. Painted sometime between 1305 and 1310, the painting (Figure 1.3) is also known as the *Ognissanti Madonna* because it was originally in the Florentine Church of Ognissanti, painted for the Order of the Humiliati, the "humble ones." Like the Franciscan and Dominicans, the Humiliati arose in the thirteenth century, with an emphasis on humility, charity, prayer, and manual labor, thus members of the order, both clerical and laypeople, worked in the wool industry. By the early fourteenth century, the Humiliati had become extremely wealthy and commissioned this enormous painting and other devotional panels from the leading artist of the time, who commanded very high fees. The "humble" origins of the order are represented by the "spiritual corporeality," of Giotto's figures, in the way "the partially transparent tunic of the Madonna reveals the contours of her breasts. The Christ Child's blessing hand also draws attention to the Madonna's breasts, while her hand on his groin [is] a pointed reference to his human nature." Moreover, the Madonna's full nursing breasts reflect the Humiliati's emphasis on charity.[1] In stark contrast to Giotto's work is another panel representing the theme of Madonna and Child: the *Madonna del Popolo* (Figure 1.2) by an anonymous Florentine artist who painted in the older style, around 1260. An object of popular devotion, it was considered a miracle-working image; the powers attributed to it ranged from helping women who had difficulty conceiving children to bringing military victory to Florence.[2]

Dante Alighieri, *Purgatory XI, 94–96, c.*1314

In painting Cimabue was thought
to hold the field, now Giotto is all the rage
and the other's fame is dimmed.

Giovanni Boccaccio, ***Decameron VI, c.*****1349–51**

Giotto had so excellent a genius that there was nothing of all which Nature, mother and mover of all things, presents to us by the ceaseless revolution of the heavens, but he with pencil and pen and brush depicted it and that so closely that not like, nay, but rather the thing itself it seemed, insomuch that men's visual sense is found to have been oftentimes deceived in things fashioned by him, taking that for real which was but depicted. Wherefore, he having brought back to the light this art, which had for many an age lain buried under the errors of certain folk who painted more to divert the eyes of the ignorant than to please the understanding of the judicious, he may deservedly be styled one of the chief glories of Florence.

Cennino Cennini, ***The Craftsman's Handbook, c.*****1398**

This Giotto changed the art of painting from the Greek to the Latin (manner), and brought it to the modern (style); and he possessed more perfect art than anyone else ever had.

Filippo Villani, ***On Florence and Her Famous Citizens, c.*****1400**

Giotto . . . restored painting to its pristine dignity and high reputation. For pictures formed by his brush follow nature's outlines so closely that they seem to the observer to live and breathe.

Lorenzo Ghiberti, ***Commentaries, c.*****1452**

He introduced the new art [of painting]. He abandoned the crudeness of the Greeks and rose to be the most excellent [painter] in Etruria. . . . Giotto saw in art what others had not attained. He brought the natural art and refinement with it, not departing from the proportions.

Giorgio Vasari, *Lives of the Artists*, 1568

Giotto became such a good imitator of nature that he completely banished that awkward Greek manner and revived the modern and good art of painting.

Notes

1 Miller and Taylor-Mitchell 27.
2 Holmes 88.

Sources

Dante Alighieri, *Purgatory* XI, 94–96, ed. Natalia Sapegno, Nuova Italia, trans. Kaborycha.

Giovanni Boccaccio, *Decameron* VI, cited by Hayden Magginis, *Painting in the Age of Giotto: A Historical Reevaluation*, Penn State UP, 1997, p. 80.

Cennino d'Andrea Cennini, *The Craftsman's Handbook*, ed. Kaborycha, Yale UP, 1933, p. 5., trans. Daniel V. Thompson.

Filippo Villani cited by Samuel Y. Edgerton, Jr. in *The Heritage of Giotto's Geometry: Art and Science on the Eve of the Scientific Revolution*, Cornell UP, 1991.

Lorenzo Ghiberti cited by Elizabeth Gilmore Holt, in *A Documentary History of Art, Vol. I, The Middle Ages and Renaissance*, Doubleday, 1957, p. 154.

Giorgio Vasari cited by Robert Brennan, in *Painting as a Modern Art in Renaissance Italy*, Brepols, 2019, p. 6.

References

Cole, Bruce. "Old in New in the Early Trecento," *Mitteilungen des Kunsthistorischen Institutes in Florenz*, Vol. 17. Bd., H. 2/3 (1973), pp. 229–48.

Derbes, Ann and Mark Sandona, eds. *The Cambridge Companion to Giotto*, Cambridge UP, 2004.

Gardner von Teuffel, Christa. "The Significance of the *Madonna del Popolo* in the Brancacci Chapel: Re-framing Assumptions," in *The Brancacci Chapel: Form, Function and Setting*, Olschki, 2007, pp. 37–51.

Holmes, Megan. *The Miraculous Image in Renaissance Florence*, Yale UP, 2013.

Miller, Julia I. and Laurie Taylor-Mitchell. *From Giotto to Botticelli: The Artistic Patronage of the Humiliati in Florence*, University Park, PA, 2015.

3 A river, a mountain, a young man's soul

Petrarch, *Sonnet* 162, *c.*1336

Petrarch, *Letter on the Ascent of Mt. Ventoux*, 1336

Francesco Petrarca (1304–1374), known as Petrarch, the Latin humanist who would become one of the greatest poets in the Italian language, spent much of his youth in the south of France close to the papal court in Avignon. Drawn to nature, in 1337 he moved to a remote, wooded area in the Vaucluse region near the source of the Sorgue River. The youthful Petrarch was passionately in love with a woman named Laura; after her death in 1348, he gathered the vernacular poem below, along with 365 others into his *Canzoniere* (Songbook), of which she is the focal point. The poet's mind was filled with thoughts of Laura while he wandered in these wild, romantic surroundings; natural imagery abounds in his verses. Towering over the landscape is a high mountain peak, and in his famous *Letter on the Ascent of Mount Ventoux*, Petrarch describes the day he decided to climb it with his brother. Dated April 26, 1336, the letter was written when Petrarch would have been in his early thirties, around the same age as Dante when he undertook the journey to the Inferno "in the middle of life's road." Like Dante, Petrarch was undergoing a spiritual crisis and seeking answers. In elegantly crafted Latin prose, he describes an experience of religious epiphany in which nature plays a central role. The letter is addressed to the Augustinian friar Dionigi da Borgo San Sepolcro (*c.*1300–1342), who taught theology and philosophy in Paris, before coming to Avignon, where the two met around 1333. In this narrative, the author breathlessly describes the day's events as if jotting them down immediately afterward; in reality, Petrarch continued reworking this text until perhaps as late as 1352.

Petrarch, *Sonnet 162, c.*1336

Happy, carefree flowers and well born grasses,
imprinted by my lady, as she walks, thinking,
riverbank that listens to her sweet words
and keeps some trace of her fair foot,

DOI: 10.4324/9781003284284-4

innocent trees and green unripened fronds,
tender, pale little violets,
shady woods where the Sun strikes
with his tall, proud rays,

O gentle countryside, O pure river[1]
that bathe her lovely face and clear eyes
and take your qualities from that living light,

how much I envy you her dear and honored movements!
By now there should not be a single stone
that does not learn to glow with my flame.

Petrarch, *Letter on the Ascent of Mt. Ventoux*, 1336

Today I made the ascent of the highest mountain in this region, which is not improperly called Ventosum.[2] My only motive was the wish to see what so great an elevation had to offer. I have had the expedition in mind for many years; for, as you know, I have lived in this region from infancy, having been cast here by that fate which determines the affairs of men.[3] Consequently the mountain, which is visible from a great distance, was ever before my eyes, and I conceived the plan of some time doing what I have at last accomplished today.

[. . .]

At the time fixed we left the house, and by evening reached Malaucène, which lies at the foot of the mountain, to the north. Having rested there a day, we finally made the ascent this morning, with no companions except two servants; and a most difficult task it was. The mountain is a very steep and almost inaccessible mass of stony soil. But, as the poet has well said, "Remorseless toil conquers all." It was a long day, the air fine. We enjoyed the advantages of vigor of mind and strength and agility of body, and everything else essential to those engaged in such an undertaking and so had no other difficulties to face than those of the region itself. We found an old shepherd in one of the mountain dales, who tried, at great length, to dissuade us from the ascent, saying that some fifty years before he had, in the same ardor of youth, reached the summit, but had gotten for his pains nothing except fatigue and regret, and clothes and body torn by the rocks and briars. No one, so far as he or his companions knew, had ever tried the ascent before or after him. But his counsels increased rather than diminished our desire to proceed, since youth is suspicious of warnings.

[. . .]

One peak of the mountain, the highest of all, the country people call "Sonny," why, I do not know, unless by antiphrasis, as I have sometimes suspected in other instances; for the peak in question would seem to be the father of all the surrounding ones. On its top is a little level place, and here we could at last rest our tired bodies.

Now, my father, since you have followed the thoughts that spurred me on in my ascent, listen to the rest of the story, and devote one hour, I pray you, to reviewing the experiences of my entire day. At first, owing to the unaccustomed quality of the air and the effect of the great sweep of view spread out before me, I stood like one dazed. I beheld the clouds under our feet, and what I had read of Athos and Olympus seemed less incredible as I myself witnessed the same things from a mountain of less fame. I turned my eyes toward Italy, whither my heart most inclined. The Alps, rugged and snow-capped, seemed to rise close by, although they were really at a great distance; the very same Alps through which that fierce enemy of the Roman name once made his way, bursting the rocks, if we may believe the report, by the application of vinegar. I sighed, I must confess, for the skies of Italy, which I beheld rather with my mind than with my eyes. An inexpressible longing came over me to see once more my friend and my country. At the same time, I reproached myself for this double weakness, springing, as it did, from a soul not yet steeled to manly resistance. And yet there were excuses for both of these cravings, and a number of distinguished writers might be summoned to support me.

Then a new idea took possession of me, and I shifted my thoughts to a consideration of time rather than place: "Today it is ten years since, having completed your youthful studies, you left Bologna. Eternal God! In the name of immutable wisdom, think what alterations in your character this intervening period has beheld! I pass over a thousand instances. I am not yet in a safe harbor where I can calmly recall past storms. The time may come when I can review in due order all the experiences of the past, saying with St. Augustine, 'I desire to recall my foul actions and the carnal corruption of my soul, not because I love them, but that I may the more love you, O my God.' Much that is doubtful and evil still clings to me, but what I once loved, that I love no longer. And yet what am I saying? I still love it, but with shame, but with heaviness of heart. Now, at last, I have confessed the truth. So it is. I love, but love what I would not love, what I would that I might hate. Though loath to do so, though constrained, though sad and sorrowing, still I do love, and I feel in my miserable self the truth of the well-known words, 'I will hate if I can; if not, I will love against my will.' Three years have not yet passed since that perverse and wicked passion which had a firm grasp upon me and held undisputed sway in my heart began to discover a rebellious opponent, who was unwilling longer to yield obedience. These two adversaries have joined in close combat for the supremacy, and for a long time now a harassing and doubtful war has been waged in the field of my thoughts."

Thus I turned over the last ten years in my mind, and then, fixing my anxious gaze on the future, I asked myself, "If, perchance, you should prolong this uncertain life of yours for yet two decades, and should make an advance toward virtue proportionate to the distance to which you had departed from your original infatuation during the past two years, since the new longing first encountered the old, could you, on reaching your fortieth year, face death, if not with complete assurance, at least with hopefulness, calmly dismissing from your thoughts the residuum of life as it faded into old age?"

These and similar reflections occurred to me, my father. I rejoiced in my progress, mourned my weaknesses, and commiserated the universal instability of human conduct. I had well-nigh forgotten where I was and our object in coming; but at last I dismissed my anxieties, which were better suited to other surroundings, and resolved to look about me and see what we had come to see. The sinking Sun and the lengthening shadows of the mountain were already warning us that the time was near at hand when we must go. As if suddenly wakened from sleep, I turned about and gazed toward the west. I was unable to discern the summits of the Pyrenees, which form the barrier between France and Spain; not because of any intervening obstacle that I know of but owing simply to the insufficiency of our mortal vision. But I could see with the utmost clearness, off to the right, the mountains of the region about Lyons, and to the left the bay of Marseilles and the waters that lash the shores of Aigues Mortes, although all these places were so distant that it would require a journey of several days to reach them. Under our very eyes flowed the Rhone.

While I was thus dividing my thoughts, now turning my attention to some terrestrial object that lay before me, now raising my soul, as I had done my body, to higher planes, it occurred to me to look into my copy of St. Augustine's *Confessions*, a gift that I owe to your love, and that I always have about me, in memory of both the author and the giver. I opened the compact little volume, small indeed in size, but of infinite charm, with the intention of reading whatever came to hand, for I could happen upon nothing that would be otherwise than edifying and devout. Now it chanced that the tenth book presented itself. My brother, waiting to hear something of St. Augustine's from my lips, stood attentively by. I call him, and God too, to witness that where I first fixed my eyes it was written: "And men go about to wonder at the heights of the mountains, and the mighty waves of the sea, and the wide sweep of rivers, and the circuit of the ocean, and the revolution of the stars, but themselves they consider not." I was abashed, and, asking my brother (who was anxious to hear more), not to annoy me, I closed the book, angry with myself that I should still be admiring earthly things who might long ago have learned from even the pagan philosophers that nothing is wonderful but the soul, which, when great itself, finds nothing great outside itself. Then, in truth, I was satisfied that I had seen enough of the mountain; I turned my inward eye upon myself, and from that time not a syllable fell from my lips until we reached the bottom again.

Notes

1 "Addressed to the landscape of Vaucluse; the river is the Sorgue." Durling 308.
2 "Ventosum" is Latin for Mount Ventoux, which means "windy mountain."
3 Petrarch's father belonged to the same political faction as Dante and was exiled from Florence in 1302 as well.

Sources

Petrarch, *Sonnet 162*, in Francesco Petrarca, *Il Canzoniere*, ed. Giancarlo Contini, Einaudi, 1964, p. 210, trans. Kaborycha.

Petrarch, *Letter on the Ascent of Mt. Ventoux*, in Robinson, James Harvey, ed. and trans. *Petrarch: The First Modern Scholar and Man of Letters*, Putnam, 1898, pp. 308–20, ed. Kaborycha.

References

Celenza, Christopher S. *Petrarch: Everywhere a Wanderer*, Reaktion Books, 2017.

Kirkham, Victoria and Armando Maggi, eds. *Petrarch: A Critical Guide to the Complete Works*, U Chicago P, 2009.

Petrarch. *Lyric Poems: The Rime Sparse and Other Lyrics*, trans. and ed. Robert M. Durling, Harvard UP, 1976.

4 A city manages a natural disaster

Ordinances for Sanitation in a Time of Mortality, *Pistoia City Council*, 1348

Marchionne di Coppo, *Chronicle*, *c.*1381

When the Black Death first struck in 1348, doctors were caught off guard. Moved by the urgency to discover a cure, many rejected the useless advice of traditional medical authorities as well as arcane astrological or theological explanations; instead they sought treatments based on direct observation of the disease. Giovanni della Penna (fl. 1344–87), a lecturer at the medical faculty in Naples, declared that the disease could flourish "because uninformed or stupid doctors say that it comes from God or heaven, whatever is seen before about the natural [or immediate] causes." Gentile da Foligno (fl. 1322–48), one of the most renowned physicians of his day, in his treatise on the plague wrote that if a house were burning or if someone were bitten by a snake you would not waste time discussing the qualities of fire or the physiology of the snake. Similarly, in the case of this disease, "a stand must be made against it to destroy it lest it destroy us."[1] Though not all medical practitioners were in agreement, it is clear from the health ordinances issued by the commune of Pistoia, a small Tuscan city (population about 11,000), that Italian communal governments took a practical approach to managing public hygiene during the pandemic. Although historians have pointed out that communities had developed effective sanitary regulations well before the Black Death,[2] this selection indicates how Pistoia embraced an empirical scientific attitude and adopted the rapid response advised by Gentile da Foligno. As for Gentile himself, he died of the plague in June of 1348. One man who survived the plague was Marchionne di Coppo di Stefano Buonaiuti (1336–1385), from a wealthy Florentine family; orphaned young, he was raised with his stepbrothers. A prosperous small landowner, Marchionne was very active in Florentine politics, held a number of government offices and military appointments; he served as *podestà* of Montecatini and as a Florentine ambassador from 1378 to 1381. He began writing his chronicle probably in the late 1370s, yet his memories of the events of the 1348 Black Death from the time he was barely twelve years old sound as vivid as if they had just occurred.

DOI: 10.4324/9781003284284-5

Ordinances for Sanitation in a Time of Mortality, *Pistoia City Council*, May 2, 1348[3]

In the name of Christ Amen. Herein are written certain ordinances and regulations made and composed by certain wise People,[4] elected and appointed by the Elders and the Standard-bearer of Justice, in order to conserve the health of the human body and to restrain and resist various and diverse pestilences which can otherwise befall the human body. And written by me Simone Buonacorsi, notary, and now notary and scribe of the same wise men deputized through the same Lords Elder and Standard-bearer to this writing in the year from the Nativity of the Lord 1348, first Indiction.[5]

These wise men ordered and ordained,

1. *Item.* So that none of the contaminated matter which presently encroaches on the areas surrounding the city of Pistoia can enter into the bodies of the citizens of Pistoia, no person—whether citizen or inhabitant of Pistoia or its territory, whether dwelling in said city or environs or territory, wherever they may be, of whatever status, condition, or authority—shall presume or dare to go to Pisa or Lucca by any means, or to their environs or territory, or nearby. And no one should or can come from either of them or their environs . . . to said city of Pistoia or its environs or territory, on penalty of 500 pence accounted in gold.[6] . . . And that the gatekeepers of the city of Pistoia guarding the gates of the said city shall not permit those coming or returning to the said city of Pistoia from the said cities of Pisa or Lucca, their environs or territory to enter the said gates on penalty of 10 pence from each of the guards responsible for the gate through which such an entry has been made. It is permitted, however, for citizens now living in Pistoia to go to Pisa and Lucca, their environs and territories if they first obtain permission from the common council—who will vote on the merits of the case presented to them. The license is to be drawn up by the notary of the Elders and Standard-bearer of the city. And this ordinance is to be upheld and observed from the day of its adoption until 1 October, or longer if the council sees fit.
2. *Item.* The said wise men ordered that no person—whether citizen, inhabitant . . . or foreigner—shall dare in any way to bring . . . any used cloth, whether linen or woolen, to the city of Pistoia, its environs or territory, for use as men's or women's clothing or for bedclothes, on penalty of 200 pence. And the cloth is to be burnt in the public piazza of Pistoia by the official who discovered it. Citizens of Pistoia . . . will be allowed to take linen or woollen cloths with them for their own use or wear, provided that they are in a pack or fardle weighing 30 pounds or less. And this rule . . . shall be observed from the day of its adoption

until next January 1. And if any quantity of cloth of said type or quality has been carried into said city, territory or environs, the carrier must remove and export it from the said city within three days of the adoption of the present ordinance—same penalty for each carrier or carriers and for each violation.

3. *Item.* They ordered that the bodies of the dead, after they have died, neither should nor shall be removed from the place in which they are found unless first such a body has been enclosed in a wooden casket covered by a lid secured with nails, so that no stench can issue forth; nor can it be covered by more than one canopy, blanket or drape, under a penalty for 50 pence paid by the heirs of the deceased or, if there are no heirs, by the nearest kinsmen in the male line. The goods of the deceased are to stand as surety for the payment of the penalty. Also, such dead bodies of the dead must be carried to the grave only in said casket; same penalty. And so that the aforesaid shall be noted by the rectors and officials of the city of Pistoia, present and future rectors of the parishes of the city of Pistoia in whose parish there is any dead person must themselves announce the death and the neighborhood in which the dead person lived to the *podestà* and captain or others of the government of said city. They must notify them . . . [of this] or pay said penalty for each violation. And the *podestà* and captain to whom such an announcement or notification has been made, must immediately send one of their officials to the same location to see if the contents of the present article and other statutes concerning funerals are being observed, and punish anyone found guilty with the same penalty. . . . The aforesaid shall neither be extended to nor enforced upon poor persons—those who are declared to be poor according to the statutes of the city.
4. *Item.* In order to avoid the foul stench that the bodies of the dead give off, they have ordered that any ditch in which a dead body is to be buried must be dug under ground to a depth of 2 ½ armlengths by the measure of the city of Pistoia [about 6 feet deep].
5. *Item.* They have ordered that no person—of whatever condition or status or authority—shall dare to return or carry to the city of Pistoia any dead body—in or out of a casket or in any manner—on penalty of 25 pence paid by whoever carries, brings, or orders [a body] to be carried or brought for each occasion. And that the gatekeepers of the city shall not permit such a body to be brought into the city on penalty of the same fine for each gatekeeper at the gate through which the body was brought.
6. *Item.* They have ordered that any person who will have come for the burial or to bury any dead person neither should nor shall be in the presence of the body itself nor with the relatives of such a dead person—except for the procession to the church where it will be buried. Nor shall such persons return to the house where the defunct person lived, nor enter into that house or any other house on said occasion on penalty of 10 pence.

7. *Item.* They have ordered that when anyone has died, no person should dare to present or send any gift before or after burial to the former dwelling place of such a dead person, or any other place on the said occasion, or to attend or to go to a meal in that house or place on said occasion, on penalty of 25 pence. . . . Children, carnal brothers and sisters,[7] nieces and nephews of such a dead person and their children, however, shall be exempted [from this provision].
8. *Item.* They have ordered that, in order to avoid useless expenses, no person should dare to dress in new clothing during the period of mourning for any dead person or during the eight days after that, on penalty of 25 pence for whoever contravenes [this] and for each time. Wives of such dead persons however, shall be exempted; they can be dressed in whatever new clothing they wish without penalty.
9. *Item.* They have ordered that no paid mourner . . . shall dare to mourn publicly or privately or to invite other citizens of Pistoia to go to the funeral or to the dead person; nor may anyone engage said mourner, horn player, crier or drummer.
10. *Item.* So that the sounds of bells might not depress the infirm nor fear arise in them, [the Wise Men] have ordered that the ringers or custodians in charge of the bell tower 12 of the cathedral of Pistoia shall not permit any bell in the said bell tower to be rung for the funeral of the dead nor shall any person dare to ring any of these bells on the said occasion. . . . At the chapel or parish church of the said dead person, or at the friary if the person is to be buried at a church of the friars, they can ring the bell of the chapel, parish church or the church of the friars so long as it is rung only one time and moderately, on the foresaid penalty in the foresaid manner [for each violation].
11. *Item.* They have ordered that no one shall dare to gather, or cause to gather, any persons for the purpose of bringing any widow from the former habitation of a dead person, unless at the time she is being returned from the church or cemetery where such a dead person was buried. [Blood relatives] of such a widow, however, wishing to bring the widow from the house at times other than at the time of burial, may send up to four women to accompany the said woman, who is to be brought from the foresaid house of the dead person. . . .
12. *Item.* They have ordered that no person should dare to raise or cause to be raised any wailing or clamor over any person or because of any person who has died outside the city, environs or territory of Pistoia; nor on the said occasion should any persons be brought together in any place, except blood relatives and associates of such a dead person, nor on the said occasion should any bell be rung or caused to be rung, nor announcements be made through the city of Pistoia by mourners, nor on the said occasion should any invitation [to join the mourners] be made, on a penalty of 25 pence. . . . It must be understood, however, in any written ordinances speaking of the dead

and of honoring the burial of the dead that the aforesaid shall not have force in the burial of the body of any soldiers of the militia, doctors of laws, judges or physicians whose bodies, because of their dignity, may be honored licitly at burial in a manner pleasing to their heirs. . . .

13. So that the bodies of the living will not fall ill from putrid or rotten food, no butcher or meat monger, even in the smallest amounts, should dare in any way to inflate[8] meat, or to keep meat inflated, or to sell, or arrange to have it kept and sold inflated, in his shop or over the counter. Penalty of 10 pence, to be paid by each butcher and meat monger for each offense. And the masters of the butchers' guild are bound, for the time being, to investigate and inquire concerning these things on every day that meat is slaughtered; they are to immediately denounce those found culpable to the lord *podestà* or Captain, or to one of their officials; same penalty, to be paid by the same masters, or by any one of them, if they or any one of the masters does not arrange for all of the aforesaid things to be carried out. And the *podestà* and Captain are each bound, for the time being, to send one of their officials to inspect and investigate and inquire concerning each and every one of the things contained in this article, and they are to fine and punish with same penalty those found guilty and those masters, or any one of them, who does not at once denounce whoever committed these same offenses. And the word or report of any official who finds any transgression against this statute is to stand and be believed, without any other proof being necessary.
14. *Item.* They have ordered that butchers and retail vendors of meat, individually and in common, neither should nor shall hold or maintain near a tavern or other place where they sell meats, or near a shop or beside or behind a shop any stable, pen or any other thing which will give off a putrid smell; nor can they slaughter meat animals nor hang them after slaughter in any stable or other place in which there is any stench on a penalty of 10 pence.

Marchionne di Coppo di Stefano Buonaiuti, *Chronicle*, c.1381

Of the Pestilence in the City of Florence, during which many people died

At all the churches, or most of them, they dug pits all the way down to the level of the ground water; they were as wide and deep as the number of people demanded. And so, those who died during the night, if they weren't very rich, were carried on the shoulder of someone whose duty it was and tossed into that pit, or else a huge amount was paid for another to do it. In the morning many were found in the pit, soil was dug up and thrown on top of them, and then others were laid on top of them, and then layer upon layer of soil, scattering earth as if sprinkling cheese on lasagne.

Notes

1 Wray 315–16.
2 Geltner.
3 This translation and notes are courtesy of Jessica Goldberg.
4 "A political and legal term, *popolani*, which denoted a status group among the citizenry of the town." (JG)
5 "This is an Egyptian, then Roman inheritance, a way of counting years in fifteen-year cycles that originally comes out of the need for tax re-assessments. At this point it was of no practical use in northern Italy." (JG)
6 "There are lots of kinds of money in medieval western Europe, but most written materials reckon by pounds (traditionally gold), shillings (traditionally silver, 20 of them make a pound), and pennies (12 make a shilling). The usage here indicates that the pennies are reckoned in gold, that is, 240 of them make a gold pound—which here in Pistoia meant the gold florin of Florence. Other Pistoian materials will express values in shillings of pence. The penalty, just over two florins, is fairly enormous." (JG)
7 "Carnal is used here to mean those to whom one is related by having a shared parent. It has to be specified because everyone had God-relatives as well—that is, all the relatives of the godmother and godfather who stood at your baptism were considered your relatives for lots of legal purposes." (JG)
8 "Many translators give this as 'hung' rather than inflated; Aberth explains that medieval butchers inflated carcasses in order to remove the skin. Aberth, *Black Death*, 142." (JG)

Sources

Chiappelli, Alberto. "Gli ordinamenti sanitari del comune di Pistoia contro la pestilenza del 1348," *Archivio Storico Italiano*, ser. 4, Vol. 20 (1887), pp. 3–21. From Archivio di Stato di Pistoia, Comune, *Statuti* 5, fols. 42v–45, trans. Jessica Goldberg.

Marchionne di Coppo di Stefano Buonaiuti's *Chronicle* in *Cronisti del Trecento*, ed. Roberto Palmarocchi, Rizzoli, 1935, pp. 649–50, trans. Kaborycha.

References

Aberth, John. *Doctoring the Black Death: Medieval Europe's Medical Response to Plague*, Rowman & Littlefield, 2021.

Arrizabalaga, Jon. "Facing the Black Death: Perceptions and Reactions of University Medical Practitioners," in *Practical Medicine from Salerno to the Black Death*, Cambridge, 1994, pp. 237–88.

Geltner, G. "The Path to Pistoia: Urban Hygiene before the Black Death," *Past and Present*, No. 246 (February 2020), pp. 3–33.

Herlihy, David. "Population, Plague and Social Change in Rural Pistoia, 1201–1430," *The Economic History Review*, New Series, Vol. 18, No. 2 (1965), pp. 225–44.

Horrox, Rosemary. *The Black Death: A Reader*, Manchester UP, 1994.

Wray, Shona Kelly. "Boccaccio and the Doctors," *Journal of Medieval History*, Vol. 30, No. 3 (September 2004), pp. 301–22.

5 Nature triumphs over nurture

Giovanni Boccaccio, *The Nymph of Fiesole*, *c.*1346

Giovanni Boccaccio, *Decameron* IV, Introduction, 1349–51

Giovanni Boccaccio's (1313–1375) *Ninfale fiesolano* is a pastoral love story in verse: it tells of the amorous adventures of a shepherd and a woodland nymph. This poem is about young love, represented in all its freshness and exuberance, set within idyllic natural surroundings, however, like nature itself, it contains violence—in the form of sexual assault, and eventually both lovers' deaths. Their names, Africo and Mensola, are those of the two rivers that run through the area where Boccaccio's family had their country home in Corbignano, about five kilometers outside Florence. It is the place where, in all probability, the author himself went to escape the plague in 1348. It is also the location of the fictional setting of his masterpiece, the *Decameron*, where a group of young Florentines go for ten days to shelter from the plague, telling ten stories per day to entertain each other. Almost halfway through this collection of one hundred tales, Boccaccio pauses and steps out from behind the curtain to address his female readers directly. He tells them that critics of his writing have accused him of going too far: "they have said that you please me too much and it is not decent for me to take such pleasure in pleasing you and consoling you." While never stating who these critics are, or how they have read the book, which at this point had not yet been completed, the implication is that these scandalously erotic tales are written for women to enjoy. Boccaccio's excuse is that he cannot help himself because the power of love is too strong for him. This he explains, inevitably, through another story. The story of Filippo Balducci and his son is a delightfully comic parable about the power of natural instinct over social mores. This is a predominant theme throughout the *Decameron*, though in many of the tales Boccaccio demonstrates that there are tragic consequences for those who, like Africo and Mensola, dare to break the rules.

DOI: 10.4324/9781003284284-6

Giovanni Boccaccio, *The Nymph of Fiesole*, *c*.1346

[Having fallen in love with the nymph Mensola, the shepherd Africo goes in search of her.]

Guided by love, he went from hill to hill
toward Fiesole, immersed in thought,
seeking his harsh, untamed beloved,
who made him sick with melancholy.
But before he had gone a mile,
he came upon a hidden place,
where a divide between two mountains:
He heard the singing of nymphs, and then he saw them.

As he drew closer to that narrow valley
he could hear an angelic voice
and two others singing with her. He paused
and crossing his arms in prayer to Jove,
fell to his knees in humble entreaty,
saying: "O Lord, could Mensola be here
in this glen amongst the others? Please God
that she is, for now I will go there too."

As he who wishes to catch a cricket
strides lightly with long, measured steps,
making not a sound, that is just how Africo
moved between those boulders.
As he came up upon that lovely song
resounding in the valley, he came so near
that he saw the stirring of some oak branches
that concealed the nymphs from sight

[Africo chases, captures, and rapes Mensola. Afterward she tries to kill herself but he stops her and implores her forgiveness, declaring his love.]

What tower has ever existed
in all the world, that was so well-built
that being shaken and attacked by many blows
did not in the end weaken and fall?
Or what woman so merciless,
with heart of steel, would not have surrendered
to Africo's entreaties and his kisses,
that would have moved mountains?

Mensola, whose heart was not made of steel,
held out under this assault for some time,
but unable to resist the power of Love,
she was ensnared and taken by him;
the sweet flavor of love she had
first tasted as most bitter outrage;
she carried such thoughts of suffering
mixed with sweetest desire.

And such was her innocence,
that she never thought anything
else would come about, like one who
scarcely, or perhaps never before had
heard of the means by which
man is created and how he is born:
she did not know that of such coupling
man's seed and childbirth could follow.

She kissed him, and said: "O my love,
I do not know what destiny or fortune
would have me do what you desire,
and have me drop my defenses
against you, so I surrender,
as she who has no longer any
strength to oppose Love; for you,
he has pierced my heart.

Then, do now what you like;
you can do with me whatever you wish,
since I have lost all my force and boldness
in the face of Love and of your pleas.
But I must beg you, if it does not displease you,
that after, you must go away as fast as you can,
for still it seems to me that I will be found
by my companions, and hunted down."[1]

Africo then felt great joy,
hearing that she was agreeable,
and giving her a profusion of kisses,
as the matter required.
Nature, more than mischief,
aided them, in lifting off their clothes,
so much did nature instruct them both,
that the two seemed made as one.

Then one kissed the other, and biting,
tightly embracing, the lips ecstatic:
"My dearest love!" they each exclaim,
"Get water, water, the fire burns!"
The mill ground on with full force,
Each swelling with desire, exclaiming:
"Hold me tight!" "Oh, oh, oh. . . ."
"Oh help me!" "In faith, I die!"

The water came, the fire was put out,
and the mill was silent. They sighed.
And it then pleased God for
Mensola to become pregnant by Africo,
with a robust male child.

[*Separated from Mensola, Africo kills himself. When the goddess Diana learns of Mensola's misbehavior, she transforms the nymph into a river.*]

Giovanni Boccaccio, *Decameron* IV, Introduction, 1349–51

In our city, some time ago, there was a citizen named Filippo Balducci, a man of rather modest background, but wealthy, well-regarded, and expert in those things necessary to his station in life. He had a wife whom he loved above all else, and the two lived together in harmony, devoted entirely to making one another happy. It came to pass, as it does all the time, that the good woman passed from this life. She left behind nothing of herself to Filippo, except the one child she had conceived of him, a boy around two years of age. The man was utterly miserable, having never lost anything he had loved so well. And being thus abandoned by the company of the one he most loved, he arranged to leave behind the things of this world and to dedicate himself to God, and his little son as well. Having given away all his possessions to charity, without hesitation he went with his up to Mount Asinaio, where they lived in a tiny cell, begging, fasting, and saying prayers. Above all, the man was careful never to mention any worldly matters, and not to let the boy see anything that might distract him from his service to God. Instead, he always spoke of eternal life, of God, and the saints, teaching the child nothing but holy prayers. And he went on like this for many years, never letting the boy leave the cell, nor showing him anything outside it.

This worthy man used to go from time to time to Florence and from there as need arose went to see various religious friends and then returned to his cell.

Now it happened that, the boy having reached the age of eighteen and Filippo become old, the son asked his father where he was going. When Filippo told him, the youth said, "Father you're old now and cannot bear this exertion. Why not take me with you to Florence this once? That way I can get to know your friends and holy men, so that I, who am young and stronger than you can take care of all we need in Florence whenever you like, and you can remain here."

The worthy man thought of how his son was grown-up and accustomed to God's service, and would be unlikely to go astray. He said to himself, "The boy is right." And since he had to go there, decided to take him.

And so, the youth, when he saw the palaces, houses, churches and all the other things the city is filled with, as one who'd never seen them before, began to marvel greatly and asked his father what they were and what they were called. The father told him, and after each question he would ask another and another. Going along like this, the son asking and the father answering, they came across a group of lovely, well-dressed young women returning from a wedding party, and thus he asked his father what these were.

To which the father replied, "My son, lower your eyes and do not look at them, because they are bad things."

The son asked, "Oh, what are they called?"

The father, in order to avoid needlessly wakening a lustful appetite in the young man, did not want to call them by their actual name—that is, women—and told him, "They are called goslings."

The youth couldn't believe his ears. As if he'd never seen any of the other things, he forgot all about the palaces, the oxen, the horses, the mule, the money, and everything else and immediately said, "Father, I beg you: let me have one of those goslings!"

"Woe is me, my son," said the father, "be silent—they are evil."

To which the youth replied, "Are evil things really shaped like that?"

"Yes," said the father.

"I don't know what you're saying or why these might be evil, for my part, I've never seen anything so beautiful or pleasing than these. They are lovelier than the painted angels that you have showed me so many times. For pity's sake! If you care for me, let me take one of these goslings back with us and I'll take care of it and feed it."

The father said, "I do not wish it and you don't know what they feed upon!"

The man grasped that nature was stronger than all his efforts and at once regretted having brought the boy to Florence.

Note

1 Mensola and the other wood nymphs go about armed for hunting and have sworn oaths of chastity to the goddess Diana; the penalty for breaking that oath is death.

Sources

Boccaccio, Giovanni. *Opere volgari*, Garzanti, 2010, trans. Kaborycha.
Boccaccio, Giovanni. *Decameron di Giovanni Boccaccio, Vol. XVII, Ninfale fiesolano*, ed. Ignazio Moutier, Magheri, 1834, trans. Kaborycha.

References

Boccaccio, Giovanni. *Decameron*, trans. Mark Musa, Signet, 2010.
Boccaccio, Giovanni. *The Nymph of Fiesole*, trans. Daniel J. Donno, Columbia UP, 1960.
Hollander, Robert. *Boccaccio's Two Venuses*, Columbia UP, 1977.
Scaglione, Aldo D. *Nature and Love in the Late Middle Ages*, UC Press, 1963.
Serafini-Sauli, Judith. "The Pleasures of Reading: Boccaccio's *Decameron* and Female Literacy," *MLN*, Vol. 126, No. 1, Italian Issue (January 2011), pp. 29–46.

6 Leonardo takes a close look at plants

Leonardo da Vinci, *Treatise on Painting*

Leonardo da Vinci, *Notes on botany*, 1510–16

Figure 1.4 Leonardo da Vinci, *Annunciation*, detail, *c.*1472–74, Uffizi.

Leonardo da Vinci (1452–1519) left behind relatively few paintings—at most fifteen that experts generally agree upon. However, more than 7,000 pages of writings and sketches in his hand still exist, gathered in various codices. These precious notebooks, kept in libraries, museums, and private collections across the world, contain the man's meticulous studies of everything from dissections of human cadavers to gears, war machinery, fossils, hydraulics, air, animals, flight, and optics. While vast, these notebook pages are significantly fewer than what originally existed; it has been estimated to be less than a third of the

DOI: 10.4324/9781003284284-7

material Leonardo left in his will to his student Francesco Melzi. One of the drawings found among his papers is of a lily (Figure 1.1), similar to the one that appears in his *Annunciation*, an early work that Leonardo painted sometime between 1472 and 1474, during his first period in Florence when the artist was in his early twenties. It has often been noted that this painting displays a certain awkwardness in the position of the Virgin Mary and sculptural stiffness in the drapery of her skirt, as well as influences of Andrea del Verrocchio, in whose workshop Leonardo was working. Martin Kemp refers to it as "the picture of a young man striving to impress just a little too hard," nevertheless noting Leonardo's "unblinking attention to natural effects."[1] Indeed, the young man's extraordinary attention to nature is everywhere evident in the atmosphere of this garden setting, its light, trees, and plants. In particular, the flower held by the angel, symbol of the purity of the Virgin Mary, stands out as a focal point of the painting. The biblical episode of the archangel Gabriel appearing to the Virgin Mary (Luke 1:26–38) is omnipresent in Florentine Renaissance art (#34) and often depicted by Florentine artists as the so-called "Florentine lily," which grows naturally in the region (not a lily at all, but an iris named the *Iris florentina*). Instead, the flower here is recognizable as a *Lilium candidum*, the white lily or Madonna lily, which is also represented in the Royal Collection drawing. Like so much about Leonardo, however, there are questions about this drawing. Included among the thousands of pages left to Melzi, it may or may not have been a study for the lily in the *Annunciation*; moreover, some scholars believe it was drawn not by Leonardo, but by Andrea del Verrocchio, in whose workshop he had trained.[2] Leaving aside this drawing, Leonardo's notebooks are filled with sketches and descriptions of plants and trees native to Italy that are undeniably in his own hand. Leonardo used these studies in his paintings, and he often comments in his notebooks on the need for artists to closely observe the natural world. Furthermore, for Leonardo, the attentive observation of the external appearance of objects in order to reproduce them accurately in painting was never an end in itself. He sought to understand the workings of nature for its own sake, as made evident below in a selection from the many botanical observations recorded in his notebooks. Leonardo explores aspects of morphology (relationships between structures) of plants; phyllotaxis (arrangement of leaves on the axis, or stem); geotropism (the effects of gravity on growth); and heliotropism (the tendency to turn toward the Sun) that would not be fully explored until the modern era. For Leonardo, the scientific study of nature and its representation in painting went hand in hand.

Leonardo da Vinci, *Treatise on Painting*[3]

He is not universal who does not love equally well all the elements in painting, as when one who does not like landscapes holds them to be a subject for cursory and straightforward investigation—just as our Botticelli said such study was of no use because by merely throwing a sponge soaked in a variety of colors at a wall there would be left on the wall a stain in which could be seen a beautiful landscape. He was indeed right that in such a stain various inventions are to be seen. I say that a man may seek out in such a stain heads of men, various animals, battles, rocks, seas, clouds, woods, and other similar things. It is like the sound of bells which can mean whatever you want it to. But although these stains may supply inventions, they do not teach you how to finish any detail. And the painter in question makes very sorry landscapes.

[. . .]

If you scorn painting, which is the sole imitator of all manifest works of nature, you will certainly be scorning a subtle invention, which with philosophical and subtle speculation considers all manner of forms: sea, land, trees, animals, grasses, flowers, all of which are enveloped in light and shade. Truly, this is science, the legitimate daughter of nature, because painting is born of that nature; but to be more correct, we should say the granddaughter of nature, because all visible things have been brought forth by nature and it is among these that painting is born. Therefore, we may justly speak of it as granddaughter of nature and as the kin of god.

Leonardo da Vinci, *Notes on botany*, 1510–16

On the birth of leaves on their branches.

The thickness of a branch is not diminished within the space between one leaf and another, except by the thickness of the eye [bud] that is above the leaf, and this thickness will be less following along the branch up to the next leaf.

Nature has placed the leaves on the last branches of many plants in a way that the sixth leaf is above the first, and continues that way if the pattern is not impeded. And this serves the plant in two useful ways: the first is that when the next year the branch or fruit is born and from the eye [bud] comes from a shoot, which is in contact with the attachment of the leaf above it, the water that wets the branch can descend to nourish the shoot, holding the drop in the concavity where the leaf is born. The second benefit is that when these branches are born the following year, one does not cover another, because five branches emerge turned in five different directions, and the sixth one that is born above the first is relatively distant from it.

[*In the margin is Leonardo's sketch of an "eye" in the juncture between a stem and a branch.*]

Notes

1 Kemp 48–9.
2 Clayton 26.
3 See pp. 138, 141 on this treatise.

Sources

Leonardo da Vinci, *Leonardo on Painting: An Anthology of Writings*, ed and trans. Martin Kemp and Margaret Walker, Yale UP, 1989, pp. 201–2; 13.

Leonardo da Vinci, *Notes on botany* in Institut de France, Manuscript G, fol. 16v, *Archivio digitale di storia della tecnica e della scienza* https://www.leonardodigitale.com/sfoglia/manoscritto-g-dell-Institut-de-france/0016-v/, trans. Kaborycha.

References

Ackerman, James S. "Leonardo Da Vinci: Art in Science," *Daedalus*, Vol. 127, No. 1, Science in Culture (Winter 1998), pp. 207–24.

Clayton, Martin. *Leonardo da Vinci: A Life in Drawing: 200 Works from the Royal Collection*, Rizzoli Electa, 2018.

Emboden, William A. *Leonardo da Vinci on Plants and Gardens*, foreword by Carlo Pedretti, Dioscorides Press, 1987.

Kemp, Martin. *Leonardo da Vinci: The Marvellous Works of Nature and Man*, Dent, 1981.

Leonardo da Vinci. *The Manuscripts of Leonardo da Vinci in the Institut de France: Manuscript G*, trans. John Venerella, Ente Raccolta Vinciana, 2002.

Leonardo da Vinci. *Notebooks*, ed. Irma A. Richter, with notes by Thereza Wells, and preface by Martin Kemp, Oxford UP, 2008

Morley, Brian. "The Plant Illustrations of Leonardo da Vinci," *The Burlington Magazine*, Vol. 121, No. 918 (September 1979), pp. 553–6+558–62.

7 How to create a realistic monster

Giorgio Vasari, *The Life of Leonardo da Vinci*, 1568

When Giorgio Vasari (1511–1574) wrote his first version of *The Lives of the Artists* in 1550, Leonardo had been dead for three decades and the genius from Vinci was already a legend. Vasari uses words such as "admirable," "celestial," "divine," "wondrous," and "superhuman" to describe the artist, and praises him above all for his "subtle and exact reproduction of every detail in nature." Beyond careful descriptions of Leonardo's paintings, some of which he might not have had access to—Vasari probably never saw the *Mona Lisa*, for instance, which was in France—the art historian needed to find a way to explain the mystery of Leonardo's extraordinary mind. Researching Leonardo, in preparation for the second edition of the *Lives*, in 1566 Vasari travelled to Milan and met Leonardo's former pupil Francesco Melzi, from whom he learnt of the master's various uncompleted projects and was able to view the famous notebooks. He also spoke with contemporaries who had been familiar with the painter: "Friends and acquaintances of Vasari's—Giovanni Francesco Rustici, Pontormo, Baccio Bandinelli—had known Leonardo and could supply their reminiscences. And there were certainly echoes of Leonardo's words still to be caught in Florence in the 1520s when Vasari arrived there."[1] As with all his biographies, Vasari enlivens the bare facts with juicy anecdotes that add a certain fictional flavor to his narrative, drawing comparison with the tales told by Boccaccio.[2] Doubtless, fantastical legends about the prodigy from Vinci were spreading already during Leonardo's lifetime. One of the most striking related by Vasari is the episode of the young artist assembling a monster to paint for his father. But did Leonardo actually do this? Leonardo wrote in one of his notebooks: "If therefore you wish to make one of your imaginary animals appear natural—let us suppose it to be a dragon—take for its head that of a mastiff or setter, for its eyes those of a cat, for its ears those of a porcupine, for its nose that of a greyhound, with the eyebrows of a lion, the temples of an old cock and the neck of a water-tortoise."[3] It is certainly possible that Leonardo created such a monster as described in Vasari's account, however, we cannot know for sure. Perhaps more interesting than the question of whether this story is true or false is what it reveals about what people at the time considered believable about Leonardo—as well as Vasari's motivation in repeating it. Beyond a hint of

DOI: 10.4324/9781003284284-8

Dr. Frankenstein in the artist's temperament, the story suggests that, while great artists are able to flawlessly produce natural effects, the greatest artists rise above mere imitation of nature—through use of artifice and imagination their creations can be superior to nature. Vasari indeed praises Michelangelo in similar terms as the one who "triumphed over ancient artists, modern artists, and even Nature herself."

Giorgio Vasari, *The Life of Leonardo da Vinci*, 1568

It is said that Ser Piero[4] who was at the country house, was sought out at home by one of the peasants who worked for him. This man had cut down a fig tree on the farm and had himself cut from it a roundel[5] that he wanted to have painted in Florence. As the man was very good at catching birds and fishing, and Ser Piero made plentiful use of his services, he was most happy to oblige. Whereupon he had the roundel taken to Florence, without telling Leonardo whose it was, and asked him to paint something on it. Leonardo, once he got the roundel into his hands, seeing it crooked and clumsily made, straightened it over the fire, and gave the rough, awkward thing to a wood turner who evened it out so it was regular and smooth. And after applying plaster and preparing the panel to his pleasing, Leonardo began to think about what to paint on it, something that would frighten anyone who came upon it, having the same effect as the head of the Medusa.[6] He brought scaly reptiles, green lizards, crickets, snakes, butterflies, locusts, bats, and all kinds of similarly strange species of animals into a room where no one else entered, and out of this multitude, variously blended together, he created a horrible and frightening beast that poisoned the air with its fiery breath. He depicted it emerging from the crack in a dark stone, breathing venom from its wide-open mouth, fire coming from its eyes, and smoke from its nose so eerily that it was a monstrous and horrible thing to behold. And he took such pains to make it, that though the room was filled with the sickening stench of dead animals, Leonardo did not smell it, such was his great love for his art. When the work was finished and no longer sought after by either the peasant or his father, Leonardo sent word that he could come to get it. When Ser Piero went one morning to get the panel and knocked on the door, Leonardo told him to wait a moment, and going back into the room, arranged the easel in the light and adjusted the window shades so that the light would be dazzling. He then let him in to see it. Ser Piero's first reaction without thinking was sudden shock; he did not believe what he was seeing was either a wooden panel or a painted image. And taking a step back, Leonardo held him there, saying, "This painting has done its job: take it away, since this is the objective of a work of art." The thing seemed beyond miraculous to Ser Piero and he praised Leonardo's fanciful subject most highly. Then he went to a shop where he discretely bought another roundel painted with a heart pierced by an arrow and gave it to the peasant who was grateful to him for the rest of his life. Afterward Ser Piero sold Leonardo's work secretly to some merchants in Florence for one hundred ducats. Not long after that it came into the hands of Francesco, duke of Milan, sold for three hundred ducats by those same merchants.

Notes

1 Rubin 39–40.
2 Barolsky 18.
3 Cited in Findlen *Inventing Nature* 307; see also **#79**.
4 Leonardo's father, Piero da Vinci (1426–1504), was a notary, thus the honorific address "Ser."
5 The word is *rotella*, sometimes translated as "buckler" or "shield."
6 The Medusa was a monster in Greek mythology, whose head, covered with serpents, was so fearsome that anyone who looked at her would be instantly turned to stone. The hero Perseus killed her by looking at her reflection in a mirror. See **#39**.

Source

Giorgio Vasari. *Le vite dei più eccellenti pittori, scultori e architetti*, Giunti, 1568, trans. Kaborycha.

References

Barolsky, Paul. *Why Mona Lisa Smiles and Other Tales by Vasari*, Pennsylvania State UP, 1991.

Findlen, Paula. "Inventing Nature: Commerce, Art and Science in the Early Modern Cabinet of Curiosities," in *Merchants & Marvels: Commerce, Science, and Art in Early Modern Europe*, Routledge, 2002.

Rubin, Patricia Lee. "What Men Saw: Vasari's Life of Leonardo da Vinci and the Image of the Renaissance Artist," *Art History*, Vol. 13, No. 1 (March 1990), pp. 34–46.

Turner, A. Richard. *Inventing Leonardo*, Knopf: Distributed by Random House, 1993.

8 Likenesses in art and in art history

Niccolò Martelli, *Letter to Rugasso*, 1544

Giorgio Vasari, *Life of Andrea del Sarto*, 1550, 1568

Figure 1.5 Andrea del Sarto, *Portrait of a Young Man*, *c.*1517–18, National Gallery, London.

Who is the young man in this painting? As depicted by artist Andrea del Sarto (Andrea d'Agnolo, 1486–1530), he is not wearing elegant aristocratic garments, rather he is dressed in the clothing of a Florentine craftsman or tradesman. Some have suggested that he might have been a sculptor, and that in his hands he appears to be holding a block of clay or a stone. Though

DOI: 10.4324/9781003284284-9

the lower left corner of the painting is in poor condition, preliminary drawings clearly show the sitter holding a book. Thus, it has alternatively been proposed that the sitter might have been someone in the bookselling trade.[1] Andrea del Sarto came from a similar social background; his surname *sarto* meaning "tailor" indicates his father's profession. Other Renaissance artists had names that likewise indicated their families' trades: Ghirlandaio's made garlands, Pollaiuolo's were poultry sellers, Tintoretto's were dyers, and Vasari's made vases. The tailor's son, it was once believed, had here painted his self-portrait. However, the features of the man in this painting do not match the two certain existing self-portraits by Andrea del Sarto.[2] Although we probably will never be able to definitively know the identity of the subject of this striking portrait, the viewer receives the impression that they "know" him. The young man is caught in a seemingly unguarded moment of reflection. Interrupted in his reading, he turns and looks over his shoulder at the viewer. The arresting pose, reminiscent of other Renaissance masterpieces—portraits for instance by Leonardo (*Portrait of Cecilia Gallerani*, **#36**) and by Raphael (*Portrait of Baldassarre Castiglione*, **#18**)—imparts the "admirable vivacity and immediacy" that Vasari praises in Andrea's works (see below). Fredrika Jacobs cites art theorist Lodovico Dolce (**#49**) who wrote in his 1557 *Dialogue on Painting*, "We take pleasure in truth and it amazes the eye of the viewer to see in stone, in canvas, or on wood an inanimate thing that seems to move."[3] She argues that it was this quality of reproducing nature, imparting the appearance of movement, that was valued above all else in Renaissance portraits. Thus, "lifelikeness" was the objective, more than achieving a "likeness" of the sitter. Long before the advent of photography, during a time when only the wealthy could afford to commission portraits, and even the cost of high-quality mirrors was out of reach for most, we must ask: what were people's expectations of seeing the exact reproduction of their own or another's individual features in a painting? Certainly, what we do see during the High Renaissance, rather than necessarily producing recognizable images of a model, is the emerging concept of portraiture as a distinct genre. Beyond merely creating images of ideally beautiful people, representation of human character imbued with psychological depth becomes a goal for many, though not all artists. For instance, Botticelli did not set out to accomplish this (*Birth of Venus*, **#47**) nor, generally, did Michelangelo. In a letter to a friend, Niccolò Martelli describes running into Michelangelo one day in July 1544 when the artist was working on sculptural portraits of the Medici dukes in the Basilica of San Lorenzo. The brief exchange with the artist reveals his nonchalance toward accurately representing even the well-known features of members of the Medici family.

Though we will probably never know much with certainty about the sitter in Andrea's portrait, we do have information about the painter, once again from Giorgio Vasari. Unlike Giotto, who had lived two centuries earlier (**#2**), and Leonardo, who died while the art historian was only a boy (**#7**), Andrea del Sarto was a contemporary of Vasari, who not only knew the painter, but also had studied with Andrea for a time. Vasari is, however, a problematic source when writing about his former master. In the first edition of the *Lives of the Artists*—published just two decades after Andrea del Sarto's death from the plague—aside from damning with faint praise, the art historian also included many sordid financial details, as well as a negative portrayal of the painter's shrewish wife, information possibly tainted by personal animosity. Eighteen years later, when he expanded and revised the book, Vasari altered the biography of the artist. All this raises the question: can a comparison be drawn between the significance of representing accurate physical details in a painted portrait and representing accurate biographical details in a written portrait?

Niccolò Martelli, *Letter to Rugasso*, 1544

Michelangelo is the only one here in Florence in the library of San Lorenzo; he's there sculpting the illustrious lords of the most fortunate house of Medici, not taking for his models Duke Lorenzo and Lord Giuliano as Nature had portrayed and composed them, but rather giving them a grandeur, proportion, and decorum, saying that, "a thousand years from now no one would know that they had been any different, so that people looking upon these very images would be amazed."

Giorgio Vasari, *Lives*, 1550 edition

Andrea del Sarto, Florentine painter

It is to be lamented with Fortune, that a man who is born in possession of a good mind and perfect judgment in painting, who makes himself recognized for his excellent abilities, creating works worthy of praise, is seen to do the contrary, lowering himself in his manner of living, unable to moderate in any way his bad habits. Certainly, those who love him are moved to compassion, afflicted and sorrowing when they see him persist in those ways. . . . This is more how he was in his life than in his art, this most excellent Florentine painter Andrea del Sarto, who was much indebted to nature for a rare talent [*ingegno*] in painting. If he had lived a more civil

Giorgio Vasari, *Lives*, 1568 edition

Life of Andrea del Sarto, most excellent Florentine painter

And here, after the lives of many most excellent artists, some using color, others through drawing, and some with their invention, we have arrived at the most excellent Andrea del Sarto, in whom nature and art showed all that can be achieved in painting, using drawing, the handling of color, and invention, to such a degree that if Andrea had possessed a prouder, more daring soul, to match his intellect and deepest judgment in this art, without a doubt, he would have been unequaled. But a certain timidity of heart, and a somewhat modest and simple nature did not permit a certain lively ardor or proud spirit to show and honorable life and not neglected himself and those near to him out of his appetite for a woman that kept him always in poverty and of base condition, he could have stayed in France, where he had been summoned by that king who adored his work, greatly esteemed him, and would have richly rewarded him. Instead, in order to satisfy his desire and their appetite for each other, he returned, and always lived in a low manner. And for all of his efforts, he received very little in return from her, whom he adored, and she abandoned him in the end when he was close to death. But let us start at the beginning.

Born in the year 1478,[4] in the city of Florence, to a respectable person who had the name Sarto, from the craft he practiced, the son's name was Andrea . . .

through, which, added to his other gifts, would have made him really divine in his painting. Therefore, for this reason his painting lacked those ornaments, grandeur, and copiousness of style [*maniere*] that is often seen in many other painters. Nonetheless his figures, even if simple and pure, well-conceived, without errors, and in all ways highly perfect; the natural and gracious air of the heads of *putti* and women alike, and those of youths and old men have admirable vivacity and immediacy; the clothing lovely, the nudes very well executed. And though he drew simply, nevertheless, his colors are rare and truly divine.

Andrea was born in the year 1478,[4] in Florence to a father who practiced the craft of a tailor, hence he was called by everyone.

Notes

1 Cecchi.
2 Freedberg 79–80.
3 Jacobs 1.
4 Andrea del Sarto was born July 16, 1486, as recorded in the Florentine baptismal registry.

Sources

Le Lettere di Niccolò Martelli 1546 fol.49, trans. Kaborycha.
Vasari *Vite* 1550, 1568, trans. Kaborycha.

References

Brooks, Julian, Denise Allen, Xavier F. Salomon, and Alessandro Cecchi. *Andrea del Sarto: The Renaissance Workshop in Action*, J. Paul Getty Museum, 2015.
Campbell, Lorne. *Renaissance Portraits: European Portrait-painting in the 14th, 15th, and 16th Centuries*, Yale UP, 1990.

Cecchi, Alessandro. "A Portrait of a Florentine 'Cartolaio' by Andrea del Sarto in the National Gallery," *The Burlington Magazine*, Vol. 158, No. 1358 (May 2016), pp. 331–5.

Freedberg, S.J. *Andrea del Sarto*, Harvard UP, 1963.

Jacobs, F.H. *The Living Image in Renaissance Art*, Cambridge UP, 2005.

Loh, Maria H. "Renaissance Faciality," *Oxford Art Journal*, Vol. 32, No. 3, Mal'Occhio: Looking Awry at the Renaissance Special Issue (2009), pp. 341, 343–63.

Mann, N. and L. Syson, eds. *The Image of the Individual: Portraits in the Renaissance*, British Museum Press, 1998.

Shearman, John. *Andrea del Sarto*, Clarendon Press, 1965.

9 Heretical belief in a "world soul"

Giordano Bruno, *Expulsion of the Triumphant Beast*, 1584

Giordano Bruno (1548–1600) was a natural philospher who explored widely diverse concepts, including Copernicanism, infinity of the Universe, multiplicity of worlds, panpsychism (everything has a mental aspect), and metempsychosis (transmigration of souls), as well as Kabbalah and Hermetic magic. He was a controversial figure who travelled widely and was everywhere driven away for his outspoken, unorthodox beliefs—Bruno was excommunicated by the Catholic, Lutheran, and Calvinist Churches. He fled to England, where he wrote *Expulsion of the Triumphant Beast*, published in London in 1584. The characters in this dialogue are the pagan gods who have been summoned to a heavenly council led by Jove (Jupiter). The head of the Olympian gods has decided that it is time to cleanse the world, ridding human society of vice, the "triumphant beast." The vices that Bruno targets are principally ignorance and intolerance. As he sets no limits to philosophical inquiry and explores the possibility of divergent belief systems, his fundamental credo is the principle of tolerance: "For Bruno, indeed, the infinite stretches of time and space bred, at least ideally, an infinite tolerance for the various ways that people have sought God and wisdom (although he never quite found the patience to tolerate Calvinists or pedant asses)."[1] Throughout *Expulsion*, although the setting is a mythological council of pagan gods, Bruno attacks basic doctrines of Christianity. After the introduction in praise of the natural world, Bruno's first dialogue contains a passage inspired by one of the Greek writer Lucian's satires (second century CE). In it, Bruno enumerates the daily chores of an all-powerful deity in minutely absurd detail, at the same time mocking the belief in an omnipotent, personal God, as well as the rigid Calvinist concept of divine predestination. In the third dialogue, Bruno elaborates on his notion of the "world soul" (or "universal soul"), an equally heretical concept. This work was considered so dangerous that it was the only one of Bruno's "singled out by the Roman Inquisition at the summation of his trial," which ended in the author being burned at the stake soon thereafter.[2]

DOI: 10.4324/9781003284284-10

Giordano Bruno, *Expulsion of the Triumphant Beast*, 1584

Introduction

Blind is he who does not see the Sun; foolish, he who does not recognize it; ungrateful he who does not give thanks to it, since so great is its light, its good, and its benefit for those upon whom it shines, excels, and supports: master of the senses, father of substances, author of life.

Dialogue 1, Part III

[*The god Mercury recounts a list of the many tasks Jove has set for him that day.*]

Mercury: He has ordained that today at noon two melons in Franzino's[3] melon patch will be perfectly ripe, but that they will not be picked for another three days, when they will be judged no longer good to eat. He wills that at the same time, thirty perfect jujubes on the tree by the house of Gioan Bruno at the foot of Mount Cicala, will be picked; seventeen will fall to the ground, of which fifteen will be eaten by worms. Vasta, Albenzio's wife, while curling her hair, burns fifty-seven of them close to her forehead because she overheated the iron, but this time she will not burn her head, and she won't curse when she smells it, but bears it with patience. From the dung of her ox, two hundred fifty-two dung-beetles will be born, of which fourteen will be stepped on by Albenzio's foot and die, twenty-six will die by flipping over on their backs, twenty-two will live in the cellar, eighty go on a pilgrimage through the courtyard, forty-two go to live under that block of wood by the door, sixteen will roll their balls of dung wherever they like and the rest run about at will. While Laurenza combs her hair, seventeen strands fall out, thirteen break, and of those, ten regrow in three days, while seven never grow back. Antonio Savolino's bitch conceives five puppies, three of which will live, two will be thrown away. Of the three that are kept, one will resemble its mother, the second will be mixed, the third will look a bit like its father and a bit like Polidoro's dog. At the same time the cuckoo is heard singing from Starza, and it lets out the cry "cuckoo" twelve times, no more, no less, then goes to the ruins of Cicala castle for eleven minutes, and from there flies away to Scaravaita. Later we will provide[4] what happens next. The gown that Master Danese is cutting on his bench will rip. Twelve bedbugs will leave the table beside Constantino's bed and go to his pillow—seven are very large, four very small, one medium size—we will provide for what happens to them this evening by candlelight. Fifteen minutes after, by the motion of her tongue across her palate, on the fourth time, the third molar belonging to Fiurulo's old woman falls out of her lower right jaw, painlessly, without bleeding, because that molar has reached the end of its wobbliness, which lasted seventeen annual lunar cycles. Ambruoggio, on the one hundred and twelfth thrust has discharged and completed his business with his wife, not impregnating her this time, but he will the next time with the semen converted from the cooked leek he now eats with fermented must and millet bread. Pubic hair will begin to sprout on Martinello's son and at the same time his voice will start to gargle and break. Meanwhile, Paulino with the effort he makes while bending to pick up a broken needle from the ground will break the red string that ties his breeches and he will let out a blasphemy. I will punish him for this tonight by making his soup too salty and smell of smoke. It will cause him to break a flask of wine for which he will swear again—we'll provide for that later. Of seven moles that began tunnelling up from the depths of the ground four days ago, each by different routes, two will come up to the surface at the same hour, one exactly at noon, the other fifteen minutes, nineteen seconds later, at a distance of three paces, one foot, and half a finger's length from one another, in the garden of Anton Faivano. The time and place of the other two will be provided for later.

Sophia:[5] You have a lot to do, Mercury! In telling me about all these acts of Providence that Father Jove has set out for you, and in recounting them one by one, you remind me of the man who wanted to count all the grains of sand on Earth. You've taken such effort to report a few miniscule actions in this tiny roadside village involving four or five not very magnificent beings, among infinite others that were occurring at the same time. What if you were to fully take into account all the things ordained to happen in the town at the base of Mount Cicada? Surely, not even a year would be enough for you to explain them one by one, as you have begun to do. What would it be like if you had to bring about all the things happening in the city of Nola, in the Kingdom of Naples, in Italy, in Europe, on the whole terrestrial globe, and on every other globe, endlessly, as the number of worlds under Jove's Providence is infinite?

[. . .]

Dialogue 3, Part 2

Jove: [*Explains to the others*] Nature, as you must know, is nothing other than God in things.

Salino: Then *natura est deus in rebus*.

Sophia: However, diverse living things represent different deities and different powers: aside from the absolute being they possess, they obtain the being communicated to all things according to their capacity and measure. Whence, all of God is in all things, although not totally, some more fully and some less. Nevertheless, Mars is found most effectively in a natural vestige and mode of substance not only in a viper and scorpion, but also in an onion or bulb of garlic, just as well as in any kind of painting or inanimate sculpture. Think in the same way of the Sun in a crocus, in a narcissus, in a heliotrope, in a rooster, or in a lion. You must think in this way of each of the gods of each of the species and of the various categories of existence.

[*The subject of the worship of plants and animals in ancient Egypt arises and the goddess Isis explains to the others about Egyptian religious worship*.]

Sophia: Those wise men knew God to be in things, and Divinity latent in Nature, operating and sparkling differently in different subjects, and taking on different physical forms, sharing various arrangements of herself, that is, in her being, life, and intellect.[6] Nevertheless, with these equally diverse arrangements they provided themselves with the means to receive as many such gifts as they desired. Thus, for victory they poured libations to magnanimous Jove as an eagle, in which attribute [symbol] is hidden his divinity; for prudence their offerings were to wise Jove as a serpent; to guard against treachery to menacing Jove as a crocodile. In this way, for so many, innumerable ends, they made offerings to other innumerable species. They did all of this not without magical and most efficacious reasoning.

Saulino: How can you say this, Sophia, if Jove was not named at the time of the Egyptian cults, but was found much later, during the time of the Greeks?

Sophia: Don't give a thought to the Greek name, Saulino, because I am speaking in the most universal way, and because even among the Greeks, names for divinities are provisional. Everyone knows that Jove was a king of Crete, a mortal man, whose body like that of other men, putrefied, or turned to ashes. It is no secret that Venus was a mortal woman, a most charming, uncommonly beautiful, gracious, and liberal queen in Cyprus. Similarly, you must have heard about all the other gods who have been known to be humans.

Saulino: Why then were they adored and worshipped?

Sophia: I will tell you. They did not adore Jove as if he were a divinity, but adored the divinity that was in Jove, because seeing a man who excelled in majesty, justice, and magnanimity, they recognized in him a magnanimous, just, and benign god. They arranged and established the tradition that such a god, or divinity, inasmuch as that it is how it was passed down, should be named Jove.

[. . .]

Here then, is why crocodiles, roosters, onions, and turnips were never worshipped, but the gods and the divinity in crocodiles, roosters, and others at certain times and in certain places were found, are found, and will be found in different objects, which although they are mortal have a relationship to Divinity according to how close and familiar they are, not according to Divinity itself, which is the highest, absolute in itself, and without association with the things produced.

[. . .]

So then, that God, as absolute, is not involved with us, except inasmuch as he communicates the effects of Nature and is more intimate with them than Nature herself. Therefore, if he is not Nature herself, he is surely the nature of Nature, and the soul of the Soul of the world, if not the Soul herself.

Notes

1 Rowland 168.
2 Imerti 21.
3 The various people Bruno names in this passage have been identified as family, friends, and neighbors from his hometown of Nola; various locations in the vicinity are also mentioned. Gioan (Giovanni) Bruno was the author's father.
4 A reference to Divine Providence.
5 The name means "wisdom" in Greek; Leone Ebreo, gives a character in his philosophical dialogue the same name; see **#36**.
6 This is a Neoplatonic hierarchy outlined by Plotinus.

Source

Giordano Bruno. "Spaccio della bestia trionfante," in *Opere Italiane di Giordano Bruno*, vol. II, UTET, 2002, pp. 247–50, trans. Kaborycha.

References

Blum, Elisabeth. "Panpsychism in Giordano Bruno and Tommaso Campanella," in *Giordano Bruno: Law, Philosophy, and Theology in the Early Modern Era*, ed. Massimiliano Traversino Di Cristo, Garnier, 2021, pp. 207–17.

Bruno, Giordano. *The Expulsion of the Triumphant Beast*, trans. and ed. Arthur D. Imerti, Rutgers UP, 1964.

Gatti, Hilary, ed. *Giordano Bruno. Philosopher of the Renaissance*, Ashgate, 2002.

Maifreda, Germano. *The Trial of Giordano Bruno*, Routledge, 2022.

Rowland, Ingrid D. *Giordano Bruno, Philosopher, Heretic*, Farrar, Straus and Giroux, 2008.

10 A scientist's method of observation

Galileo Galilei, Notes on Lagalla's *De phaenomenis*, 1612

Galileo Galilei, "Parable of the Sounds," *The Assayer*, 1623

Galileo Galilei (1564–1642) famously wrote that, in order to understand the workings of the universe, one had to first learn "the language of mathematics." Observation using mathematical measurement and precision instruments was crucial to his scientific method. Nevertheless, the Tuscan recognized that he needed to use a more easily understandable language to explain this "new science" to the general public. Rather than write in Latin, which would have been the usual way to communicate with the scholarly community, Galileo chose to publish *Il Saggiatore* in the Italian language, in order to reach a wider audience among his countrymen. The title means *The Assayer*—an assay balance is a tool used for precision measurement of gold—and in this work Galileo metaphorically weighs the value of various opinions, carefully analyzing and assessing their merits. By 1623, Galileo felt a need to address his critics and to explain his empirical scientific method in terms that anyone could understand, so he wrote a fable, the so-called "Parable of the Sounds." It is a charming tale, told with literary verve, in which the author paints a vivid picture of a man discovering various sounds in nature— birds, insects, musical instruments, and other auditory phenomena. He did not employ this poetic imagery solely out of a desire to popularize his research, however. Galileo genuinely viewed scientific inquiry not as something separate from the arts, painting, music, and literature, but sharing with those disciplines the same goal, namely, of learning directly from nature and celebrating her wonders. Around ten years before writing *The Assayer*, he had scrawled some notes about a book recently published by Giulio Cesare Lagalla.[1] In these notes, found among his private papers, Galileo expresses the conviction that science and the arts are profoundly interrelated. In his own life he practiced both: "His last disciple and first biographer, Vincenzo Viviani, boasted that his master could compete with the best lutenists in Tuscany, advise painters and poets on matters of artistic taste, and recite vast stretches of Petrarch, Dante, and Ariosto by heart."[2] Incidentally, Galileo's father, the lutenist and composer Vincenzo Galilei (*c.*1520–1591), wrote highly influential works on music theory, performed experiments with sound, and is considered a

DOI: 10.4324/9781003284284-11

pioneer in the science of acoustics. And finally, Galileo's own drawings of the Moon, based on his observations through the telescope, display an extraordinary artistry (#76).

Galileo Galilei, Notes on Lagalla's *De phaenomenis*, 1612

The difference between philosophizing and studying philosophy is that which exists between drawing from nature and copying pictures. In order to become accustomed to handling the pen or crayon in good style, it is right to begin by redrawing good pictures created by excellent artists. Likewise in order to stimulate the mind and guide it toward good philosophy, it is useful to observe the things that have already been investigated by others in their philosophizing; especially those which are true and certain, these being chiefly mathematical.

But men who go on forever copying pictures and never get around to drawing from nature can never become perfect artists, or even good judges of painting. For they remain unpracticed in separating the good from the bad, or the accurately from the poorly drawn, by means of recognizing in nature itself (as a result of countless experiences) the true effects of foreshortening, of backgrounds, of lights and shadows, of reflections, and of the infinite variations in differing viewpoints.

In the same way a man will never become a philosopher by worrying forever about the writings of other men, without ever raising his own eyes to nature's works in the attempt to recognize there the truths already known and to investigate some of the infinite number that remain to be discovered. This, I say, will never make a man a philosopher, but only a student of other philosophers and an expert in their works. I do not believe that you would esteem as a good painter a man who had made so great a study of the drawings and canvases of all painters that he could promptly identify the style of each one, even if he could also imitate them.

Galileo Galilei, "Parable of the Sounds," *The Assayer*, 1623

> *It seems to me, having observed through long experience, that such is the human condition concerning intellectual matters: the less someone knows about something, the more resolutely he is determined to hold forth on it. While on the contrary, the multitude of things to be known and understood ought to render one more hesitant and slower to pass judgment on new phenomena.*

Once upon a time, in an isolated place a man was born whom nature had gifted with a most observant intellect and extraordinary curiosity, and it was his pastime to raise many kinds of birds, delighting in their song. With greatest wonder he observed how with marvelous skill they were able to form, at will, a variety of lovely songs using the same air they breathed. It happened that one night, near his house he heard a delicate sound and never imagining that it could be anything but a small bird, went to catch it. On the street he found a shepherd boy, who by blowing into a wooden tube pierced with holes and moving his fingers along the wood, opening and closing various holes, drew out various voices, similar to those of birds, but in a very different manner from them. Stunned, and moved by his natural curiosity, he gave the shepherd a calf in exchange for the flute. When he was on his own, the man reflected that if he had not chanced upon the shepherd, he never would have learned that there were two ways to produce voices and gentle songs, and decided to go away from his home, thinking to encounter some other adventure. And on the next day, when passing by a small hut, the man heard similar tones being sounded, and in order to ascertain whether it was a flute or a blackbird, he went inside where he found a boy holding a bow in his right hand and sawing at some sinews stretched over a concave piece of wood, while with the left he supported the instrument, moving his fingers along it. And without using any breath, he drew from it different, very lovely sounds. Now, you who share the man's curiosity of intellect, imagine his amazement at finding, in addition to the two other ways of producing sound, such an unexpected one; he began to believe that there might be even more in nature. But how great was his amazement, when upon entering a temple, there was a sound; the man looked behind the door to see who had made it, and became aware that it came from the metal hinges when the door opened. Another time, driven by curiosity, he went into a tavern expecting to see a bow lightly touching the strings of a violin, and saw someone running their fingertip around the edge of a glass, drawing out the sweetest sound. But when he observed wasps, mosquitoes, and bluebottles, who unlike the birds he had first heard, did not form separate notes with their breath, but with the most rapid beating of their wings created a continuous sound, how much greater his sense of wonder grew. Nor could all his previous experiences have sufficed to make him understand or believe that crickets, not with their breath, but by rubbing together their wings, though they did not fly, could emit such sweet and sonorous hissing. But when the man believed it could hardly be possible to make sounds in any other way, after having observed in addition to the aforesaid ways, also many organs, trumpets, fifes, string instruments of all kinds—even including that sort of little tongue of iron that when placed between the teeth, makes odd use of the mouth cavity as a resonance chamber and the breath for vehicle of the sound—when, as I said, he believed he had seen everything, the man found himself again shrouded in ignorance. For he was astonished when he chanced to hold a cicada in his hand, and neither by shutting its mouth nor stopping its wings could he diminish its deafening screeching. Neither did he see movement of its scales or any other part, and finally lifting its breastplate and seeing some hard but fine strips of cartilage there, and believing the noise came from their movement, he resolved to break them in order to silence the insect. But nothing happened, until by piercing it and pushing the needle deeper inside, he took away not only the creature's voice, but also its life, so that he could not even determine whether the song came from there or not. After this the man was reduced to such distrust of his own knowledge, that when he was asked how sounds were generated, he responded frankly that he understood some ways, but that he knew for certain that there might be a hundred other unknown and unforeseeable ones as well.

> *I could explain with many other examples Nature's bounty in producing her effects in ways that are inscrutable to us, without our sensory experiences to demonstrate them, and even those sometimes do not suffice. And so, if I cannot determine precisely how a comet is produced, I ought to be allowed to admit that—all the more so, as I never claimed to be able to do so.*[3]

Notes

1 *De phaenomenis in orbe lunae novi telescopii usu a domino Gallileo Galileo*, 1612. Lagalla questions Galileo's method of representing the surface of the Moon in his 1610 *Sidereus Nuncius* (*The Starry Messenger*).

2 Heilbron v.

3 In 1618 a comet had appeared and Galileo's views on the phenomenon had been challenged. By the time he wrote *The Assayer*, Galileo's discoveries with the telescope had become widely known. Viewed as an expert on all things astronomical, he was often asked to explain a variety of heavenly phenomena, including the composition and movements of comets.

Sources

Galileo's Notes on Lagalla's *De phaenomenis*, trans. by Stillman Drake, in *Discoveries and Opinions of Galileo*, Random House, 1957, pp. 224–5.

Galileo Galilei. *Il Saggiatore*, 1623, in Ed. Naz. VI, trans. Kaborycha.

References

Heilbron, John. *Galileo*, Oxford UP, 2010.

Panofsky, Erwin. "Galileo as a Critic of the Arts: Aesthetic Attitude and Scientific Thought," *ISIS*, Vol. 47, No. 1 (March 1956), pp. 3–15.

Part II

Under the influence of the ancients

Figure 2.1 Belvedere Torso, First century BCE, Vatican Museums

11 Rival humanists fight a war of words

Antonio Loschi, *Invective Against the Florentines*, 1401

Coluccio Salutati, *Reply to a Slanderous Detractor*, 1403

Leonardo Bruni, *Panegyric to the City of Florence*, 1403–4

Pier Candido Decembrio, *Panegyric in Praise of the City of the Milanese*, 1436

By the beginning of the fifteenth century, Florence had been at almost constant war with Milan for a dozen years. Moreover, hostilities did not end on the battlefield; inflamed Latin rhetoric was exchanged as well. The renowned Milanese humanist Antonio Loschi (1368–1441), who had studied in Florence, was chancellor for Giangaleazzo Visconti, duke of Milan, when he wrote his scathing *Invectiva in Florentinos* (*Invective against the Florentines*) in 1401. Loschi's former teacher, Florentine chancellor Coluccio Salutati (1331–1406) struck back in 1403. Writing in florid Ciceronian Latin, the Florentine humanist slashed Loschi's Latin prose to pieces—Visconti had famously declared that a letter by Salutati was worth a thousand horsemen.[1] Salutati could well permit himself the triumphant tone, as Florence was no longer directly threatened by Milan at this point, having narrowly escaped defeat with Giangaleazzo's sudden death in 1402. Though military conflict had ceased, the humanist battle of words continued to rage. Leonardo Bruni (1370–1444), another former pupil of Salutati who succeeded him as chancellor, picked up where his predecessor left off. Bruni soundly struck back at Loschi in his *Laudatio Florentinae Urbis* (*Panegyric to the City of Florence*) in 1403–4. It is a lengthy work of praise for Florence, its physical setting, citizens, and laws, in which the author constructs a republican genealogy for the city. Bruni makes the claim that because it was founded during the time of the Roman Republic, Florence inherited its ancient traditions of self-government and love of liberty. The debate hardly ended here, though; it continued to rage for decades between the opposing camps of humanists living under rival signorial and republican regimes. When Florence decided to reissue Bruni's *Panegyric* in 1434—as part of a campaign to supplant Basel as the site for the Church council—Pier Candido Decembrio (**#14**) produced a rebuttal on behalf of Milan. In his 1436 *De laudibus Mediolanensium urbis panegyricus*

DOI: 10.4324/9781003284284-13

(*Panegyric in Praise of the City of the Milanese*), Decembrio pointed out that Bruni conveniently omitted the detail that Florence was actually founded during the time when the dictator Lucius Sulla (138–78 BCE), "the most wicked of tyrants," was in command of Rome. Though by no means the end of the contest, these examples demonstrate how humanists often deployed classical learning in political conflicts, manipulating and weaponizing their knowledge of ancient history on behalf of their governments.

Antonio Loschi, *Invective Against the Florentines*, 1401

Will that day ever dawn, O most evil citizens, enemies of your country and disturbers of the peace in Italy, when you will pay the penalty your crimes deserve, when you will have to undergo the punishment you merit? Will it ever come about that the example of your special undoing will frighten those like you and make them comprehend, in light of your disasters, the risks they run, such that your ruin will be not only a fitting vindication, but also a useful example? And will your deceptions be revealed and thus foiled, deceptions that you rely upon wholly, so that other nations may be found to be clear-sighted and so that you may appear to be what you are: utterly empty and utterly blind?

So shall it surely be, I am certain; the times have arrived, destiny is about to be fulfilled, and with great strides there approaches the collapse of your pridefulness, long wished-for by the human race. We shall see—and how we shall see!—your celebrated constancy and "Roman" tenacity in defending that repulsive liberty, or rather cruel tyranny. You are accustomed to boast of the name of Rome and declare to all that you descend from the Romans. This impudent lie I will refute another time. Now I continue: we shall see, I say, that Florentine presumption and insolence is as empty as the wind, and we shall learn how much the praise that more than any other nation, you claim for yourselves, truly corresponds to virtue.

People can no longer hear your name without vexation; Italy can no longer bear that those who have afflicted her with many disasters, and in the end even sought to strangle her with wretched slavery, remain unpunished; divine justice herself can no longer tolerate you. I can hardly see how you can hold out when yearnings and hopes of nearly all humanity are aroused against you; if Italy—which you harassed and summoned to servitude—hates you, and if heaven's wrath itself, vexed by so many misdeeds, is in arms against you. Yes, heavenly wrath too makes war upon you, believe me, wicked ones; it too thirsts for your guilty blood; it too requires the total ruin of the most scheming and criminal of nations. That is why it has injected this madness into your minds, so that you hatch pernicious plots to destroy Holy Mother Church, to undermine the Roman Empire and ruin the most glorious of dukes. What else can one imagine but that God Himself, outraged by your wickedness, has blinded you, driving you to the height of madness, so that he might arouse hatred and arms against you? You cannot bear even the gleam of your enemies' arms, to say nothing of their power.

Coluccio Salutati, *Reply to a Slanderous Detractor Who Has Written Many Wounding Things Against the Renowned City of Florence*, 1403

Certain distinguished and venerable men have placed in my hands a copy of an invective, transcribed from an authoritative copy, said to be the work of my dear brother Antonio Loschi of Vicenza; an invective, they said, written against the good name and the honor of the Florentines, as the text itself makes clear. The author, they added, had most certainly written with the desire and intent to defame, and they besought me to write a reply to every accusation in defense of my country. Informed of the matter and exhorted to act, I confess that I felt at once the impulse to write, whether driven more by indignation or by pain I know not: both attacked me at the same time. I was pained that someone dared to defame my country, and I was indignant that my Antonio had elected to take on such a task without pay.

But once I had scanned the text and found that there was no foundation to the accusations, no order or purpose, nothing proven or convincing, and that the beginning, to leave aside its commonplace clichés, could easily be turned upon the accuser just by reversing the names, I had to laugh to myself and think: "The fellow who dictated this is immature either in age or in learning, motivated entirely by impulse and lacking any power of speech or reason; the accusations cast in the face of his enemy are so weak that simple denial would be enough to disprove them all, and he would have to retract them and start all over again from the beginning, as though he had said nothing at all."

Indeed it is schoolboy error to speak at such length without realizing that, by simply denying what is said, the entire case falls to pieces. The force of an argument lies not only in what is said and how prettily, but in whether you prove it, whether you persuade, whether you give incontrovertible evidence of what you say. Is there a sin or a vice that cannot be attributed to anyone, however immune from vice and crime? Moreover, neither is elegance of style enough to produce belief, since it can be applied equally to true things and to false. All this leads me to affirm without the least doubt that my Loschi—who is an able man not only because of his natural gifts but thanks to culture and education—could never have gone in for such trifling and petty speech or such impudently caustic reproaches. To be sure, the words *do* bear a superficial resemblance to Cicero's, such that it would be hard to attribute them to anyone besides Antonio, who knows how to write in that manner. But, again, the lack of both coherence in the discourse and force in the arguments makes it hard for me to believe that Antonio could have composed it.

Leonardo Bruni, *Panegyric to the City of Florence*, 1403–4

Now that we have described what Florence is, we should next consider what manner of citizens there are here. As one usually does in discussing an individual, so we want to investigate the origins of the Florentine people and to consider from what ancestor the Florentines derived and what they have accomplished at home and abroad in every age. As Cicero says: "Let's do it this way, let's begin at the beginning."

What, therefore, was the stock of these Florentines? Who were their progenitors? By what mortals was this outstanding city founded? Recognize, men of Florence, recognize your race and your forebears. Consider that you are, of all races, the most renowned. For other peoples have as forebears refugees or those banished from their fathers' homes, peasants, obscure wanderers, or unknown founders. But your founder is the Roman people—the lord and conqueror of the entire world. Immortal God, you have conferred so many good things on this one city so that everything—no matter where it happens or for what purpose it was ordained—seems to redound to Florence's benefit.

For the fact that the Florentine race arose from the Roman people is of the utmost importance. What nation in the entire world was ever more distinguished, more powerful, more outstanding in every sort of excellence than the Roman people? Their deeds are so illustrious that the greatest feats done by other men seem like child's play when compared to the deeds of the Romans. Their dominion was equal to the entire world, and they governed with the greatest competence for many centuries, so that from a single city comes more examples of virtue than all other nations have been able to produce until now. In Rome there have been innumerable men so outstanding in every kind of virtue that no other nation on Earth has ever been equal to it. Even omitting the names of many fine and outstanding leaders and heads of the Senate, where do you find, except in Rome, the families of the Publicoli, Fabricii, Corruncani, Dentati, Fabii, Decii, Camilli, Pauli, Marcelli, Scipiones, Catones, Gracchi, Torquati, and Cicerones? Indeed, if you are seeking nobility in a founder you will never find any people nobler in the entire world than the Roman people; if you are seeking wealth, none more opulent; if you want grandeur and magnificence, none more outstanding and glorious; if you seek extent of dominion, there was no people on this side of the ocean that had not been subdued and brought under Rome's power by force of arms. Therefore, to you, also, men of Florence, belongs by hereditary right dominion over the entire world and possession of your parental legacy. From this it follows that all wars that are waged by the Florentine people are most just, and this people can never lack justice in its wars since it necessarily wages war for the defense and recovery of its own territory. Indeed, these are the sorts of just wars that are permitted by all laws and legal systems. Now, if the glory, nobility, virtue, grandeur, and magnificence of the parents can also make the sons outstanding, no people in the entire world can be as worthy of dignity as are the Florentines, for they are born from such parents who surpass by a long way all mortals in every sort of glory. Who is there among men who would not readily acknowledge themselves subjected to the Roman people? Indeed, what slave or freedman strives to have the same dignity as the children of his lord or master, or hopes to be chosen instead of them? It is evident that it is no trifling ornament to the city of Florence to have had such an outstanding creator and founder for itself and its people.

But at what point in history did the nation of the Florentines arise from the Romans? Now I believe that in the case of royal successions there is a custom observed by most peoples, namely, that the person who is finally declared to be heir to the king must be born at the time his father possessed the royal dignity. Those offspring who are born either before or after are not considered to be the sons of a king, nor are they permitted to have the right of succession to their father's kingdom. Surely whoever rules when in his best and most flourishing condition also accomplishes his most illustrious and glorious deeds. Indeed, it is evident that, for whatever reasons, prosperous times stimulate men's minds and call forth great spirits, so that at such moments in history great men are able to do only what is important and glorious, and what is accomplished then is always especially outstanding.

Accordingly, this very noble Roman colony was established at the very moment when the dominion of the Roman people flourished greatly and when very powerful kings and warlike nations were being conquered by the skill of Roman aims and by virtue. Carthage, Spain, and Corinth were levelled to the ground; all lands and seas acknowledged the rule of these Romans, and these same Romans suffered no harm from any foreign state. Moreover, the Caesars, the Antonines, the Tiberiuses, the Neros—those plagues and destroyers of the Roman Republic—had not yet deprived the people of their liberty. Rather, still growing there was that sacred and untrampled freedom that, soon after the founding of the colony of Florence, was to be stolen by those vilest of thieves.[2] For this reason I think something has been true and is true in this city more than in any other; the men of Florence especially enjoy perfect freedom and are the greatest enemies of tyrants. So I believe that from its very founding Florence conceived such a hatred for the destroyers of the Roman state and underminers of the Roman Republic that it has never forgotten to this very day. If any trace of or even the names of those corrupters of Rome have survived to the present, they are hated and scorned in Florence.

Now this interest in republicanism is not new to the Florentine people, nor did it begin (as some people think) only a short time since. Rather, this struggle against tyranny was begun a long time ago when certain evil men undertook the worst crime of all—the destruction of the liberty, honor, and dignity of the Roman people. At that time, fired by a desire for freedom, the Florentines adopted their penchant for fighting and their zeal for the republican side, and this attitude has persisted down to the present day. If at other times these political factions were called by different names,[3] still they were not really different. From the beginning Florence has always been united in one and the same cause against the invaders of the Roman state and it has constantly persevered in this policy to the present time. By Jove, this was caused by a just hatred of tyranny more than by the well-deserved respect due to the ancient fatherland. For who could bear that the Roman state, acquired with the kind of virtue that Camillus, Publicola, Fabricius, Curtius, Fabius, Regulus, Scipio, Marcellus, the Catos, and countless other very honorable and chaste men displayed, fell into the hands and under the domination of Caligula and other monsters and vile tyrants who were innocent of no vice and redeemed by no virtue? To excel in this these monsters were in a competition of mighty proportions, striving with all their power.

[*There follows an extended description of the excesses of cruelty and sexual perversions under the reigns of the Roman emperors Caligula and Tiberius derived from Suetonius's* Lives of the Caesars. *Bruni lays the blame for this decadence at the feet of Julius Caesar, who undermined the Roman Republic.*]

O Gaius Caesar, what manifest crimes have you visited upon the city of Rome! . . . you paved the way for so many evils and outrages that your successors perpetrated with every kind of iniquity and cruelty.

But to what end? someone will ask. Really there are two reasons: first, to show that Florence has not, without good cause, developed its political allegiances; and second, to make it understood that at the time when Florence was founded the city of Rome flourished greatly in power, liberty, genius, and especially with great citizens. Now, after the Republic had been subjected to the power of a single head, "those outstanding minds vanished," as Tacitus says. So it is of importance whether a colony was founded at a later date, since by then all the virtue and nobility of the Romans had been destroyed; nothing great or outstanding could be conveyed by those who left the city.

Since Florence had as its founders those who were obeyed everywhere by everyone and dominated by their skill and military prowess, and since it was founded when a free and unconquered Roman people flourished in power, nobility, virtues, and genius, it cannot be doubted at all that this one city not only stands out in its beauty, architecture, and appropriateness of site (as we have seen), but that Florence also greatly excels beyond all other cities in the dignity and nobility of its origin.

Pier Candido Decembrio, *Panegyric in Praise of the City of the Milanese*, 1436

You therefore, o most learned Leonardo [Bruni], wrote that the founders of Florence were the Romans; I want to trace the origins of the Milanese from the kings of the Gauls. So which people has a more noble origin? . . . Pay attention, o Milanese, and appreciate your lineage, when you realize to what extent your origin makes you supremely illustrious and distinguished among all peoples, since you do not excel in nobility only compared to foreigners, but you exceed in glory and prestige the Florentines, who descend from the Roman people. Was not the colony of Fiesole founded by Lucius Sulla while besieging the [Roman] state with force and arms? So where did the Florentines' bitter hatred of tyrants come from, [those Florentines] who descend from Sulla, the most wicked of tyrants?

[. . .]

Not unjustly did the ancients give this city [Milan] the name of "Second Rome," a civic glory that both Florence and the other illustrious Italian cities have always lacked. It seems to me that such preeminence was attributed to the Milanese people because they would restore to its original splendor the empire's strength, declining in favor in another part of the world [that is, the Eastern Roman Empire], and they would not allow the name of Italy to be robbed of the ancient dignity of their ancestors.

Notes

1 Salutati xxvii. See also Salutati's letter cited in **#24**.

2 Florence was founded *c.* 200 BCE by the Etruscans, destroyed by the dictator Sulla in 82 BCE, and restored under Julius Caesar in 59 BCE. His adopted son Caesar Augustus became the first Roman emperor in 27 BCE.

3 Either a reference to Guelf and Ghibelline factionalism or to the Roman civil wars.

Sources

Antonio Loschi, *Invective Against the Florentines*, in Salutati, Coluccio, *Political Writings*, ed. Stefano U. Baldassarri, trans. Rolf Bagemihl, Harvard UP, 2014, pp. 145–7.

Coluccio Salutati, *Reply to a Slanderous Detractor Who Has Written Many Wounding Things Against the Renowned City of Florence*, in Salutati, Coluccio. *Political Writings*, ed. Stefano U. Baldassarri; trans. Rolf Bagemihl, Harvard UP, 2014, pp. 175–7.

Leonardo Bruni, *Panegyric to the City of Florence*, Benjamin Kohl translation in Witt, *The Earthly Republic*, U Pennsylvania P, 1978, pp. 149–54.

Pier Candido Decembrio. *Panegyric in Praise of the City of Milan*, in Paolo Ponzù Donato, "Between Dante and Caesar. The Vernacular Policy of Filippo Maria Visconti," *Humanistica Lovaniensia*, Vol. 69, No.1/2 (Fall 2020), 9–33, pp. 12, 14.

References

Baron, Hans. *The Crisis of the Early Italian Renaissance*, Princeton UP, 1955.

Bruni, Leonardo. *History of the Florentine People*, ed. and trans. James Hankins, Harvard UP, 2001.

Hankins, James, ed. *Renaissance Civic Humanism: Reappraisals and Reflections*, Cambridge UP, 2000.

Witt, Ronald. *In the Footsteps of the Ancients: The Origins of Humanism from Lovati to Bruni*, Brill, 2003.

12 Antiquity as inspiration for painters

Leon Battista Alberti, *On Painting*, 1435

Figure 2.2 Sandro Botticelli, *The Calumny of Apelles*, 1490s, Uffizi.

Leon Battista Alberti (1404–1472), the quintessential "Renaissance man," was a polymath who studied and wrote on a wide variety of scholarly and artistic topics. He is best known today as the architect of buildings such as the Palazzo Rucellai and the façade of Santa Maria Novella in Florence, and as the author of *On Painting*. It was long believed that Alberti first wrote this treatise in Latin in 1435 and translated it into the vernacular afterward in 1436; however, recent scholarship has demonstrated that he probably wrote it in Italian first, with input from Filippo Brunelleschi, to whom the work is dedicated. In this treatise, Alberti praises the genius of Brunelleschi and his contemporary Florentine artists, and puts their talent on a par with the ancients.

DOI: 10.4324/9781003284284-14

Advocating that these artists study the liberal arts as the noble Greeks and Romans once did, he thereby raises the Renaissance artist's status from that of a mere artisan or manual laborer to a creative intellectual. The term "liberal arts" derives from the Latin *liber*, meaning free, and refers to the study of skills befitting a free man, as distinguished from manual labor performed by servants or slaves. Hence, an elevation in social status is implied, as well as access to higher education: the seven liberal arts studied in universities at the time were grammar, rhetoric, logic, music, geometry, arithmetic, and astronomy. Alongside the study of geometry for developing technical skills, Alberti emphasizes the need for a painter to have a broad knowledge of literature. In order to devise a compelling "*historia*"—the narrative that forms the subject for a painting—he further advises the artist to discuss ideas with "poets and orators," who will be able to suggest themes from antiquity. The example he provides is a complex composition by the fourth-century BCE painter Apelles.[1]

This theme, the so-called *Calumny of Apelles*, was adopted two decades after Alberti's death by Florentine painter Sandro Botticelli (Alessandro di Mariano di Vanni Filipepi, 1445–1510), one of a number of the artist's paintings on classical or mythological themes.[2] This small panel, painted in the 1490s, reflects the turbulent spiritual and political atmosphere in Florence during his day. Botticelli is said to have been a *piagnone*, a supporter of Girolamo Savonarola (#54), and the nude figure of Truth on the far left of the painting perhaps reveals the influence of the friar. "In a sermon of 1497, Savonarola claimed that 'Naked truth is more pleasing, just as an undressed figure, without a veil, is more pleasing than one that is covered.' Significantly, he explicitly described David as being naked in his fight against Goliath: 'know that truth will conquer and, in the end, will prove stronger; truth does not seek to attach itself to another power; rather on its own, alone and naked, it wins always.'"[3] Botticelli's Truth is physically almost identical to his Venus, painted perhaps half a dozen years earlier (*Birth of Venus*, Figure 5.4). However, rather than being gracefully poised at the center of the composition lost in sweet thoughts of her own, the lovely nude woman is shunted to the far end of the canvas and mostly ignored; she gestures upward, turning her imploring gaze toward Heaven. The emotional impact of this gesture is yet another element that Alberti would have approved of, as he describes how the positions of the body and the features of the face reflect the state of an individual's mind. By causing the viewer to identify with the emotions expressed in the painting, their heart will be moved, which according to Alberti is the objective of art.

Leon Battista Alberti, *On Painting*, 1435

Book 2

28. There were certainly a great number of sculptors and painters in those [ancient] times, when princes and plebeians, the learned and the unlearned

enjoyed painting, and among the first spoils brought from the provinces were painted panels and other images. It reached such a point that Paulus Aemilius and many other Roman citizens taught their children painting, a worthy custom that had been widely practiced by the Greeks. They wanted their children to be raised well, learning painting along with geometry and music. Indeed, even among females it was considered an honor to know how to paint. Martia, the daughter of Varro, is praised by writers for her skill in painting. Painting was so highly prized by the Greeks that they passed a law banning servants from learning how to paint. Indeed, they did well, since the art of painting was always the most fitting for free minds and noble souls.

And for myself, I consider it an excellent indicator of a most perfect intellect if a person takes great delight in painting. Even though it happens that this art is appealing to both the learned and the unlearned, it rarely occurs with other arts that the same thing pleases both expert and inexpert alike. Nor will you often find a person who does not greatly desire to become skilled in painting. Indeed, Nature herself seems to delight in painting, as we see the shapes of hippocentaurs and the hairy bearded faces of kings in the crevices of marbles. It is even said by many that in a certain gem belonging to Pyrrhus, all nine Muses were depicted by Nature each with her own symbol. Moreover, no other art is to be found in which the educated and uneducated of all ages so willingly strive to exert themselves to learn it. Let me confess, about myself, that for pleasure I give myself over to painting, a thing I do frequently whenever I find some leisure from my greater tasks. Then, with what pleasure I remain at my work, often amazed when three or four hours have gone by.[4]

29. Thus, the practice of this art brings praise, riches, and perpetual fame to a person who becomes a master. This being so, if painting be the best and most ancient ornament of things, worthy of free men, welcome to both learned and unlearned, I highly encourage young scholars to devote themselves as much as possible to painting.

[*Alberti describes techniques such as use of the velo (veil), measurement, principles of linear perspective, representation of proportions of the body, as well as depiction of light and shade.*]

40. The *historia* that will cause you to praise and marvel will be the one that shows itself to be rich and agreeable, capturing the attention and moving the soul for an extended time, regardless of whether or not the viewer is educated. The first element that gives pleasure in the *historia* comes from abundance and variety of things. As in food and music, freshness and plenty are always pleasing, so different from old, customary things that the mind is charmed by every type of abundance and variety. Thus, in painting, a multitude of bodies and colors is pleasing. I will say that a painting is richest that contains the presence of old people, mature men, youths, boys, women, maidens, children, domestic animals, puppies, small birds, horses, sheep,

buildings, country scenes, and every such thing, each in its appropriate place. And I will always praise any abundance appropriate to the *historia*. . . .

41. Furthermore, the *historia* will move the viewer's heart when the persons depicted there express their feelings strongly. Nature sees to it that nothing moves us more powerfully than when something is similar to our own selves: we cry with those who cry, laugh with those who laugh, and sorrow with those who sorrow. But these emotions—movements of the heart—are made known through motions of the body. We see how those who are dispirited, oppressed by care and assailed by worry, remain as if dazed in their powers and feelings, moving slowly and sluggishly, their limbs pale and unstable. You will see the brow of a melancholy person compressed, their neck languidly bent, every limb drooping, almost overwhelmed with exhaustion and neglect. However, in the person who is irate—since anger stirs the heart and irritation fills the eyes and face—when agitated by such burning fury the entire body is aflame with color. Men who are happy and joyous move about freely, their joints bending gracefully. They say Aristides of Thebes, a contemporary of Apelles, was expert at representing emotions, just as we are sure to be when we come to recognize them through diligent study.

[. . .]

Book 3

53. I would like for the painter to be educated, as much as possible, in all the liberal arts, but most of all, I desire for him to know geometry. I like the opinion of Pamphilus, a most noble ancient painter from whom young noblemen began to learn to paint. He held that no painter could paint well if he was not well-versed in geometry. Our rudiments, which expound all of the perfect, complete art of painting, can be easily grasped by a geometrician. But whoever is ignorant of geometry will never understand those basics, nor any other principles of painting. Therefore, I affirm that it is necessary for the painter to study geometry. And I would further desire them to take pleasure in the company of poets and orators. These men have many qualities in common with painters, and their abundant information on many topics will help them greatly in composing a *historia*, which is praised most for its invention. This quality has such force that we see, even alone without the painting, a beautiful invention is appealing. Reading it, one admires Lucian's description of *Calumny* that he recounts as painted by Apelles. I think it is not inappropriate here to tell the story, in order to advise painters how they ought to be watchful for this kind of invention. In that picture there was a man with enormous ears, and near him, were two women, one on each side; the name of one was Ignorance, the other Suspicion. A little farther off was Calumny, a woman most lovely to look at, but with a face that was somewhat too cunning. In her right hand she held a burning torch, and with the other she dragged by his hair a youth who had his hands raised to the sky. There was an ugly, pallid, deformed man, filthy all over—he looked as a soldier might,

who was emaciated and sunbaked in the fields—he was guiding Calumny and his name was Envy. And Calumny had other female companions, who arranged her ornaments and clothes: one was called Deceit, and the other Fraud. Behind these was Penitence, a woman dressed in mourning, rending her garments. Behind followed a young girl, modest and chaste, and she was called Truth. If this story gives such pleasure when it is told, just think how charming and delightful it would be to see it painted by the hand of Apelles.

54. It would also be pleasing to see those three sisters—named by Hesiod as Aglaea Euphrosyne and Thalia—who were depicted holding hands and laughing, wearing loose and transparent garments.[5]

Notes

1 The original painting has not survived from antiquity; its composition is known to us from a description by Greek satirist Lucian of Samosata, a second-century CE satirist who wrote in Greek. According to Lucian, Apelles was slandered by a rival painter named Antiphilus, who accused him of conspiracy before the Egyptian King Ptolemy. After being proved innocent, Apelles created this painting in retaliation.
2 Botticelli, who probably read little Latin and no Greek, might have been inspired by Alberti's description of the scene, although there were other numerous vernacular translations of Lucian that Botticelli could have drawn upon. Dressen 326. See also Botticelli's inspiration for the *Birth of Venus* (#47).
3 Burke 72.
4 Apart from a medal that is believed to be a self-portrait, we have no surely attributed artistic works by Alberti's hand.
5 A description of the three Graces, depicted by Botticelli in his *Primavera*, *c.*1482, Uffizi.

Source

Leon Battista Alberti. *De Pictura*, 1435 in *Opere volgari*, vol. III, Laterza, 1973; trans. Kaborycha.

References

Alberti, Leon Battista. *On Painting. A New Translation and Critical Edition*, ed. and trans. Rocco Sinisgalli, Cambridge UP, 2011.

Barker, Emma, Nick Webb and Kim Woods. *The Changing Status of the Artist*, Yale UP in association with the Open University, 1999.

Burke, Jill. *The Italian Renaissance Nude*, Yale UP, 2018.

Dressen, Angela. "From Dante to Landino: Botticelli's *Calumny of Apelles* and its Sources," *Mitteilungen des Kunsthistorischen Institutes in Florenz*, Vol. 59. Bd., H. 3 (2017), pp. 324–39.

Grafton, Anthony. *Alberti Master Builder of the Italian Renaissance*, Cambridge UP, 2002.

Olszewski, Edward J. "Michelangelo's *David*: Full Frontal Nudity in the Age of Savonarola," *Notes in the History of Art*, Vol. 35, No. 1–2 (Fall 2015/Winter 2016), pp. 118–25.

13 Philology deployed against the papacy

Lorenzo Valla, *On the Forgery of the Alleged Donation of Constantine*, 1440

The man who debunked "the most infamous forgery in the history of the world" was Roman humanist Lorenzo Valla (1407–1457).[1] For centuries the church had used the document known as the *Donation of Constantine* to declare possession of enormous territories and to justify political intervention in secular matters. The text of the *Donation* purports that, shortly after converting to Christianity in 313 CE, Emperor Constantine (r.306–37 CE) gave or "donated" the entire Western Roman Empire to Pope Sylvester I (r.314–35 CE), who is said to have cured the emperor of leprosy. Before Valla, others had objected to this document, including Marsilius of Padua (**#22**), Petrarch, and Dante (**#52**). In the *Inferno*, Dante condemned the *Donation* as the root of the corruption of the church: "Ah, Constantine, what wickedness was born—and not from your conversion—from the dower that you bestowed upon the first rich father!"[2] And Valla's contemporary, the theologian Nicholas of Cusa (1401–1464) denounced the document as a forgery in 1433. No one before Valla, however, had launched such a scathing, irrefutable attack on it. Written in Latin and titled *De falso credita et ementita Constantini Donatione*, in this diatribe, Valla systematically tears to shreds all claims to its authenticity. He accomplishes this by using tools of humanist philology, the field that regards language within its historical context, recognizing that language is never static, but that grammar and use of words evolve over time. In his analysis, Valla effectively demonstrates that the Latin language as it was used during the time of the Roman Empire was very different than the medieval Latin employed in the text of the *Donation*. Modern scholarship has confirmed Valla's conclusions, dating the forgery of the document to sometime during the middle to late eighth century.

The historical context of Valla's own writing is also significant. He wrote this polemical discourse in 1440 (between April 2 and May 25) while he was employed at the court of King Alfonso of Aragon ("the Magnanimous," 1396–1458, **#15**) in Naples. Alfonso was involved in a power struggle with Pope Eugenius IV during this time. After the death of Queen Johanna (Giovanna) II of the Anjou dynasty in 1435, succession to the throne of Naples was contested, with Eugenius supporting the Angevin claim over the Aragonese. Eventually

DOI: 10.4324/9781003284284-15

the dispute with the pope was resolved on June 14, 1443, with the Treaty of Terracina, after Valla strengthened Alfonso's hand in negotiation by undermining the papacy's claim to dominion in southern Italy. Thus, an impeccable piece of humanist scholarship also served the political ends of the ruler: "Valla's treatise illustrates better than any other work of the Neapolitan humanists the way the needs of a patron and the talents of a client could combine to produce a work of genius."[3] And beyond the immediate political context of the Kingdom of Naples, Valla's analytical method was admired by scholars across Europe. Dutch humanist Desiderius Erasmus (1466–1536) praised him as "a man who with so much energy, zeal and labor, refuted the stupidities of the barbarians, saved half-buried letters from extinction, restored Italy to her ancient splendor of eloquence, and forced even the learned to express themselves henceforth with more circumspection."[4] Furthermore, Valla's critique of the *Donation* continued making waves during the Protestant Reformation. In 1537, Martin Luther published it in German—calling its author a "learned and accurate man" and the pope the Antichrist[5]—while the papacy retaliated by placing Valla's work on the *Index of Prohibited Books* in 1559.

Lorenzo Valla, *On the Forgery of the Alleged Donation of Constantine*, 1440

I know that for a long time now men's ears are waiting to hear the offense with which I charge the Roman pontiffs. It is, indeed, an enormous one, due either to supine ignorance, or to gross avarice which is the slave of idols, or to pride of empire of which cruelty is ever the companion. For during some centuries now, either they have not known that the *Donation of Constantine* is spurious and forged, or else they themselves forged it, and their successors walking in the same way of deceit as their elders have defended as true what they knew to be false, dishonoring the majesty of the pontificate, dishonoring the memory of ancient pontiffs, dishonoring the Christian religion, confounding everything with murders, disasters and crimes. They say the city of Rome is theirs, theirs the kingdom of Sicily and of Naples, the whole of Italy, the Gauls, the Spains, the Germans, the Britons, indeed the whole West; for all these are contained in the instrument of the *Donation* itself. So all these are yours, supreme pontiff? And it is your purpose to recover them all? To despoil all kings and princes of the West of their cities or compel them to pay you a yearly tribute, is that your plan?

> [*Valla argues that the Emperor Constantine would never have given away his empire and that Pope Sylvester would never have accepted such a "donation."*]

But I want to take the forger himself, truly a "straw" man without wheat, by the neck, and drag him into court. What do you say, you forger? Whence comes it that we do not read this grant in the *Acts of Sylvester*? This book, forsooth, is rare, difficult to get, not owned by the many but rather kept as the Fasti once were by the pontifices, or the Sibylline books by the Decemvirs! It was written in Greek, or Syriac, or Chaldee! Gelasius testifies that it was read by many of the orthodox; Voragine mentions it; we also have seen thousands of copies of it, and written long ago; and in almost every cathedral it is read when Sylvester's Day comes around. Yet nevertheless no one says that he has read there what you put in it; no one has heard of it; no one has dreamt of it. Or is there perhaps some other history of Sylvester? And what can that be? I know no other, nor do I understand that any other is referred to by you, for you speak of the one which Gelasius says is read in many churches. In this, however, we do not find your grant. But if it is not found in the *Life of Sylvester*, why do you declare that it is? How did you dare to jest in a matter of such importance, and to make sport of the cupidity of silly men?

But I am foolish to inveigh against the audacity of this [forger], instead of inveighing against the insanity of those who give him credence. If any one should say that this had been recorded for remembrance among the Greeks, the Hebrews, the barbarians, would you not bid him name his author, produce his book, and the passage, to be explained by a reliable translator, before you would believe it? But now your own language, and a very well-known book are involved, and either you do not question such an incredible occurrence, or when you do not find it written down you have such utter credulity as to believe that it is written down and authentic! And, satisfied with this title, you move heaven and earth, and, as though no doubt existed, you pursue with the terrors of war and with other threats those who do not believe you!

> [*Valla criticizes the language used in the document, finding in it incorrect and anachronistic vocabulary, crude Latin style.*]

O you scoundrel, you villain! The same history [the *Life of Sylvester*] which you allege as your evidence, says that for a long time none of senatorial rank was willing to accept the Christian religion, and that Constantine solicited the poor with bribes to be baptized. And you say that within the first days, immediately, the Senate, the nobles, the satraps, as though already Christians, with the Caesar passed decrees for the honoring of the Roman church! What! How do you want to have satraps come in here? Numskull, blockhead! Do the Caesars speak thus; are Roman decrees usually drafted thus? Whoever heard of satraps being mentioned in the councils of the Romans?[6] I do not remember ever to have read of any Roman satrap being mentioned, or even of a satrap in any of the Roman provinces. But this fellow speaks of the emperor's satraps, and puts them in before the Senate, though all honors, even those bestowed upon the ruling prince, are decreed by the Senate alone, or with the addition "and the Roman people." Thus, we see carved on ancient stones or bronze tablets or coins two letters,

"S.C.," that is "By decree of the Senate," or four, "S.P.Q.R.," that is, "The Senate and the Roman People."

[. . .]

I will not speak here of the barbarisms in [the forger's] language when he says "chief over the priests" instead of chief of the priests; when he puts in the same sentence "*extiterit*" and "*existat*" [confusing meanings, moods and tenses]. . . . How in the world—this is much more absurd, and impossible in the nature of things—could one speak of Constantinople as one of the patriarchal sees, when it was not yet a patriarchate, nor a see, nor a Christian city, nor named Constantinople, nor founded, nor planned! For the "privilege" was granted, so it says, the third day after Constantine became a Christian; when as yet Byzantium, not Constantinople, occupied that site.

[. . .]

And how is it that he speaks of a province of "Byzantia," when it was a town, Byzantium by name? The place was by no means large enough for the erection of so great a city; for the old city of Byzantium was included within the walls of Constantinople. And this man says the [new] city is to be built on the most fitting place in it! Why does he choose to put Thrace, in which Byzantium lies, in the East, when it lies to the north? I suppose Constantine did not know the place which he had chosen for the building of the city, in what latitude it was, whether it was a town or a province, nor how large it was!

"On the churches of the blessed apostles Peter and Paul, for the providing of the lights, we have conferred landed estates of possessions, and have enriched them with different objects; and through our sacred imperial mandate, we have granted them of our property in the east as well as in the west; and even in the north and in the southern quarter; namely, in Judea, Greece, Asia, Thrace, Africa and Italy and the various islands; under this condition indeed, that all shall be administered by the hand of our most blessed father the supreme pontiff, Sylvester, and his successors."

O you scoundrel! Were there in Rome churches, that is, temples, dedicated to Peter and Paul? Who had constructed them? Who would have dared to build them, when, as history tells us, the Christians had never had anything but secret and secluded meeting-places?

[*Valla notes that the dating of the document is impossible.*]

"Given at Rome, on the third day before the Kalends of April, Constantine Augustus consul for the fourth time, and Gallicanus consul for the fourth time."

He took the next to the last day of March so that we might feel that this was done in the season of holy days, which, for the most part, come at that time. And "Constantine consul for the fourth time, and Gallicanus consul for the fourth time." Strange if each had been consul thrice, and they were colleagues in a fourth consulship! . . . And by this argument alone the whole "privilege" is confuted outright, destroyed, and overturned.

Notes

1 Fried 1.
2 *Inferno* 19.115–17, Mandelbaum trans.
3 Bentley 114.
4 Cited by Coleman 3.
5 Whitford 49.
6 Coleman notes that the term was not used until the eighth century.

Source

Lorenzo Valla. *On the Forgery of the Alleged Donation of Constantine* in Latin with English translation by Christopher B. Coleman, Yale UP, 1922, pp. 25–27, 79–81, 85–87, 93–97, 137, ed. Kaborycha.

References

Bentley, Jerry H. *Politics and Culture in Renaissance Naples*, Princeton UP, 1987.

Black, Robert. "The Donation of Constantine: A New Source for the Concept of the Renaissance," in *Language and Images of Renaissance Italy*, ed. Alison Brown, Clarendon Press, 1995, pp. 51–85.

Celenza, Christopher S. "Valla, Latin Christianity, Culture," in *The Italian Renaissance and the Origins of the Modern Humanities: An Intellectual History, 1400–1800*, Cambridge UP, 2021, pp. 200–27.

Fried, Johannes. *Donation of Constantine and Constitutum Constantini: The Misinterpretation of a Fiction and its Original Meaning*, Walter de Gruyter, 2007.

Lorch, Maristella. "Italy's Leading Humanist: Lorenzo Valla," in *Renaissance Humanism. Foundations, Forms, and Legacy*, ed. A. Rabil, vol. 1, U Pennsylvania P, 1988, pp. 332–49.

Valla, Lorenzo. *On the Donation of Constantine*, trans. G.W. Bowersock. I Tatti Renaissance Library, Harvard UP, 2007.

Whitford, David M. "The Papal Antichrist: Martin Luther and the Underappreciated Influence of Lorenzo Valla," *Renaissance Quarterly*, Vol. 61, No. 1 (Spring 2008), pp. 26–52.

14 The duke of Milan likened to Caesar

Suetonius, *Lives of the Caesars*, *c.*119 CE

Pier Candido Decembrio, *Life of Filippo Maria Visconti*, 1447

Pier Candido Decembrio (1399–1477), "probably the most important representative of humanism in Milan during the first half of the fifteenth century,"[1] was born in Pavia to a distinguished and learned family. He was the son of humanist Uberto Decembrio (1350–1427), who had succeeded Antonio Loschi (**#11**) as chancellor to the duke of Milan. Though humanism is most associated with Florence—scholars from all over the Italian Peninsula were attracted to study there with luminaries such as Salutati, Bruni, Marsilio Ficino, and Angelo Poliziano—Decembrio belonged to a well-established tradition of humanists in northern Italy. This included Petrarch, who had spent significant time in Milan, Pavia, Padua, and Venice, and corresponded with scholars throughout the Italian Peninsula. Not only did humanists thus create a sort of Renaissance republic of letters, they also disseminated cultural cross-pollination by moving from one city to another in search of patronage. For example, Lorenzo Valla, born in Rome, and Panormita (Antonio Beccadelli, **#15**), from Palermo, each resided for a time at the courts of both the king of Naples and the duke of Milan, Filippo Maria Visconti (1392–1447). Filippo Maria, who became duke of Milan after the death of his elder brother Giovanni Maria in 1412, surrounded himself with humanist scholars, including Francesco Filelfo (1398–1481), Gasparino Barzizza (1360–1430), and Panormita. The presence of so many men of letters increased the prestige of his court, and though not as learned as his father, (Giangaleazzo Visconti **#11**), Filippo Maria recognized the propaganda value of humanists' rhetoric. Part of the duke's inner circle for twenty-eight years, Pier Candido Decembrio wrote a detailed biography soon after his employer died and included sordid details of sadism, torture of political prisoners, sexual relations with young boys, as well as the duke's many irrational superstitions and reliance on astrology.[2] Decembrio's model for writing the *Life of Filippo Maria Visconti* was the ancient biographer Gaius Suetonius Tranquillus (*c.*69 CE–post 122 CE). In his *Lives of the Caesars*, Suetonius provided similarly scandalous details about the Roman emperors, including information about Julius Caesar's youthful homosexual encounters and the Emperor Augustus's numerous extramarital affairs. In one passage, after a

DOI: 10.4324/9781003284284-16

description of Augustus's political and military victories, Suetonius lists the emperor's personal traits, including his fears and superstitions, which are strikingly similar to Filippo Maria's own quirks. One wonders whether, had he been alive to read it, Pier Candido's patron would have been entirely displeased by the contents of a biography that showed him to be similar in so many ways to the Caesars. We know that Duke Filippo Maria admired the work of Suetonius: for the ducal library of Pavia that his father had founded, Filippo Maria had many Latin works translated into the vernacular, the first being *Lives of the Caesars* by Suetonius and the *Historia Augusta*, which similarly contains biographies of Roman emperors. The dedication copy of the latter was copied by Angelo Decembrio, brother to Pier Candido, who was probably the translator.[3] Moreover, Pier Candido translated a life of Alexander the Great and writings of Julius Caesar for the library, with dedications to Filippo Maria Visconti and inscriptions comparing the duke with these great men from antiquity. "Caesarism"—drawing the comparison between themselves and the Caesars—was an important incentive for Renaissance despots to patronize humanism.

Suetonius, *Lives of the Caesars*, *c.*119 CE

The Emperor Augustus

We have the following account of him respecting his belief in omens and such like. He had so great a dread of thunder and lightning that he always carried about him a seal's skin, by way of preservation. And upon any apprehension of a violent storm, he would retire to some place of concealment in a vault underground; having formerly been terrified by a flash of lightning, while travelling in the night. . . . Some signs and omens he regarded as infallible. If in the morning his shoe was put on wrong, the left instead of the right, that boded some disaster. If when he commenced a long journey, by sea or land, there happened to fall a mizzling rain, he held it to be a good sign of a speedy and happy return. He was much affected likewise with anything out of the common course of nature. A palm tree, which chanced to grow up between some stones in the court of his house, he transplanted into a court where the images of the household gods were placed, and took all possible care to make it thrive in the island of Capri, some decayed branches of an old ilex, which hung drooping to the ground, recovered themselves upon his arrival; at which he was so delighted, that he made an exchange with the Republic of Naples, of the island of Oenaria [Ischia], for that of Capri. He likewise observed certain days; as never to go from home the day after the Nundiae [market day], nor to begin any serious business upon the Nones; avoiding nothing else in it, as he writes to Tiberius, than its unlucky name.

Pier Candido Decembrio, *Life of Filippo Maria Visconti*, 1447

67. His superstitious nature and his fear of lightning

People unfamiliar with the private lives of Augustus and other Roman emperors might well be forgiven for thinking that Filippo Maria was the most superstitious prince that ever lived. He ordered service trees to be chopped down wherever they grew, his reason being (as he said) that he had heard how noxious the shade cast by this kind of tree could be, inflicting sharp pains on its victims. And he offered a reward to anyone who obeyed his standing order to kill all crows, paying up once their dead bodies were brought to him. He had a special place marked off in his sleeping quarters where his former valet Silvester had lain, prior to his death. This space was sacred and no one was allowed to enter it. So when once it happened that the chief steward Todeschino, while serving the prince's meal, accidentally put his foot in the forbidden zone, Filippo Maria ordered that the food be carried back to the kitchen, and that the meal be started all over again from scratch.

In the very center of his palace there stood an ancient pear tree. It was customary to tie wild animals to this tree for sport, and to let the dogs of the house torment them. The demise of this tree saddened Filippo Maria to such an extent that he ordered five trees of a similar kind to be planted in exactly the same spot. He wanted full grown loquat trees to be especially well cared for, out of respect for the fruit that appeared emblazoned on the Visconti coat of arms.

Every year on the first of January he would order that a horse of whitest white be finely arrayed and brought before him, a ritual that was supposed to bring him good luck. If it happened that he accidentally slipped his left shoe onto his right foot, he took this as a bad omen. If he heard birds crying out with strange sounds, especially in the middle of the night, he immediately took fright. He regarded it as unlucky to encounter on a Friday anyone who had just shaved, or to go catching birds, especially quail, in the fields on that day; it was equally wrong to mount a horse on the day set aside to commemorate the beheading of Saint John the Baptist, or to do likewise thereafter throughout the year on similar holy days, just as it was absolutely forbidden to do anything improper on the feast days devoted to the Virgin Mary. He was also most assiduous in worshipping the images of these two holy figures, as well as those of Saints Anthony, Christopher, Sebastian, Guiniforte, Peter Martyr, and Mary Magdalene and Elizabeth, as shown by his prayerful devotions.

There was however nothing he feared more than lightning. When once lightning bolts struck the Castle of Porta Giovia, causing a fire to spread out in all directions, he ordered his men to fight off the conflagration; he himself could not bear to look upon the flames, such was his horror of fiery lightning.

After that incident he ordered the room where he slept to be reinforced with double-vaulted walls, to protect it against sudden and unexpected lightning strikes. As soon as he heard thunder in the sky, he would hide himself away in a corner of this room, surrounded by his retinue of servants. He venerated the image of Saint Barbara for this very reason. In addition to which he had a gold medal cast that drew upon the power of the stars to drive away storm clouds.

68. His respect for astrologers and his observance of the lunar cycles

So strong was his belief in the teachings and pronouncements of the astrologers that he summoned to his court the most skilled practitioners of the art, and followed their advice in virtually everything he undertook to do.

Notes

1 Kristeller 282.
2 On Renaissance rulers and astrology, see Azzolini.
3 Ponzù Donato 18.

Sources

Suetonius, *Lives of the Twelve Caesars*, trans. Alexander Thomson, Gebbie & Co. 1889.

Pier Candido Decembrio, *Lives of the Milanese Tyrants*, trans. Gary Ianziti, Harvard UP, 2019, pp. 135–9.

References

Azzolini, Monica. *The Duke and the Stars. Astrology and Politics in Renaissance Milan*, Harvard UP, 2013.

Kristeller, Paul Oskar. "Pier Candido Decembrio and His Unpublished Treatise on the Immortality of the Soul," *The Classical Tradition: Literary and Historical Studies in Honor of Harry Caplan*, ed. L. Wallach, Cornell University Press, 1966, 536–558.

Ponzù Donato, Paolo. "Between Dante and Caesar. The Vernacular Policy of Filippo Maria Visconti," *Humanistica Lovaniensia*, Vol. 69, No.1/2 (Fall 2020), pp. 9–33.

Rabil, Jr. Albert. "Humanism in Milan," in *Renaissance Humanism. Foundations, Forms, and Legacy*, vol. 1, U Pennsylvania P, 1988, pp. 235–63.

Robin, Diana. *Filelfo in Milan: Writings 1451–1477*, Princeton UP, 1991.

15 A triumphal arch for the king of Naples

Panormita, *King Alfonso's Triumph*, 1455

Panormita, *On the Sayings and Deeds of King Alfonso*, 1455

Figure 2.3 Pere Joan, Pietro da Milano, et al. *Triumphal Arch of King Alfonso of Aragon*, 1444–51; 1465–86, detail of middle section, Castel Nuovo, Naples. The upper Latin inscription reads: "Alfonso, first among kings, built this arch"; the lower one reads: "Alfonso King of Spain, Sicily, Italy: Pious, Merciful, Invincible."

After defeating René of Anjou in 1442, like a victorious Roman emperor, Alfonso of Aragon (see Valla, **#13**) made a grand triumphal entry into the city of Naples. For the official ceremony, which occurred on February 26, 1443, he had a temporary arch erected. Soon afterward, plans began for a magnificent freestanding triumphal arch to permanently commemorate that entry. Later, the structure was fitted as the monumental entrance to the royal residence, the Castel Nuovo, also known as the Maschio Angioino (the Angevin fortress, built in 1266 by Charles of Anjou). Framed by a pair of massive circular, turreted stone towers, the marble arch was created over the course of the following decades "by a changing tribe of anonymous workers."[1] There were more than thirty-three sculptors from various parts of Italy—the influence of the Florentine school of sculpture, especially

DOI: 10.4324/9781003284284-17

of Donatello, is evident—as well as from the Iberian Peninsula and Dalmatia. Knowledgeable of ancient history, Alfonso was aware of the self-image he wanted to project, and the stone carvers were eager to satisfy their generous patron with classically inspired friezes, reliefs, and sculptures celebrating the king's virtues. Moreover, the structure recalls the Arch of Trajan (*c.*114 CE), in nearby Benevento, associating King Alfonso with the ancient Roman emperor who ruled between 98 and 117 CE. As a new ruler, and a foreigner, Alfonso appreciated the comparison to Trajan who, like himself, was born in Spain. Their common birthplace is also emphasized by Panormita (Antonio Beccadelli 1394–1471) in his biography *The Sayings and Deeds of King Alfonso* (*De dictis et factis Alphonsi regis*), for which Alfonso rewarded the humanist with 1,000 gold coins.

The central frieze represents, in simplified form, Alfonso's actual triumphal entry into the city, with Alfonso sitting atop a chariot, the orb of empire in one hand, and in the other, there was once a scepter. There are also chivalric elements in the frieze: at the king's feet a flame is burning, representing the Siege Perilous (the "perilous seat") of Arthurian legend, on which only the hero capable of rescuing the Holy Grail could sit safely. The chariot is accompanied by the local barons on foot, who "walk in a quiet, swaying manner, though with nervous urgency."[2] Behind them is the Tunisian ambassador and a group of bearded Moors wearing turbans, and to the far left are a group of admiring townspeople looking on. Four prancing horses draw the chariot, bringing to mind the *Triumphal Quadriga* of St. Mark's Basilica in Venice (second or third century CE). At the head of the procession are sculpted images of musicians and dancers reminiscent of the figures of Donatello and Luca della Robbia in their *Cantorie*, while to the far right is a group of mounted heralds, cheeks puffed out blowing on wind instruments and banging drums. The background is filled with classical architectural elements—coffered ceilings, pilasters topped by a pediment with scrollwork, decorative friezes, allegorical busts, and putti—yet the total effect is a harmonious blend of ancient, medieval, and Christian imagery. Military symbols are nowhere present; there are no signs of the spoils of war that were normally on display in ancient Roman triumphs, no bound prisoners or piles of booty, rather, the emphasis in this triumphal frieze is on King Alfonso as bringer of peace. Alfonso's rule, however, was anything but peaceful. His takeover of Naples created enemies both foreign and domestic, with a constant threat of conflict during his reign. Many within the kingdom continued to support the ousted Angevin king, and Alfonso was resented for bringing in so many Catalans and awarding them important offices and privileges over local Neapolitan subjects. Despite the grand images created by his sculptors and the lavish praise bestowed on him by humanists, "Alfonso the Magnanimous" actually had a somewhat precarious hold on power. Just as much as they benefitted from his generosity, the artists and scholars who were employed by Alfonso provided a priceless service to their patron. Due to their efforts, it is easy to overlook the fact that Alfonso was neither the legitimate hereditary ruler nor chosen by the people. Rather than depicting yet another Renaissance "new prince"—to use Machiavelli's language intent on nothing more than the conquest and domination of a foreign land, what his sculptors and humanists created was the image of the king of Naples as a wise and benevolent ruler, loved and admired by his people.

Panormita, *King Alfonso's Triumph*, 1455

Thus, on the day of February 26, the king appeared with his princes at the Carmine Gate, near a portion of the city walls that the citizens themselves had torn down in order to make a wider opening in honor of the king's entry. There the tall triumphal chariot, all of gold, had been prepared, at its summit a golden throne covered with purple. To draw the chariot were harnessed four spirited white horses, with silk bridles and golden bits. On the chariot before the king's throne was the Siege Perilous, certainly the most important insignia of the king, which seemed to give off flames. To the sides of the chariot were twenty noblemen, and each of these held aloft a pole, at the top of which were attached the corners of a precious golden pallium, the likes of which had never been used in this way before. The edges decorated with the coats of arms of the Kingdom and the city hung down elegantly, fluttering in the breeze.

> [*Alfonso pauses to award titles of nobility to various gentlemen in his service.*]

When he appeared, mounted high atop the chariot, great jubilation and applause rose up from the crowd of men all around and from the women watching from the rooftops. So great was the clamor that they raised that no one could hear the sound of trumpets and fifes, even though they were most numerous. Some could be seen crying with joy, others laughing with pleasure, others astonished by these extraordinary, unheard-of things.

> [*A description of the Florentine contingent with their extravagant clothes, jewels, and horses, followed by allegorical figures. Fortuna is drawn on a cart, followed by the three theological virtues and four cardinal virtues. Hope, Faith, Charity, Fortitude, Temperance, and Prudence ride on horseback. Last of all is Justice, dressed as a queen atop an elaborate platform*]

Following this gorgeous throne was a large multitude of knights, who had the costumes and manners of many diverse peoples, princes, and nobles. They followed the throne, however, giving precedence to a chariot that carried a personification of Caesar. Indeed, carried on a very ornate platform that he mounted on a carpeted staircase, Caesar came forward. He stood there, his head crowned with laurel, dressed in armor and a cloak, holding a scepter in his right hand and an orb in his left. Beneath his feet was the world, shaped like a sphere, continually turning. He stopped before Alfonso and spoke in this in vernacular rhymed verse to this effect:

"Alfonso, most excellent amongst kings, I exhort you to keep with you, until the end these seven virtues, which you have just now seen pass before you and which you have always cultivated. If you do that—and I know that you will—those [virtues] which you triumphantly display before these people will one day make you worthy of the imperial throne."

Panormita, *On the Sayings and Deeds of King Alfonso*, 1455

Each of the transmarine provinces was accustomed to supply Rome and Italy with its own produce. Sicily, the most famous of its islands, supplied wheat and sugar; Sardinia leather and cheese; Corsica wine; Ibiza salt; and other provinces other goods. Only Spain used to give Rome and Italy emperors and kings. And what kind of emperors and kings? Trajan, Hadrian, Theodosius, Arcadius, Honorius, Theodosius II. Finally, Alfonso, the living image of all the virtues, who stands forth as equal to those mentioned above in every form of commendation; but in terms of religion—true wisdom, that is, which distinguishes us from brutish animals—he is very greatly superior and more famous by far.

Notes

1 Hersey xiii. Various artists associated with the project include Pere Joan, Pietro da Milano, Guillermo Sagrera, Francesco Laurana, Paolo Romano, Isaia da Pisa, Andrea dell'Aquila, Domenico Gagini, Onofrio di Giordano, Antonio Chellino, and Mino da Fiesole. It has been suggested that designs were by Pisanello or Alberti, but neither is universally accepted by scholars.
2 Hersey 48.

Sources

Panormita (Antonio Beccadelli). *Alfonsi regis Triumphus = Il Trionfo di re Alfonso*, ed. and Italian trans. Fulvio Delle Donne. Centro Europeo di Studi su Umanesimo e Rinascimento Aragonese, Basilicata UP, 2021, trans. Kaborycha.

Stacey, Peter. "Hispania and Royal Humanism in Alfonsine Naples," *Mediterranean Historical Review*, Vol. 26, No. 1 (2011), 51–65, p. 56.

References

De Divitiis, Bianca. "Castel Nuovo and Castel Capuano in Naples: The Transformation of Two Medieval Castles into 'All'antica' Residences for the Aragonese Royals," *Zeitschrift für Kunstgeschichte*, Vol. 76. Bd., H. 4 (2013), pp. 441–74.

Hersey, George L. *The Aragonese Arch at Naples, 1443–1475*, Yale UP, 1973.

Santoro, Mario. "Humanism in Naples," in *Renaissance Humanism. Foundations, Forms, and Legacy*, ed. A. Rabil, vol. 1, U Pennsylvania P, 1988, pp. 296–331.

Schadee, Hester. "Alfonso 'the Magnanimous' of Naples as Portrayed by Facio and Panormita: Four Versions of Emulation, Representation, and Virtue," in *Portraying the Prince in the Renaissance: The Humanist Depiction of Rulers in Historiographical and Biographical Texts*, ed. Patrick Baker et al., De Gruyter, 2016, pp. 95–115.

16 Man's unique place in the cosmos

Marsilio Ficino, *Commentary on Plato's* Timaeus, 1484

Giovanni Pico della Mirandola, *Oration on the Dignity of Man*, 1486

Giovanni Pico della Mirandola (1463–1494) was born into a wealthy, noble family in their castle of Mirandola near Modena, and he began his studies early. At the age of fourteen, he began study of canon law in Bologna, then a couple of years later went to Ferrara to learn philosophy and ancient Greek instead. His scholarly interests would take him to Padua, Paris, and eventually Florence, where he became closely associated with Florentine Platonists and was particularly influenced by Marsilio Ficino (#46). Possessing a restless, inquiring mind, in addition to Latin and Greek, Pico plunged into the study of Hebrew, Arabic, and Aramaic, pursuing knowledge derived from a startling variety of philosophical and religious traditions. The learned men who gathered at Pico's home in Florence included Hebrew scholars Elijah del Medigo (1458–1493), Johannan Alemanno (c.1435–after 1504), and Flavius Mithridates (fl.1466–87). Pico's grand intellectual project was his *900 Theses* (*Conclusiones*), in which he attempted to integrate disparate spiritual, philosophical, and mystical traditions with Christian theology, drawing on the Jewish Kabbalah as well as ancient magical practices. In 1486, the twenty-three-year-old philosopher planned to present his *Conclusiones* at a conference in Rome, opening these ideas to public debate. The introduction to his presentation, known as the *Oration on the Dignity of Man*,[1] was meant to be a sparkling rhetorical flourish with which to open the conference. The ideas he expresses in this speech—the uniqueness and dignity of human beings above all other creatures—echo those voiced earlier by Ficino in his commentary on Plato's dialogue, the *Timaeus*.[2] However, the broader scope of Pico's research and his more daring approach are evident from the words of the opening salvo of the *Oration*. The work turned out to be too daring—it was condemned by the pope, and the conference was cancelled. Pico never published it; significantly, neither the *900 Theses* nor its introduction circulated until after the author's death. And it is important to remember that this brilliant speech—that has resonated to the present day and is widely viewed as a powerful celebration of free will and human potential—was never actually delivered, but remained largely forgotten until the nineteenth century. Today, Pico's *Oration on the Dignity of Man* is generally cited as a fundamental text of Renaissance humanism.

DOI: 10.4324/9781003284284-18

Marsilio Ficino, *Commentary on Plato's Timaeus*, 1484

Man is a creature to be wondered at, being composed from the immortal and the mortal, for it was necessary to have here a creature who would worship the gods, a creature midway between the highest beings, which are immortal in body as well as in soul, and the lower beings, which are transient in both respects, a creature who is mortal in his body but immortal in his soul and who, for these reasons, not only descends to the Earth but also, while here, would subsequently imitate the contemplation of old as well as divine providence.

Giovanni Pico della Mirandola, *Oration on the Dignity of Man*, 1486

I have read, most revered fathers,[3] in Arab documents, that Abdala the Saracen, when asked what was most admirable on the world's stage, answered, "There is nothing to look on more wonderful than man!"[4] This belief is supported by Hermes: "O Asclepius, what a great miracle is man!"[5] Still, when I pondered the reasons for these opinions, I was not satisfied with the explanations given for the magnificence of human nature: that man is the intermediary between the creatures, the familiar of superior beings and the king of inferior ones, that by means of his keen senses, use of reason, and through the light of his intellect he can interpret nature, that he is fixed midway between eternity and flowing time, and (as the Persians say) the coupling or rather wedding hymn of the world, as David said, only a little lower than the angels.[6] These reasons are indeed great, but they are not the principal basis for humans to claim the privilege of the highest admiration. For why should the angels and the blessed heavenly choirs themselves not command more admiration? At last, I seem to have understood why man is the most fortunate of all living beings, and consequently worthy of all admiration, and what condition he is assigned in the universal order, to be envied not only by brute beasts, but by the stars and celestial intelligences [angels]. It is a thing so wondrous as to be unbelievable—yet why not? For it is because of this that man is rightly judged and said to be a great miracle, a being worthy of all admiration. But hear, O fathers, exactly what this condition is, and in the name of your humanity, lend your kindly ears to my work.

Already had God, the Supreme Father and Architect, constructed this cosmic home that we see, the most august temple of divinity by the laws of his mysterious wisdom. He had adorned the heavenly spheres with intelligences, infused the ethereal globes with eternal souls, and filled the filthy dungheap of the lower world with a multitude of every kind of animal life. But, having finished the work, the Craftsman desired to have someone to ponder the meaning of such a work, to love its beauty, and to be awed by its magnitude. Therefore, when everything was done (as Moses and Timaeus testify), he at last thought of bringing forth man.[7] But there was nothing in his archetypes from which he could model a new offspring, nothing in his treasury to endow his heir, nor any bench for him to sit on as a contemplator of the universe. Every place was already filled, everything in its designated order—high, middle, and low. But the Heavenly Father was not to fail, as if exhausted in this final act of creation; his Wisdom would not hesitate, as if lacking counsel, to carry out a necessary deed. Nor was it in the nature of his benevolent love, that he who would praise God's generosity toward all other things, would condemn its absence in regard to himself. So, at last the Master Builder decided that the creature to whom nothing entirely of his own could be given should share in all that belonged to every other being. Therefore, he took man, this creation with undefined appearance, and put him in the middle of the world saying:

"We have made no fixed place for you, O Adam, nor given you a particular appearance, or function, in order that whatever place, appearance, or function you choose, of your own will you may have and possess according to your desire and judgment. Defined by us, the nature of all other things must adhere to our rules; only you, without narrow limits, governed by your own will which we have placed in your hands, you may determine it for yourself. We have placed you in the middle of the world so that you may look around with ease at all there is to see in the world. Neither earthly nor celestial have we made you, neither mortal nor immortal, so that with free choice and dignity you may shape yourself into any form you choose. You are capable of lowering yourself to the position of the brute animals; you are capable through the judgment of your soul of rebirth, raising yourself up to the divine."

O supreme generosity of God! Most wonderful happiness of man! To man it is given to be whatever he desires and chooses to be!

Notes

1 The first edition of the introduction was published in 1496 by Pico's nephew, Gianfrancesco Pico della Mirandola (#77), with the title "*A Very Elegant Oration*," leaving out the text of the *900 Theses*. The subtitle "*De hominis dignitate*" first appeared in the 1504 Strasbourg edition.

2 There were various other Renaissance works on the topic of the dignity of man, notably Florentine humanist Giannozzo Manetti's *On Human Worth and Excellence*, written about fifty years earlier.

3 The oration is addressed to the audience of theologians at Pico's intended conference in Rome.

4 Scholars have not succeeded in identifying this source.

5 This is a reference to Hermes Trismegistus, the name in Greek for the Egyptian god Thoth, whose name was attached to a number of spiritual and magical texts from late Antiquity, known as the hermetic writings. Ficino translated many of these from Greek into Latin. Asclepius was the Greek god of healing.
6 Psalm 8:5: "For thou hast made him a little lower than the angels, and hast crowned him with glory and honour."
7 This is a reference to the biblical story from Genesis, as well as the Creation described by Plato, in the *Timaeus*.

Sources

Marsilio Ficino. *All Things Natural: Ficino on Plato's Timaeus*, trans. Arthur Farndell, Shepheard-Walwyn, 2010, p. 127.

Giovanni Pico della Mirandola. *Oratio de hominis dignitate*, Brown University Pico Project. www.brown.edu/Departments/Italian_Studies/pico/oratio.html, trans. Kaborycha

References

Cassirer, Ernst. "Giovanni Pico della Mirandola: A Study in the History of Renaissance Ideas," *Journal of the History of Ideas*, Vol. 3, No. 2 (1942), pp. 123–44.

Celenza, Christopher S. "'We Barely Have Time to Breathe,' Poliziano, Pico, Ficino, and the Beginning of the End of the Florentine Renaissance," in *The Intellectual World of the Italian Renaissance: Language, Philosophy, and the Search for Meaning*, Cambridge UP, 2018, pp. 313–37.

Copenhaver, Brian. *Magic and the Dignity of Man*, Belknap, Harvard UP, 2019.

Pico della Mirandola, Giovanni. *Oration on the Dignity of Man: A New Translation and Commentary*, ed. Francesco Borghesi, Michael Papio and Massimo Riva, Cambridge UP, 2012.

Wirszubski, Chaim. *Pico della Mirandola's Encounter with Jewish Mysticism*, Harvard UP, 1989.

17 Women's place among humanists

Isotta Nogarola, *Letter to Antonio Borromeo*, *c.*1436

Laura Cereta, *Letter to Lucilia Vernacula*, 1487

Cassandra Fedele, *Oration in Praise of Learning*, *c.*1490

During the Renaissance, it was uncommon for women to receive a humanist education, and those who achieved high levels of erudition became well known in their day. There was, for instance, Cassandra Fedele (1465–1558), a prodigy who learned Greek and Latin by the age of twelve. Recognized for her knowledge of ancient history, literature, philosophy, and logic, while still a teenager she was often called upon to deliver high-profile public speeches (orations). In 1491, Angelo Poliziano (#53) wrote to Fedele: "I used to marvel at Pico della Mirandola, than whom no mortal is more beautiful or more outstanding (I believe) in all branches of learning. Now behold, Cassandra, I have begun to venerate you next after Pico, perhaps now, also along with him."[1] Although admired for their accomplishments, because of their gender, women humanists were never allowed to forget their inferior place in Renaissance society. Isotta Nogarola (1418–1466), author of numerous Latin poems, orations, and letters, was aware from an early age of the challenges of competing in this field of learning dominated by men, as is clear from an elegantly composed Latin letter she wrote to her uncle Antonio Borromeo. Around that same time, Nogarola wrote a letter to Guarino of Verona (Guarino Guarini, 1374–1460), after the humanist had enthusiastically praised her. When he failed to respond, she complained that his silence was making her the object of ridicule, and Guarino wrote a scathing response mocking her as a pathetic female.[2] Later in life, and after suffering unfair criticism and slander, in 1451, Nogarola would challenge attitudes about gender in a groundbreaking philosophical dialogue titled *Of the Equal or Unequal Sin of Adam and Eve*.[3] Like Nogarola, Laura Cereta (1469–1499) also directly addressed gender issues, "anticipating modern feminism"[4] in her writing. At the time she wrote them, Cereta's Latin letters were so well-composed that it was rumored her father had written them for her. One recipient of her letters sent his wife to Cereta's home in order to directly observe the female scholar with pen and paper as she wrote a Latin letter.[5] Moreover, other women's assessments of female scholarship could be just

DOI: 10.4324/9781003284284-19

as damaging as men's criticism, as Cereta explains in a letter that is a masterpiece of Latin invective.

Isotta Nogarola, *Letter to Antonio Borromeo, c.*1436

I had often planned to send you my unpolished and unworthy writings, but when I thought of how many men there are—if they deserve to be called men—who consider learning in women a plague and public nuisance, this deterred me from the task. But it seems to me that these men—who approve of nothing except what they themselves do and think—are themselves a different kind of plague, that of men envious of others' glory, which comes from ignorance and baseness of spirit. I know for a certainty that they have not read with how much fame and renown those illustrious and remarkable women are celebrated, who each in her own era spent all her energy, care, and effort in study. The Muses themselves were women, who instructed and inspired great men and godlike poets. Clearly Virgil was not ashamed to invoke their aid when he wrote, "Come Sicilian Muses, let us sing of loftier themes." Certainly in Plato's circle women were not unoccupied with divine philosophy: for example, Lasthenia of Mantinea and Axiothea of Phlius, and she, they say, wore men's clothing in order to study with him. In how many poems has Cornelia the mother of the Gracchi been honored! Our ancestors have rightly preserved for later ages the memory of that remarkable woman Proba, the wife of Adelphus, a Christian by religion, who was so learned that they say she knew Virgil by heart and composed a clear and beautiful version of the New Testament. And so, does not learning exist among women—although woman is considered the origin and source of evil? Does not their learning letters warrant respect for women? Has it not made them more worthy of admiration that these women have surpassed not only other women in learning, but men as well?

Given all of this, I have decided to throw off my embarrassed timidity and send you these trifling works, since I am aware that you, for the sake of honor, will punish and destroy the envy and slander of those cowardly and malevolent men, and if there were anyone who wished to injure me, I do not doubt that you, in accord with your usual kindness and generosity toward me, will stand firm and defend me when I am not with you.

It remains to be said that by these crude works I hope to impress upon you that I am in need of your help, for at the moment I lack only money to be able, even if I am not worthy to be numbered in the circle of those women whom I have named above, at least to run in their footsteps. The lovely, the most beautiful *Decades* of Livy of Padua are in my hands and offered to me for purchase. To buy it I would need to raid fifty gold florins from my money chest, which I cannot do; and so I fly to you and humbly beg for your assistance. For I know that your benevolence and love for me is so great that you will choose to humor me in this matter—you are my father, my patron, and I have put all my hope in you. And so I beg you, if it is possible, to take care to send it, since there is an amazing shortage of such books here and those that are here are much sought after, they say. If you do this, I shall be most grateful to you, both because the book is useful to me and because it will give me extraordinary delight. But since I know that you know this, I do not wish to pile on more words; rather I shall put an end to my writing and implore you to help me in this, since I believe that you will and it no burden to do so. Farewell; I commend myself to you.

Laura Cereta, *Letter to Lucilia Vernacula*, 1487[6]

I should think that the tongues should be cut to pieces and the hearts brutally lacerated of people whose minds are so wicked and whose envious rage is so incredible that they deny, in their ignorant rantings the possibility that any woman might master the most elegant elements of Roman oratory. I would pardon the morally hopeless and even people destined for a life of crime, whom wagging tongues are accustomed to castigate with obvious fury. But I cannot tolerate the gabbing and babbling women who, burning with wine and drunkenness, harm with their petulant talk not only their sex but themselves. These mindless women—these female counselors who emerge victorious from the cookshop jar after a prodigious vote among their neighbors—hunt down with their bilious poison those women who rise to greater distinction than they. The bold and undisguised passion these women have for destruction and disgrace, this hunger of theirs for calamity, which strives to smear even those who are completely above reproach, deserves to bring a worse disgrace on itself. For the man who does not take care to have himself absolved of wrongdoing wants his own moral lapses to be excused.

Besides, these women, being idle with time on their hands and no interests of their own, occupy themselves with keeping watch over other people's business, and, like scarecrows hung up in the gardens to get rid of sparrows, they shoot poison from the bows of their tongues at those who cross their paths. What after all is the purpose of honor if I were to believe that the barking roars of these sharp-tongued women were worth tolerating, when decent and cultivated women always extol me with honorable words? I am not a woman who wants the shameful deeds of insolent people to slip through under the pardon of silence, either so that in the end I'll be said to approve of what I'm silent about or so that the very women who lead their lives with shame will continue to entice a great many people into their licentiousness as accomplices. Nor would I want, because of my speaking out, someone to criticize me for intolerance; even dogs are allowed to protect themselves from more aggressive fleas by crushing them with their nails. An infected sheep must always be isolated from the healthy flock. For the greatest number are often harmed by the least. Who would believe that disease in trees is caused by ants?

Those insolent women are therefore silent about every law of honor who, burning with the fires of hatred, would silently gnaw away at themselves, if they didn't feast in their slanderous talk on others. Mildew of the mind afflicts certain demented mothers, who being veritable Megaeras[7] can't stand to hear even the epithet "learned women." Their faces are spongy-looking, and in the vehemence of their speech they sometimes produce the words of a very large louse from their wrinkled cheeks, and sometimes in the presence of onlookers whose eyes grow round with horror at their thunderous idiocies. Human error causes us to be ashamed and disgusted that those women who are themselves caught in a tangle of doubt have given up hope of attaining knowledge of the humane arts, when they could easily acquire such knowledge with skill and virtue. For an education is neither bequeathed to us as a legacy, nor does some fate or other give it to us as a gift. Virtue is something that we ourselves acquire, nor can those women who become dull-witted through laziness and the sludge of low pleasures ascend to the understanding of difficult things. But for those women who believe that study, hard work, and vigilance will bring them sure praise, the road to attaining knowledge is broad. *Vale*. November 1, 1487.

Cassandra Fedele, *Oration in Praise of Learning*, *c.*1490[8]

Most Serene Prince, Gentlemen of the Senate, and most distinguished men,

As the great orator and philosopher Giorgio Valla[9] considered the question of whether young ladies ought to immerse themselves in rigorous studies, he regarded me as worthy to be admitted to his presence, encouraging and urging me to pursue immortality in these occupations. I was persuaded by his vehemently insistent arguments to bring my thoughts to light—although being of the female sex and aware of the limitations of my mind, his honest and urgent demands made me blush—so that the common rabble will be ashamed of itself and cease to trouble me when I dedicate myself to the liberal arts.

No one, therefore, ought to take it amiss if I, Cassandra, at first hesitate in my mind or spirit, or stumble somewhat in my speaking. To be sure, when I began to reconsider the magnitude of the subject upon which I decided to speak in public, before this most respected and splendid assembly, I realized that nothing so eloquent, brilliant, or polished could be said even by the most perfect orator, that would not seem meager, pallid, and vile compared with the greatness of your learning and excellence. Who possesses such force of mind and eloquence to praise the literary arts as to fully satisfy your erudite ears? On account of these difficulties, and aware of my modest abilities, I might easily have become frightened out of this opportunity to speak, if it had not been for the kindness and understanding with which you encouraged me. Obviously, I am aware that you would hardly demand a task that was too great, or be in the habit of expecting more than the subject allows;

you would not require anyone to take more upon their shoulders than they are capable of. I am, moreover, driven to speak by the same thing that initially deterred me, namely by your benevolence, which makes me confident that nothing could be sweeter or more agreeable to erudite men—such as most of you are, as well as to those of you who are especially interested in learning—than hearing an oration praising literature and the liberal arts.

Thus encouraged, and seeing that you are listening to me attentively, I shall speak, though briefly, on how knowledge of the liberal arts is useful to people, how it is honorable, both delightful and splendid. That it is precisely the possession of reason which distinguishes man from beast, not only philosophers, but even the most ignorant realize and admit. What then is it that so much helps, increases, and embellishes them both [learned and ignorant] if not the teaching and knowledge of the liberal arts? These things surely not only set human beings apart from herd animals, but indeed separate freeborn[10] gentlemen from the stupid and uncultivated. Certainly, to my mind, paintings and shadows differ less from real, living men than ignorant, unskilled men from those immersed in learning. However, crude unlettered men, even if they have an innate seed of reason, if left uncultivated over a lifetime, neglected and disused, it will entirely perish, and they will render themselves incapable of noble deeds. For, wandering in darkness, they stumble through all actions, and through imprudence, ignorance, and inexperience run into calamities, and in some ways live all their lives almost by accident. These are men who make Fortune their goddess, placing all things on her lap; they praise her and kiss her when things go well, but when things go badly, they vehemently blame her and grieve.

> "Soldiers, who have conquered the world, and on whom my destiny depends, behold the chance of battle you have so often prayed for. Prayer is no longer needed; with your swords you must now summon fate. So true to her bargain, did Fortune continue to the end the prosperity of Magnus; so true to her bargain, she summoned him at his death from his pinnacle of glory, and ruthlessly made him pay in a single day for all the disasters from which she protected him for many years; and Pompey was the only man who never experienced good and evil together: his prosperity no god disturbed, and on his misery no god had mercy. Fortune held her hand for long and then overthrew him with one blow. He is tossed on the sands."[11]

But learned men filled with knowledge of diverse human and divine matters aim all their thoughts and intellect toward reason, as if at a target; exposed to worries, they free their minds from all anxieties. It is less likely for them to be exposed to the countless arrows of Fortune, and they are prepared in every way to live well and happily. In all things they are guided by reason, considering not only themselves in any situation, but are also in the habit of helping many others with their energy and counsel in public and in private.

Thus Plato, a man almost divine, wrote that republics would be blessed if they were administered either by philosophers or by those who received guidance from philosophers. He mentions, I believe, that those whom Fortune has enriched with bodily or worldly goods more often turn to vice than those who are lacking. Without training, those naturally born with good minds, but who otherwise fail to cultivate them with learned studies, he held to be unfit for managing public matters, and he was not mistaken.

The study of literature polishes, ennobles, and shapes the intellect, cleanses the mind and entirely washes away faults, or removes most of them. It abundantly perfects natural endowments, adding distinction and elegant ornaments. Moreover, states and princes who protect and cultivate such studies become more humane, more gracious, and more noble; surely this is the reason why the sweetest name of "humanities" is claimed by these studies. Certainly, those whose minds are harsh and rustic become milder and more civilized by means of these studies, while those who because of their worldly goods or natural gifts tend to be brash, unruly, and arrogant, by exposure to the liberal arts assume modesty, mildness, and an amazing kindness toward all men. Indeed, it is similar to places that are by nature desolate when they lie uncultivated, and are by means of men's labor and industry rendered not only fertile and luxuriant with fruit, but also charmingly pleasant. So too, are our talents developed, polished, and illuminated by the liberal arts.

Philip, king of Macedon—who with his virtue and industry greatly enlarged his empire, conquering many peoples and nations—clearly understood this. In a letter to the philosopher Aristotle, announcing the birth of his son Alexander, he explained charmingly and skillfully that though his son would be the heir to such a great empire, he rejoiced even more that his son happened to be born in Aristotle's lifetime. O excellent sound sentiments, worthy of such a prince! O most weighty judgment of an emperor! Having spent all of his life in the business of war and victories, that king and emperor surely was affected by that, and knew that an empire could hardly be ruled gloriously, prudently, and well, by one who was not steeped in the arts, as was proven by Alexander shortly after. Instructed in liberal arts by Aristotle, he greatly surpassed all princes and emperors who came before or after him in ruling, protecting, and increasing an empire. For this reason, the ancients rightly held all leaders lacking in letters, no matter how skillful in military matters, to be rough and uncultured.

But this is enough on the usefulness of literature. Not only is this divine field abundant, generous, and precious, it also brings forth the sweetest, most plentiful, perpetual fruit in great profusion. Of these fruits I have tasted a little, and when I reflect—on the idea of going forth in life with distaff and needle, the pitiful weapons of a little woman—that I have followed my vocation, I nevertheless believe that even if a woman is not rewarded with any advantage or prestige from it, she ought to undertake the study of literature, nourishing her interest, if for no other reason than the pleasure and delight it brings.

Notes

1 King and Rabil 127.
2 Cited in Jardine 808.
3 "The importance of this work and its place among inaugural texts in the history of the European controversy over gender and nature cannot be overstated. It confronts squarely the prevalent assumptions about female inferiority attached to the reading of a canonical text." Robin and King 2004, 143.
4 Robin, Cereta, *Collected Letters* 3.
5 Rabil 1981 12–13.
6 The name of the addressee is a pseudonym; the identity of this woman has never been discovered.
7 Megaera was the one of the Furies in Greek mythology; her name means "the jealous one."
8 Though the exact date she wrote it is uncertain, Fedele was in her twenties when she delivered this speech before Doge Agostino Barbarigo and the Senate of Venice.
9 Giorgio Valla (1447–1499) was a prominent humanist polymath, author of a multi-volume encyclopedic work on literature, the sciences, and philosophy. He was also well-known for his large library of Greek and Latin manuscripts.
10 See p.59 on the liberal arts.
11 Fedele is citing first a speech of Julius Caesar and then recounting the tragic end of Pompey. Both are quotations from *Pharsalia* (7:250–2, 8:701–8) written by the Roman poet Lucan, *c.* 61–5 CE; translation is by Duff, Harvard UP, 1977.

Sources

Isotta Nogarola, *Letter to Antonio Borromeo*, in *Complete Writings: Letterbook, Dialogue on Adam and Eve, Orations*, ed. and trans. Margaret L. King and Diana Robin, U Chicago P, 2004, pp. 38–9.

Laura Cereta, *Letter to Lucia Vernacula*, in *Collected Letters of a Renaissance Feminist*, trans. and ed. Diana Robin, U Chicago P, 1997, pp. 81–2.

Cassandra Fedele. *Orazioni e epistole*, ed. Antonino Fedele, Poligrafo, 2010, trans. Kaborycha.

References

Fedele, Cassandra. *Letters and Orations*, ed. and trans. Diana Robin, U Chicago P, 2000.

Grafton, Anthony and Lisa Jardine. "Women Humanists: Education for What?" in *From Humanism to the Humanities: Education and the Liberal Arts in Fifteenth- and Sixteenth-century Europe*, Harvard UP, 1986.

Jardine, Lisa. "'*O Decus Italiae Virgo*', or The Myth of the Learned Lady in the Renaissance," *The Historical Journal*, Vol. 28, No. 4 (December 1985), pp. 799–819.

King, Margaret L. "Book-lined Cells: Women and Humanism in the Early Italian Renaissance," in *Beyond Their Sex: Learned Women of the European Past*, ed. Patricia H. Labalme, New York UP, 1980.

King, Margaret L. and Albert Rabil, Jr., ed. and trans. *Her Immaculate Hand: Selected Works by and about the Women Humanists of Quattrocento Italy*, Center for Medieval & Early Renaissance Studies, 1983.

Rabil, Albert, Jr. *Laura Cereta, Quattrocento Humanist*, Center for Medieval & Early Renaissance Studies/(Medieval & Renaissance Texts & Studies [Series] v. 3.), 1981.

18 A plea for architectural conservation

Pope Leo X, *Appointment of Raphael as Commissioner of Antiquities*, 1514

Raphael, *Letter to Baldassarre Castiglione*, 1519

Raphael and Castiglione, *Letter to Pope Leo X*, 1519

Figure 2.4 Raphael, *Portrait of Baldassarre Castiglione*, *c.*1515, Louvre.[1]

DOI: 10.4324/9781003284284-20

The portrait of humanist Baldassarre Castiglione manifests the deep regard that the painter Raphael (Raffaello Santi or Sanzio 1483–1520) had for his friend. The admiration was mutual, as is clear from the high praise that Castiglione expresses for the artist in *The Courtier* (#56).[2] At the time he painted this portrait, Raphael was at the height of his fame, the darling of Roman society. In the half dozen years since arriving in Rome, the young man from Urbino had painted the frescoes in two of the Vatican Stanze for Pope Julius II, and those of the grand salon in the Villa Farnesina of banking tycoon Agostino Chigi, in addition to many sacred paintings and private commissions carried out with the assistance of his large workshop. When seemingly the painter could ascend no higher, in 1514, Pope Leo X (#27) appointed Raphael architect of St. Peter's. In order to learn more about ancient architecture, the artist had his friends the humanists Marco Fabio Calvo and Angelo Colocci (#26) translate Vitruvius's first century BCE *De architectura* for him, since he did not know Latin well. The following year, Leo appointed Raphael commissioner of antiquities, putting the artist in charge of requisitioning stone and antiquities for papal projects, a position which had "more to do with eminent domain in acquiring marble for the construction of St. Peter's than with humanist preservation."[3] In response to what he viewed as the continued pillaging of Roman ruins, Raphael reached out to his friend Castiglione for assistance with a draft of his letter to the pope in 1519.[4] Castiglione did contribute to Raphael's letter, the two making an eloquent plea for architectural conservation. Leon Battista Alberti had advocated that painters seek out "the company of poets and orators" for such kinds of assistance in his 1435 treatise *On Painting* (#12). Moreover, the relationship between the writer and painter was mutually beneficial, comparable to that of Aretino and Titian (#38). Titian, too, painted a stunning portrait of his literary friend which, like Raphael's portrait of Castiglione, provides posterity with a psychological depth and insight into the author's character that writings alone could never convey.

Pope Leo X, *Appointment of Raphael as Commissioner of Antiquities*, 1515

It is of utmost importance for the work on the Roman temple of the Prince of the Apostles that the stones and marble, of which a great quantity are needed, be easily obtained in the neighborhood rather than imported from afar. . . . We create you, because we have entrusted you with the direction of the work, inspector in chief for all the marble and all the stone which will be excavated from now on within Rome or within ten miles around it, so that you can purchase them if they are useful for the work on the temple.

Raphael, *Letter to Baldassarre Castiglione*, 1519

Our Lord [Pope Leo X], along with honoring me, has put a great weight on my shoulders. This is the responsibility for the *fabbrica* of Saint Peter's.

I really hope that I will not fall beneath it, and the more so since the model that I made pleases His Holiness, and is praised by many fine geniuses. But I raise myself with higher thoughts. I hope to find the beautiful forms of ancient buildings, but I don't know if my flight will be like that of Icarus.[5] Vitruvius sheds a great light for me, but not enough.

Raphael and Baldassarre Castiglione, *Letter to Pope Leo X*, 1519

There are many people, Most Holy Father, who when measuring their own limited abilities against the great achievements of the ancient Romans—the feats of arms, the wondrous art, the adornments and greatness of their buildings—are liable to consider those more legendary than true. But to me it is quite different, because the divinity of those ancient minds is visible in the ruins still in Rome; many things that seem impossible to us today, to them were very easy. As I have closely studied these antiquities, and with great care examined and diligently measured them, reading the great authors, comparing the works with the writings, I think I have attained some appreciation of ancient architecture. On the one hand the knowledge of such excellence is a source of the greatest pleasure to me; on the other, it is the greatest sorrow to see the cadaver of that noble fatherland, once queen of the world, so wretchedly torn to pieces.

Thus, as every person owes reverence towards parents and country, I feel obligated to expend all my abilities, meager as they are, in order to keep alive even a shadowy image of what is truly the universal fatherland of all Christians. For a time, it was so noble and powerful that men began to believe that, alone of all [civilizations] under the Sun, despite fortune, and against the course of nature, she could last forever. However, it seemed that time, envious of the glory achieved by mortals, lacking confidence in the powers of his devouring rasp, arranged with fortune that unholy, immoral barbarians would add impious furor, fire, iron, and all necessary means to ruin her. Hence, those famous works, which today would have been even more robust and beautiful than ever, were by the unholy rage and cruel urges of evil men, or rather beasts, burned and destroyed. Although the destruction is not entire, the structure almost completely remains, but without its ornaments, almost in a way like the bones of a body without its flesh.

But why should we be pained by the deeds of Goths, Vandals, and other wicked enemies, when the very men, who as fathers and protectors should have defended these poor relics of Rome, themselves have been intent on destroying them? How many pontiffs, Most Holy Father—who held the same office as your holiness, but without your wisdom, greatness of soul, nor godlike clemency—how many popes have aimed at ruining ancient temples, statues, arches, and other glorious edifices? How many simply in order to extract *pozzolana*[6] have dug up foundations so that those buildings soon fell down? How many statues and other antique decorations were ground into lime for building? I dare say that this new Rome that we see now, great as she is, adorned with palaces, churches, and other buildings, is all built of lime from ancient marble.

Nor can I remember without being stirred to pity, that since I came to Rome not eleven years ago, how many beautiful things, such as the Meta that was on the Via Alexandrina,[7] the ill-fated arch, so many columns and temples, destroyed, most of all by Messer Bartolomeo della Rovere.[8]

Thus, Holy Father, it ought not be the last among your concerns to take care of the little that remains of this ancient mother of glory and Italian fame.

Notes

1 "According to the principles of portraiture of the time, Raphael's objective would have been to capture both a physical likeness and a sense of the *spirito* or *animo* of his sitter; to reproduce both the appearance and the character of a man who was actively thinking about perfect courtiers and promoting grace as their supreme virtue. Raphael would have wanted to compliment his friend, to endow him with the qualities with which he would most like to be associated." Mac Carthy 38.
2 See Shearman for a detailed analysis of Castiglione's mentions of Raphael in *The Courtier*.
3 Barkan 37.
4 Raphael did not have time to develop many architectural projects, as he died in 1520, and the letter to the pope was apparently never sent (Leo died in 1521). The draft of this letter was found among the artist's papers bound in a manuscript containing the translation of Vitruvius.
5 The figure from Greek mythology who, ignoring his father's advice, flew with his fabricated wings too close to the Sun, which melted the wax and caused him to plunge to his death.
6 A type of volcanic ash mined in Pozzuoli; it was used as a building material by the ancient Romans.
7 The Meta Romuli (Pyramid of Romulus) was an ancient monumental burial site. Pope Donus I (r.76–78 CE) had stripped the marble from it to pave the atrium of St. Peter's, and it was entirely demolished by Pope Alexander VI in 1498 to inaugurate the Via Alexandrina, now Borgo Nuovo.
8 The nephew of Pope Julius II.

Sources

Pope Leo X, *Appointment of Raphael*, in Robert Klein and Henri Zerner. *Italian Art, 1500–1600; Sources and Documents*, Prentice-Hall, 1966, p. 45.

Raphael, *Letter to Castiglione*, in Richard J. Betts, "Raphael and the Ruins of Rome: Archeology and Architecture," in *Raphael and the Ruins of Rome: The Poetic Dimension* [exhibition] November 12, 1983 through January 22, 1984, Krannert Art Museum, U Illinois P at Urbana-Champaign, p. 19.

Raphael, *Letter to Pope Leo X*, in *Lettera a Leone X di Raffaello e Baldassarre Castiglione*, ed. Francesco Paolo Di Teodoro, Olschki, 2020, trans. Kaborycha.

References

Barkan, Leonard. *Unearthing the Past: Archaeology and Aesthetics in the Making of Renaissance Culture*, Yale UP, 1999.

Jacks, Philip J. *The Antiquarian and the Myth of Antiquity: The Origins of Rome in Renaissance Thought*, Cambridge UP, 1993.

Mac Carthy, Ita. "Grace and the 'Reach of Art' in Castiglione and Raphael," *Word & Image*, Vol. 25, No. 1 (2009), pp. 33–45.

Rowland, Ingrid D. "Raphael, Angelo Colocci, and the Genesis of the Architectural Orders," *The Art Bulletin*, Vol. 76, No. 1 (March 1994), pp. 81–104.

Shearman, John. "Castiglione's Portrait of Raphael," *Mitteilungen des Kunsthistorischen Institutes in Florenz*, Vol. 38. Bd., H. 1 (1994), pp. 69–97.

19 Benefits of civil strife in ancient Rome

Niccolò Machiavelli, *Discourses on Livy*, 1519

Niccolò Machiavelli (1469–1527) was appointed to his first government job when he was twenty-nine years old, and for the next fourteen years he held crucial positions within the office of the chancery. Located in the Palazzo Vecchio, the chancery was the nerve center of the Florentine Republic where official correspondence was drafted, documents redacted, and official deliberations recorded. Despite his apparent lack of notarial and secretarial training, through sheer talent and energy, Machiavelli's abilities were recognized, and he swiftly rose in rank. He became a trusted envoy, was sent on diplomatic missions across Europe, and provided confidential intelligence to Piero Soderini, chief executive of the Republic, as well as to the Council of Ten of War and other government committees. When in late 1512 the Florentine Republic was overthrown and the Medici suddenly returned to power, Machiavelli was excluded from government, compelled to spend the rest of his life as a commentator, rather than active participant in politics. He consoled himself by reading the classical authors, as well as by engaging in political discussions with like-minded Florentines, often in his friend Bernardo Rucellai's gardens, the Orti Oricellari. Though they could not openly criticize the Medici who had overturned their government, conversation centered on what caused republics to succeed or fail. Machiavelli focused special attention on the ancient Roman Republic as described by the Roman author Livy (Titus Livius Patavinus 59 BCE–17 CE), who wrote *Ab urbe condita* ("From the founding of the city"), during the reign of Emperor Augustus. Livy recounts the history of Rome from its founding through the growth of the republic through his own time when, like Machiavelli and his friends in the Rucellai gardens, the republican form of government had been replaced by an autocracy. Written between 1512 and 1519,[1] the *Discourses on the First Ten Books of Titus Livius* (or *Discourses on Livy*) applies examples from ancient Roman history to provide insights for republics in Machiavelli's own day. Machiavelli had been immersed in studies of ancient Rome from childhood when he received a thoroughly humanist education.[2] The conclusions that he drew from those classical studies, however, were strikingly different from those of fellow humanists. The dominant humanist stance was praise of civic

DOI: 10.4324/9781003284284-21

harmony as expressed by Marcus Tullius Cicero (106–43 BCE) when he was consul, as "*concordia ordinum,*" or concord between the classes. In opposition to this view, Machiavelli considered political conflict a potential force for good. In this text he argues that when opposing segments of society are able to work out their contentious rivalries, government can become better regulated, pass laws that are fairer, and contribute to the well-being of all citizens.

Niccolò Machiavelli, *Discourses on Livy*, 1519

Preface

Consider how much honor is attributed to antiquity, and how often—to take just one of many examples—a fragment of an ancient statue is purchased at a high cost to have it near, to honor one's home, how it is imitated by those who delight in that art, and how they use all their efforts to portray it in all their works (#20). On the other hand, I see that history's greatest deeds of *virtù*—achieved by ancient kingdoms and republics, by kings, generals, citizens, lawgivers, and others who worked tirelessly for their fatherlands—are more readily admired than imitated. Indeed, even the smallest details are avoided, so that not a single trace of that ancient *virtù* remains, and I can only be amazed and saddened by this.

Book I, Chapter 4. How discord between the plebeians and the Roman Senate made that republic free and powerful

I do not want to leave out a discussion of the conflicts that occurred in Rome from the death of the Tarquins through the creation of the tribunes, and to oppose the opinion of many who believe that Rome was an unruly republic, full of such turmoil that, if good fortune and military *virtù* had not compensated for its defects, it would have been inferior to all other republics. I cannot deny that Fortuna and their military were reasons for Roman power, however, it seems to me that those people do not realize that where there is a good military, there must also be good government, and rarely does it happen that there is not good fortune as well. But let us come to the details of that city. I say that those who condemn the conflict between the nobles and the plebs are criticizing the very thing that kept Rome free; and they are paying more attention to the noise and shouting of the rioting, than the positive results born of it. They do not take into consideration that in every republic there are two different humors—that of the people, and that of the nobles—and that every law which favors liberty is born of the discord between the two. The way this occurred in Rome is clearly seen, as from the time of the Tarquins to the Gracchi, a period of more than three hundred years, conflict in Rome rarely led to exile and rarely to bloodshed. Nor should these uprisings be judged harmful, nor the republic divided, when in all that time no more than eight or ten citizens were sent into exile, few were killed, and not many were fined. A republic can in no way be called disorderly where there are so many examples of *virtù*, since good examples derive from good education, and good education from good laws, and the good laws from the conflicts so many people thoughtlessly condemn. Because, if you look closely at the outcome of those clashes you will not find that they led to any exile or violence against the common good, but to laws that benefitted public freedoms. And some might say: the means for achieving this were extreme and almost ferocious, seeing the populace shouting together against the Senate, and the Senate against the populace, people running riot in the streets, shops shut down, the plebeians leaving Rome, things that make everyone afraid, even just reading about it. I respond that every city must have its own ways for the people to be able to give vent to their ambitions, especially in those cities that want to engage the citizenry in important undertakings. Among these was Rome, which functioned in this way: when the people wanted a law passed, either they did some of the aforementioned things or refused to go to war, and in order to placate them, it was necessary to satisfy them to some extent. The desires of free peoples are rarely harmful to liberty because they arise either from oppression or of the fear of being oppressed. And if it happens that these opinions be false or dangerous to liberty, there is a remedy in public discourse and a righteous man will speak out and show them that they are mistaken; the populace, as Cicero says, although they are ignorant, are receptive to truth, and easily yield to it when a trustworthy man speaks truth to them.

Notes

1 Machiavelli composed the *Discourses on Livy* roughly at the same time he was writing *The Prince*; neither work was published during his lifetime.

2 On Machiavelli's humanist education, see Black 73–5: "In his education, in his literary interests, in his technical command of language and style, Machiavelli was a fully-fledged humanist when he entered the chancery in the summer of 1498, a worthy successor to the pre-eminent figures who had previously filled the office of second chancellor."

Source

Niccolò Machiavelli, *Discourses on Livy*, in *Tutte le Opere di Niccolò Machiavelli*, ed. Mario Martelli, Sansoni Editore, Firenze, 1971, trans. Kaborycha.

References

Atkinson, James B. and David Sices, trans. and ed. *The Sweetness of Power: Machiavelli's Discourses & Guicciardini's Considerations*, Northern Illinois UP, 2002.

Black, Robert. "Machiavelli, Servant of the Florentine Republic," in *Machiavelli and Republicanism*, ed. Gisela Bock, Quentin Skinner and Maurizio Viroli, Cambridge UP, 1990, pp. 71–99.

Clarke, Michelle T. "Machiavelli and the Imagined Rome of Renaissance Humanism," *History of Political Thought*, Vol. 36, No. 3 (Autumn 2015), pp. 452–70.
Najemy, John M. "Society, Class, and State in Machiavelli's *Discourses on Livy*," in *The Cambridge Companion to Machiavelli*, ed. John M. Najemy, Cambridge UP, 2010.
Pocock, J.G.A. "Machiavelli and Rome: The Republic as Ideal and as History," in *The Cambridge Companion to Machiavelli*, ed. John M. Najemy, Cambridge UP, 2010, pp. 144–56.
Skinner, Quentin. "Machiavelli's *Discorsi* and the Pre-humanist Origins of Republican Ideas," in *Machiavelli and Republicanism*, ed. Gisela Bock, Quentin Skinner and Maurizio Viroli, Cambridge UP, 1990, pp. 119–42.

20 Ancient fragmented statues speak

Anonymous, *Pasquinade*, 1541

Figure 2.5 *Pasquino*, Second century BCE, Piazza Pasquino, Rome.

Many ancient statues were discovered during the Renaissance, usually broken or badly damaged, having laid hidden for centuries under fields or gardens. The work known as the *Belvedere Torso* (Figure 2.1) is a fragment of an ancient statue; its name comes from the Belvedere Courtyard in the Vatican Palace, where it is located. It had been unearthed sometime early in the fifteenth century and was recorded as being in the collection of Cardinal Prospero Colonna between 1432 and 1435, transferred to the papal collection in the 1530s. Created during the first

DOI: 10.4324/9781003284284-22

century BCE and signed by the Athenian sculptor "Apollonios son of Nestor," it has variously been said to represent Hercules, Ajax, Prometheus, or Marsyas.

The *Belvedere Torso* was universally admired during the Renaissance and highly influential on artists, especially Michelangelo. Echoes of the vigorous, muscled torso can be seen in Michelangelo's sculptures of *Day* (Medici Chapel, San Lorenzo, Florence) and his *Victory* (Palazzo Vecchio, Florence), as well as in many of his paintings, including the figures of Christ and St. Bartholomew in his *Last Judgment* (**#29**). Unlike other classical sculptures such as the *Apollo Belvedere* and the *Laocoön*, which were repeatedly restored—it was common for Renaissance sculptors to refashion various missing body parts and attach them to ancient statues—the *Belvedere Torso* was left as is, without head and limbs. Since then, the incomplete state of the figure has invited viewers to imagine the rest, as vividly described by the German art historian Johann Joachim Winckelmann in the mid-eighteenth century:

> It seems inconceivable that one could depict the power of thinking in any other part [of the body] than the head; yet witness here how the hand of a creating master has the capacity to render material into spirit. I have the sensation as though the statue's back, bent over by lofty acts of contemplation, manages to create for me the image of a head which is busied with happy recollection of its extraordinary deeds. And just as the head, so full of majesty and wisdom, rises before our eyes, so the other missing limbs start to form themselves in my thoughts. Out of the present condition of the work a new creation assembles itself, producing, as it were, a sudden complete restoration.[1]

Not only was the statue left as is, and admired despite its mutilated condition, it has been suggested that this gave rise to an aesthetic of the *non finito*, or "unfinished" artwork in the Renaissance. The many unfinished statues of Michelangelo—twenty-six out of his forty-three extant marble sculptures[2]—have caused some modern viewers to wonder whether the artist, under the influence of ancient fragments, intentionally left them in that state.

Unlike the *Belvedere Torso*, other works of art uncovered from ancient times were treated with less reverence. The so-called *Pasquino* (Figure 2.5) is another fragment of an ancient statue; it was dug up near Piazza Navona in 1501 and placed on a pedestal on a neighborhood street corner. The custom for Romans to attach satirical notes or poems known as *pasquinate* (pasquinades) to the statue began soon after, and continues to this day. Whether targeting politicians or the pope and members of his curia, these anonymous lampoons composed in crude doggerel comment on current events and provide unusual access to popular opinion. One of the many pasquinades that were collected and copied down was an anonymous sonnet about Michelangelo's *Last Judgment* in the Sistine Chapel, dashed off soon after the painting was unveiled to the public.

Anonymous, *Pasquinade*, 1541

Judgment of Michelangelo, the Florentine

Don't you scold the Florentine
who's just painted the Sistine;
he's really done a splendid job
showing Jesus and all the mob.

Old St. Cathy's right up there,
with naked backside in the air,
and all the other saints are jolly,
flashing asses at Pope Pauly![3]

Meanwhile Cesena's[4] there as well,
his sins having landed him in Hell.
He hangs around behind a rock,
while a serpent munches some guy's cock.

Notes

1 Cited in Barkan 189.
2 Bambach 30.
3 Pope Paul III r.1534–9.
4 Biagio da Cesena was papal master of ceremonies and a critic of Michelangelo. Tradition has it that the artist included his nemesis among the damned in this painting.

Source

Anonymous *Pasquinade*, in *Pasquinate romane del Cinquecento*, ed. Valerio Marucci, Antonio Marzo e Angelo Romano, Salerno Editrice, 1983, vol. 1, p. 498, trans. Kaborycha.

References

Bambach, Carmen. "Leonardo, Michelangelo, and Notions of the Unfinished in Art," and Bayer, Andrea. "Renaissance Views of the Unfinished," in *Unfinished: Thoughts Left Visible*, ed. Kelly Baum, Andrea Bayer and Sheena Wagstaff, The Metropolitan Museum of Art, 2016.

Barkan, Leonard. *Unearthing the Past: Archaeology and Aesthetics in the Making of Renaissance Culture*, Yale UP, 1999.

Fiorio, Maria Teresa. "Broken Sculpture: Michelangelo and the Aesthetic of the Fragment," in *The Genius of the Sculptor in Michelangelo's Work*, ed. Pierre Théberge, Montreal Museum of Fine Arts, 1992, pp. 68–84.

Haskell, Francis and Nicholas Penny. *Taste and the Antique: The Lure of Classical Sculpture 1500–1900*, Yale UP, 1981.

Steinberg, Leo. "A Corner of the *Last Judgment*," *Daedalus*, Vol. 109, No. 2 (Spring 1980), pp. 207–73.

Part III

The sacred and the secular

Figure 3.1 Melozzo da Forlì, *Sixtus IV Appoints the Papal Librarian*, *c.*1476, Pinacoteca Vaticana (originally painted directly on the wall of the old Vatican Library, transferred to canvas, now exhibited in the Vatican Museum). Melozzo da Forlì (Melozzo degli Ambrosi, 1438–1494) enjoyed a high reputation for his use of perspective and mastery of portraiture; unfortunately, few paintings have survived that can be attributed with certainty to the artist.

21 The pope asserts supreme authority

Boniface VIII, *Unam Sanctam*, 1302

"Render therefore unto Caesar the things which are Caesar's; and unto God the things that are God's" (Matt. 22:21). These words, recorded by the Apostle Matthew, were spoken by Jesus to explain to his followers how they ought to balance their obligations to the Roman emperor with their obedience to God, as he urged them to obey the law and pay their taxes. Christians have cited this biblical passage for centuries when trying to negotiate the conflicting demands of spiritual and secular authorities, of church versus state. However, at the time these words were uttered, there was no official Christian Church, so the divide between sacred and secular was clearer. After the Emperor Constantine converted in 313 CE and made Christianity the official religion of the empire, the lines began to blur. The issue did not seem to overly trouble the philosopher and theologian St. Augustine (Augustine of Hippo, 354–430 CE), who regarded secular government in an earthly city as a temporary arrangement, inferior to the perfect arrangement in heaven, which he described in his *City of God*. Living during the time of the Sack of Rome (410 CE), Augustine was primarily concerned with political stability, and he advocated obedience to temporal powers and supported their coercive authority, citing St. Paul: "Everyone must submit to governing authorities. For all authority comes from God, and those in positions of authority have been placed there by God."[1] Though human justice was faulty, the Day of Judgment, it was believed, would soon arrive and sort good from evil. Eventually, over the centuries while waiting for that day to come, a church hierarchy developed. Land was acquired, churches and monasteries built, armies raised, tithes collected. Over the course of the following millennium, local bishops began to amass ever greater worldly power, influence, and wealth. And the one who stood above them all was the bishop of Rome—the pope. Though there were many forceful popes who challenged secular authority and battled with dukes and kings for dominance, none asserted the claim to supreme power more powerfully than Benedetto Caetani (1230–1303), who reigned as Pope Boniface VIII from 1294 until his death in 1303. His papal bull *Unam Sanctam* was proclaimed on November 18, 1302.

DOI: 10.4324/9781003284284-24

Pope Boniface VIII, *Unam Sanctam*, 1302

The true faith compels us to believe that there is one holy catholic apostolic church,[2] and this we firmly believe and plainly confess. And outside of her there is no salvation or remission of sins, as the Bridegroom says in the Song of Solomon: "My dove, my undefiled is but one; she is the only one of her mother, she is the choice one of her that bare her" [Song of Sol. 6:9]; which represents the one mystical body, whose head is Christ, but the head of Christ is God [1 Cor. 11.3]. In this church there is "one Lord, one faith, one baptism" [Eph. 4:5]. For in the time of the flood there was only one ark, that of Noah, prefiguring the one church, and it was "finished above in one cubit" [Gen. 6:16], and had but one helmsman and master, namely, Noah. And we read that all things on the Earth outside of this ark were destroyed. This church we venerate as the only one, since the Lord said by the prophet: "Deliver my soul from the sword; my darling from the power of the dog" [Ps. 22:20]. He prayed for his soul, that is, for himself, the head; and at the same time for the body; and he named his body, that is, the one church, because there is but one Bridegroom [cf. John 3:29], and because of the unity of the faith, of the sacraments, and of his love for the church. This is the seamless robe of the Lord which was not rent but parted by lot [John 19:23]. Therefore, there is one body of the one and only church, and one head, not two heads, as if the church were a monster. And this head is Christ and his vicar, Peter and his successor; for the Lord himself said to Peter: "Feed my sheep" [John 21:16]. And he said "my sheep," in general, not these or those sheep in particular; from which it is clear that all were committed to him. If therefore Greeks or anyone else say that they are not subject to Peter and his successors, they thereby necessarily confess that they are not of the sheep of Christ. For the Lord says in the Gospel of John, that there is one fold and only one shepherd [John 10:16]. By the words of the gospel we are taught that the two swords, namely, the spiritual authority and the temporal are in the power of the church. For when the apostles said "Here are two swords" [Luke 22:38]—that is, in the church, since it was the apostles who were speaking—the Lord did not answer, "It is too much," but "It is enough." Whoever denies that the temporal sword is in the power of Peter does not properly understand the word of the Lord when he said: "Put up thy sword into the sheath" [John 18:11]. Both swords, therefore, the spiritual and the temporal, are in the power of the church. The former is to be used by the church, the latter for the church; the one by the hand of the priest, the other by the hand of kings and knights, but at the command and permission of the priest. Moreover, it is necessary for one sword to be under the other, and the temporal authority to be subjected to the spiritual; for the apostle says, "For there is no power but of God: and the powers that are ordained of God" [Rom. 13:1]; but they would not be ordained [i.e., arranged or set in order; note the play on the words] unless one were subjected to the other, and, as it were, the lower made the higher by the other. For, according to St. Dionysius, it is a law of divinity that the lowest is made the highest through the intermediate. According to the law of the universe all things are not equally and directly reduced to order, but the lowest are fitted into their order through the intermediate, and the lower through the higher. And we must necessarily admit that the spiritual power surpasses any earthly power in dignity and honor, because spiritual things surpass temporal things. We clearly see that this is true from the paying of tithes, from the benediction, from the sanctification, from the receiving of the power, and from the governing of these things. For the truth itself declares that the spiritual power must establish the temporal power and pass judgment on it if it is not good. Thus the prophecy of Jeremiah concerning the church and the ecclesiastical power is fulfilled: "See, I have this day set thee over the nations and over the kingdoms, to root out, and to pull down, and to destroy, and to throw down, to build, and to plant" [Jer. 1:10]. Therefore if the temporal power errs, it will be judged by the spiritual power, and if the lower spiritual power errs, it will be judged by its superior. But if the highest spiritual power errs, it can not be judged by men, but by God alone. For the apostle says: "But he that is spiritual judgeth all things, yet he himself is judged of no man" [1 Cor. 2:15]. Now this authority, although it is given to man and exercised through man, is not human, but divine. For it was given by the word of the Lord to Peter, and the rock was made firm to him and his successors, in Christ himself, whom he had confessed. For the Lord said to Peter: "Whatsoever thou shalt bind on Earth shall be bound in heaven: and whatsoever thou shalt loose on Earth shall be loosed in heaven" [Matt. 16:19]. Therefore, whosoever resisteth this power thus ordained of God, resisteth the ordinance of God [Rom. 13:2], unless there are two principles (beginnings), as Manichæus pretends there are. But this we judge to be false and heretical. For Moses says that, not in the beginnings, but in the beginning, God created the heaven and the Earth [Gen. 1:1]. We therefore declare, say, and affirm that submission on the part of every man to the bishop of Rome is altogether necessary for his salvation.

Notes

1 Rom. 13.
2 The Latin word *catholicus* derives from the Greek *katholikos* meaning "universal." "Apostolic" refers to Christ's Apostles; here it indicates the direct succession of the popes from the Apostle Peter.

Source

Boniface VIII, *Unam Sanctam*, in Oliver J. Thatcher and Edgar Holmes McNeal, eds. *A Source Book for Medieval History*, Scribners, 1905, pp. 314–17, ed. Kaborycha.

References

Caspary, Gerald E. *Politics and Exegesis: Origen and the Two Swords*, U California P, 1979.

Tierney, Brian. *The Crisis of Church and State 1050–1300*, U Toronto P, 1988.

22 A scholar denies secular power of papacy

Marsilius of Padua, *Defender of the Peace*, 1324

Marsilio dei Mainardini (*c.*1275–1342), better known as Marsilius of Padua, was a daring and original thinker who argued that the rulers of the church had no right to exercise any political or legal power in the secular realm. After studying medicine either in Padua or Paris, he obtained an arts degree from the University of Paris sometime before 1311 and became a rector there in 1313. His political theories were well known by 1319 when, from Avignon, Pope John XXII (Jacques Duèze, r.1316–34) denounced him as a Ghibelline (the pro-imperial, anti-papal faction). And it was in Paris that Marsilius wrote the treatise *Defensor pacis* (*Defender of the Peace*) in 1324, condemning the papacy using the rigorous system of Aristotelian logic current at the university since Thomas Aquinas (**#52**) taught there a generation earlier. In October 1327, the pope declared *Defensor pacis* heretical and excommunicated its author. By this time, Marsilius had become counselor to Ludwig the Bavarian (Louis IV of Bavaria) when he arrived in Rome in 1327. The pope had also excommunicated Ludwig, who retaliated by declaring John XXII a heretic. Ludwig was crowned Emperor Louis IV in January 1328, and Marsilius returned from the Roman expedition with Ludwig, living at the imperial court in Munich until his death.

Marsilius worked for the emperor, and the model he proposes for an elective monarchy is compatible with the institution of Holy Roman Emperor, thus, his patron used this treatise as a weapon against the Avignon popes. However, though Marsilius—like his contemporary Dante in *On Monarchy* (**#52**)—attacks the papacy for arrogating too much power in the secular sphere, the Paduan philosopher holds more nuanced views concerning monarchy and popular sovereignty. Marsilius advocates for an elective monarchy, chosen by the entire community. It is the community which makes the laws, and the term he uses for this body of citizens is the "legislator." The ruler or prince he refers to as the "principate," which can be an individual *or* a group of people, but either must serve with the citizens' consent. At the end of his treatise, Marsilius explains the title of the work: the primary concern of the government is to defend "civil peace or tranquility." During a time of extreme factionalism and civil unrest among the Italian city-states,

DOI: 10.4324/9781003284284-25

Marsilius, like Aquinas and Dante, aims to eliminate discord and to establish what he considers to be the most just, stable system of government.

Marsilius of Padua, *Defender of the Peace*, 1324

Discourse II, Chapter 1

As I embark upon something so difficult, then, I am quite assured that there is nothing in the way that could have a claim to truth. But nevertheless I see three entrenched enemies of that very truth readying their weapons against this work. One is persecution from the violent power of the Roman bishops and their accomplices. For they will strive with all their forces to destroy both it and those heralds of the truth who spread it abroad, as the direct adversaries of their purpose of unjustly seizing and keeping possession of temporal goods, as well as their burning desire for principate [autocratic rule]. To recall them from all this with words of truth will be a difficult business, however evident those words may be. But may merciful God in his grace deign to recall them nonetheless: may he curb their violent might, and may all his faithful, both princes and subjects, curb it likewise; for it is everyone's peace that is menaced by these men.

A second old enemy of almost any truth is no less readying its weapons against this work, viz. the habit of listening to and believing things that are false: I mean falsehoods that have long been sown and taken root in the souls of many simple Christian faithful by certain priests or bishops and their adherents. For in various of their speeches and writings these priests have implicated both divine and human judgements about human acts in multiple convolutions that are extremely laborious to unfold. And from this tissue of opinions they have inferred, although without any justification, certain interpretations by means of which they have introduced their unjust despotism upon the Christian faithful. For these in their simplicity believe, from various bits of misreasoning on the part of these priests—along with a threat of eternal damnation—that they are bound by divine ordinance to obey these spoken and written sophistries (in which the conclusion frequently fails to follow from the premises). For the true opinions of these matters of inquiry and dispute, and their true and uncomplicated beginnings, have been driven from men's minds and falsehoods gradually insinuated in their place, so that the ability to discern either is now hidden from most. And this is because, in any discipline, the habit of listening to what is false confuses and diverts men from the truth in no small measure: as Aristotle attests, *Metaphysics* II, last chapter. And because of this habit those who read and hear this work, especially those who have no training in philosophy or practice in Holy Scripture, will from the outset be greatly hindered from understanding and fully believing the truths contained in this volume.

The remaining and third entrenched enemy of the truth will present a major obstacle to this teaching: and this is the bitterness of those who, although they believe we have told the truth, will nevertheless set themselves against this true opinion because they realize someone has developed it before them; prompted by the malignant spirit of smoldering envy to tear at it with the hidden teeth of detractors or with noisy yaps of presumption.

[. . .]

Discourse II, Chapter 3

Let us first, then, bring in the authorities of Holy Scripture which might make someone think that the Roman bishop who is called the pope is the supreme judge . . . over all bishops or priests and other ecclesiastical ministers of the world, and also over all princes, communities, collective bodies and individual persons of this world, whatever their condition.

Let us set down as the first of these authorities the passage of Scripture in which Christ, addressing Saint Peter, says: "And I will give unto thee the keys of the kingdom of heaven: and whatsoever thou shalt bind on Earth shall be bound in heaven: and whatsoever thou shalt loose on earth shall be loosed in Heaven" [Matt. 16:19]. For it is from this passage that certain Roman bishops have assumed for themselves the authority of supreme jurisdiction just mentioned. For by the keys that Christ granted to Peter, they want it to be understood that plenitude of power over the entire government of humanity was handed to them.

[*Marsilius presents many arguments in support of the papal position, which he summarizes below, before going on to refute those arguments in the next chapter.*]

From all this, therefore, it would seem that it can be convincingly established that bishops or priests have coercive jurisdiction[1], and that the one who is supreme among them, the Roman pontiff, has as his due supreme overall principate in the world. We seem to have supported this sufficiently both with authorities of Holy Scripture and with certain quasi-political and human arguments.

Discourse II, Chapter 4

We now wish to continue by bringing in from the opposite side the truths of Holy Scripture that, in both the literal and the mystical sense of Scripture and according to the interpretation of the saints and the exposition of other approved doctors of the Christian faith, explicitly command or counsel that neither the bishop of Rome who is called the pope, nor any other bishop, priest, or deacon, has and should have any principate or judgement or coercive jurisdiction over any priest or non-priest, prince, community, collective body or individual person of whatever condition.

[. . .]

We wish to show that Christ in his purposed intention, words and actions wanted to and did exclude himself and the apostles from the office of prince or of contentious jurisdiction, government or coercive judgement of whatever sort in this world. This is plain and undoubted, firstly, from the passage of the gospels in John 18. For when Christ was accused before Pontius Pilate, vicegerent of the Roman prince in Judea, for having said he was king of the Jews, Pilate asked him whether he had indeed said this and whether he called himself a king. Christ replied to Pilate's question with, among others, the following words: "My kingdom is not of this world," i.e., I did not come into this world to reign with temporal government or dominion, in the way that kings of the world reign. And Christ himself added the proof of this with a manifest sign when he said: "If my kingdom were of this world, then would my servants fight, that I should not be delivered to the Jews." As if his argument went like this: If I had come into the world to reign with worldly or coercive government, I would have servants of this government, sc. fighting men to coerce transgressors, like other kings; but I have no such servants, as you can plainly see.

[. . .]

Thus Christ said: "The princes of the Gentiles exercise dominion over them. But ye" (sc. the apostles) "shall not be so." Christ, king of kings and lord of lords, did not therefore hand on to them the power to exercise the secular judgements of princes, nor coercive power over anyone; on the contrary he explicitly forbade them this when he said: "But ye shall not be so." And we should in consequence maintain the same of all the successors of the apostles, the bishops or prelates. . . . It is clear: dominion is forbidden to the apostles. Therefore go ahead and dare to usurp the apostolic office as a lord, or as an apostle to usurp dominion. Clearly you are forbidden to do either. If you want to have both of these at the same time, you will lose both.

[. . .]

Discourse III, Chapter 2

Of the conclusions to be drawn, we shall set down as the first:

1 That in order to gain eternal beatitude, it is necessary to believe only in the truth of divine or canonic Scripture, what follows from it with any kind of necessity, and the interpretation of it that has been made by a common council of the faithful. . . .
2 That only a general council of the faithful or its prevailing multitude or part should determine the senses of divine law where there is doubt over the definition, especially those matters which are called the articles of the Christian faith, and anything else that must be believed of necessity of salvation. . . .

3 That no one is commanded in evangelical scripture to be compelled to observe the commands of divine law by temporal penalty or punishment.

[. . .]

5 That no mortal can give a dispensation from things that are commanded or prohibited by God or in the evangelical law; and that only a general council or the faithful human legislator can prohibit things that are permitted, binding people to fault or penalty for the status of this present world or of that to come. . . .
6 That only the universal body of the citizens or its prevailing part is the human legislator. . . .
7 That the decretals or decrees of the Roman or any other pontiffs, laid down either collectively or individually without the concession of the human legislator, oblige no one with temporal penalty or punishment. . . .
8 That only the legislator or someone else by its authority can give a dispensation from human laws. . . .
9 That elected principate, or any other office, depends solely upon the election of the body that has the authority for it, and upon no other confirmation or approval.

[. . .]

12 That to decide upon persons and their nature and number for the offices of the city, and any other civil matters, belongs solely to the authority of the faithful prince, in accordance with the laws or approved customs. . . .
13 That no one who exercises the office of prince, and still less any partial collective body or individual person of whatever rank, has plenitude of command or power over the personal or civil acts of others without the decision of the mortal legislator. . . .
14 That no bishop or priest, as such, has any principate or coercive jurisdiction over any clergyman or layperson, even if that person is a heretic.

[. . .]

16 That it is not licit for any bishop or priest or college of them to excommunicate anyone without the authority of the faithful legislator. . . .
17 That all bishops are of equal authority directly through Christ. . . .
18 That by divine authority, and if the faithful human legislator consents or allows it, the other bishops can either collectively or individually excommunicate the Roman bishop. . . .
19 That no mortal can grant a dispensation in marriages prohibited by divine law, and that in the case of those prohibited by human law, this belongs to the authority of the legislator alone or of him who is prince through the legislator. . . .

20 That it belongs to the authority of the faithful legislator alone to legitimize children born out of wedlock so that they can succeed as heirs and accept other civil functions and ecclesiastical offices and benefices.

[. . .]

24 That it does not belong to any bishop as such, either collectively or individually, to institute notaries or other public officials. . . .

25 That no bishop as such, either collectively or individually, has the ability to grant a license to teach or to practice publicly in respect of any art [guild] or discipline.

[. . .]

27 That the legislator can, licitly and in accordance with divine law, use the temporal goods of the church (and also those things that are a part of divine worship) either wholly or in part for the sake of common or public utility or defense, when once the needs of the priests and other ministers of the gospel, and of the poor who are unable to provide for themselves, have been satisfied. . . .

28 It belongs solely to the prince, in accordance with the decision of the legislator and the intention of the person who made the bequest or gift, to dispose of all temporal goods that have been established for pious causes or works of mercy, for example things that are bequeathed in wills for crossing overseas to resist the infidel, or for redeeming those captured by them.

[. . .]

38 That one whose duty it is to observe the evangelical perfection of supreme poverty can have no immoveable goods in his power without the specific intention of selling any such thing he has at the first opportunity, and of giving its price to the poor.

[. . .]

41 That the Roman bishop or any other minister of the church or temple in respect of divine law should be promoted to an ecclesiastical office which is separable solely by the faithful legislator or the prince by its authority or by a general council of the faithful; and that if a fault on his part requires it, he should be suspended and deprived of that office by the same. . . .

42 Many other useful conclusions could be inferred of necessity from the two first discourses; but we are content with those that we have deduced here, since they offer an easy and adequate entry-point for cutting out the said plague together with its cause; and in order to keep our discourse short.

Discourse III, Chapter 3, On the title of this book

This treatise will be called *The Defender of the Peace*, because it discusses and explains the particular causes by which civil peace or tranquility is preserved and exists, and also those through which its opposite, strife, arises, is prevented and is removed. For by it the authority, cause, and harmony of divine and human laws and of coercive principate of any kind—which are the rules of human actions—can be known: and it is in the appropriate and unhindered measurement of these actions that the peace or tranquility of the city consists.

Furthermore, both prince and subject, the primary elements of any civil order, can understand by this treatise what they must do in order to preserve the peace and their own liberty. For the first citizen or part of a civil regime, sc. the princely—be it one man or several—will understand from the human and divine truths written down in this book that they alone have the authority to command the subject multitude, collectively or individually, and to constrain any individual, if it is expedient to do so, according to the laws that have been laid down. They will also understand that they can do nothing more than this, particularly anything involving difficulty, without the consent of the subject multitude or the legislator; and that the multitude or legislator should not be provoked by injustice, because the force and authority of principate consists in the express will of this same multitude. The subject multitude and each of its individuals can, for its part, learn from this book what kind of man or men it should institute to exercise the function of prince. It will also learn that it is obliged to obey only the commands of the princely part as being coercive for and in the status of this present world, although these commands must nonetheless be in accordance with the laws. . . .

Once these things have been understood, committed to memory and carefully guarded or stored, a realm and any other temperate civil community shall be preserved in its peaceable or tranquil existence: through which those who live in a civil manner obtain a sufficient earthly life, and without which they are necessarily deprived of it and are badly disposed in respect of heavenly beatitude as well. These we have assumed in the foregoing discussions, as self-evident to all, to be the ends and what is ultimately desirable for humanity, but in different worlds. We add to what we have said above that if anything is there found determined, defined or otherwise enunciated or written less than catholically, it was not said in obstinacy; and we submit it to the authority of the catholic church or general council of Christian faithful to correct and determine.

In the year one thousand three hundred and twenty-four
the *Defender* was finished, on the feast of the Baptist.
Praise and glory be unto thee, Christ!

Note

1 The Church has "the right to admonish or warn its members, ecclesiastical or lay, who have not conformed to its laws and also, if needful to punish them by physical means, that is, *coercive* jurisdiction," from "Ecclesiastical Jurisdiction," in *New Advent Catholic Encyclopedia, www.newadvent.org. Retrieved 2023-08-31.*

Source

Marsilius of Padua. *The Defender of the Peace*, ed. and trans. Annabel Brett, Cambridge UP, 2005, pp. 139–40; 152–75; 547–58.

References

Gewirth, Alan. "Republicanism and Absolutism in the Thought of Marsilius of Padua," *Medioevo*, Vol. 5 (1979), pp. 23–48.

Moreno-Riaño, Gerson and Cary J. Nederman, eds. *A Companion to Marsilius of Padua*, Brill, 2012.

Moreno-Riaño, Gerson, ed. *The World of Marsilius of Padua*, Brepols; Marston, 2006.

Rubinstein, Nicolai. "Marsilius of Padua and Italian Political Thought of his Time," in *Europe in the Late Middle Ages*, ed. J.R. Hale, Northwestern UP, 1965, pp. 44–75.

Skinner, Quentin. "Scholasticism and Liberty," in *The Foundations of Modern Political Thought, Vol. I The Renaissance*, Cambridge UP, 1978, pp. 49–65.

23 A cardinal's lavish party in Avignon

Anonymous, *Letter from Avignon*, 1343

The following is an excerpt from an eyewitness account of a celebration given for Pope Clement VI (r.1342–52) in a villa on the outskirts of Avignon in 1343. The host of this opulent feast was Cardinal Annibale Caetani di Ceccano (*c*.1282–1350), descended from a powerful and wealthy line of noble lords in southern Italy. He studied and later taught theology in Paris, became archbishop of Naples, and then was made cardinal by Pope John XXII (r.1316–34), who showered Caetani with numerous lucrative benefices in England and France. He was a noted patron of the arts, who commissioned Simone Martini to paint frescoes over the portal of Notre-Dame des Doms, the cathedral of Avignon. The cardinal threw this party for the Frenchman Pierre Roger, who had only recently been elected to the papacy as Clement VI. Aside from the fact that he was a Florentine, the identity of the author of this letter is unknown, although it is unmistakable from his appraisal of the luxurious surroundings that he has a merchant's eye.

Anonymous, *Letter from Avignon*, 1343

"The room where the Pope and sixteen cardinals and twenty other prelates dined was decorated as follows: the walls were hung from ceiling to floor with gold and silk draperies. In the center, behind the seat was a luxurious piece of vermilion samite [satin] cloth, of the richest color ever seen. Then, in another hall, with the finest and grandest canopies overhead, and likewise thick carpets and rugs under one's feet. The tables were laid, as can be imagined with the finest and most elegant table linens.

The menu was comprised of nine courses, each one of three dishes, making a total of twenty-seven dishes, that trying to write of it, my memory fails me. . . .

After the first three of the nine courses, a castle appeared, loaded with game: an enormous cooked stag that seemed alive, a wild boar, roe deer, wild hare, and rabbits. And all of them appeared to be alive, but were cooked. It

DOI: 10.4324/9781003284284-26

was carried in by squires accompanied by knights playing all kinds of musical instruments. I think the sound of these instruments mixed with the cheers of all the company echoed all the way to Avignon!

After the fourth course, the clerics and squires of Lord Anibaldo [Cardinal Annibale Ceccano] came in and one of the clerics said to Our Lordship, "Holy Father, here is a most noble white war-horse, and two rings, and a goblet with a lid. The cardinal begs Your Holiness to accept these things." Our Lordship took the rings—an enormous sapphire and a huge topaz—and put them on his fingers. He commanded the steed to be conducted away and gave the goblet to one of the knights who served him. It was said that the horse was worth 400 gold florins, the two rings valued at 150 florins, and the goblet 100 florins. . . .

After the fifth course a fountain was brought in, topped with a tower and a column, from which five different wines flowed. The margins of the fountain were decorated with peacocks that were cooked, yet seemed to be alive, with their tails spread like tents; there were pheasants, partridges, cranes, white swans, and every kind of wild bird. All this was accompanied as before, with the sound of people's voices and musical instruments.

After this came the sixth course, and then after the seventh, ten enormous steeds entered the hall, one by one, ridden by knights in armor, the first carrying a banner with the arms of Lord Anibaldo. Once they had all entered, they began a tournament, one against the other, striking marvelous, resounding blows lasting for an hour. . . .

After this came the eighth course. Six fencers appeared in the hall dressed all in the same livery, and with a cry, they brandished swords, striking bucklers, and in front of the pope's table they began an unusually fierce and bitter skirmish that really seemed, with all the sounds of many heavy blows, as if thirty men were battling. This went on for a while and then they left the hall.

The ninth course arrived, and as an intermission, the singing of churchmen was heard, but they were not seen. There were voices of every kind: low, medium, high, and those very high and boyish, with a sweetness that silenced the entire hall, as attentively listening ears silenced their tongues, such was the gentle delicacy of the music.

When the singing ended and the last plates removed, all kinds of fruit were served. Two trees were brought to the pope's table: one that looked like it was silver, with apples, pears, figs, peaches, and golden grapes; the other was green like a laurel, bearing candied fruits of many colors.

Source

Anonymous, *Letter from Avignon* in Carte del Bene in the ASF, transcribed by Eugenio Casanova. "Visita di un papa avignonese," in *Archivio della Società Romana di storia patria*, vol. XXII, 1899, pp. 371–81, trans. Kaborycha.

References

Falkeid, Unn. *The Avignon Papacy Contested: An Intellectual History from Dante to Catherine of Siena*, Harvard UP (I Tatti Studies in Italian Renaissance History), 2017.

Mollat, Guillaume. *The Popes at Avignon, 1305–1378*, trans. from the 9th French ed., 1949, Harper & Row, 1963.

Weiss, Stefan. "Luxury and Extravagance at the Papal Court in Avignon and the Outbreak of the Great Western Schism," in *A Companion to the Great Western Schism (1378–1417)*, ed. Joelle Rollo-Koster and Thomas M. Izbicki, Brill, 2009, pp. 67–88.

24 A holy woman urges the pope to reform

Catherine of Siena, *Letter to Gregory XI*, 1376

Less than a century after her death, Caterina di Jacopo di Benincasa (1347–1380) was canonized as St. Catherine of Siena. During her lifetime, Catherine was recognized for her extraordinary piety and was renowned as much for her fasting, her experience of the stigmata, and her religious visions (**#42**) as for her public role in the civic life of Siena. She wrote a number of spiritual works and 375 letters that she dictated to her confessor Raymond of Capua, and these circulated widely. Many of the letters are addressed to various men and women of Siena, whom she admonishes to lead more upright lives. Catherine also wrote to powerful people—*condottieri*, queens, and popes—administering not only spiritual but also political advice. Deeply concerned about violence in the society around her, she tried whenever possible to use her religious authority to make peace. The leaders of the Republic of Siena, recognizing the young woman's influence, sent her on various delegations to negotiate on behalf of the city. When, in 1376 Catherine went to Avignon to meet with Pope Gregory XI (Pierre Roger de Beaufort, r.1370–78), Tuscany was in the midst of armed conflict with the papacy, the War of the Eight Saints. During this crisis, Coluccio Salutati, chancellor of Florence (**#11**), composed letters filled with forceful humanist oratory urging cities across the Italian Peninsula to join Florence and rise up against the tyranny of the papacy. Writing in Latin to the citizens of Rome in January 1376, Salutati appealed to a shared sense of ancient Roman heritage: "How sad to see noble Italy, whose right it is to rule other nations, itself suffer slavery! What a sight to see this abject barbarism seize upon Latium with ferocious cruelty, creating havoc and preying upon the Latins! Therefore, arise . . . and expel this abomination from Italian territory, and protect those who desire liberty. Do not allow these Gallic devourers to oppress your Italy with such cruelty!"[1]

Catherine had her own criticisms of the papacy. She arrived in Avignon with her companions on June 18, 1376, and met with the pope two days later. According to her biographer, Catherine's first impression of the papal court was that "where there ought to be a paradise of heavenly virtues, she found instead the stench of infernal vices."[2] Catherine wrote to a papal

DOI: 10.4324/9781003284284-27

nuncio that the pope was surrounded with clerics who were "wolves and devils incarnate." She lamented the bad pastors who "care about nothing but food and beautiful houses and pretty youths and big horses. Ah me, that what Christ acquired on the wood of the cross is being thus spent on prostitutes."[3] In the letter below, possibly presented to Gregory XI at the time of her arrival, Catherine is both blunt and ingratiating. She alternately threatens and cajoles the pope to convince him not only to reform what she perceives as the immoral behavior at the papal court, but also to bring peace to Tuscany. Moreover, she adds her voice to those calling for a crusade, hoping to deflect violent conflict away from Italy, directing it toward the Holy Land instead. Her larger mission, of course, was to convince the pope to leave France and to return the papal court to Italy, which he did toward the end of 1376, arriving in Rome the following year.

Catherine of Siena, *Letter to Pope Gregory XI,* 1376

In the name of crucified Jesus Christ and sweet Mary, holiest and sweetest father,

Your unworthy, miserable daughter in sweet Jesus Christ, Catherine, commends herself to you through his precious blood, with the desire to see you manly and steadfast, fearless, and without selfish worldly love for yourself or towards anyone related to you by bodily ties. In contemplating God's gentle presence, I see that nothing can prevent this good, holy desire of yours, or interfere with God's honor and the reformation and exaltation of the Holy Church as much as this. You ought to wish with all your soul for God in his infinite mercy to remove every passion and weakness from your heart and to reform you into another man, that is, to work a reformation in burning and most ardent desire, as there is no other way for you to fulfill God's will, as well as the desires of His servants.

Alas, alas, my dearest Daddy,[4] pardon my presumption, what I have said and am saying now: I am compelled by sweet Foremost Truth to tell you this. This is his will, Father; this is what he demands of you. He asks you to bring justice amidst the abundant iniquities committed by those who feed themselves, grazing in the garden of the holy Church, for he says that animals should not eat the food of men. Since he has given you authority and you have taken it, you ought to use your virtue and power, if not, it would be better—more honorable for God and for the salvation of your soul—for you to resign.

There is another thing that he desires and asks of you and it is this: he wants you to make peace with all of Tuscany, with whom you are in conflict. You must take away as much and whatever you can from your rebellious, wicked children, but without waging war, disciplining them as a father punishes an offending child. Rather, God in his gentle goodness requires you to give full authority to those who ask to go on a Holy Crusade; though it may seem impossible to you, it is possible through the gentle goodness of God, who has ordained it and wills it to happen.

Take care, as you value your life, that you do not neglect your duties, nor treat the works of the Holy Spirit as a joke: you must carry out the things that are required of you. If you want justice, you can make it happen. You can have peace, withdrawing from the perverse pomp and delights of the world, preserving only the honor of God and everything rightfully due to the Holy Church. And what's more, you have the authority to give it to those who ask for it. So, since you are not poor, but rich, and you hold in your hand the keys of Heaven—its gates are opened for people when you open them, and shut for others when you shut them.

If you do not do these things, you will be chastised by God. If I were in your place, I would fear Divine Judgment would fall on me. And yet, on behalf of crucified Christ, I beg you most tenderly to obey the will of God, for I know that you desire nothing else than to do his bidding, so that you do not receive this harsh rebuke: "May you be cursed, as time and strength were given to you, but you did not make use of them!" Father, through God's goodness, and taking hope from your Holiness, I believe that you will act so that it will not fall on you.

I say no more. Forgive me! Forgive me! I am forced to speak by the great love I have for your salvation, and the great pain I feel when I see its opposite. In order to unburden my conscience, I would gladly have said all this in your presence. When it pleases you Holiness for me come to you, I will come willingly. Do not make me reprimand you before Christ crucified, for there is no one else I can go to, as you are the highest person on Earth. May you continue to enjoy God's holy and sweet love. In humility I ask your blessing.

Sweet Jesus! Jesus love!

Notes

1 Salutati addressed this letter to citizens of Rome in January 1376. "Gallic devourers" is a reference to the papal court, composed largely of Frenchmen during the period in Avignon. The letter is in Gene Brucker. *Florentine Politics and Society, 1343–1378*, Princeton UP, 1962, p. 300.
2 These are the words of Raymond of Capua (**#42**); Beattie 82.
3 Luongo 164.
4 The word Catherine uses is *babbo*. In Tuscan dialect, this is still the affectionate term children use for their father; the literal translation is "daddy."

Sources

Catherine of Siena, *Letter CCLV* in *Le Lettere di S. Caterina da Siena—ridotte a miglior lezione e in ordine nuovo disposte con proemio e note*, ed Niccolò Tommaseo, G. Barbera, editore, 1860, trans. Kaborycha.

References

Beattie, Blake. "Catherine of Siena and the Papacy," in *A Companion to Catherine of Siena*, ed. Carolyn Muessig, George Ferzoco and Beverly Mayne Kienzle, Brill, 2012, pp. 73–98.

Catherine of Siena. *An Anthology*, ed. Suzanne Noffke, Arizona Center for Medieval and Renaissance Studies, 2011–2012.

Catherine of Siena. *The Letters of Catherine of Siena*, Translated with introduction and notes by Suzanne Noffke, O.P., Arizona Center for Medieval and Renaissance Studies, 2001.

Luongo, F. Thomas. *The Saintly Politics of Catherine of Siena*, Cornell UP, 2006.

Peterson, David S. "The War of the Eight Saints in Florentine Memory and Oblivion," in *Society and Individual in Renaissance Florence*, ed. William J. Connell, UC Press, 2002, pp. 173–214.

25 Papal patronage, largesse, and nepotism

Bartolomeo Platina, *Inscription in honor of Sixtus IV, c.*1475

Bartolomeo Platina, *The Lives of Christ and the Popes,* 1475

Francesco della Rovere (1414–1484), who would become Pope Sixtus IV, was born in Celle Ligure, a small seaside town in the Republic of Genoa, into a large, respectable family of modest means. Francesco was destined from childhood for a religious career: he joined the Franciscan order at the age of nine, received an excellent education, and became an accomplished scholar of natural philosophy and theology. Recognized for his learning, Francesco gradually rose in the hierarchy of the church, becoming Minister General of the order in 1464, and appointed Cardinal of San Pietro in Vincoli in 1467. When he was elected pope in 1467, he took the name Sixtus IV. This fresco commemorates the expansion of the papal library in 1475 under Sixtus, a project begun under Pope Nicholas V two decades earlier. Building upon his predecessor's collection, enlarging and enhancing the library's physical space, Sixtus lavished funds on this project. The splendor of this library, "in its time must have ranked alongside Sixtus's other grand achievements, the Sistine Chapel, sculpture collection on the Capitol, the Hospital of Santo Spirito, and the Ponte Sisto."[1] The inscription at the bottom of the painting describes some of those other cultural initiatives and urban renewal projects, which included churches, buildings, streets, walls, marketplaces, and the aqueduct of Rome. Sixtus dedicated vast papal funds to these and many other renovation and building projects, both in the city at large as well as within the Vatican. Even more well-known than the papal library is the Sistine Chapel, the structure that Sixtus had built between 1479 and 1481 and that is named for him. The pope employed some of the most celebrated painters of the day—Botticelli, Domenico Ghirlandaio, Cosimo Roselli, Luca Signorelli, Pietro Perugino, and Pinturicchio—to decorate its walls. Work on these frescoes took place between 1481 and 1483, with the participation of the Florentine artists facilitated by Lorenzo de' Medici once he and the pope had reconciled following the Pazzi Conspiracy (#53).

In addition to his expenditures as a patron of the arts and benefactor to the city of Rome, Sixtus spent vast sums to advance the careers and

DOI: 10.4324/9781003284284-28

increase the private fortunes of his own family members, several of whom are represented in the painting by Melozzo da Forlì (Figure 3.1). They are four of the pope's nephews: Raffaele Riario, Girolamo Riario, Giovanni della Rovere, and Giuliano della Rovere, the future Pope Julius II, who is standing at the center of the painting facing Sixtus.[2] These papal nephews ("*nipoti*" in Italian, hence the term "nepotism") all benefitted from their uncle's influence, through either lucrative church offices if they were pursuing a religious career or socially advantageous arranged marriages if they preferred a secular lifestyle. Further emphasizing their prosperity, on the pilasters on either side of this portrait, the della Rovere are represented by abundant oak leaves and acorns (*rovere* in Italian is a species of oak), celebrating the literal flourishing of the family tree.

The man kneeling in the foreground of the painting and the author of the inscription in Latin elegiac couplets at its base is the humanist Bartolomeo Platina (Bartolomeo Sacchi of Piadena, 1421–81). For a scholar, Platina had an unusual job history, serving early in his career as a soldier for four years under Francesco Sforza and Niccolò Piccinino. When he reached adulthood, he threw himself into humanist pursuits, studying first in Mantua and later in Florence, where he came to know Lorenzo de' Medici and the Florentine humanists in his circle. Like many humanists, Platina found employment in the papal chancery of Pius II (#44), who greatly increased the number of papal secretaries during his reign. The following pope, Paul II, fired many of the secretaries upon taking office in 1464 and demanded they return the salaries they had received. When Platina objected, he was arrested and imprisoned in the Castel Sant'Angelo where he was tortured and accused of having been involved in a plot to assassinate the pope. After his release, he was unable to find work in the Vatican until Sixtus IV was elected. He wrote his *Lives of Christ and the Popes* and dedicated it to Sixtus, who the following year appointed him as papal librarian. In this work Platina draws continual parallels between the grandeur of Emperor Augustus, the majesty of Christ, and implicitly, the greatness of Sixtus IV. Though lavish in flattering his patron, the humanist nevertheless condemns the corruption he witnessed regularly in the Vatican, as evident in the selection below from his *Life of Pope Dionysius*. Platina was the author of numerous philosophical, historical, biographical, and literary works, as well as a very popular cookbook.

Bartolomeo Platina, *Inscription in honor of Sixtus IV*, *c.*1475

[*Words in Latin beneath Melozzo da Forlì's painting.*]

WITH CHURCHES AND PALACE RESTORED, AND THE STREETS, FORA, CITY WALLS, BRIDGES,

NOW THAT THE AQUA VIRGO AT TREVI IS BACK IN REPAIR,

NOW YOU MAY OPEN OUR AGE-OLD PORT FOR THE SHIPPERS' CONVENIENCE,

AND GIRDLE THE VATICAN GROUNDS, SIXTUS, WITH A NEW WALL.

STILL, ROME OWES YOU MORE THAN THIS: WHERE A LIBRARY LANGUISHED IN SQUALOR,

NOW IT IS VISIBLE IN A SETTING BEFITTING ITS FAME.

Bartolomeo Platina, *The Lives of Christ and the Popes*, 1475

The life of Christ

Augustus had inherited the empire from Julius Caesar by right of kinship and hereditary succession—or rather, he defeated and killed the traitors and usurpers who were trying to usurp the Republic—and reformed the monarchy of the world into a better form, bestowing wondrous happiness on his age. After pacifying foreign and domestic affairs, he was held in such great honor, not only by his people but also by foreign kings, that they built cities in his name, which they called Sebaste and Caesarea. Many kings came to Rome to see him, and he received them with such kindness and courtesy that he turned them into his best friends. He lived most humanely with his own citizens; he was held to be clement toward criminals and very generous to his friends. He made friends sparingly, but kept them with the greatest constancy. He was so fond of the liberal arts that hardly a day passed without his reading, writing or declaiming something. He delighted in the wit and learning of Sallust, Livy, Virgil, Horace, Asinius Pollio, and the outstanding orator Messala Corvinus; and they immortalized all his deeds in their writings. He so beautified Rome that he boasted that he had found a city of brick and was leaving a marble one.

The felicity of his rule was great, honestly, but it was certainly made greater still by the most salutiferous birth of Christ our King. Now between the creation of the world and this most joyous birthday there had elapsed 5190 years. . . . Orosius reports that on that same day Augustus Caesar commanded that no one should henceforth call him "lord," foreseeing, I believe, that the true prince of the whole world had been born. He also ordered that all the people in the Roman world be registered in a census, as if he would some day render an account of the empire he governed to a greater prince; and by senatorial decree he placed the consul Cyrinus in charge of the census.

There had never been such great peace and tranquility at home or abroad. For the prophets called Christ the prince of justice and of peace.

[. . .]

The foregoing is more or less what I have decided to write, in the briefest possible way, about the royal life of Christ and of our pontiff, so that I might more easily approach my intended work, and so that readers might enjoy my text the more, because like a refreshing spring it flows from the emperor of the Christians and continues in order through the Roman pontiffs up until the time of Sixtus IV.

The Life of Dionysius I [r.260–68]

In the time of Dionysius, Paul of Samosata left the orthodox faith and revived the heresy of Artemon. After replacing as bishop of Antioch a man who had died, he behaved with excessive arrogance. Out of pride, while walking, he would read through and dictate letters to a throng of followers behind and in front of him. On account of this man's arrogance, many people despised the Christian religion. But what would they make of our time, when no pride or pomp, not to say luxury, is lacking? What if they were to see the many silk- and scarlet-clad youths parading on high-spirited, prettily caparisoned horses, and a crowd of priests following them with parti-colored, gold-embossed riding cloaks hanging from their horses? I know well that they would despise them; they would say that they have nothing in common with Christ apart from a kind of similarity of religion.

Notes

1 Clark 21.
2 Julius II della Rovere (r. 1503–13), who initiated the rebuilding of St. Peter's, was the patron of Bramante, Michelangelo, and Raphael.

Sources

Platina, *Inscription in honor of Sixtus IV* in Ingrid Rowland. *The Culture of the High Renaissance: Ancients and Moderns in Sixteenth-century Rome*, Cambridge UP, 1998, p. 32.

Platina, *Lives of the Popes*, ed. and trans. Anthony F. D'Elia, Harvard UP, 2008, pp. 11–13; 19–21; 139–41.

References

Clark, Nicholas. *Melozzo da Forlì: Pictor Papalis*, Sotheby's Publications; Distributed in the USA by Harper & Row, 1990.

Grafton, Anthony, ed. *Rome Reborn: The Vatican Library and Renaissance Culture*, Library of Congress, in association with Biblioteca Apostolica Vaticana, 1993.

Howe, Eunice D. *Art and Culture at the Sistine Court: Platina's "Life of Sixtus IV" and the Frescoes of the Hospital of Santo Spirito*, Biblioteca Apostolica Vaticana, 2005.

Lee, Egmont. *Sixtus IV and Men of Letters*, Edizioni di storia e letteratura, 1978.

Shearman, John. "The Chapel of Sixtus IV," in *The Sistine Chapel: The Art, the History, and the Restoration*, ed. Carlo Pietrangeli, Harmony Books, 1986, pp. 22–91.

26 Accounts of the 1527 Sack of Rome

Jacopo Buonaparte (attrib.), *Account of the Sack of Rome*

Marcello Alberini, *Memoirs*, 1547

Antonio Tebaldeo, *Letter to Angelo Colocci*, Nov. 20, 1527

Luigi Guicciardini, *History of the Sack of Rome*, 1537

The Sack of Rome began on the morning of May 6, 1527, when Spanish, German, and Italian troops serving Emperor Charles V breeched the city's crumbling walls. The conflict had its roots in the decades-long geopolitical power struggles between Spain, France, and the Papal States; the more immediate causes of the crisis were poor diplomatic and tactical decisions made by Pope Clement VII. But the ones to bear the brunt of the humanitarian disaster were the people of Rome. Although it is impossible to calculate the numbers precisely, it has been estimated that the invasion and the subsequent occupation, which lasted for nine months, reduced the city's population by nearly half, due to deaths caused by violence, famine, and disease, as well as the flight of many residents.[1] The following four accounts by contemporaries convey the magnitude of the disaster and the impact it had on Italians at the time.

Jacopo Buonaparte (d.1541) was a Florentine who was a friend and counsellor to Pope Clement VII. The account attributed to him[2] describes the carnage observed from the safety of the Castel Sant'Angelo, where the pope and his court had taken refuge. Other inhabitants of the city, such as Marcello Alberini (1511–1580) were not as lucky. Born in Rome in 1511, he was the son of Marzia Picchi and Giovanni Battista Alberini, wealthy supporters of the Colonna faction who opposed the secular power of the papacy. Marcello was sixteen years old when the Sack of Rome took place, and in his *Memoirs*, begun in 1547, he vividly recalls the hardships his family endured following the invasion by Imperial troops, which included being taken hostage and held for ransom. Angelo Colocci (1467–1549) was a humanist originally from the south who had moved to Rome, where he held a succession of high offices under Pope Leo X and later under Clement VII. The owner of numerous properties in Rome, and an art collector, Colocci was extorted twice during the Sack, and in July of 1527, he fled to his hometown of Jesi, not to return to Rome until the next year. Colocci asked one of his friends, the poet Antonio Tebaldeo (or Tebaldi, 1463–1537) who was

DOI: 10.4324/9781003284284-29

in Rome, to go check on his things. Known for his vast personal library, Colocci was worried in particular about his treasured books. In his letter, Tebaldeo describes what he found when he went there. Tebaldeo himself had been living in Rome at the time of the Sack and lost everything; he died ten years later in great hardship.

Luigi Guicciardini (1478–1551), like his more well-known younger brother Francesco (#27) and his even more well-known friend Niccolò Machiavelli, was both an author of works concerning historical and political events, as well as someone who helped shape those events. Although Luigi Guicciardini was not an eyewitness to the Sack of Rome, in preparing his narrative, he drew on written and oral accounts of his contemporaries, analyzing political events from a perspective similar to that of Machiavelli. Luigi Guicciardini was the "earliest documented reader of *The Prince*,"[3] and like Machiavelli, he offered this work to a member of the Medici family. Around ten years after the Sack took place, in his dedication to the young Duke Cosimo I de' Medici, Luigi wrote the following words: "Part of the historian's task is to teach the advisers of republics and princes how to live by using the true example of others. His greater role is to encourage the great men of the future to imitate the noblest virtues and the best customs of celebrated men and to shun the negative qualities of those who have counseled or acted unwisely in service of their countries."[4]

Jacopo Buonaparte, *Account of the Sack of Rome*

On the streets you saw nothing but looters and the vilest scoundrels carrying away enormous heaps of the most precious vestments and ecclesiastical ornaments and innumerable sacks full of candelabras and vases of silver and gold. You could also see huge numbers of prisoners, of every quality of life, shouting and screaming, in much torment as they were deliberately led back to their residences—which already had been violently sacked—by Spaniards and Germans, to keep them wretchedly locked up inside in hopes of extracting yet more wealth from them. On those same streets heaps of dead bodies were to be found covered in mud, among these many nobles who had resisted and were cut to pieces. Many of these were still half-alive, lying on the bare ground with no hope of aid. Amid that wild chaos could be seen, at times, men, women, and children of every age and condition, here and there forced to jump out of windows, and some even did so voluntarily. Others, in order not to be taken alive by such fierce men, tried to flee. When the enemy caught them, they were horribly treated, slaughtered on the spot, and they ended their unhappy lives there on the streets. The spectacle was so harsh and pitiable that it cannot be recounted without the utmost horror.

The evil doings of those men, the mockery and maltreatment of both secular and religious persons, the lack of regard for sacred, divine things and the disdain for the orders and rites of the Catholic Church, had made Rome—that before had been the nest of religion, almost the city of God on Earth—into a place that no longer held Masses or holy offices, no more processions or devout prayers were said, as in earlier times was done in times of adversity. Rather, disgraceful words rang out through the city, cruel curses and abhorrent blasphemies, mixed with the screams and laments of the wretched Roman people.

[. . .]

Furthermore, it happened that a troop of Germans had captured a prelate, who in addition to other jewels he had on his vestments, wore a diamond ring that might have been worth around three or four hundred scudi, and one of the soldiers was trying to pull it off his finger. He was losing patience; a corporal in the company saw this, and turning to his companion said, "Now I'll get it off of him!" And taking hold of a sharp dagger, right away cut off the finger and handed it to his comrade, who removed the ring and threw the finger in the man's face.

Marcello Alberini, *Memoirs*, 1547

We were left miserable and helpless since celestial mercy did not save us. We were prey to the wrath and fury of those barbarians, whom I will never be able to call humans; they possessed no humanity, those appalling beasts. Nor were the Italians less cruel, but what can I say of all those men and the cruelty they practiced? It often happens that victory makes the victors insolent and those who moderate themselves deserve twice the triumph for having conquered first their enemies, and afterwards their own impulses, which is more difficult.

This disordered rabble entered Rome; they were from various countries, speaking many different languages and without obedience to their superiors, having lost their leader; it was such a thing as had not been endured for many years. As night fell, our afflictions increased; such was the terror and dread we experienced that everyone had fear and death written on their faces. And in the shadowy darkness, besides the murders, there were greater horrors: smashing of doors, breaking of strongboxes, taking of prisoners everywhere, and torturing them so they would confess secret hiding places [of money] or raise large sums to ransom them and be freed. I will remain silent about the acts of violation and sacrilege, since neither persons' bodies, nor holy places, nor even God himself were respected. Those wretched, ragged soldiers, who absorbed in their plunder, robbed us, would themselves have been the prey of others, had the duke of Urbino been more concerned with his honor and less content with the horrible spectacle we presented—vilely seized, whipped, burned and murdered—nearly under his eyes, that he could have liberated us. In short, we were humiliated as the vanquished, subject to the will of the victors, who in their pride, employed the harshest severity in their triumph, without any regard even for God. I believe that in Heaven St. Peter himself most bitterly wept for us, but on account of our sins, the Lord would not heed him nor take pity on us. Wretched Church, to what end did you see your priests and pastor reduced!

[*The pope and some cardinals take refuge in the Castel Sant'Angelo; Alberini describes the activities of the Colonna faction; imperial troops sack homes, demand ransom, and commit acts of brutality.*]

Added to so many calamities, either from corruption in the air or contamination of the blood—caused by the hardships and outrages suffered, as well as from extreme poverty and being forced to feed themselves on things other than bread—or by the will of God, without which nothing is accomplished, a pestilence arose, so great that it would be impossible to recount the number of the dead, that every day, for weeks and months, were buried in June, July, and August. Whereas, in other times people fled as far as possible to avoid being infected, there were so many other evils at the time that the plague was hardly considered, indeed, many longed to be released from their troubles as soon as possible.

And thus God provided for me: having lost all my goods, I was to lose those who shared that loss with me, namely my sisters Livia, Diana, and Laura, the youngest of whom was ten years old. What pained me the most was the death of my brother Oratio, with whom I would have willingly shared my life, not to mention that miserable portion that remained to us amid such ruins, which I never knew of before his death, until my father made his will. And because no element of the scourge of the plague was lacking, hunger was intolerable. Thus, those thieves went searching from house to house and when they found anything to keep them alive, let alone bread or wine, there was no way to guard yourself and protect it. And those who had people who were infected or sick with the plague in the house, when they heard such people at the door, what little bread they had, was hidden under the mattresses of the sick in order to save it. It didn't matter, however, because those wicked men cared neither about the plague nor God and took it, leaving for the household's nourishment only the straw and wool of the beds.

Antonio Tebaldeo, *Letter to Angelo Colocci*, Nov. 20, 1527

Reverend Messer Angelo,

I received, along with another, a letter of yours to which I respond. You cannot know what great difficulty it is staying in Rome, due to the extensive plague and the beatings that soldiers give anyone wanting to see the homes, as they did before to Messer Pietro Cursio, and recently to me in the presence of your neighbors. My housekeeper had the plague, from which I was in great danger, yet God saved us from it.

When I was at your house the soldiers had left and your housekeeper was dead, thus I went with Philippa your godmother; and I found your books in the room above the roof, and I began to sort through them. While doing this, the Spanish captain returned and struck me, so I couldn't go there anymore. Afterwards, the whole army came into Rome and other persons entered your house, so that there was yet another Sack and I believe that all your books came to a bad end. I will not be able to find out what happened if the soldiers don't leave, as one hopes they soon will.

All the people who were in Messer Benedetto da Porto's home have died of the plague, and all the chests were taken away, according to the neighbors, to Santo Apostolo, where I was able to find those belonging to Messer Benedetto. However, I believe that those too have been lost, since the soldiers returned.

As regards recovering your books, I tell you that it will not be possible because they have ended up in many different hands.

Messer Pietro Cursio stayed a month in Tivoli, and since then has remained in Rome.

There was someone saying that one of your homes was his—I wasn't told who he was—but he didn't go back there. All the houses are in very bad condition, except the one where the cooking was done, the place where Philippa used to live. But Philippa ran away and I don't know how that house ended up, because the soldiers burn all the wood in the houses, so that they are all empty inside. If you return, you will see Rome torn apart.

When the Prior returns I will write to you, and I commend myself to you. In Rome, 20 November, 1527

Luigi Guicciardini, *The Sack of Rome*, 1537[5]

I know I am about to say things that many people will have difficulty in believing. Namely that the German and Lutheran soldiers, even though they are thought to be more inhumane and more prejudiced against Italians than the Spanish, this time showed themselves to be more benign, less greedy, and much more tractable by nature than either the Spanish or Italian troops of the emperor. Many Germans, after the first furious wave of the attack was over, did not force their prisoners to undergo extensive torture, but they were content and satisfied with the sums of money that they were offered freely. And many of them were both humane and respectful towards gentlewomen (even when they were young and beautiful). They brought them food and kept them at a distance from other prisoners, where they would not be insulted or injured by others. Consequently, many prisoners at any early point in their capture, offering a small amount of money in comparison to what they could actually pay, were liberated without difficulty. This liberality and easygoing nature of the Germans is not to be attributed to their inexperience or to the fact that because they were very poor, every little offer of money seemed a lot to them. But it reflects a more humane and moderate nature. Certainly no one ever heard that the Spanish in their first raids, even though they were extremely poor, ever behaved towards their prisoners with such compassion and respect.

If it were not for the example of the other nationalities, I have no doubt, except for the prelates and clerics (these being the principal enemies of the Lutheran sect), the Germans would not have shown much cruelty against laypeople, either Roman citizens or foreigners. After hearing and seeing again and again, however, that in order to avoid torture, the prisoners of the other nationalities paid hundreds and thousands of scudi, and that many whom they had freed were secretly recaptured by the Spanish and then paid out huge sums of money to avoid torture; then they changed their nature and their methods. It is a common trait among people that they learn bad habits from each other more readily than good ones: especially when it is to their own advantage. And so after this the Germans exerted themselves to surpass every other nationality in the invention of barbarous torments.

[. . .]

The sumptuous palaces of the cardinals, the proud palaces of the pope, the holy churches of Peter and Paul, the private chapel of His Holiness, the Sancta Sanctorum, and other holy places, once full of plenary indulgences and venerable relics, now became the brothels of German and Spanish whores. And in place of the false ceremonies and lavish music, now you could hear the horses cough and neigh, and men cursing God and all the saints. They committed shameful acts on the altars and in the most sanctified places, in contempt of contemporary religion. Many sacred pictures and sculptures that had once been worshipped with vain ceremonies were burned and broken by iron and fire. Crucifixes were shattered by shots from arquebuses and lay on the ground; the relics and calvaries of saints lay among the dung of men and animals.

All the sacraments of the modern Church were scorned and vilified as if the city had been captured by Turks or Moors or some other barbarous and infidel enemy. There was no sin or villainy that these mad and impious Lutherans did not commit. When they saw the Germans dishonoring the churches and the most holy relics, the Spanish took this very badly; they began to curse the Germans, and they came very close to violence on this score. But in the end this disagreement was settled, and the situation quieted down; the Germans stopped destroying holy images and gave their full attention to tormenting their prisoners and revisiting the same houses. And the booty continually grew, since they always found something that had been hidden before but newly revealed by their prisoners.

I will not write of the anguish and confusion that those in Castel Sant'Angelo are enduring. With the pope, there are thirteen cardinals, innumerable prelates, lords, noblewomen, merchants, couriers and soldiers, all in terror and despairing of their safety. . . .

One can easily imagine the anguish and torment of the pope, constantly seeing and hearing such a scourge of punishment raised against himself and against Rome. Like the rest of those under siege, he is suffering in fear that he will soon fall into the hands of cruel enemies, obviously thirsting for his blood. And though he enjoyed great honors and sweet pleasures in the past, now he is paying for them with humiliation and pitiful distress. If he ever considered himself a wise and glorious prince, now he must acknowledge himself to be the most unfortunate and the most abject pontiff who ever lived. And since it is his fault that the Church, Rome, and Italy all find themselves in such extreme danger, we can easily imagine that he often looks toward the sky with tears in his eyes and with the bitterest and deepest sighs demands:

"Wherefore, then, hast thou brought me forth out of the womb? Oh, that I had died, and no eye had seen me!" [Job. 110:18]

Notes

1 Hook 177.
2 There is some controversy concerning the authorship of this work. Milanese believes that Buonaparte might have been the "compiler" of this account, but that the printed version of the text that has come down to us has been somewhat corrupted (xxi–xxii), while Goethals refers to it simply as one of the "spurious works inspired by Guicciardini" (177).
3 Goethals 178.
4 McGregor 5.
5 Although McGregor gives 1527 as the date of composition of this text, and indeed much of the writing is meant to give the impression that the author is recounting events as they unfold, most historians believe it was written in 1537.

Sources

Jacopo Buonaparte. *Il Sacco di Roma del MDXXVII*, ed. Carlo Milanesi, Barbera Editore, 1867, pp. 369–70; 373–74, trans. Kaborycha.

Marcello Alberini. *Il sacco di Roma: L'edizione Orano de I ricordi di Marcello Alberini*, ed. Paola Farenga and Domenico Orano, Roma nel Rinascimento, 1997, pp. 268–76; 293–98, trans. Kaborycha.

Antonio Tebaldeo, *Letter to Angelo Colocci* in Santorre Debenedetti. "Le ansie di un bibliofilo durante il sacco di Roma," in *Mélanges offerts à M. Émile Picot*, Damascène Morgand, 1913, vol. I, pp. 511–14, trans. Kaborycha.

Luigi Guicciardini. *The Sack of Rome*, trans. James H. Mc Gregor, Italica Press, 1993, pp. 110–1; 114–16.

References

Chastel, André. *The Sack of Rome*, trans. Beth Archer, Princeton, 1983.

Esposito, Anna and Manuel Vaquero Piñeiro. "Rome During the Sack: Chronicles and Testimonies from an Occupied City," in *The Pontificate of Clement VII: History, Politics, Culture*, ed. Kenneth Gouwens and Sheryl E. Reiss, Ashgate, 2005, 124–42.

Goethals, Jessica. "Spectators of the Sack: Rhetorical 'Particularity' and Graphic Violence in Luigi Guicciardini's *Historia del sacco di Roma*," *Italian Studies*, Vol. 68, No. 2 (2013), pp. 175–201.

Hook, Judith. *The Sack of Rome 1527*, 2nd ed., Palgrave Macmillan, 2004.

27 The characters of two popes compared

Francesco Guicciardini, *The History of Italy*, 1540

Born into a prominent Florentine family belonging to the elite, powerful class in Florence known as the *ottimati*,[1] Francesco Guicciardini (1483–1540) was destined to play a role in Florentine political life. By nature, he yearned for glory and looked to a career in the Church to achieve this. In his twenties, Francesco wrote that when his father forbade it, he was disappointed because he wanted to become "great in the Church . . . with the hope of becoming a cardinal." Nonetheless, after attaining his law degree and serving the Florentine Republic for two years as ambassador to Spain, in 1515 the young man came to the attention of the recently elected pope and thereafter would occupy a prominent place in papal politics. The two popes he served for nearly twenty years belonged to the most powerful Florentine family: Leo X (Giovanni de' Medici, r.1513–21) and Clement VII (Giuliano de' Medici, r.1523–34). Leo put Guicciardini in charge of the administration of the cities of Modena, Reggio, and Parma, at that time part of the Papal States. Clement VII, Leo's cousin, later appointed Guicciardini as governor of the Romagna, with full powers everywhere in the region, apart from Bologna. Guicciardini served as papal advisor and was instrumental in arranging the 1526 League of Cognac, an alliance of the papacy with the republics of Venice and Florence, the Duchy of Milan, and France, which was intended to counter the military threat of Emperor Charles V. Afterwards, Clement rewarded Guicciardini by appointing him lieutenant general of the papal forces. None of these measures, however, prevented the advance of the troops of Charles V into the Italian Peninsula or the Sack of Rome, which occurred the following year. Francesco Guicciardini was not only a man of action, but also a prolific, expert writer of history who was finely attuned to the subtleties of language. His humanist, literary education in Latin and Greek involved the study of ancient history, and his legal training in examining evidence certainly contributed to his close analysis of the causes of historical events. As a historian, it is Guicciardini's attention to character, in particular, that makes his work uniquely modern. In the excerpt below, he contrasts the characters of the two Medici popes in order to assess the impact of their personalities on the way events played out. Contemporaries were well aware that character played an important part in the way an individual carried out his role as pope, but few

DOI: 10.4324/9781003284284-30

had such intimate access to the papacy as Guicciardini, and even fewer possessed his ability for astute psychological analysis.

Francesco Guicciardini, *The History of Italy*, Book 16, Chapter 12, 1540

Leo, who first brought ecclesiastical grandeur to the house of Medici, and with his authority as cardinal so greatly supported both himself and the family, which had fallen from such heights into base decline,[2] so that they could hope for the return of good fortune. He was a man of enormous generosity, if that, however, is the right word for excessive spending beyond all measure. Once he achieved the pontificate, he displayed such splendor and magnificent spirit that it would have been marvelous even had he descended from a long succession of kings or emperors. Not only was he lavish with money, but with all the favors that are in a pope's power; he granted these so excessively that he debased papal authority, upset the style of the court, and by spending too much made it necessary to always be looking for money by extraordinary means. To this easy manner of his was added a most elaborate act through which he manipulated everyone in his pontificate and it made him seem like a very good prince—I am not referring to apostolic goodness, because with our corrupt customs, a pope is praised for being good when he does not surpass the malignancy of other men. Nevertheless, he had a reputation for being clement, eager to benefit everyone, and utterly incapable of any action that would do offense to anyone. The same man was greatly devoted to music, jests, and buffoons, in which entertainments his mind was immersed most of the time, otherwise he would have turned to great enterprises and goals, for which he had a most capacious intellect. Many believed during the early days of his papacy that he was completely chaste, but later it was discovered that he was excessively dedicated to those pleasures that cannot be decently named, and day by day he became ever more so.

Among his many fortuitous circumstances, was the not inconsiderable fortune of having by his side his cousin Giulio de' Medici, whom he raised from knight of Rhodes to the rank of cardinal, even though he was of illegitimate birth. Because Giulio was by nature serious, diligent, and assiduous in official matters, disinclined to pleasure, organized and disciplined in all things, and Leo had placed all important matters of the papacy in his hands, he put up with much disorder that derived from the other's indulgent, easy-going ways and was able to moderate it. And even more, not following the custom of other nephews and brothers of popes, he placed Leo's honor and grandeur ahead of any backing he would gain after his death and was so utterly faithful and obedient that he seemed really to be Leo's other self. For this, the pope was always raising him to greater heights and daily turned more affairs over to him, which in the hands of two such different natures demonstrated how sometimes the mixture of two opposites can fit well together.

The assiduousness, diligence, order, and seriousness of one, and the easy prodigality, pleasures, and hilarity of the other caused many to believe that Leo was governed by Giulio, and that by himself he could not have managed such a heavy burden, unable to harm anyone and craving only the enjoyment of the comforts of the papacy, that it was Giulio who possessed the spirit, ambition, and yearning for new things. Thus, all harsh measures, changes, and enterprises that were carried out during Leo's time were believed to have come about through Giulio's instigation; he was reputed to be a malevolent man, but with a great, ingenious mind. This opinion of his worth was confirmed after Leo's death, because with all the contradictions and difficulties he had, he held himself with such dignity that he seemed nearly papal, and in this way, he maintained his authority with many cardinals, so that when entered in two conclaves, he came out absolute master of sixteen votes. And finally, despite infinite objections from the majority, and from most of the older members of the College, after Adrian's death,[3] not even two years had passed since Leo's, when he attained the pontificate.

So great were expectations, that it was the universal opinion that he would be the greatest pope and would accomplish greater things than anyone who had ever sat on that throne until then. But the opinions held of both Leo and Giulio were soon recognized as false. For Leo was filled with condescension more than goodness, but Giulio had many qualities different from those he was first believed to possess: he was neither so desirous of innovation, nor the greatness and inclination of the spirit toward generous and magnanimous ends that had been previously believed; and he had been Leo's executor and minister of his plans, rather than the director and counselor who introduced his own counsel and wishes. Even though he had the most capacious intellect, and marvelous knowledge of everything in the world, nonetheless it was not matched by resoluteness or ability to carry out deeds. He was impeded not only by his considerable timidity of spirit and by his aversion to spending, but also by a certain irresolution and perplexity, that came naturally to him. Almost always he remained unresolved and ambiguous when pressed for a decision about things that had long been foreseen, considered, and practically resolved. Hence, between the deliberation and the execution of what had been deliberated, every little detail that he discovered, every slight impediment that he came across, seemed enough to make him return to his confusion prior to making his decision. It always seemed to him, once he had decided, that the advice he had rejected was the best, because when he remembered them, he only thought of those reasons that he had overlooked, without recalling the reasons that had caused him to choose, whereas the contrast and comparison would have weakened the weight of the opposing reasons. He remembered that he had very often been mistakenly afraid, yet the experience was not enough to overcome his fear. His nature thus tangled up in such a confused manner of proceeding, he let himself often be carried away by his ministers, who seemed more to lead him than advise him.

Notes

1 The Italian word derives from a term used to describe the elite class during the time of the late Roman Republic. In Latin, *optimates* means "the best ones"; the opposing group was known as the *populares*.
2 Piero di Lorenzo de' Medici (1472–1503), the son of Lorenzo the Magnificent, was driven out of Florence in 1494.
3 The Dutchman Adriaan Florensz Boeyens was Pope Adrian VI (r.1522–23).

Source

Francesco Guicciardini. *Storia d'Italia*, ed. Silvana Seidel Menchi, Einaudi, 1971, pp. 1588–92, trans. Kaborycha.

References

Bedini, Silvio A. *The Pope's Elephant*, Carcanet, 1997.
Cummings, Anthony M. "Leo's Jesters," *Revue belge de Musicologie/Belgisch Tijdschrift voor Muziekwetenschap*, Vol. 63 (2009), pp. 31–65.
Francesco Guicciardini. *The History of Italy*, trans. and ed. Sydney Alexander, Princeton UP, 1984.
Kruse, Jeremy. "Hunting, Magnificence and the Court of Leo X," *Renaissance Studies*, Vol. 7, No. 3 (September 1993), pp. 243–57.
Mitchell, Bonner. *Rome in the High Renaissance: The Age of Leo X*, U Oklahoma P, 1973.
Phillips, Mark. *Francesco Guicciardini: The Historian's Craft*, U Toronto P, 1977.
Stinger, Charles L. "The Place of Clement VII and Clementine Rome in Renaissance History," and T.C. Price Zimmermann, "Guicciardini, Giovio, and the Character of Clement VII," in *The Pontificate of Clement VII: History, Politics, Culture*, ed. Kenneth Gouwens and Sheryl E. Reiss, Ashgate, 2005.

28 Art, both sacral and sensuous

Leonardo da Vinci, *On the sacred in painting*, 1540

Vittoria Colonna, *Sonnet on the Magdalene by Titian*, 1530s–40s

Council of Trent, *Session XXV: On sacred images*, 1563

Figure 3.2 Titian, *Penitent Mary Magdalene*, 1531, Pitti Palace, Florence. The artist painted numerous versions of this image of the Magdalene for a variety of patrons. It is believed that this painting was given by Duke Federico Gonzaga to Vittoria Colonna as a present.

DOI: 10.4324/9781003284284-31

One of the criticisms Protestants leveled at the Roman Catholic Church concerned what some of them viewed as inappropriate use of images depicting the Holy Family, saints, and biblical scenes. Citing the Old Testament passage in which God condemns idolatry—"Thou shalt not make unto thee any graven image, or any likeness of any thing that is in heaven above, or that is in the Earth beneath, or that is in the water under the Earth" (Exod. 20:4)—various Protestants engaged in iconoclasm, defacing or totally destroying holy images in churches.[1] Moreover, as Renaissance art became more naturalistic, representing human anatomy with greater realism, artists lavished attention on portrayal of the often scantily clad bodies of saints and martyrs, inspiring what critics considered prurient interest. To some, beauty itself was suspect in sacred art, as the physical appearance of a saint such as Mary Magdalene could distract worshippers from their devotions. Along with the Virgin Mary and St. Catherine of Alexandria, Mary Magdalene was one of the most popular female saints during the Middle Ages and Renaissance. According to legend, Mary Magdalene, renowned for her beauty, had been a prostitute before becoming a follower of Christ.[2] Her subsequent repentance and holy life made her a role model for laymen and laywomen who were guilty of the sins of greed or lust; the example of the Magdalene offered them hope of salvation. As Renaissance artists created increasingly voluptuous depictions of the saintly former prostitute—and it has been suggested that especially in Venetian art actual courtesans posed for these alluring paintings—the debate intensified. Although not originally convened to consider matters of aesthetics—the Council of Trent met over the course of eighteen years (1545–63) to settle issues of doctrine and to address institutional reform—eventually the question of the "legitimate use of images" arose during the final session. As a direct result of the decisions of the Council of Trent, the style of painting shifted afterward. So-called "Tridentine" art, with its principal aim of inspiring piety while rigidly adhering to Church doctrine, has certain recognizable features: the story from the Bible or life of a saint is depicted clearly and accurately; the artist refrains from adding distracting or extraneous details; at all times decorum and decency are observed, while aiming at achieving a powerful emotional impact on the viewer. Though these were the objectives, which many artists followed exactly, in reality these strictures were rarely enforced. Though one outcome of the Council of Trent was the creation of the Sacred Congregation of the Index in 1571 to further crack down on the publication of writings banned by the Catholic Church, no concerted effort was ever made to censor art. Moreover, while sacred paintings exhibited in religious locations—notably Michelangelo's *Last Judgment* and Veronese's *Feast in the House of Levi* (**#29**)—could be denounced for excessive nudity, eroticism, or lack of decorum, these same standards did not apply to private commissions, whether by laypeople or clergy; indeed, some of the most generous and enthusiastic Renaissance patrons of art were bishops, cardinals, and popes. Moreover, though the *Penitent Magdalene* by the Venetian artist

Titian (#38) might appear to have been created to excite the male gaze, it is probable that this was the exact painting that was presented as a gift to the devout noblewoman Vittoria Colonna (*c.*1490–1547) who, in one of her sacred poems, describes the inspiration she finds in the spiritual message of the painting. It is worthy of note that at the Council of Trent the sacred use of images was considered comparable to the worship of relics, an observation made a generation earlier by Leonardo da Vinci in his meditations on the sacrality of painting.

Leonardo da Vinci, *Treatise on Painting*, 1540[3]

On the sacred in painting

Do we not see pictures representing the divine beings constantly kept under coverlets of the greatest price? And whenever they are unveiled there is first great ecclesiastical solemnity with much hymn singing, and then at the moment of the unveiling the great multitude of people who have gathered there immediately throw themselves to the ground, worshipping and praying to the deity, who is represented in the picture, for the repairing of their lost health and for their eternal salvation, exactly as if this goddess were there as a living presence. This does not happen with any other science or other works of man, and if you claim that this is not due to the power of the painter but to the inherent power of the thing represented, it may be replied that in this case the minds of men would be satisfied were they to remain in their beds rather than going to wearisome and dangerous places on pilgrimages, as may be continually witnessed. But since such pilgrimages continue to take place, what causes their inessential travels? Certainly you will concede that it is the visual image. All the writings could not do this, by representing so potently the form and spirit of this deity. Accordingly it would seem that the deity loves this painting and loves those who love and revere it, and takes delight in being adored in this way rather than in any other form of imitation, and thus bestows grace and gifts of salvation in accordance with the faith of those who gather in that location.

Vittoria Colonna, *Sonnet on the Magdalene by Titian Sent to Her by the Duke of Mantua*, 1530s–40s

A fiery passionate woman, and far from the errant
masses in solitary residence
appears to me joyous, leaving behind
whatever is not pleasing to the true eternal beloved;
and desire arrested, arrested her steps,

atop a great mountain,
whence I mirror myself and back
in the beautiful example, and straighten and raise up my soul,
following in the blessed footsteps and the saintly deeds.
In such thought from the vile knot I free myself
praying to her with ardent and daring voice
to beseech the Lord a place for me next to her.

Decrees of the Council of Trent, *Session XXV*, 1563

On the invocation, veneration, and relics of saints, and on sacred images

The holy Synod enjoins on all bishops, and others who sustain the office and charge of teaching, that, agreeably to the usage of the Catholic and Apostolic Church, received from the primitive times of the Christian religion, and agreeably to the consent of the holy Fathers, and to the decrees of sacred Councils, they especially instruct the faithful diligently concerning the intercession and invocation of saints; the honor (paid) to relics; and the legitimate use of images: teaching them that the saints, who reign together with Christ, offer up their own prayers to God for men; that it is good and useful suppliantly to invoke them, and to have recourse to their prayers, aid, (and) help for obtaining benefits from God, through His Son, Jesus Christ our Lord, who is our alone Redeemer and Savior: but that they think impiously who deny that the saints, who enjoy eternal happiness in heaven, are to be invocated; or who assert either that they do not pray for men; or that the invocation of them to pray for each of us even in particular is idolatry; or that it is repugnant to the word of God; and is opposed to the honor of the one mediator of God and men, Christ Jesus; or that it is foolish to supplicate, vocally or mentally, those who reign in heaven. Also, that the holy bodies of holy martyrs, and of others now living with Christ—which bodies were the living members of Christ, and the temple of the Holy Ghost, and which are by Him to be raised unto eternal life, and to be glorified—are to be venerated by the faithful, through which (bodies) many benefits are bestowed by God on men; so that they who affirm that veneration and honor are not due to the relics of saints; or that these and other sacred monuments are uselessly honored by the faithful; and that the places dedicated to the memories of the saints are in vain visited with the view of obtaining their aid; are wholly to be condemned, as the Church has already long since condemned, and now also condemns them.

Moreover, that the images of Christ, of the Virgin Mother of God, and of the other saints, are to be had and retained particularly in temples, and that due honor and veneration are to be given them; not that any divinity, or virtue, is believed to be in them, on account of which they are to be worshipped; or that anything is to be asked of them; or that trust is to be reposed in images, as was of old done by the Gentiles who placed their hope in idols; but because the honor which is shown them is referred to the prototypes which those images represent; in such wise that by the images which we kiss, and before which we uncover the head, and prostrate ourselves, we adore Christ; and we venerate the saints, whose similitude they bear: as, by the decrees of Councils, and especially of the second Synod of Nicaea, has been defined against the opponents of images.

And the bishops shall carefully teach this—that by means of the histories of the mysteries of our Redemption, portrayed by paintings or other representations, the people is instructed, and confirmed in (the habit of) remembering, and continually revolving in mind the articles of faith; as also that great profit is derived from all sacred images, not only because the people are thereby admonished of the benefits and gifts bestowed upon them by Christ, but also because the miracles which God has performed by means of the saints, and their salutary examples are set before the eyes of the faithful: that so they may give God thanks for those things; may order their own lives and manners in imitation of the saints; and may be excited to adore and love God, and to cultivate piety. But if anyone shall teach, or entertain sentiments, contrary to these decrees; let him be anathema.

And if any abuses have crept in amongst these holy and salutary observances, the holy Synod ardently desires that they be utterly abolished; in such wise that no images, (suggestive) of false doctrine, and furnishing occasion of dangerous error to the uneducated, be set up. And if at times, when expedient for the unlettered people; it happen that the facts and narratives of sacred Scripture are portrayed and represented; the people shall be taught that not thereby is the Divinity represented, as though it could be seen by the eyes of the body, or be portrayed by colors or figures.

Moreover, in the invocation of saints, the veneration of relics, and the sacred use of images, every superstition shall be removed, all filthy lucre be abolished; finally, all lasciviousness be avoided; in such wise that figures shall not be painted or adorned with a beauty exciting to lust; nor the celebration of the saints, and the visitation of relics be by any perverted into revellings and drunkenness; as if festivals are celebrated to the honor of the saints by luxury and wantonness.

In fine, let so great care and diligence be used herein by bishops, as that there be nothing seen that is disorderly, or that is unbecomingly or confusedly arranged, nothing that is profane, nothing indecorous, seeing that holiness becometh the house of God.

And that these things may be the more faithfully observed, the holy Synod ordains, that no one be allowed to place, or cause to be placed, any unusual image, in any place, or church, howsoever exempted, except that image have been approved of by the bishop: also, that no new miracles are to be acknowledged, or new relics recognized, unless the said bishop has taken cognizance and approved thereof; who, as soon as he has obtained some certain information in regard to these matters, shall, after having taken the advice of theologians, and of other pious men, act therein as he shall judge to be consonant with truth and piety. But if any doubtful, or difficult abuse has to be extirpated; or, in fine, if any more grave question shall arise touching these matters, the bishop, before deciding the controversy, shall await the sentence of the metropolitan and of the bishops of the province, in a provincial Council; yet, so that nothing new, or that previously has not been usual in the Church, shall be resolved on, without having first consulted the most holy Roman Pontiff.

Notes

1 For a description of incidents of iconoclasm during the Sack of Rome see p. 26.

2 This tradition derives from a conflation of three biblical female figures: Mary of Magdala, Mary of Bethany, and the woman at the house of Simon the Pharisee. This last one "was a sinner" (Luke 7:36–50) who washed Christ's feet, anointed them with oil, and dried them with her hair, hence the many images of her long golden hair and the ointment jar. The episode in which Christ casts seven devils from her (Matt. 9–11 and Luke 8:1–3) further confirmed Mary Magdalene's reputation as a sinner, although sexual sin is not specified in any of the biblical accounts. The presence of Mary Magdalene at the Crucifixion and afterward at Christ's tomb is recorded in the Gospels, and significantly she is mentioned as the first witness of his Resurrection in the Garden of Gethsemane.

3 The *Treatise on Painting* was compiled from Leonardo's notes by his student Francesco Melzi around 1540. Though Leonardo had intended to write this book, he never completed it, and only about a quarter of the work exists in Leonardo's hand.

Sources

Leonardo da Vinci, *On the sacred in painting* in *Leonardo on Painting: An Anthology of Writings*, ed and trans. Martin Kemp, Yale UP, 1989, p. 20.

Vittoria Colonna, *Sonnet on the Magdalene by Titian,* in Rona Goffen, "Saint Mary Magdalen: Sanctity and Sexuality," *Titian's Women*, Yale UP, 1997, pp. 170–92, 179.

Council of Trent, *Session XXV: On sacred images* in *The Canons and Decrees of the Sacred and Oecumenical Council of Trent*, ed. and trans. J. Waterworth, Dolman, 1848, pp. 233–36, ed. Kaborycha.

References

Debby, Nirit Ben-Aryeh. "Vittoria Colonna and Titian's Pitti *Magdalen*," *Woman's Art Journal*, Vol. 24, No. 1 (2003), pp. 29–33.

Erhardt, Michelle A. and Amy M. Morris, eds. *Mary Magdalene, Iconographic Studies from the Middle Ages to the Baroque*, Brill, 2012.

Hall, Marcia B. *The Sacred Image in the Age of Art: Titian, Tintoretto, Barocci, El Greco, Caravaggio*, Yale UP, 2011.
Haskins, Susan. *Mary Magdalene. The Essential History*, Pimlico, 2005.
O'Malley, John. "Trent, Sacred Images, and Catholics' Senses of the Sensuous," in *The Sensuous in the Counter-Reformation Church*, ed. Marcia B. Hall and Tracy E. Cooper, Cambridge UP, 2013.

29 An artist fleshes out religious doctrine

Pietro Aretino, *Letter to Michelangelo*, 1545

Transcript of Paolo Veronese's trial before the Holy Tribunal, 1573

Figure 3.3 Michelangelo Buonarroti, *The Last Judgment*, 1541, detail, Sistine Chapel, Vatican.

DOI: 10.4324/9781003284284-32

When Michelangelo Buonarroti (1475–1564) unveiled his majestic fresco of *The Last Judgment* on the wall above the altar of the Sistine Chapel on October 31, 1541, the effect was stunning. Before viewers' eyes, a vast cosmic drama unfolded with hundreds of figures—the damned sinking downward, dragged and shoved by demons toward the underworld, and the blessed rising, swirling upward to heaven—with Christ and his mother at the center, surrounded by a throng of saints. It was not only the enormous scope of the artist's vision that astonished them, but also the way he had chosen to represent the scene. For Michelangelo does not depict the judgment itself, but the moment when, after rising from the dead, souls are reunited with their bodies and experience the "resurrection of the flesh." The Apostles' Creed, regularly recited by all the faithful, includes the phrase "I believe in the Holy Spirit, the holy Catholic Church, the communion of saints, the forgiveness of sins, the resurrection of the body" [*carnis resurrectionem*, in Latin, literally means resurrection of the flesh]. Indeed, the central doctrine of Christianity is that God became flesh in order to save mankind. So, fittingly, to his mind, Michelangelo covered the immense wall with nude bodies, everywhere displaying flesh. A key figure in the painting who appears just beneath Christ is St. Bartholomew, one of the twelve apostles. According to legend, Bartholomew was martyred by being flayed alive; thus, he is usually represented holding the knife and/or his skinned flesh. Michelangelo portrays the saint holding the knife in one hand and, in the other, an empty sack of flesh dangled over the side of the cloud he straddles. The face on the skin is usually identified as a self-portrait of the artist expressing despair at the possibility of his own salvation, though another interpretation is that Michelangelo is comparing himself with the mythological satyr Marsyas who challenged the pagan god Apollo to an art contest and was punished by being skinned alive.

It has also been suggested that St. Bartholomew bears the features of Pietro Aretino (1492–1596) who had "flayed" Michelangelo with his criticism of his work. Aretino was a celebrated writer who earned the nickname "the scourge of princes" for his habit of blackmailing powerful people. If he wrote in praise of a prominent individual and they failed to reward him, Aretino would publish a poison pen letter damaging their reputation. He first wrote a flattering letter to Michelangelo in 1537 hoping to begin corresponding with the artist and perhaps receive some artwork in return. Not satisfied with the painter's polite, but curt responses to his letters, in November 1545, Aretino wrote a scathing letter from Venice "To the great Michelangelo Buonarroti in Rome." Aretino subsequently edited and published the letter in 1550, and it circulated widely. By that point, many were scandalized by the pervasive nudity in the *Last Judgment*, and especially with the decree of the Council of Trent banning inappropriate images, and it was decided to paint over the offending anatomical details. Thus, the cloth that covers Bartholomew's genitals was added in 1565 by Michelangelo's student Daniele da Volterra (Daniele Ricciarelli, 1509–1566). He and the other painters who participated in the censorship of many of the naked figures were given the nickname "*braghettoni*" meaning "breeches painters." Less than a decade later in 1573, Paolo Veronese (#58) was brought before the Venetian Inquisition and accused of including inappropriate characters in his painting of the *Last Supper*. In his defense, the artist invoked the celebrated case of Michelangelo's *Last Judgment*. Fortunately, Veronese's work was not tampered with; a compromise was reached, in which the painter agreed to change the title of the painting. It is known today as *Feast in the House of Levi* (1573, Accademia, Venice).

Pietro Aretino, *Letter to Michelangelo Buonarroti*, 1545

Sir,

When I inspected the complete sketch of the whole of your *Last Judgment*, I arrived at recognizing the eminent graciousness of Raphael in its agreeable beauty of invention. Meanwhile, as a baptized Christian, I blush before the license, so forbidden to man's intellect, which you have used in expressing ideas connected with the highest aims and final ends to which our faith aspires. So, then, that Michelangelo stupendous in his fame, that Michelangelo renowned for prudence, that Michelangelo whom all admire, has chosen to display to the whole world an impiety of irreligion only equaled by the perfection of his painting! Is it possible that you, who, since you are divine, do not condescend to consort with human beings, have done this in the greatest temple built to God, upon the highest altar raised to Christ, in the most sacred chapel upon Earth, where the mighty hinges of the Church, the venerable priests of our religion, the Vicar of Christ, with solemn ceremonies and holy prayers, confess, contemplate, and adore his body, his blood, and his flesh?

If it were not infamous to introduce the comparison, I would plume myself upon my virtue when I wrote *La Nanna*.[1] I would demonstrate the superiority of my reserve to your indiscretion, seeing that I, while handling themes lascivious and immodest, use language comely and decorous, speak in terms beyond reproach and inoffensive to chaste ears. You, on the contrary, presenting so awful[2] a subject, exhibit saints and angels, these without earthly decency, and those without celestial honors.

The pagans, when they modelled a Diana, gave her clothes; when they made a naked Venus, hid the parts which are not shown with the hand of modesty. And here there comes a Christian, who, because he rates art higher than the faith, deems it a royal spectacle to portray martyrs and virgins in improper attitudes, to show men dragged down by their shame, before which things houses of ill-fame would shut the eyes in order not to see them. Your art would be at home in some voluptuous bagnio [brothel], certainly not in the highest chapel of the world. Less criminal were it if you were an infidel, than, being a believer, thus to sap the faith of others. Up to the present time the splendor of such audacious marvels has not gone unpunished; for their very superexcellence is the death of your good name. Restore them to repute by turning the indecent parts of the damned to flames, and those of the blessed to sunbeams; or imitate the modesty of Florence, who hides your David's shame beneath some gilded leaves.[3] And yet that statue is exposed upon a public square, not in a consecrated chapel.

As I wish that God may pardon you, I do not write this out of any resentment for the things I begged of you.[4] In truth, if you had sent me what you promised, you would only have been doing what you ought to have desired most eagerly to do in your own interest; for this act of courtesy would silence the envious tongues which say that only certain Gerards and Thomases[5] dispose of them.

Well, if the treasure bequeathed you by Pope Julius, in order that you might deposit his ashes in an urn of your own carving, was not enough to make you keep your plighted word, what can I expect from you? It is not your ingratitude, your avarice, great painter, but the grace and merit of the Supreme Shepherd, which decide his fame. God wills that Julius should live renowned for ever in a simple tomb, inurned in his own merits, and not in some proud monument dependent on your genius. Meantime, your failure to discharge your obligations is reckoned to you as an act of thieving.

Our souls need the tranquil emotions of piety more than the lively impressions of plastic art. May God, then, inspire his Holiness Paul with the same thoughts as he instilled into Gregory of blessed memory, who rather chose to despoil Rome of the proud statues of the Pagan deities than to let their magnificence deprive the humbler images of the saints of the devotion of the people.

Lastly, when you set about composing your picture of the universe and hell and heaven, if you had steeped your heart with those suggestions of glory, of honor, and of terror proper to the theme which I sketched out and offered to you in the letter I wrote you and the whole world reads, I venture to assert that not only would nature and all kind influences cease to regret the illustrious talents they endowed you with, and which to-day render you, by virtue of your art, an image of the marvelous: but Providence, who sees all things, would herself continue to watch over such a masterpiece, so long as order lasts in her government of the hemispheres.

Your Servant, The Aretine

PS Now that I have blown off some of the rage I feel against you for the cruelty you used to my devotion, and have taught you to see that, while you may be divine, I am not made of water, I bid you tear up this letter, for I have done the like, and do not forget that I am one to whose epistles kings and emperors reply.

Transcript of Paolo Veronese's trial before the Holy Tribunal, 1573

Venice, July 18, 1573. The minutes of the session of the Inquisition Tribunal of Saturday, the 18th of July, 1573. Today, Saturday, the 18th of the month of July, 1573, having been asked by the Holy Office to appear before the Holy Tribunal, Paolo Caliari of Verona,[6] domiciled in the Parish Saint Samuel, being questioned about his name and surname, answered as above.

Questioned about his profession:
Answer: I paint and compose figures

Question: Do you know the reason why you have been summoned?
A: No, sir.

Q: Can you imagine it?
A: I can well imagine.

Q: Say what you think the reason is.
A: According to what the Reverend Father, the Prior of the Convent of SS. Giovanni e Paolo, whose name I do not know, told me, he had been here and Your Lordships had ordered him to have painted [in the picture] a Magdalen in place of a dog. I answered him by saying I would gladly do everything necessary for my honor and for that of my painting, but that I did not understand how a figure of Magdalen would be suitable there for many reasons which I will give at any time, provided I am given an opportunity.

Q: What picture is this of which you have spoken?
A: This is a picture of the Last Supper that Jesus Christ took with His Apostles in the house of Simon.

Q: Where is this picture?
A: In the Refectory of the Convent of SS. Giovanni e Paolo.[7]

[. . .]

Q: At this Supper of Our Lord have you painted other figures?
A: Yes, milords.

Q: Tell us how many people and describe the gestures of each.
A: There is the owner of the inn, Simon; besides this figure I have made a steward, who, I imagined, had come there for his own pleasure to see how the things were going at the table. There are many figures there which I cannot recall, as I painted the picture some time ago.

[. . .]

Q: In this Supper which you made for SS. Giovanni e Paolo, what is the significance of the man whose nose is bleeding?
A: I intended to represent a servant whose nose was bleeding because of some accident.

Q: What is the significance of those armed men dressed as Germans, each with a halberd in his hand?
A: This requires that I say twenty words!

Q: Say them.
A: We painters take the same license the poets and the jesters take and I have represented these two halberdiers, one drinking and the other eating nearby on the stairs. They are placed here so that they might be of service because it seemed to me fitting, according to what I have been told, that the master of the house, who was great and rich, should have such servants.

Q: And that man dressed as a buffoon with a parrot on his wrist, for what purpose did you paint him on that canvas?
A: For ornament, as is customary.

[. . .]

Q: Does it seem fitting at the Last Supper of the Lord to paint buffoons, drunkards, Germans, dwarfs and similar vulgarities?
A: No, milords.

Q: Do you not know that in Germany and in other places infected with heresy it is customary with various pictures full of scurrilousness and similar inventions to mock, vituperate, and scorn the things of the Holy Catholic Church in order to teach bad doctrines to foolish and ignorant people?
A: Yes, that is wrong; but I return to what I have said, that I am obliged to do as my superiors have done.

Q: What have your superiors done? Have they perhaps done similar things?
A: Michelangelo in Rome in the Pontifical Chapel painted Our Lord, Jesus Christ, His Mother, St. John, St. Peter, and the Heavenly Host. These are represented in the nude—even the Virgin Mary—and in different poses with little reverence.

Q: Do you not know that in painting the Last Judgment in which no garments or similar things are presumed, it was not necessary to paint garments, and that in those figures there is nothing that is not spiritual? There are neither buffoons, dogs, weapons, or similar buffoonery. And does it seem because of this or some other example, that you did right to have painted this picture in the way you did and do you want to maintain it is good and decent?
A: Illustrious Lords, I do not want to defend it, but I thought I was doing right. I did not consider so many things and I did not intend to confuse anyone, the more so as those figures of buffoons are outside of the place where Our Lord is represented.

After these things had been said, the judges announced that the above named Paolo would be obliged to improve and change his painting within a period of three months from the day of this admonition and that according to the opinion and decision of the Holy Tribunal all the corrections should be made at the expense of the painter and that if he did not correct the picture he would be liable to the penalties imposed by the Holy Tribunal.

Notes

1 Aretino is making a reference to his book about the courtesan Nanna who gives advice about the trade to her daughter.
2 The word "awful" is meant in the sense of inspiring awe or reverence.
3 A metal belt with a garland of gilt leaves was hung around Michelangelo's *David* soon after the statue was placed in front of the Palazzo Vecchio in 1504; the garland was removed around 1550. John Paoletti, *Michelangelo's David: Florentine History and Civic Identity*, Cambridge UP, 2015, 52.
4 Aretino had written a letter to Michelangelo on January 20, 1538, asking for some of the artist's drawings.
5 This is an innuendo about some of Michelangelo's close male friendships. Giorgio Vasari relates that Michelangelo gave various drawings to Gherardo Perini and Tommaso de' Cavalieri (**#50**).
6 The painter Paolo Cagliari, known as Veronese (**#58**).
7 This painting is today in the Accademia in Venice with the title *The Feast in the House of Levi.*

Sources

Pietro Aretino, *Letter to Michelangelo* in John Addington Symonds. *The Life of Michelangelo Buonarroti*, 1892, Project Gutenberg, pp. 519–23, ed. Kaborycha.

Transcript of Paolo Veronese's Trial before the Holy Tribunal in Elizabeth Gilmore Holt, *A Documentary History of Art*, Vol. II, Doubleday, 1957, pp. 66–70.

References

Barnes, Bernadine. *Michelangelo's Last Judgment: The Renaissance Response*, UC Press, 1997.

Barnes, Bernadine. "Skin, Bones, and Dust: Self-Portraits in Michelangelo's *Last Judgment*," *The Sixteenth Century Journal*, Vol. 35, No. 4 (Winter 2004), pp. 969–86.

Cocke, Richard. *Paolo Veronese: Piety and Display in an Age of Religious Reform*, Ashgate, 2001

Hall, Marcia. "Michelangelo's *Last Judgment* and the Failure of the Sacred Image at Midcentury," in *The Sacred Image in the Age of Art: Titian, Tintoretto, Barocci, El Greco, Caravaggio*, Yale UP, 2011.

Hartt, Frederick. "Michelangelo in Heaven," *Artibus et Historiae*, Vol. 13, No. 26 (1992), pp. 191–209.

O'Malley, John W. "The Council of Trent (1545–63) and Michelangelo's *Last Judgment* (1541)," *Proceedings of the American Philosophical Society*, Vol. 156, No. 4 (December 2012), pp. 388–97.

30 Religious diversity promoted in Tuscany

Ferdinando I de' Medici, *The Livornine Charter*, 1591, 1593

During the period when the Holy Office of the Inquisition was at the height of its powers, an official decree in the Grand Duchy of Tuscany granted extraordinary liberties to Jews, Muslims, Protestants, and peoples of other faiths. The so-called *Livornine Charter* (*la Costituzione Livornina*) was first issued on July 30, 1591, and later reissued with slight changes on June 10, 1593. That same year on February 25, 1593, Pope Clement VIII's papal bull *Caeca et obdurata* reinforced and intensified repressive measures against the Jewish community that had been introduced by preceding popes. Despite such official policy, during the sixteenth century many states in Italy including Ferrara, Savoy, and Venice were competing to attract Jewish merchants who were involved in lucrative trade with the Levant. In Tuscany, Grand Duke Ferdinando I de' Medici (1549–1609) issued this forty-four-clause charter with the objective of enticing foreign merchants, especially Jews, to move to Livorno and Pisa. Driven by religious persecution from the Iberian Peninsula—in the wake of the expulsions from Spain (1483, 1492), the forced conversions in Portugal (1497), and the 1506 Lisbon massacre—Jews flocked to Italy.[1]

In Italy, policies toward the Jewish people were more lenient, despite requiring them to live enclosed within crowded, walled areas known as ghettos, the first of which was established in 1516 in Venice. Then, with the papal bull *Cum nimis absurdum* in 1555, Pope Paul IV officially created the ghetto in Rome, and his successor extended the policy throughout Italy. Under this decree, Jews were forced to live isolated from the rest of the city unless they converted to Christianity. Once they converted, however, returning to Judaism was forbidden; it was condemned by the Holy Office as the crime of apostasy and punished severely. As the majority of Jews fleeing Portugal had been forced to become Christian converts (*conversos*) on pain of death, it was an open secret that many of those who came to Italy were apostates. In flagrant disregard for Church policy, Tuscany's 1591 *Livornine Charter* protected Jews, including those from Spain and Portugal, regardless of whether they had previously lived as Christians elsewhere. In 1589, Venice had issued a similar, but briefer charter granting privileges to Jews, but it never went as

DOI: 10.4324/9781003284284-33

far as condoning apostasy. And although a ghetto had been created in 1570 in Florence, Tuscany's capital, Ferdinando I's *Livornine Charter*, among other freedoms, granted Jews the right to live anywhere in the cities of Livorno and Pisa, and to move about freely. Those cities flourished as word of the exceptionally tolerant laws in Tuscany spread. Menasseh Ben Israel (1604–1657), the Portuguese-born rabbi, printer, and man of letters published a pamphlet in 1655 urging Oliver Cromwell to permit Jews—who had been officially prohibited from entering England since their expulsion in 1290—to be readmitted to the country. He proposed as model the *Livornine Charter*: "In the Government of the great Duke of Tuscany, they are by that Prince most graciously & bountifully dealt with, having power from him graunted, to have their Judicatory by themselves, and to judge in all matters, both Civill and Criminall; besides many other Priviledges, whereof I myself have the Copies in hand."[2]

Ferdinando I de' Medici, *The Livornine Charter*, 1591, 1593

DON FERDINANDO

Medici, by the Grace of God, Third Grand Duke of Tuscany, Florence and Siena, Lord of Portoferraio on the Island of Elba, Castiglione della Pescaia, and the Island of Giglio, Grand Master of the Holy Order of St. Stephen &c. to all of you merchants of any nation—Levantines, Ponentines, Spanish, Portuguese, Greeks, Germans, & Italians, Jews, Turks, Moors, Armenians, Persians, & others gives salutations.

With this Our charter, moved by worthy respect and deepest desire for the public good, We intend to enhance the willingness of foreigners to frequent, with their business and merchandise Our beloved City of Pisa and Port and commercial center of Livorno, granting permission to reside here, with or without your families, in the hope that this will result in utility to all of Italy, to Our subjects, and especially to the poor. Moreover, driven by the aforesaid reasons & others, We grant you the following rights, privileges, immunities and exemptions:

I

First, We grant all merchants, Jews, Turks, Moors & other royal merchants [i.e. those working on behalf of foreign sovereigns] free and broad safe-conduct and free passage and license to come and go, to trade, pass through, residing either alone or with your families, to leave, return, and do business in our City and Port of Livorno and also to remain to do business on behalf of others, in all our Ducal dominion without harm, either to goods or self, for the next twenty-five years,[3] with an advance notice of five-years' prior, so that within that term you can sell, give up, or otherwise assign your real estate to whomever you designate. . . .

II

You are guaranteed that during the aforementioned period while you reside in said city, no tribunal or prince will bother or inconvenience you, your families, servants, or agents for any denunciation, accusation, or lawsuit brought against you and your families outside of our State in the past, no matter how great the crime.

III

We furthermore desire that for the said period of time, no inquisition, investigation, denunciation, or accusation be made against you or your families, even if you lived in the past outside of our dominion in custom or in name as Christians[4] you can come to live in our Cities of Pisa and Livorno, doing business freely in our Dominion, practicing all your ceremonies, rituals, and customs according to Jewish Law. . . .

IV

We further render you free, exempt, and safe in your persons, goods, and merchandise from any outstanding civil or criminal liabilities incurred by you or your families outside of Our States and Dominion, for which debts or misdeeds you will be under the authority of the Massari[5] of your synagogue and no outside Judge, Forum, Tribunal, or Magistracy can take action, pass sentence, or ruling on aforesaid debts as they hold Our favor dear and fear Our wrath and should this be pronounced, they will be null and void by law.

V

We free you of any and all taxation that either We, or our successors might impose during the said time period, for which you are never to be troubled or inconvenienced, except for the payment of the usual customs duties on your merchandise; We desire that you not be subject to payments, levies, laws and statutes, which the Jews residing in Florence or Siena are subject to, or will be subject to in the future.

VI

We grant you the right to traffic and conduct business in all the cities, lands, fairs, markets, towns, and territories of our state and to navigate in the east and west, to the Barbary Coast & Alexandria & elsewhere, under your own name, or that of Christians or others, as you wish; and that you, your merchandise, your associates, customers, and agents, will be safe in Livorno; and that we guarantee you immunity from our galleys and we request all Christian Princes, their ministers, Captains of galleys and other vessels that they do the same, in order that you may arrive safely to our Port of Livorno and Pisa, paying only the usual customs duties that our own Florentine and Pisan merchants customarily pay, as long as you maintain a principal residence in either aforesaid city of Pisa or within the territory of Livorno.

VII

We further grant that your merchandise be assured, and once you have paid the first instalment, you will have the option of freely keeping it in our customs house one additional year without incurring extra payments or penalties.

[. . .]

X

We will appoint a Judge, a lay doctor of jurisprudence, neither Florentine nor Pisan, to whom we will give the authority to resolve and summarily decide all your differences and cases, whether civil or criminal, once the truth of the matter has been learned, admitting the testimony of Jewish people under oath according to Jewish custom, justice will be carried out and there will be no appealing his sentences, except by Our special favor.

[. . .]

XVII

We grant you the right and permission to possess books of any kind, printed or in manuscript form, in Hebrew or in another language, as long as they are reviewed by the Inquisitor or others delegated to that task.

XVIII

We desire that all your Jewish medical doctors, whether physicians or surgeons, without any impediment or prejudice be permitted to treat and cure not only you, but any Christian or other person whosoever.

XIX

We desire that you may all be permitted to study & acquire university degrees.

XX

We grant that you may have in said City of Pisa and territory of Livorno, a place for a Synagogue in which you can practice all your Jewish ceremonies, rules, & rituals & observing all these rites, both inside outside of it. We do not want anyone to dare to commit insult, outrage, or violence there under pain of our displeasure, just as none of you shall dare, under any pretext or in any manner whatsoever, to try to persuade any Christian to follow your rites, for which you shall be severely castigated and punished in conformity with our laws.

[. . .]

XXIV

We furthermore desire that your Sabbath days & other Jewish festivals, in addition to those celebrated in the city of Florence, shall be observed and celebrated as non-working days and legal holidays. Nor may anyone stir discord or contention, nor make accusations against you, or others; from this point forward, We admit and declare these non-working days.

XXV

That your Jewish Massari in your Synagogues shall have authority to decide, to make rulings, and to impose punishments as they please, according to your Jewish custom and rites, on all differences that arise between one Jew and another, and they may make their usual rulings & other censures in their own way, desiring that the Jurisdiction & other authorities of your said Judge be limited and that the Massari shall have the de facto power to send into exile all those Jews who they consider to be scandalous.

XXVI

It is prohibited for any Christian to dare to take away or reclaim any member of your family, male or female, in order to force them to become Christian, unless they have passed thirteen years of age. And those who have attained their majority that are attending the usual school for catechumens, can be reminded [of their Jewish faith] and spoken to by their Fathers, Mothers, or other Relations in their quarantine [trial period] before Baptism. We desire that any Jewish man or woman who becomes Christian, if a son or daughter in a family, the father and mother are not held nor obliged to give them any legitimate possessions or inheritance during their lifetime, and that such Baptized persons cannot be witnesses in Jewish legal cases.

XXVII

We grant that your slaves cannot be freed.

XXVIII

We desire that all the butchers' shops prepare every kind of meat that you need, and in a timely fashion, without any alteration of prices that they charge our Christians, under penalty of a ten scudi fine for each offense, above other penalties imposed at the discretion of your aforesaid Judge. And you can, if you wish, choose one or more Jewish butchers to prepare the meat that you need, and they can go out freely to purchase any type of livestock, paying the usual customs duties at the gate.

XXIX

We grant all the Privileges that our Florentine Merchants and Citizens and Pisan Christians enjoy, namely, to exercise any kind of Profession and business, and that none of you or members of your families are obliged to wear any sign[6] distinguishing you from said Christians, and you can also buy real estate.

[. . .]

XXXVII

We grant that you may buy a plot of land in Pisa & in Livorno for the purpose of burying your dead, and that you will not be bothered by anyone who holds our favor dear.

[. . .]

XL

We desire that you are not burdened or charged with lodging soldiers, nor are you obliged to provide things of any kind from your homes or stables to them or any other officials.

XLII

We grant that you may have Christian servants and wet nurses to nourish your children, keeping them as the need arises, to live freely in your homes, in the same manner as is practiced in Ancona, Rome, and Bologna.

Notes

1 At the time of the 1492 edict of expulsion, the Jewish community in Spain was the largest, most flourishing Jewish community in Europe, with a population of around 200,000 Jews and 300,000 *conversos* (Jewish converts to Christianity).
2 Wolf 87.
3 Clause #36 states that this charter is subject to automatic renewal for another twenty-five years if five-years' notice of cancellation is not given.

4 This was a very important clause guaranteeing that there would not be prosecutions for apostasy, which was a criminal offense.
5 The executive board of leaders of the Jewish community.
6 Jews elsewhere were generally required to wear an identifying mark, often a yellow patch or star of David attached to the front of their garment.

Source

Livornine Charter in Renzo Toaff. *La nazione ebrea a Livorno e a Pisa (1591–1700)*, Olschki, 1990, pp. 419–35, trans. Kaborycha.

References

Cooperman, Bernard Dov. "Trade and Settlement: The Establishment and Early Development of the Jewish Communities in Leghorn and Pisa (1591–1626)," (PhD Dissertation, Harvard University, 1976) I thank Stefano Villani for calling my attention to this source.

Frattarelli Fischer, Lucia and Stefano Villani. "'People of Every Mixture'. Immigration, Tolerance and Religious Conflicts in Early Modern Livorno," in *Immigration and Emigration in Historical Perspective*, ed. Ann Katherine Isaacs, PLUS-Pisa UP, 2007, pp. 93–107.

Ravid, Benjamin. "A Tale of Three Cities and Their *Raison d'Etat*: Ancona, Venice, Livorno, and the Competition for Jewish Merchants in the Sixteenth Century," in *Jews, Christians, and Muslims in the Mediterranean World After 1492*, ed. Alisa Meyuhas Ginio, Frank Cass, 1992.

Trivellato, Francesca. *The Familiarity of Strangers: The Sephardic Diaspora, Livorno, and Cross-Cultural Trade in the Early Modern Period*, Yale UP, 2009.

Wolf, Lucien. *Menasseh Ben Israel's Mission to Oliver Cromwell: Being a Reprint of the Pamphlets Published by Menasseh Ben Israel to Promote the Re-admission of the Jews to England, 1649–1656*, Macmillan, 1901.

Part IV

The arts in social context

Figure 4.1 Nanni di Banco, *Four Crowned Saints*, *c.*1416, Orsanmichele, Florence. This sculpture is a replica; the original is inside the building, while the framed niche on the outside and the relief of the stone carvers in their workshop below it is original. In the predella from left to right: a mason building a wall with blocks of stone; a carpenter carving a spiral column; a stonecutter taking measurements of a capital; and a sculptor with a chisel putting the finishing touches to the statue of a child.

31 Painting as profession, craft, and art

Cennino Cennini, *The Craftsman's Handbook*, *c.*1398

The artistic works of Cennino Cennini (1370–1427) are little known today, but his treatise on art is famous: it is the most accurate and detailed contemporary source on painting and workshop methods from this period of the Renaissance. While there are later examples of handbooks that deal with various aspects of art, such as the *Treatise on Architecture* by Filarete (Antonio Averlino, *c.*1400–*c.*1469), the *Treatise on Perspective* by Piero della Francesca (*c.*1412–1492), and Leonardo da Vinci's *Treatise on Painting*,[1] there is nothing comparable to Cennini's work from the early Quattrocento. Furthermore, when compared with two later Florentine treatises in particular—Alberti's 1435 *On Painting* (**#12**) and Ghiberti's *Commentaries*, written in the 1450s (**#32**)—an entirely different attitude toward the profession is evident in Cennini's *Handbook*. While he clearly expresses pride in his craft and recognizes that painting is both a mechanical as well as intellectual activity, the author does not make exalted claims for the painter's intellectual capacity or attempt to raise his social standing through display of literary pretensions involving comparisons with classical antiquity.

The author explains that the hands-on techniques which he describes were passed down from one generation to the next—Cennini had studied under Agnolo Gaddi, son of Taddeo Gaddi, who learned from Giotto. He shares practical painting advice, "tricks of the trade," writing as one craftsman to another. In Italian, the book is called *Il Libro dell'arte*, usually translated into English as *The Craftsman's Handbook*. It might seem that a better and more literal translation would be "the Book of Art," since the Italian word *arte* translates into English as "art" and the subject matter of this work is, after all, art. However, the term *arte* is complex. The word, especially as it was used during the Renaissance, also means "craft," "skill," or "profession." For instance, a professional guild in Florence during Cennini's day such as the Bakers' Guild would have been known as the *Arte dei Fornai*; the Cobblers' Guild, the *Arte dei Calzolai*. Thus, as one would expect in a work titled *The Craftsman's Handbook*, the author sets forth practical advice for practicing the trade: "The content and tenor of these instructions reflect a solid,

DOI: 10.4324/9781003284284-35

meticulously careful artistic practice, still thoroughly couched in artisan tradition. . . . All these procedures are expounded by Cennini as knowledge to be learned gradually in a long series of greater or smaller chapters, almost as recipes."[2] Indeed, Cennini's work contains many references to cooking: "In his instructions for working over the mass of lapis lazuli, pine rosin, gum mastic, wax, and lye 'just in the same way' as bread dough to make ultramarine blue or in tempering *gesso sottile* by mixing it 'as if you were making batter for pancakes.'"[3] Cennini's down-to-earth description of the manual labor that the painter's craft involved—tasks such as mixing and applying plaster, making glue from goat carcasses, or brushes from strands of squirrel fur—demonstrates a side to Renaissance art not visible in the immaculate images within glided frames that hang in museums. To become a master entailed decades of training in which both stamina and discipline were required, and only once he had acquired the necessary expertise and manual skill could the artist create a masterpiece—if, that is, he also happened to be a genius.

Cennino Cennini, *The Craftsman's Handbook*, c. 1398

Here begins the Craftsman's Handbook, made and composed by Cennino of Colle, in the reverence of God, and of The Virgin Mary, and of Saint Eustace, and of Saint Francis, and of Saint John Baptist, and of Saint Anthony of Padua, and, in general, of all the Saints of God; and in the reverence of Giotto, of Taddeo and of Agnolo, Cennino's master; and for the use and good and profit of anyone who wants to enter this profession.

The first chapter of the first section of this book

In the beginning, when Almighty God created heaven and Earth, above all animals and foods he created man and woman in his own image, endowing them with every virtue. Then, because of the misfortune which fell upon Adam, through envy, from Lucifer, who by his malice and cunning beguiled him—or rather, Eve, and then Eve, Adam—into sin against the Lord's command: because of this, therefore, God became angry with Adam, and had him driven, him and his companion, forth out of Paradise, saying to them: "Inasmuch as you have disobeyed the command which God gave you, by your struggles and exertions you shall carry on your lives." And so Adam, recognizing the error which he had committed, after being so royally endowed by God as the source, beginning, and father of us all, realized theoretically that some means of living by labor had to be found. And so he started with the spade, and Eve, with spinning. Man afterward pursued many useful occupations, differing from each other; and some were, and are, more theoretical than others; they could not all be alike, since theory is the most worthy. Close to that, man pursued some related to the one which calls for a basis of that, coupled with skill of hand: and this is an occupation known as painting, which calls for imagination, and skill of hand, in order to discover things not seen, hiding themselves under the shadow of natural objects, and to fix them[4] with the hand, presenting to plain sight what does not actually exist. And it justly deserves to be enthroned next to theory, and to be crowned with poetry. The justice lies in this: that the poet, with his theory, though he have but one, it makes him worthy, is free to compose and bind together, or not, as he pleases, according to his inclination. In the same way, the painter is given freedom to compose a figure, standing, seated, half-man, half-horse, as he pleases, according to his imagination. So then, either as a labor of love for all those who feel within them a desire to understand; or as a means of embellishing these fundamental theories with some jewel, that they may be set forth royally, without reserve; offering to these theories whatever little understanding God has granted me, as an unimportant practicing member of the profession of painting: I, Cennino, the son of Andrea Cennini of Colle di Val d'Elsa—(I was trained in this profession for twelve years by my master, Agnolo di Taddeo of Florence; he learned this profession from Taddeo, his father; and his father was christened under Giotto, and was his follower for four-and-twenty years; and that Giotto changed the profession of painting from Greek back into Latin, and brought it up to date; and he had more finished craftsmanship than anyone has had since)—to minister to all those who wish to enter the profession, I will make note of what was taught me by the aforesaid Agnolo, my master, and of what I have tried out with my own hand; first invoking [the aid of] High Almighty God, the Father, Son, and Holy Ghost; then [of] that most delightful advocate of all sinners, Virgin Mary; and of Saint Luke, the Evangelist, the first Christian painter; and of my advocate, Saint Eustace; and, in general, of all the Saints of Paradise, A M E N.

Chapter II: How some enter the profession through loftiness of spirit, and some, for profit.

It is not without the impulse of a lofty spirit that some are moved to enter this profession, attractive to them through natural enthusiasm. Their intellect will take delight in drawing, provided their nature attracts them to it of themselves, without any master's guidance, out of loftiness of spirit. And then, through this delight, they come to want to find a master; and they bind themselves to him with respect for authority, undergoing an apprenticeship in order to achieve perfection in all this. There are those who pursue it, because of poverty and domestic need, for profit and enthusiasm for the profession too; but above all these are to be extolled the ones who enter the profession through a sense of enthusiasm and exaltation.

Chapter III: Fundamental provisions for anyone who enters this profession.

You, therefore, who with lofty spirit are fired with this ambition, and are about to enter the profession, begin by decking yourselves with this attire:

Enthusiasm, Reverence, Obedience, and Constancy. And begin to submit yourself to the direction of a master for instruction as early as you can; and do not leave the master until you have to.

[. . .]

Chapter XXIX: How you should regulate your life in the interests of decorum and the condition of your hand; and in what company; and what method you should first adopt for copying a figure from high up.

Your life should always be arranged just as if you were studying theology, or philosophy, or other theories, that is to say, eating and drinking moderately, at least twice a day, electing digestible and wholesome dishes, and light wines; saving and sparing your hand, preserving it from such strains as heaving stones, crowbar, and many other things which are bad for your hand, from giving them a chance to weary it. There is another cause which, if you indulge it, can make your hand so unsteady that it will waver more, and flutter far more, than leaves do in the wind, and this is indulging too much in the company of woman. Let us get back to our subject. Have a sort of pouch made of pasteboard, or just thin wood, made large enough in every dimension for you to put in a royal folio, that is, a half; and this is good for you to keep your drawings in, and likewise to hold the paper on for drawing. Then always go out alone, or in such company as will be inclined to do as you do, and not apt to disturb you. And the more understanding this company displays, the better it is for you. When you are in churches or chapels, and beginning to draw, consider, in the first place, from what section you think you wish to copy a scene or figure; and notice where its darks and half tones and high lights come; and this means that you have to apply your shadow with washes of ink; to leave the natural ground in the half tones; and to apply the high lights with white lead.

[. . .]

Chapter LXVII: The method and system for working on a wall, that is, in fresco.

In the name of the Most Holy Trinity I wish to start you on painting. Begin, in the first place, with working on a wall; and for that I will teach you, step by step, the method which you should follow.

When you want to work on a wall, which is the most agreeable and impressive kind of work, first of all get some lime and some sand, each of them well sifted. And if the lime is very fat and fresh it calls for two parts sand, the third part lime. And wet them up well with water; and wet up enough to last you for two or three weeks. And let it stand for a day or so, until the heat goes out of it: for when it is so hot, the plaster which you put on cracks afterward. When you are ready to plaster, first sweep the wall well, and wet it down thoroughly, for you cannot get it too wet. And take your lime mortar, well worked over, a trowelful at a time; and plaster once or twice, to begin with, to get the plaster flat on the wall. Then, when you want to work, remember first to make this plaster quite uneven and fairly rough. Then when the plaster is dry, take the charcoal, and draw and compose according to the scene or figures which you have to do; and take all your measurements carefully, snapping lines first, getting the centers of the spaces. Then snap some, and take the levels from them. And this line which you snap through the center to get the level must have a plumb bob at the foot. And then put one point of the big compasses on this line, and give the compasses a half turn on the underside. Then put the point of the compasses on the middle intersection of one line with the other, and swing the other semicircle on the upper side. And you will find that you make a little slanted cross on the right side, formed by the intersection of the lines. From the left side apply the line to be snapped, in such a way that it lies right over both the little crosses; and you will find that your line is horizontal by a level. Then compose the scenes or figures with charcoal, as I have described. And always keep your areas in scale, and regular. Then take a small, pointed bristle brush, and a little ocher without tempera, as thin as water; and proceed to copy and draw in your figures, shading as you did with washes when you were learning to draw. Then take a bunch of feathers, and sweep the drawing free of the charcoal.

Then take a little sinoper[5] without tempera, and with a fine pointed brush proceed to mark out noses, eyes, the hair, and all the accents and outlines of the figures; and see to it that these figures are properly adjusted in all their dimensions, for these[6] give you a chance to know and allow for the figures which you have to paint. Then start making your ornaments, or whatever you want to do, around the outside; and when you are ready, take some of the aforesaid lime mortar, well worked over with spade and trowel, successively, so that it seems like an ointment. Then consider in your own mind how much work you can do in a day; for whatever you plaster you ought to finish up. It is true that sometimes in winter, in damp weather, working on a stone wall, the plaster will occasionally keep fresh until the next day; but do not delay if you can help it, because working on the fresh plaster, that is, that day's, is the strongest tempera and the best and most delightful kind of work. So then, plaster a section with plaster, fairly thin, but not excessively, and quite even; first wetting down the old plaster. Then take your large bristle brush in your hand; dip it in clear water; beat it, and sprinkle over your plaster. And with a little block the size of the palm of your hand, proceed to rub with a circular motion over the surface of the well-moistened plaster, so that the little block may succeed in removing mortar wherever there is too much, and supplying it wherever there is not enough, and in evening up your plaster nicely. Then wet the plaster with that brush, if you need to; and rub over the plaster with the point of your trowel, very straight and clean. Then snap out lines in the same system and dimensions which you adopted previously on the plaster underneath.

And let us suppose that in a day you have just one head to do, a youthful saint's, like Our Most Holy Lady's. When you have got the mortar of your plaster all smoothed down, take a little dish, a glazed one, for all your dishes should be glazed and tapered like a goblet or drinking glass, and they should have a good heavy base at the foot, to keep them steady so as not to spill the colors.

[. . .]

Chapter CIV: The system by which you should prepare to acquire the skill to work on panel

Know that there ought not to be less time spent in learning than this: to begin as a shopboy studying for one year, to get practice in drawing on the little panel; next, to serve in a shop under some master to learn how to work at all the branches which pertain to our profession; and to stay and begin the working up of colors; and to learn to boil the sizes, and grind the gessos; and to get experience in gessoing *anconas*,[7] and modeling and scraping them; gilding and stamping; for the space of a good six years. Then to get experience in painting, embellishing with mordants, making cloths of gold, getting practice in working on the wall, for six more years; drawing all the time, never leaving off, either on holidays or on workdays. And in this way your talent, through much practice, will develop into real ability. Otherwise, if you follow other systems, you need never hope that they will reach any high degree of perfection. For there are many who say that they have mastered the profession without having served under masters. Do not believe it, for I give you the example of this book: even if you study it by day and by night, if you do not see some practice under some master you will never amount to anything, nor will you ever be able to hold your head up in the company of masters.

Beginning to work on panel, in the name of Most Holy Trinity: always invoking that name and that of the Glorious Virgin Mary.

[. . .]

Chapter CIX: How goat glue is made, and how it is tempered; and how many purposes it will serve.

And there is a glue which is known as leaf glue; this is made out of clippings of goats' muzzles, feet, sinews, and many clippings of skins. This glue is made in March or January, during those strong frosts or winds; and it is boiled with clear water until it is reduced to less than a half. Then put it into certain flat dishes, like jelly molds or basins, straining it thoroughly. Let it stand overnight. Then, in the morning, cut it with a knife into slices like bread; put it on a mat to dry in the wind, out of the sunlight; and an ideal glue will result. This glue is used by painters, by saddlers, and by ever so many masters, as I shall show you later on. And it is a good glue for wood, and for many things. We shall discuss it thoroughly, showing what it may be used for, and how, for gessos, for tempering colors, making lutes, tarsias, fastening pieces of wood and foliage ornament together, tempering gessos, doing raised gessos; and it is good for many things.

Notes

1 Over the course of his lifetime, Leonardo made notes for a treatise that he never completed. After Leonardo's death, his pupil Francesco Melzi compiled the master's various writings into a text, which for a century circulated in dozens of manuscripts, before being published in 1651.
2 Wackernagel 316.
3 Smith 112.
4 "*Fermarle*. Perhaps read *formarle* 'give them shape.'" (DT)
5 This reddish-brown pigment came from Sinop in Turkey and was used in laying out the *sinopia*, or underdrawing, that Cennini is describing.
6 "That is, the preliminary layout on the rough plaster, over which the finish plaster and final painting are applied." (DT)
7 "By *ancona* is to be understood a compound panel, one with its moldings integrally attached. It may be large or small; complex, as a polyptych, or merely a 'self-framed' panel. The *tavola*, the simple 'panel,' has no moldings." (DT)

Source

Cennino d'Andrea Cennini. *The Craftsman's Handbook*, trans. Daniel V. Thompson, Yale UP, 1933.

References

Ames-Lewis, Francis. *The Intellectual Life of the Early Renaissance Artist*, Yale UP, 2000.

Cennini, Cennino. *Il libro dell'arte: A New English Translation and Commentary with Italian Transcription*, by Lara Broecke, Archetype Publications Ltd, 2015.

Long, Pamela O. "Artisan-authors in Italy," in *Openness, Secrecy, Authorship. Technical Arts and the Culture of Knowledge from Antiquity to the Renaissance*, Johns Hopkins UP, 2001, pp. 129–42.

Pedretti, Carlo. *Leonardo da Vinci on Painting: A Lost Book (Libro A)*, UC Press, 1964.

Smith, Pamela. *The Body of the Artisan: Art and Experience in the Scientific Revolution*, U Chicago P, 2004.

Wackernagel, Martin. *The World of the Florentine Artist: Projects and Patrons, Workshop and Art Market* (1938), trans. Alison Luchs, Princeton UP, 1981.

32 Sculptors in corporation and in combat

Lorenzo Ghiberti, *Commentary* II, *c.*1450

Antonio Manetti, *Life of Filippo Brunelleschi*, 1480s

Nanni di Banco (Giovanni di Antonio di Banco, *c.*1374–1421) was one of a group of youthful Florentine sculptors that included Donatello (Donato di Niccolò di Betto Bardi, *c.*1386–1466), who contributed important works to the façade of the Duomo. Nanni came from a family of expert stone carvers. His father, Antonio di Banco, was a stone carver who served as *capomastro* (master mason) of the workshop of the Duomo of Florence; on his mother's side, too, he descended from a line of stonemasons who had held positions of importance in the cathedral workshop. Both Nanni and Donatello were members of the Stonemasons' and Carpenters' Guild (*Arte dei Maestri di Pietra e Legname*) that, in addition to sculptors, comprised a wide variety of workers in the building trades, including "almost all workers above the level of manual laborers who had a degree of specialization or a certain economic independence. Besides masons they included quarriers, kiln operators, roofers, stucco-workers, house painters, vendors of sand, gravel, and wood, founders, cesspool diggers, and even carters of stone and dirt."[1] Nanni matriculated in the guild in 1405 and was elected consul in 1414. When, in 1339, the Signoria of Florence had decreed that guilds should decorate each of the twelve niches on the exterior of Orsanmichele with statues of their respective patron saints, one of these niches was assigned to the Stonemasons' and Carpenters' Guild. Although this guild was far from being the wealthiest or most important, it had the most members. The artist who was eventually selected by the guild was Nanni di Banco, who sculpted the *Four Crowned Saints* around 1416 (Figure 4.1). These patron saints were Roman sculptors who, according to legend, lived during the era of Emperor Diocletian (r.284–305 CE). Having converted to Christianity, the four men refused to carve pagan statues and were put to death. In the predella, instead of depicting stories from the lives of the saints, Nanni carved a relief representing members of the guild; dressed in contemporary workers' clothing, they are hard at work. At the top of the niche in the triangular tympanum is an image of Christ, his hand raised to bless the figures beneath. After all, what could be more natural than Jesus blessing them, since he also

DOI: 10.4324/9781003284284-36

grew up among woodworkers, as the New Testament has it: "Is this not the carpenter's son?" (Matt. 13:55).

Another sculptor of Donatello's generation was Lorenzo Ghiberti (1378–1455), most famous for his *Gates of Paradise* (1425–52, Museo del Opera del Duomo, Florence). He was raised by the goldsmith Bartolo di Michele, possibly his natural father, who taught him the trade. Barely twenty years old when he began work on the first set of doors for Florence's Baptistry, Ghiberti joined the Goldsmiths' Guild in 1409 and the Stonemasons' and Carpenters' Guild in 1426. In his *Commentary*,[2] Ghiberti describes the many sculptural projects he completed during his lifetime, but he neglects to mention the numerous assistant sculptors in his workshop who helped him carry out those projects. The contracts, which still exist, show that Ghiberti had eleven assistants when he worked on the Baptistry doors in 1403, while up to twenty people worked for him in 1407. Donatello sometimes had as many as eighteen or twenty assistants at times, and the practice was common in painting as well. Large-scale projects required not only the participation of assistants working under the master but sometimes the collaboration of two or more masters, as in the case of Ghiberti and Brunelleschi who were compelled to work together on the construction of the cupola of Florence's Duomo (1420–36). The rivalry between the two men is hinted at by Ghiberti in his second *Commentary*, in which he describes the competition for the Baptistry panels as a "*combattimento*" (combat) and proudly recounts his undisputed victory. His competitor's biographer Antonio di Tuccio Manetti (1423–1497) tells a different story: unlike the purely aesthetic triumph Ghiberti proclaims for himself, Manetti, in his account, though clearly biased, reveals the extent of behind the scenes lobbying actually involved in obtaining this important commission. Furthermore, by comparing these two versions of the story, the very different temperaments of Brunelleschi and Ghiberti emerge, as well as the motives for their fierce antagonism.

Lorenzo Ghiberti, *Commentary II*, *c.*1450

I, O most excellent reader, did not have to obey [a desire for] money, but gave myself to the study of art, which since my childhood I have always pursued with great zeal and devotion. In order to master the basic principles [of art] I have sought to investigate the way nature functions in art; and in order that I might be able to approach her, how images come to the eye, how the power of vision functions, how visual [images] come, and in what way the theory of sculpture and painting should be established.

In my youth in the year of Christ 1400, because of the corrupt air in Florence and the bad state of the country, I left the city with an excellent painter whom Signor Malatesta of Pesaro had summoned. He had a room made which was painted by us with great care. My mind was in a large part turned to painting[3] because of the work the prince promised us, and also the companion with whom I was, continually showed me the honor and benefit we would acquire. However, at this time my friends wrote me that the governors of the church of S. Giovanni Battista [in Florence] were sending for skilled masters whom they wished to see compete. From all countries of Italy a great many skilled masters came in order to take part in this trial and contest.[4] I asked permission of the prince and my companion to leave. The prince, hearing the reason, immediately gave me permission [to go]. Together with the other sculptors I appeared before the *Operai*[5] of that church [Baptistry of S. Giovanni]. To each was given four tables of bronze. As the trial piece the *Operai* and the governors of the church wanted each [artist] to make one scene for the door. The story they chose was the Sacrifice of Isaac and each contestant was to make the same story. The trial pieces were to be executed in one year, and he who won had to be given the victory. These were the contestants: Filippo di Ser Brunellesco, Symone da Colle,[6] Nicholò d'Arezzo,[7] Jacopo della Quercia da Siena, Francesco di Valdombrina,[8] Nicholò Lamberti.[9] We six were to take part in the contest, which was to be a demonstration of the art of sculpture. To me was conceded the palm of victory by all the experts and by all those who had competed with me. To me the honor was conceded universally and with no exception. To all it seemed that I had at that time surpassed the others without exception, as was recognized by a great council and an investigation of learned men. The *Operai* of the governing [board] wanted the judgment of these men written by their own hands. They were men highly skilled from the painters and sculptors of gold, silver, and marble. There were thirty-four judges from the city and other surrounding countries. The testimonial of the victory was given in my favor by all, the consuls, the *Operai*, and the entire merchants' guild which has charge of the church of S. Giovanni. It was granted to me and determined that I should make bronze doors for this church. This I executed with great care. This is my first work: the door with the frame around it cost about twenty-two thousand florins. Also in the door are twenty-eight compartments; in twenty are stories from the New Testament, and at the bottom are the Four Evangelists and the four [church] Doctors, and around the work are a great number of human heads. With great love the door was diligently made, together with frames of ivy leaves, and the door jambs with a very magnificent frame of many kinds of leaves. The work weighed thirty-four thousand pounds. It was executed with the greatest skill and care. At the same time was made of fine bronze the statue of St. John the Baptist,[10] four and a third *braccia* high. It was erected in 1414. . . .

[*Ghiberti goes on to describe his numerous sculptural and goldsmithing projects including large statues in Orsanmichele in Florence; panels for the Baptistry in Siena; tombs for Florentine notables in bronze and marble miters for popes; a casket for St. Zenobius for the Duomo in Florence; and his second set of doors for the Florentine Baptistry*—The Gates of Paradise.]

But not to tire my readers, I shall omit a great many works I have produced. I know that one can find no pleasure in such material. Nevertheless I ask pardon of all readers and all to have patience. Also by making sketches in wax and clay for painters, sculptors, and stone carvers and by making designs of many things for painters, I have helped many of them to achieve the greatest honors for their works. . . . Few things of importance were made in our country that were not designed and planned by me. Especially in the building of the cupola [of the Duomo] Filippo and I worked together at the same salary for eighteen years while we were building it.

Antonio Manetti, *Life of Filippo Brunelleschi*, 1480s

It happened while he was still in his youth, in the year of Our Lord 1401 when he was twenty-four years old, and was practicing the trade of goldsmith, that the *Operai* of the building of the temple of San Giovanni, in carrying out their restorations, had to commission the making of the second bronze doors for the aforesaid temple, which are today on the north side. And knowing the reputation of masters of figure casting, and of the Florentines, in order to commission the best one, after much debating amongst themselves, and consulting with citizens and artisans, they came to the conclusion that two, the best that could be found, were both Florentines, and neither in Florence, nor anywhere else did they hear of anyone better. One of these two was the aforesaid Filippo, and the other Lorenzo di Bartolo, whose name on the doors is written as Lorenzo di Cione Ghiberti, for he was the son of Cione.[11] At the time when the business of the doors was just beginning, Lorenzo was a young man as well. . . . They gave each one a story to sculpt in bronze, with the principal intention of assigning the doors to the one who did best in this test.

[. . .]

Filippo sculpted his story in the way that can still be seen today,[12] and he made it quickly, as he possessed a vigorous way with the art. Once he had cast, cleaned, and polished it all, he was not inclined to discuss it with anyone, since, as I have said, he was not a braggart, and he waited for the time fixed for the contest. Lorenzo, it was said, was somewhat afraid of Filippo's skill, which was very apparent, and he did not feel he had such mastery of the art, so he worked quite slowly. Having been told something about the beautiful thing that Filippo had made, as he was a clever man he made use of his industriousness, humbling himself, asking advice from everyone he esteemed—knowledgeable men who would be judging him, such as goldsmiths, painters, sculptors etc.—so that he would not fail at the contest. And while he was modelling the wax he was always consulting and asking advice, bowing low to those types of people, and tried to discover as much as he could about Filippo's work. And deferring to those above-mentioned people, he repeatedly unmade and remade the whole and parts of his work whenever it was the opinion of the majority of the experts that he should. He did this tirelessly while working the wax, and eventually it was finished and brought to the competition. The *Operai* and building officials took counsel from the very people Lorenzo had singled out.

[*The judges, though predisposed toward Ghiberti's panel, with which they were already familiar, are astonished when they see Brunelleschi's at last, and are forced to rethink their decision and meet for a second time.*]

Gathering together once more, they arrived at a decision and made this report to the *operai*: that both models were very beautiful and for their part, in comparing every aspect, they could not determine which one was superior, and since it was a large enterprise, which would take much time and great expense, it should be assigned equally to them both and they should be partners. When Filippo and Lorenzo were summoned and made aware of the tenor of the decision, Lorenzo remained silent, but Filippo would not agree unless he was put in charge of the entire project, and he would not budge from that position.

Notes

1 Goldthwaite 254.
2 The sculptor wrote a treatise on sculpture known as *The Commentaries* (*I commentarii*) toward the end of his life, around five decades after Cennini and more than one hundred years before Vasari. In this work, echoing themes in Alberti's treatise (*On Painting*, **#12**), Ghiberti expresses the view that sculptors to have knowledge of a wide variety of subject matter, as did the ancients, and he draws an implied parallel between himself and the ancient Greek sculptor Phidias (*fl.* 490–450 BCE), who it is said also wrote a book of commentaries.
3 "Ghiberti began as a painter. He was not admitted to the goldsmith's guild until 1409." (EGH)
4 The word used by Ghiberti is "*combattimento*" meaning "combat" or "trial."

5 "The *Operai* are the committee in charge of a building. The term is also used to designate the chairman of the committee. The responsibility for the maintenance of certain public buildings was assigned to different guilds, in this case, the *Arte di Calimala* (the foreign wool merchants' guild). The church of the patron saint of a guild was usually maintained by the guild." (EGH)
6 "Nothing more is known of Simone da Colle." (EGH)
7 "Niccolò d'Arezzo was the brother of the painter Spinelli." (EGH)
8 "Francesco di Valdambrino, an excellent Sienese sculptor and a collaborator of Jacopo della Quercia." (EGH)
9 "Niccolò di Piero Lamberti had been active on the Duomo since 1338." (EGH)
10 This statue is in Orsanmichele.
11 This is a sly dig at Ghiberti's alleged illegitimate birth.
12 Both competition panels are at the Museum of the Bargello in Florence.

Sources

Ghiberti, *Commentary* II in *A Documentary History of Art, Vol. I, The Middle Ages and Renaissance*, selected and ed. Elizabeth Gilmore Holt, Doubleday, 1957, pp. 156–63.

Manetti, *Life of Brunelleschi* in *Operette Istoriche di Antonio Manetti*, ed. Gaetano Milanesi, Le Monnier, 1887, pp. 87–92, trans. Kaborycha.

References

Bergstein, Mary. *The Sculpture of Nanni di Banco*, Princeton UP, 2000.

Goldthwaite, Richard A. *The Building of Renaissance Florence: An Economic and Social History*, Johns Hopkins UP, 1980.

Hurd, Janice L. "The Character and Purpose of Ghiberti's Treatise on Sculpture," in *Lorenzo Ghiberti nel suo tempo, Atti del Convegno internazionale di Studi, Florence, 18–21 October 1978*, vol. 2, L.S. Olschki, 1980, pp. 292–315.

Krautheimer, Richard, in collaboration with Trude Krautheimer-Hess. *Lorenzo Ghiberti*, Princeton UP, 1956.

Manetti, Antonio di Tuccio. *The Life of Brunelleschi*, introd., notes, and critical text ed. Howard Saalman. English translation of the Italian text by Catherine Enggass, Penn State UP, 1970.

Seymour Jr., Charles. *Sculpture in Italy 1400–1500*, Penguin, 1966.

33 The patronage of Cosimo de' Medici

Vespasiano da Bisticci, *Lives of Illustrious Men*, *c.*1480

If someone in mid-fifteenth-century Florence wanted the finest luxury manuscript, they went to the stationer's shop of Vespasiano da Bisticci (1422–1498). Known as a *cartolaio*, a stationer sold writing supplies such as paper, parchment, quills, ink, and occasionally, books.[1] Rather than having shelves full of books to choose from, Vespasiano generally took orders for bespoke volumes and had them copied by scribes and illuminated by expert miniaturists. His foreign clientele included popes Eugenius IV and Nicholas V; the king of Naples, Alfonso the Magnanimous; and the Duke of Urbino. Locally, foremost among the wealthy Florentine book collectors who were his customers was Cosimo de' Medici. In addition to books ordered for his own extensive private collection, Cosimo had Vespasiano provide books for two monastic libraries—the Convent of San Marco in Florence and the Badia in Fiesole. Eventually, Vespasiano sold the business in 1480 and retired to the town of Antella in the countryside south of Florence where he wrote a number of books, including his *Lives of Illustrious Men*. The retired bookseller drew on his long acquaintance with the famous individuals who had once been his patrons to write incisive biographies about them. He knew Cosimo de' Medici particularly well, and his biography provides rich details of Cosimo's generous patronage of architecture, sculpture, and, of course, manuscripts.

Vespasiano da Bisticci, *Lives of Illustrious Men*, *c.*1480

The life of Cosimo de' Medici (1389–1464)

Cosimo di Giovanni de' Medici was of most honorable descent, a very prominent citizen, and one of great weight in the republic. He was well versed in Latin letters, both sacred and secular, of capable judgment in all matters and able to argue thereupon . . . he had a knowledge of Latin which would scarcely have been looked for in one occupying the station of a leading citizen engrossed with affairs. He was grave in temperament, prone to associate with

DOI: 10.4324/9781003284284-37

men of high station who disliked frivolity, and averse from all buffoons and actors and those who spent time unprofitably. He had a great liking for men of letters and sought their society.

[*Vespasiano describes Cosimo's involvement in politics; his exile from Florence; subsequent return; and relations with Pope Eugenius IV.*]

Now Cosimo, having applied himself to the temporal affairs of the state, the conduct of which was bound to leave him with certain matters on his conscience—as is the case with all those who are fain to govern states and take the leading place—awoke to a sense of his condition, and was anxious that God might pardon him, and secure to him the possession of his earthly goods. Wherefore he felt he must needs turn to pious ways, otherwise his riches would be lost to him. He had prickings of conscience that certain portions of his wealth—where it came from I cannot say—had not been righteously gained, and to remove this weight from his shoulders, he held conference with Pope Eugenius, who was then in Florence, as to the load which lay on his conscience. Pope Eugenius had settled the Observantist Order in S. Marco; but, as their lodging there was inadequate, he remarked to Cosimo that, if he was bent on unburdening his soul, he might build a monastery. After he had spent ten thousand without providing all that was wanted, he afterwards completed the monastery, spending more than forty thousand florins over the work. Beyond building the house he fitted it with everything necessary for residence. He gave all the musical books for the church and the greater part of those are now in the library, and furthermore provided the sacristy with everything needful for Divine worship. And because the Dominican brothers may not hold goods of their own, he paid all the charges of their life in common in order that they might enjoy their fine convent during their lives. For the daily outlay he settled with his bank what weekly sum should be paid to them, thus providing all they wanted. To save personal application to himself, much occupied with affairs, he gave orders to the bank that whatever sum of money might be marked on the bill should be paid and charged to his account.

[*Cosimo's transfer of books from Niccolò Niccoli's estate to the Library of San Marco; his funding of renovation of the Basilica of San Lorenzo and the Badia of Fiesole*]

He next considered how he might best gather together in these lodgings a company of worthy and learned men. First, he determined to collect a suitable lot of books, and one day, when I was with him, he said: "What plan can you suggest for the formation of this library?" I replied that if the books were to be bought, it would be impossible, for the reason that they could not be found. Then he went on, "Then tell me what you would do in the matter." I said it would be necessary to have the books transcribed, whereupon he wanted to know whether I would undertake the task. I said that I would, whereupon he replied that I might begin when I liked, that he left everything to me, and that, as for the money for daily costs, he would order Don Archangelo, the prior, to present the checks at the bank where they would be duly paid. He was anxious I should use all possible despatch, and, after the library was begun, as there was no lack of money, I engaged forty-five scribes and completed two hundred volumes in twenty-two months, taking as a model the library of Pope Nicolas and following directions written by his own hand, which Pope Nicolas had given to Cosimo.

Note

1 These were manuscripts, which literally means "handwritten," as all European books were before the mid-fifteenth century with the advent of Gutenberg's printing press and its system of moveable type. It would be decades, however, before the new technology really took off.

Source

Vespasiano da Bisticci, *The Life of Cosimo de' Medici* in *The Vespasiano Memoirs: Lives of Illustrious Men of the XVth Century*, trans. William George and Emily Waters, ed. Myron P. Gilmore, Torchbook, 1963, pp. 213; 218–21.

References

De la Mare, Albinia C. "Vespasiano da Bisticci as Producer of Classical Manuscripts in Fifteenth-Century Florence," in *The History of the Book in the West: A Library of Critical Essays*, vol. 1, Ashgate, 2010.

Kanter, Laurence B. et al. *Painting and Illumination in Early Renaissance Florence, 1300–1450*, Metropolitan Museum of Art: Distributed by H.N. Abrams, c1994.

Kent, Dale. *Cosimo de' Medici and the Florentine Renaissance: The Patron's Oeuvre*, Yale UP, 2000.

Melograni, Anna. "The Illuminated Manuscript as a Commodity: Production, Consumption and the Cartolaio's Role in Fifteenth-century Italy," in *The Material Renaissance*, ed. Michelle O'Malley and Evelyn Welch, Manchester UP; Distributed exclusively in the USA by Palgrave, 2007.

Ullman, Berthold L. and Philip A. Stadter. *The Public Library of Renaissance Florence: Niccolò Niccoli, Cosimo de' Medici and the Library of San Marco*, Antenore, 1972.

34 A masterpiece in a friar's cell

Fra Roberto Caracciolo, *Sermon on the Annunciation*, 1489

Figure 4.2 Fra Angelico, *Annunciation*, *c*.1440. This fresco is painted on the wall of Cell 3, in the east (clerics') dormitory, Convent of San Marco, Florence.

The city of Florence is dedicated to the Virgin Mary. Its cathedral, Santa Maria del Fiore (St. Mary of the Flower), is named after her, and its native flower is associated with her (**#6**). Historically, the Florentine New Year began not on January 1, but on March 25, the day, nine months before Christmas, when the archangel Gabriel announced to Mary that she was to give birth to Jesus. Thus, the Annunciation was a popular subject, especially

DOI: 10.4324/9781003284284-38

for Florentine artists of the Renaissance; they painted the scene over and over, often positioned near the entry of churches, symbolically echoing the entry of the Christian savior into the world. The scene often appears within monastic settings as well, for instance, in the fresco by Fra Angelico (Giovanni da Fiesole; Guido di Piero, *c.*1395–1455) at the top of the stairs as one enters the dormitory area of the Dominican Convent[1] of San Marco (north corridor, *c.*1440–45). Beneath the fresco is an inscription that reads, "When you come before the figure of the intact Virgin, do not fail to say a Hail Mary," reminding the friars to genuflect when they entered the hall. The artist, who was one of the friars who lived at San Marco, also happened to be the most admired Florentine painter of his generation, and he was called upon to represent the Annunciation in various ways, for instance, in riotous color and lavish gold leaf for San Domenico in Cortona (*c.*1432, Museo Diocesano, Cortona). For Fra Angelico and the other Observant friars at San Marco especially, the Virgin Mary's posture in this scene carried the central meaning of humility. The image by Fra Angelico shown in Figure 4.2—yet another *Annunciation* in the convent—is located in an extremely secluded place and painted on the wall of a friar's tiny cell. For, in addition to the common areas in the building, Angelico and his team of assistants frescoed each individual cell in the three rows of dormitories for the novices, the clerics, and the lay brothers.[2] Though portions of the San Marco building complex were public or semipublic—in addition to the church, the chapter room, sacristy, and guest quarters were accessible to laypeople—access to the upper floor where the dormitories and library were located was strictly limited to men closely associated with the Dominican order. In Cell 3, the artist chose to represent the familiar scene very simply, placing it within the stark setting of a convent cloister, not unlike the cloister of San Marco; the austerity of the muted tones and the stuccoed vaults in the painting echo the curves of the ceiling and window embrasure of the cell itself. There are no superfluous details to divert the viewer's attention from scene: the Virgin Mary kneels, listening to the angel, her upper body bent forward, arms crossed over her chest in a pose chosen to represent humility and submission. Art historian Michael Baxandall has described the way popular Quattrocento preachers such as the Franciscan friar Roberto Caracciolo (*c.*1425–1495) suggested the range of postures assumed by the Virgin Mary in sacred paintings: "The preachers coached the public in the painters' repertory, and the painters responded within the current emotional categorization of the event."[3] In his sermon, Caracciolo explains how Mary's posture symbolizes humility, the appropriate attitude for the kind of person who would have been viewing this painting within San Marco. Behind the angel, the artist has added the figure of the Dominican preacher St. Peter Martyr (1205–1252). The saint, hands folded in prayer, stands in the background reverently contemplating the scene, just as the friar who lived in that cell would have done.

Fra Roberto Caracciolo, *Sermon on the Annunciation*, 1489

The third mystery to declare concerning the Annunciation of the Madonna is called the angelic conversation; it contains five laudable conditions of the Blessed Virgin:

The first is called perturbation (*conturbatione*)
The second is cogitation (*cogitatione*)
The third is interrogation (*interrogatione*)
The fourth is humility (*humiliatione*)
The fifth is merit (*meritatione*)

The first laudable condition is called perturbation, according to the writing of St. Luke [I: 26–36]. The Virgin, having heard the Angel's salutation, was troubled—this perturbation was not out of incredulity, as Nicholas of Lyra writes, but from wonderment, as she was accustomed to seeing angels and did not marvel so much at the Angel's apparition, as at the lofty and grand salutation, in which the Angel explained such great and stupendous things, and because of her humility it left her dazed and stupefied.

The second laudable condition is called cogitation, as she thought about what that salutation was: in this the prudence of that most sacred Virgin is shown. Then the Angel said, "Fear not, Mary: for thou hast found favor with God. And behold, thou shalt conceive in thy womb, and bring forth a son, and shalt call his name Jesus." . . .

The third laudable condition is called interrogation. "The Virgin asked, 'How shall this be, seeing I know not a man?'" . . .

The fourth laudable condition is called humility. What tongue could ever express, what mind could contemplate her gesture, the way and manner she placed her holy knees on the ground, and lowered her head, saying, "Behold the handmaid of the Lord." She did not say "lady"; she did not say "queen". O profound humility! O unheard-of meekness! "Behold," she said, "the slave and servant of my Lord." And then, raising her eyes to Heaven, clasping her hands, and with her arms in the form of a cross, she did as God, the Angels, and the Holy Fathers desired: "Be it unto me according to thy word."

Notes

1 In current English usage, "convent" often is understood to refer exclusively to female monastic institutions; historically, it is the standard term for the place where Christian communities of either sex, live under monastic vows. "Nunnery" is a more precise term for a building that houses nuns.

2 A man admitted to the convent would spend a year as a novice before being admitted to the order as a full friar and would move to the clerics' dormitory. Lay brothers—tertiaries—did not take full vows, but participated in the life of the order. There were three separate wings with dormitories for each group. Notably, as patron of the convent, Cosimo de' Medici had not just one, but two adjoining cells located in the wing of the lay brothers for his private devotional use.

3 Baxandall 55.

Source

Roberto Carcciolo. "Sermone XL de la Annuntiatione," in *Spechio della fede christiana volgare*, Venice, 1555, pp. 217–8, trans. Kaborycha.

References

Baxandall, Michael. *Painting and Experience in Fifteenth-Century Italy*, Oxford UP, 1972.

Drummond, Sarah. *Divine Conception: The Art of the Annunciation*, Unicorn, an imprint of Unicorn Publishing Group, LLP, 2018.

Hood, William. *Fra Angelico at San Marco*, Yale UP, 1993.

Kennedy, Trinita. "In Search of Authenticity: The Art of the Dominican and Franciscan Orders in the Age of Observant Reform," in *Sanctity Pictured: The Art of the Dominican and Franciscan Orders in Renaissance Italy*, ed. Trinita Kennedy, Frist Center for the Visual Arts, 2014.

Verdon, Timothy. *Fra Angelico*, Brepols, 2020.

35 An artist seeks employment at court

Leonardo da Vinci, *Draft of letter to the duke of Milan*, *c.*1481–2

Leonardo da Vinci (1452–1519) was barely thirty years old when he decided to leave Florence and move to the Duchy of Milan, seeking employment with its ruler, Lodovico Sforza (Lodovico "il Moro," 1452–1509). Reliable sources document that Leonardo was in Milan by April of 1483, although it is likely he moved there the year before. Thus, the artist must have written the following letter sometime between 1481 and 1482. The present document, found among Leonardo's papers in the immense *Atlanticus Codex* kept in the Biblioteca Ambrosiana in Milan, is an undated, unsigned draft. The letter is not written in Leonardo's hand, rather, he probably dictated it to a secretary; it is composed of an introduction, ten paragraphs numbered in the left-hand margin, and a closing paragraph. The editing marks here reproduce the words and phrases that are crossed out in the manuscript. This "job application letter" reveals the sort of projects Leonardo was working on, as well as the versatility expected of Renaissance artists, not to mention what Leonardo himself considered the most pressing needs of the Milanese state. In particular, he draws attention to his expertise in military matters, and indeed, there are many drawings in Leonardo's notebooks of various ingenious, deadly weapons. He owned a book by Francesco di Giorgio Martini (1439–1501) on military architecture, which is heavily annotated in Leonardo's hand. Moreover, the civil engineering and hydraulic projects that he refers to are reflected in many studies in his notebooks as well. Toward the end of the letter, Leonardo mentions his abilities in architecture and sculpture; importantly, he emphasizes his ability to cast bronze; he knew that Lodovico had for a long time wanted to erect an equestrian monument of his father, Francesco Sforza. Although there are no existing sculptures credibly attributed to Leonardo, these are techniques he would have learned as an apprentice in Verrocchio's studio in the 1470s. As to Leonardo's designs for weapons and siege machinery, we have no idea whether any effort was made at the time to actually construct these. However, once he got the job, Leonardo's ability to paint—mentioned almost as an afterthought at the end of the letter—was definitely put to good use in Milan. It was there that he produced both versions of the *Virgin of the Rocks* (1480s, Louvre, Paris; 1490s, National Gallery, London), his *Portrait of Lady with Ermine* (#36),

DOI: 10.4324/9781003284284-39

and, most famous of all, the *Last Supper* (1495–98, S. Maria delle Grazie, Milan).

Leonardo da Vinci, *Draft of Letter to the duke of Milan, c.*1481–2

My Most Illustrious Lord,

Having seen and sufficiently considered the attempts of all those who believe themselves masters and designers of instruments of war, whose inventions are nothing out of the ordinary—no offense intended toward anyone—I will strive to reveal to Your Excellency my secrets, presenting them to you at your pleasure, whenever opportune for you and bring into effective operation all those things, which in part, are briefly noted below. ~~& also many more as needs arise in various cases.~~

1 I have the means for [making] very light, strong, and easily portable bridges with which to pursue and, ~~sometimes when necessary~~, to flee the enemy, and others, sturdy and indestructible either by fire or in battle, easy and convenient to lift and place in position. Also the means for burning and destroying those of the enemy.

2 I know how, during a siege, to remove water from moats and how to make an infinite number of bridges, mantlets,[1] ladders, and other instruments appropriate for such an expedition.

3 *Item.* If, on account of the height of an embankment, or the strength of position, bombardment cannot be used during a siege, I have means for destroying any castle or fortification, provided that it is not founded on bedrock.

4 I also have types of bombards[2] that are very convenient and easy to carry, which hurl those tiny stones ~~almost~~ like a hailstorm, and its smoke frightens the enemy, causing grave damage and confusion.

5 *Item.* I have the means of arriving at a certain designated spot through caves and secret winding tunnels created entirely without noise. If needs be, these can even pass beneath moats or rivers.

6 *Item.* I can make secure and protected covered chariots that can penetrate enemy lines with artillery; there is no ~~huge~~ great number of armed troops that they cannot break through. And behind these, many foot soldiers can follow, unharmed and without impediment.

7 Item. When needed, I will make cannons, mortars, and *passavolanti*[3] in most lovely and useful shapes that are out of the ordinary.

8 *Item.* Where cannons cannot be used, I will create catapults, mangonels, trebuchets, and other instruments of admirable efficacy that are not commonly used.

9 And if one happens to be at sea, I have the means of many instruments most suitable to attack and defend, and vessels that can resist the shots of the most powerful bombard, powder & smoke.
10 In peacetime I believe I can give as complete satisfaction as any other in architecture, design of public and private buildings, and in conducting water from one place to another.

Item. I can undertake sculptures in marble, bronze and clay. Likewise, in painting, I can do as well as anyone, whoever he may be.

Furthermore, work could begin on the bronze horse that will be the immortal glory and eternal honor of the happy memory of His Lordship your father and of the noble house of Sforza.

And if any of the above-mentioned things seem to anyone impossible or unfeasible, I am most readily prepared to demonstrate them in your park or in whatever place shall please Your Excellency, to whom with all possible humility I commend myself.

Notes

1 Portable walls for protecting attacking soldiers from projectiles.
2 A short-barreled artillery piece.
3 A variety of long-barreled artillery designed to fire long range.

Source

Leonardo, *Draft of letter to duke of Milan* in *Atlanticus Codex*, fol.1082r, Biblioteca Ambrosiana, trans. Kaborycha with assistance from Maurizio Arfaioli.

References

Arnold, Thomas F. *The Renaissance at War*, Cassell, 2001.
Landrus, Matthew. *Leonardo da Vinci's Giant Crossbow*, Springer, 2010.
Syson, Luke. "The Rewards of Service: Leonardo da Vinci and the Duke of Milan," in *Leonardo da Vinci: Painter at the Court of Milan*, National Gallery, 2011.

36 Two ladies consider a portrait

Isabella d'Este and Cecilia Gallerani, *Letters*, 1498

Bernardo Bellincioni, *Sonnet: Dialogue on Leonardo's portrait of Cecilia Gallerani*, *c.*1490–1

Figure 4.3 Leonardo da Vinci, *Portrait Sketch of Isabella d'Este*, 1500, Louvre.

Figure 4.4 Leonardo da Vinci, *Portrait of Cecilia Gallerani (Lady with Ermine)*, *c.*1490–1, Czartoryski Museum, Kraków.

Among the various projects Leonardo worked on during the seventeen years he remained at the court in Milan was the painting known as *Portrait of Lady with Ermine*, believed to be an image of the duke's mistress, Cecilia Gallerani (1473–1536). Cecilia was not only beautiful—"as lovely as a flower" in the words of the Ferrarese ambassador—she was also charming and well-educated, wrote poetry in the vernacular, and delivered orations in Latin. She and Lodovico Sforza were lovers in 1489 when Cecilia was sixteen years old, and in 1491 she bore the duke a son. When later that same year Sforza married Beatrice d'Este (1475–1497), Cecilia was obliged to leave the Milanese court, and she was married to

DOI: 10.4324/9781003284284-40

a local nobleman in 1492. Afterward, Cecilia remained on good terms, not only with the duke of Milan, but with his sister-in-law Isabella d'Este (1474–1539), who was the marchesa of Mantua. When the invasion of French troops in 1499 forced Cecilia and her family to flee, Isabella offered them shelter. A discerning patron of the arts and owner of an impressive collection of art, both ancient and contemporary, Isabella in her letter to Cecilia, expresses curiosity about the artist's ability to create an image that was true to life. A contemporary who also expressed an opinion concerning the lifelike quality of Leonardo's portrait of Cecilia Gallerani was Bernardo Bellincioni (1452–1492), court poet in Milan, whose sonnet is the earliest documented source concerning the painting. Convinced of Leonardo's mastery, Isabella yearned to have him paint her portrait. So, in 1500 when the artist also took refuge from the French troops, staying briefly at the Mantuan court, she posed for him. Leonardo drew a stunning preliminary sketch of the marchesa, but never produced a painting of her.

Isabella d'Este Letter to Cecilia Gallerani, April 26, 1498

Lady Cecilia Bergamini,[1]

Having today viewed some beautiful portraits by the hand of Giovanni Bellini, we began to discuss the works of Leonardo, and desire to compare them with some that we have. Remembering that he painted you from life, we would request you to be pleased to send this portrait by the present courier, whom we have sent specially for this purpose. For, beyond satisfying us in making this comparison, we would most gladly see your face. And as soon as the comparison has been made, we will send it back to you. Recommending ourselves to your gracious satisfaction, we await your pleasure. From Mantua, April 26, 1498.

Cecilia Gallerani Letter to Isabella d'Este, April 29, 1498

Most illustrious, most excellent, and my most highly honored lady Marchesa of Mantua,

I have seen what your Excellency has written about having a desire to see my portrait, which I do send to you. I should send it more willingly if it more closely resembled me. Your Excellency ought not believe this to be a defect on the part of the master, because I truly believe there is no [painter] to be found who can equal him. It is only because this portrait was made when I was at such an undeveloped age. I have since changed so much from that image that seeing it and myself together, there is no one who would judge it to have been made of me. Nevertheless, I beg your Excellency to appreciate my good will, that I long to please you, not only with the portrait, but I am prepared to do even more to gratify you, whose devoted servant I am, and to whom I commend myself endlessly. From Milan on the 29th day of April, 1498.

From your excellency's servant Cecilia Viscountess Bergamini

Bernardo Bellincioni, *Sonnet: Dialogue on Leonardo's portrait of Cecilia Gallerani, c.*1490–1

The poet: Nature, who stirs your wrath, who arouses your envy?
Nature: It is Vinci, who has painted one of your stars!
Cecilia, today so very beautiful, is the one
Beside whose beautiful eyes the Sun appears as a dark shadow.
The poet: All honor to you [Nature], even if in his picture
She seems to listen and not talk.
Think only, the more alive and more beautiful she is,
The greater will be your glory in future times.
Be grateful therefore to Ludovico, or rather
To the talent [*ingegno*] and hand of Leonardo
Which allows you to be part of posterity.
Everyone who sees her—even if too late
To see her alive—will say: that suffices for us
To understand what is nature and what art.

Note

1 Cecilia's husband was Count Lodovico Carminati de Brambilla, also known as Bergamino.

Sources

Isabella d'Este and Cecilia Gallerani, *Letters* in Francis Ames-Lewis. *Isabella and Leonardo: The Artistic Relationship between Isabella d'Este and Leonardo da Vinci, 1500–1506*, Yale UP, 2012, pp. 223–24, trans. Kaborycha.

Bernardo Bellincioni, *Sonnet* in Frank Zöllner, "Leonardo da Vinci's Portraits: Ginevra de' Benci, Cecilia Gallerani, La Belle Ferronière, and Mona Lisa," in *Rafael i jego spadkobiercy. Portret klasyczny w sztuce nowozytnej Europy; materialy ses-ji naukowej, 24–25 October 2002*, Nicholas Copernicus University, 2003 (Sztuka i kultura) 4, 157–83, p. 167.

References

d'Este, Isabella. *Selected Letters*, ed. and trans. Deanna Shemek, Iter Press Arizona Center for Medieval and Renaissance Studies, 2017.

Musacchio, Jacqueline Marie. "Wives, Lovers, and Art in Italian Renaissance Courts," in *Art and Love in Renaissance Italy*, The Metropolitan Museum of Art, Yale UP, 2008, pp. 29–41.

Shaw, Christine. *Isabella d'Este: A Renaissance Princess*, Routledge, 2019.

Shell, Janice and Grazioso Sironi. "Cecilia Gallerani: Leonardo's Lady with an Ermine," *Artibus et Historiae*, Vol. 13, No. 25 (1992), pp. 47–66.

37 Networks of musical patronage

Raffaele Brandolini, *On Music and Poetry*, 1513

King Ferrante of Naples, *Letter to Lorenzo de' Medici*, 1473

Antonio Squarcialupi, *Letter to Guillaume Dufay*, 1467

Throughout the Renaissance, music was enjoyed in many contexts: to magnify the pageantry of civic ceremonies, for dancing and entertainment at private gatherings, and to increase devotion in sacred services in church. Crucially, music played a central role at Renaissance courts. Baldassarre Castiglione, in one of the many passages he dedicated to music in *The Courtier* (#56), expresses the following opinion: "I am not satisfied with the courtier unless he is also a musician, and besides being able to read music, he must be able to play various instruments as well." Not only courtiers, but many Renaissance rulers themselves were highly trained, expert musicians, who sought out the finest performers and composers of the day to entertain them. And beyond the obvious pleasure of listening to music, as with art patronage, the presence of top-notch musicians at court provided a special kind of cultural capital. In particular, polyphony became the rage in Italian courts during the second half of the Quattrocento. Written and often performed by musicians imported from northern Europe, the sounds of the latest complex polyphonic compositions of sacred music resounded in elegant court chapels. Music functioned as a soundtrack that enhanced the aura of magnificence surrounding the prince; one musicologist refers to "the investment in polyphony as an instrument of the theatricalization of princely power."[1] This is made especially clear in the treatise written by Raffaele Lippo Brandolini (1465–1517). A humanist man of letters, Brandolini was also a blind *improvvisatore*, renowned for his ability to compose and perform extemporaneous verses in Latin. In 1513, he wrote *On Music and Poetry* and dedicated the book to his friend and patron, then Cardinal Giovanni de' Medici, who soon after became Pope Leo X (#27). In this work, Brandolini exalts the lyric arts, citing the honored position music and poetry held not only in noble ancient settings but also in Italian Renaissance courts, both papal and secular. Encouraging his patron to be ever more generous in supporting artists like himself, Brandolini draws attention to two well-known patrons of the arts: a former pope with a distinct love of music, Pius II (#44), as well as the current pope's father, Lorenzo the Magnificent. Furthermore, two letters indicate just

DOI: 10.4324/9781003284284-41

how far patronage networks extended throughout the Italian Peninsula and across Europe: one was sent by the king of Naples to Lorenzo de' Medici in Florence, and another was written by Antonio Squarcialupi (1416–1480), cathedral organist in Florence, to the celebrated Franco-Flemish composer Guillaume Dufay (1397–1474) in Cambrai, France.

Raffaelle Brandolini, *On Music and Poetry*, 1513

In our fathers' time Alfonso, the most illustrious King of Aragon, and Borso d'Este—as you know the former most laudably governed the Kingdom of Naples, the latter the Duchy of Ferrara—honored and supported above all, men distinguished in the discipline of music. And Pope Pius II, not much after, delighted so much in poetic verses accompanied on the lyre that he preferred this diversion to all others; not only did he enjoy listening to the lyre, but he was also accustomed to playing it most sweetly himself. . . .

Ferdinand [Ferrante], moreover, who received the Kingdom of Naples from his father Alfonso (**#13, #15**) and ruled in peaceful manner for thirty-six years, in both private and in public, was so dedicated to the pursuit of musical science that not only did he often practice it himself in his leisure time, but attracted to his court with great rewards, those most learned in the discipline and the most skillful makers of instruments from all of Europe. As we all know, he kept a very flourishing throng of singers selected from France, Britain, Spain, and Germany, engaged solely to participate in divine services and praises. At his chapel in Naples, which can be seen in the main hall of the new castle, two organs, though different, are both sweet and harmonious. They were as delightful to see as to hear, and pleasing to the eye and ear of the severest judge, due to the excellence of their craftsmanship and the sweetness of their sound. . . .

In addition to numerous domestic servants whom he called "chamber musicians" for the comforts and charms of voices and strings performed in private, not far from his chambers, he had a certain hall most elegantly adorned with paintings and sculptures, where he retired on his own, and it was lacking in no musical instrument that could be sounded by hand, plectrum, or mouth. . . .

His emulator, Lorenzo de' Medici, lest his fatherland were surpassed, or failed to possess any possible dignity or ornament, and lest he seem not to have accepted any favor from that King, whom he himself [Lorenzo] had inspired to build a private library, [Lorenzo] adorned the church of San Giovanni [the Baptistry] most beautifully with the sweetest concord of voices in praise of God.

King Ferrante of Naples, *Letter to Lorenzo de' Medici*, 1473

Magnificent Lord, and Our Dearest Friend,

Our esteemed and beloved servant and counsellor the Count of Altavilla has under our order sent to Florence a young son he has raised by the name of Angelo so that he will learn to play the organ and other musical instruments and that he will be taught by Maestro Antonio [Squarcialupi]. And since we would be most pleased that the aforesaid boy reaches perfection in these matters that he studies, knowing that Maestro Antonio is entirely at your disposal, we entreat and urge most warmly and heartily that it please you to recommend said boy, in such a way that the greatest possible care and diligence is taken in his instruction; this would give us exceptional pleasure and we would be much obliged to you. In our land of San Severino, on February 5, 1473.

Antonio Squarcialupi, *Letter to Guillaume Dufay*, 1467

My venerable father, rightly to be honored above all others!

With the greatest joy to my soul, I have read and often reread your most humane letter; and I embraced with all my heart the fellow-singers whom you sent, the best of your church, just as you wrote, and having heard them, I am easily induced to believe it. They are, indeed, absolutely excellent, both in sweetness of voice and in the knowledge and the art of singing, and worthy of you, their teacher. It is not possible to tell you how much this has pleased our Magnificent Piero de' Medici, who loves you very much, dear father, and always speaks of you with great respect. And he asserts what I can freely agree to, that you are the greatest ornament of our age. Also Lorenzo de' Medici, the son of Piero, regards you with admiration. Because of the excellence of his divine talent, [Lorenzo] enjoys quality in all the arts, and thus he delights exceedingly in the greater refinement of your music. And for that reason he admires your art and respects you as a father.

Note

1 Borghetti 194.

Sources

Brandolini, Raffaele Lippo. *De musica et poetica opusculum,* Roma, Bibl. Casanatense, MS. 805, ff. 84v-87v, trans. Kaborycha

King Ferrante, *Letter to Lorenzo de' Medici* in Ernesto Pontieri, "La dinastia aragonese di Napoli e la casa de' Medici di Firenze," in *Archivio Storico per le Province Napoletane*, N.S. Anno XXVI, 1940, p. 300, cited by Atlas, p. 113, trans. Kaborycha.

Squarcialupi, *Letter to Dufay* in Frank D'Accone, "The Singers of San Giovanni in Florence during the 15th Century," *Journal of the American Musicological Society*, Vol. 14, No. 3 (Autumn 1961), 307–58, p. 322.

Further reading

Atlas, Allan W. *Music at the Aragonese court of Naples*, Cambridge UP, 1985.

Borghetti, Vincenzo. "Music and the Representation of Princely Power in 15th and 16th Century," *Acta Musicologica*, Vol. LXXX, No. 2 (2008).

Brandolini, Raffaele Lippo. *On Music and Poetry = De musica et poetica*, 1513 translated with an introduction and notes by Ann E. Moyer; with the assistance of Marc Laureys, Arizona Center for Medieval and Renaissance Studies, 2001.

Cummings, Anthony M. *The Lion's Ear: Pope Leo X, the Renaissance Papacy, and Music*, U Michigan P, 2012.

D'Accone, Frank. "Lorenzo the Magnificent and Music," in *Lorenzo il Magnifico e il suo mondo*, ed. Gian Carlo Garfagnini, Olschki, 1994.

38 Titian, his patron, and his guests

Titian, *Letter to Philip II*, 1560

Francesco Priscianese, *Letter to Lodovico Becci*, 1550

The Venetian artist Titian (Tiziano Vecellio, *c.*1488–1576) was recognized as one of the greatest painters in Europe during his lifetime; he accumulated honors and wealth far beyond the dreams of the average Renaissance artist. His international celebrity increased after he was introduced to Emperor Charles V in 1529; then, after being summoned to Augsburg in 1547 to paint for the emperor, Titian was awarded the Order of the Golden Spur and the title of Count Palatine. Thereafter, Titian created various works for Charles V (r.1519–56). However, it was the emperor's son Philip II who, as king of Spain (r.1556–98), became the greatest of Titian's patrons. The painter first met Philip, then crown prince, during his stay in Milan in 1549, and Titian painted *Danaë*, the first in a series of his large-scale paintings for Philip on erotic mythological themes (**#49**). The second time they met in person was in Augsburg in the winter of 1550–1. Titian essentially became court artist to the king of Spain, though without residing at the Spanish court. He was paid an annual salary to send regular shipments of religious and secular paintings, an arrangement that lasted for twenty-five years until Titian's death. In 1560, after sending Philip paintings on the *Diana and Acteon* theme, Titian had still not received a response or payment from the king, as indicated in the letter below. It is highly likely that Titian received help drafting this "daringly sarcastic letter"[1] from Pietro Aretino (**#29**). The friendship between the writer and painter was a close one, and mutually beneficial to the two men's careers. "He [Titian] developed an aristocratic and princely clientele only after Pietro Aretino arrived in Venice in 1527. Almost immediately the two men became close friends, virtually partners, with Aretino using his pen to advertise Titian to the nobility of Europe, and in turn acquiring prestige as an arbiter of taste and an intimate of the greatest painter of the day."[2] Titian, in turn, painted a flattering portrait of Aretino (1545, Pitti Palace, Florence), which burnished the writer's otherwise somewhat scurrilous reputation. Due to the stratospheric prices that his works commanded, Titian was able to enjoy life in luxurious surroundings, as described in a letter written by the Tuscan humanist Francesco Priscianese (1494–*c.*1575), who was a guest at a dinner party held at the artist's home one balmy summer night in 1550.

DOI: 10.4324/9781003284284-42

Titian, *Letter to Philip II, 1560*

Most perspicacious and most powerful king,

Seven months have elapsed since I sent the pictures which your Majesty ordered of me, and as I have received no notice of their arrival, I should greatly rejoice to hear that they gave pleasure, because if they should not have done so, according to the perfect judgment of your Majesty, I should take care to paint them afresh so as to correct past errors. If received at last with favor, I should have more courage to proceed with the *Fable of Jupiter and Europa* [*The Rape of Europa*] and the *Story of Christ in the Garden*, [*Agony in the Garden*, Prado, Madrid] and so to do something that might not be thought altogether unworthy of so great a King. The letters with which I was favored by your Majesty in respect of the money assigned to me at Genoa have not had any effect; from which it appears that he who can conquer the most powerful and proud of his enemies is not able to secure the obedience of his ministers, and I do not see how I can hope ever to obtain the sums granted to me by your Majesty's grace. I therefore humbly beg that the obstinate insolence of these subordinates may be chastised, either by ordering that my claims should be instantly satisfied, or by transferring the order for payment to Venice or elsewhere, so that your humble servant shall be enabled to obtain the fruits of your Majesty's liberality. My devotion further prompts me to ask your Majesty to order that the glorious and immortal victories of Caesar should be painted as a memorial to posterity, and of these I should wish to be the first to paint one, as a sign of my gratitude for the many benefits I have received from their Caesarean and Catholic Majesties. So I should esteem it a favor of your Majesty to let me know the light and configuration of the rooms where these pictures are to hang, and meanwhile, & etc. From Venice, April 22, 1560.

Your Majesty's humble servant.

Francesco Priscianese, *Letter to Lodovico Becci*, 1550

To the Very Reverend Messer Lodovico Becci and his [friend] Messer Luigi del Riccio,

I was invited on the calends of August to celebrate that type of Bacchanal which—I could not say why—is called *ferrare Agosto*,[3] so that for most of the evening it was debated in a delightful garden belonging to Messer Tiziano Vecellio, the superb Venetian painter (as everyone knows), a person truly suited to spice every worthy banquet with his pleasantries. There were gathered together with the said Messer Tiziano (because like seeks like) some of the most original minds to be found in this city, and of our own,[4] principally Messer Pietro Aretino,[5] the new miracle of nature, and beside him, one who is as great an imitator of nature with his chisel as the host of our gathering is with his paintbrush, Messer Jacopo Tatti called Sansovino,[6] as well as Messer Jacopo Nardi,[7] and myself being the fourth amidst such wisdom. Here, before the tables were put out, since the Sun (despite the shady setting) was making his power felt, we went inside. There we passed the time in contemplation of lifelike representation in most excellent paintings, of which the house was full. And everyone spoke with singular pleasure of the rare beauty of the garden, marveling at its charm. The house is located at the extreme part of Venice, on the sea, overlooking the lovely Island of Murano and other most beautiful views. As soon as the Sun went down, that part of the sea was filled with a thousand little gondolas adorned with the loveliest women and the air was ringing with many harmonious voices and musical instruments, which accompanied our joyous meal until midnight.

Notes

1 Wittkower 267.
2 Hope 8.
3 Ferragosto, celebrated on August 15, is the Catholic Feast of the Assumption of the Virgin Mary.
4 The guests were Tuscans, as was the writer and addressee.
5 See **#29**.
6 Known as Sansovino (Jacopo Tatti, 1486–1570), the Florentine sculptor and architect.
7 Jacopo Nardi (1476–1563) was a Florentine republican exile, author of various works including a history of Florence. He frequented the Orti Oricellari group along with Niccolò Machiavelli.

Sources

Titian, *Letter to Philip II* in J.A. Crowe and G.B. Cavalcaselle. *Titian: His Life and Times*, J. Murray, 1877, Vol. II, pp. 305–6, ed. Kaborycha.

Priscianese, *Letter to Becci* in Francesco Priscianese. *Della Lingua Latina Libri Sei*, Vincenzio Valgrisi alla bottega d'Erasino, 1550, pp, 398–401, trans. Kaborycha.

References

Hale, Sheila. *Titian: His Life*, Harper Collins, 2012.

Hope, Charles. "Titian as a Court Painter," *Oxford Art Journal*, Vol. 2, No. 2, Art and Society (April 1979), pp. 7–10.

Humfrey, Peter. *Titian: The Complete Paintings*, Abrams, 2007.

Padoan, Giorgio. "Titian's Letters," in *Titian: Prince of Painters*, ed. J. Manca, Marsilio Editori, 1990, pp. 43–52.

Wittkower, Rudolf and Margot Wittkower. *Born under Saturn: The Character and Conduct of Artists, a Documented History from Antiquity to the French Revolution*, Random House, 1963.

39 Perseus and his heroic sculptor

Benvenuto Cellini, *Autobiography*, 1562

Figure 4.5 Benvenuto Cellini, *Perseus and Medusa*, 1545–54 (Loggia dei Lanzi, Florence), is in the foreground, with Michelangelo's *David* (reproduction) beside the entry of the Palazzo Vecchio.

DOI: 10.4324/9781003284284-43

Benvenuto Cellini (1500–1571) was commissioned to create *Perseus and Medusa* by Duke Cosimo de' Medici. It is one of a group of impressive statues clustered around Florence's seat of power that represent triumphant male figures asserting the force of the Medici dynasty. The statue stands in the Loggia dei Lanzi[1] located beneath the Uffizi, once the official administrative center of the Grand Duchy of Tuscany, and directly across from the entrance of the Palazzo Vecchio. Cellini's sculpture faces Michelangelo's *David* (1501–4) and Baccio Bandinelli's *Hercules and Cacus* (1524–34), which frame the entrance to the building, while Giambologna's *Rape of a Sabine* (1581–83) looms behind *Perseus*. Across the Piazza della Signoria is Bartolomeo Ammannati's towering *Fountain of Neptune* (1550–75), and beside it stands Giambologna's *Equestrian Statue of Cosimo I* (1587–94). With the exception of the *David*, all these Renaissance statues were carried out under the patronage of the Medici, and apart from Donatello's *Judith and Holofernes* (*c.*1460), the piazza is dominated by victorious male figures. Cellini's muscular nude *Perseus* triumphantly raises aloft a severed female head; it belongs to Medusa, and though dead, the head is still writhing with snakes. Standing perfectly poised and untroubled, the hero tramples her decapitated body under his feet. Whereas the Medusa was shown as a horrid monster in antiquity—a single glance from the gorgon instantly turned men to stone and Perseus was only able to take aim and kill her by looking at her reflection in his shield—the body depicted by the Florentine artist is "a sensual, supine, albeit headless female, a titillating sexual fantasy. Though mutilated, the body is writhing with energy and desire."[2]

Duke Cosimo commissioned Cellini to sculpt the work in 1545. However, because of the difficulties of casting such a large figure in bronze, it was not completed until 1554. We know about the process of its casting, and much more, from Cellini's autobiography. It is a work in which, in the words of Oscar Wilde, "the supreme scoundrel of the Renaissance relates the story of his splendor and his shame." In this swashbuckling, over-the-top tale of his life, Cellini claims that during the Sack of Rome he fired the arquebus that shot and killed the Constable of Bourbon. He also describes in detail his sexual affairs with both women and men. He portrays himself as an irascible bully and braggart involved in numerous street brawls and as the darling of popes, dukes, and kings. He also tells us that Vasari had a nasty skin disease and that Baccio Bandinelli's *Hercules and Cacus* resembles a sack of melons. Cellini exposes the backbiting, competitive world of the Renaissance artist, while promoting his own legacy. Like the hero Perseus, the sculptor who created him is triumphant after overcoming staggering odds. In the following passage, the artist provides a firsthand account of the tumultuous final stages of the creation of his masterpiece after the duke had suggested that Cellini would be incapable of completing the statue.

Benvenuto Cellini, *Autobiography*, 1562

Description of the casting of Perseus

Abandoned thus to my own resources, I took new courage, and banished the sad thoughts which kept recurring to my mind, making me often weep bitter tears of repentance for having left France; for though I did so only to revisit Florence, my sweet birthplace, in order that I might charitably succor my six nieces, this good action, as I well perceived, had been the beginning of my great misfortune. Nevertheless, I felt convinced that when my *Perseus* was accomplished, all these trials would be turned to high felicity and glorious well-being.

Accordingly, I strengthened my heart, and with all the forces of my body and my purse, employing what little money still remained to me, I set to work. First, I provided myself with several loads of pinewood from the forests of Serristori, in the neighborhood of Montelupo. While these were on their way, I clothed my *Perseus* with the clay which I had prepared many months beforehand, in order that it might be duly seasoned. After making its clay tunic (for that is the term used in this art) and properly arming it and fencing it with iron girders, I began to draw the wax out by means of a slow fire. This melted and issued through numerous air-vents I had made; for the more there are of these, the better will the mold fill. When I had finished drawing off the wax, I constructed a funnel-shaped furnace all round the model of my *Perseus*. It was built of bricks, so interlaced, the one above the other, that numerous apertures were left for the fire to exhale at. Then I began to lay on wood by degrees, and kept it burning two whole days and nights. At length, when all the wax was gone, and the mold was well baked, I set to work at digging the pit in which to sink it. This I performed with scrupulous regard to all the rules of art. When I had finished that part of my work, I raised the mold by windlasses and stout ropes to a perpendicular position, and suspending it with the greatest care one cubit above the level of the furnace, so that it hung exactly above the middle of the pit, I next lowered it gently down into the very bottom of the furnace, and had it firmly placed with every possible precaution for its safety. When this delicate operation was accomplished, I began to bank it up with the earth I had excavated; and, ever as the earth grew higher, I introduced its proper air-vents, which were little tubes of earthenware, such as folk use for drains and such-like purposes. At length, I felt sure that it was admirably fixed, and that the filling-in of the pit and the placing of the air-vents had been properly performed. I also could see that my work people understood my method, which differed very considerably from that of all the other masters in the trade. Feeling confident, then, that I could rely upon them, I next turned to my furnace, which I had filled with numerous pigs of copper and other bronze stuff. The pieces were piled according to the laws of art, that is to say, so resting one upon the other that the flames could play freely through them, in order that the metal might heat and liquefy the sooner. At last, I called out heartily to set the furnace going. The logs of pine were heaped in, and, what with the unctuous resin of the wood and the good draft I had given, my furnace worked so well that I was obliged to rush from side to side to keep it going. The labor was more than I could stand; yet I forced myself to strain every nerve and muscle. To increase my anxieties, the workshop took fire, and we were afraid lest the roof should fall upon our heads; while, from the garden, such a storm of wind and rain kept blowing in, that it perceptibly cooled the furnace.

Battling thus with all these untoward circumstances for several hours, and exerting myself beyond even the measure of my powerful constitution, I could at last bear up no longer, and a sudden fever, of the utmost possible intensity, attacked me. I felt absolutely obliged to go and fling myself upon my bed. Sorely against my will having to drag myself away from the spot, I turned to my assistants, about ten or more in all, what with master-founders, hand-workers, country-fellows, and my own special journeymen, among whom was Bernardino Mannellini of Mugello, my apprentice through several years. To him in particular I spoke: "Look, my dear Bernardino, that you observe the rules which I have taught you; do your best with all dispatch, for the metal will soon be fused. You cannot go wrong; these honest men will get the channels ready; you will easily be able to drive back the two plugs with this pair of iron crooks; and I am sure that my mold will fill miraculously. I feel more ill than I ever did in all my life, and verily believe that it will kill me before a few hours are over." Thus, with despair at heart, I left them, and betook myself to bed.

No sooner had I got to bed, than I ordered my serving-maids to carry food and wine for all the men into the workshop; at the same time I cried: "I shall not be alive tomorrow." They tried to encourage me, arguing that my illness would pass over, since it came from excessive fatigue. In this way I spent two hours battling with the fever, which steadily increased, and calling out continually: "I feel that I am dying." My housekeeper, who was named Mona Fiore da Castel del Rio, a very notable manager and no less warm-hearted, kept chiding me for my discouragement; but, on the other hand, she paid me every kind attention which was possible. However, the sight of my physical pain and moral dejection so affected her, that, in spite of that brave heart of hers, she could not refrain from shedding tears; and yet, so far as she was able, she took good care I should not see them. While I was thus terribly afflicted, I beheld the figure of a man enter my chamber, twisted in his body into the form of a capital S. He raised a lamentable, doleful voice, like one who announces their last hour to men condemned to die upon the scaffold, and spoke these words: "O Benvenuto! your statue is spoiled, and there is no hope whatever of saving it." No sooner had I heard the shriek of that wretch than I gave a howl which might have been heard from the sphere of flame. Jumping from my bed, I seized my clothes and began to dress. The maids, and my lads, and everyone who came around to help me, got kicks or blows of the fist, while I kept crying out in lamentation: "Ah! traitors! enviers! This is an act of treason, done by malice aforethought! But I swear by God that I will sift it to the bottom, and before I die will leave such witness to the world of what I can do as shall make a score of mortals marvel."

When I had got my clothes on, I strode with soul bent on mischief toward the workshop; there I beheld the men, whom I had left erewhile in such high spirits, standing stupefied and downcast. I began at once and spoke: "Up with you! Attend to me! Since you have not been able or willing to obey the directions I gave you, obey me now that I am with you to conduct my work in person. Let no one contradict me, for in cases like this we need the aid of hand and hearing, not of advice." When I had uttered these words, a certain Maestro Alessandro Lastricati broke silence and said: "Look you, Benvenuto, you are going to attempt an enterprise which the laws of art do not sanction, and which cannot succeed." I turned upon him with such fury and so full of mischief, that he and all the rest of them exclaimed with one voice: "On then! Give orders! We will obey your least commands, so long as life is left in us." I believe they spoke thus feelingly because they thought I must fall shortly dead upon the ground. I went immediately to inspect the furnace, and found that the metal was all curdled; an accident which we express by "being caked." I told two of the hands to cross the road, and fetch from the house of the butcher Capretta a load of young oak-wood, which had lain dry for above a year; this wood had been previously offered me by Madame Ginevra, wife of the said Capretta. So soon as the first armfuls arrived, I began to fill the grate beneath the furnace. Now oak-wood of that kind heats more powerfully than any other sort of tree; and for this reason, where a slow fire is wanted, as in the case of gun-foundry, alder or pine is preferred. Accordingly, when the logs took fire, oh! how the cake began to stir beneath that awful heat, to glow and sparkle in a blaze! At the same time I kept stirring up the channels, and sent men upon the roof to stop the conflagration, which had gathered force from the increased combustion in the furnace; also I caused boards, carpets, and other hangings to be set up against the garden, in order to protect us from the violence of the rain.

When I had thus provided against these several disasters, I roared out first to one man and then to another: "Bring this thing here! Take that thing there!" At this crisis, when the whole gang saw the cake was on the point of melting, they did my bidding, each fellow working with the strength of three. I then ordered half a pig of pewter to be brought, which weighed about sixty pounds, and flung it into the middle of the cake inside the furnace. By this means, and by piling on wood and stirring now with pokers and now with iron rods, the curdled mass rapidly began to liquefy. Then, knowing I had brought the dead to life again, against the firm opinion of those ignoramuses, I felt such vigor fill my veins, that all those pains of fever, all those fears of death, were quite forgotten.

All of a sudden an explosion took place, attended by a tremendous flash of flame, as though a thunderbolt had formed and been discharged amongst us.

Unwonted and appalling terror astonished everyone, and me more even than the rest. When the din was over and the dazzling light extinguished, we began to look each other in the face. Then I discovered that the cap of the furnace had blown up, and the bronze was bubbling over from its source beneath. So I had the mouths of my mold immediately opened, and at the same time drove in the two plugs which kept back the molten metal. But I noticed that it did not flow as rapidly as usual, the reason being probably that the fierce heat of the fire we kindled had consumed its base alloy. Accordingly I sent for all my pewter platters, porringers, and dishes, to the number of some two hundred pieces, and had a portion of them cast, one by one, into the channels, the rest into the furnace. This expedient succeeded, and every one could now perceive that my bronze was in most perfect liquefaction, and my mold was filling; whereupon they all with heartiness and happy cheer assisted and obeyed my bidding, while I, now here, now there, gave orders, helped with my own hands, and cried aloud: "O God! Thou that by Thy immeasurable power didst rise from the dead, and in Thy glory didst ascend to heaven!" . . . even thus in a moment my mold was filled; and seeing my work finished, I fell upon my knees, and with all my heart gave thanks to God.

After all was over, I turned to a plate of salad on a bench there, and ate with hearty appetite, and drank together with the whole crew. Afterwards I retired to bed, healthy and happy, for it was now two hours before morning, and slept as sweetly as though I had never felt a touch of illness. My good housekeeper, without my giving any orders, had prepared a fat capon for my repast. So that, when I rose, about the hour for breaking fast, she presented herself with a smiling countenance, and said: "Oh! is that the man who felt that he was dying? Upon my word, I think the blows and kicks you dealt us last night, when you were so enraged, and had that demon in your body, as it seemed, must have frightened away your mortal fever! The fever feared that it might catch it too, as we did!" All my poor household, relieved in like measure from anxiety and overwhelming labor, went at once to buy earthen vessels in order to replace the pewter I had cast away. Then we dined together joyfully; nay, I cannot remember a day in my whole life when I dined with greater gladness or a better appetite.

Notes

1 A loggia is a covered patio or porch; this one takes its name from the duke's personal body guards, the company of lancers who were stationed there beginning in the sixteenth century.

2 Even 11.

Source

Benvenuto Cellini. *Autobiography*, trans. John Addington Symonds, 1887, pp. 430–36, ed. Kaborycha.

References

Corretti, Christine. *Cellini's Perseus and Medusa and the Loggia dei Lanzi: Configurations of the Body of State*, Brill, 2015.

Even, Yael. "The Loggia dei Lanzi: A Showcase of Female Subjugation," *Woman's Art Journal*, Vol. 12, No. 1 (Spring–Summer 1991), pp. 10–4.

Gallucci, Margaret A. *Benvenuto Cellini: Sexuality, Masculinity, and Artistic Identity in Renaissance Italy*, Palgrave Macmillan, 2003.

Gardner Coates, Victoria C. "'Ut vita scultura': Cellini's *Perseus* and the Self-fashioning of Artistic Identity," in *Fashioning Identities in Renaissance Art*, ed. Mary Rogers, Ashgate, 2000, pp. 149–61.

Mandel, Corinne. "Perseus and the Medici," *Storia dell'arte*, Vol. 87 (1996), pp. 168–87.

Pope-Hennessy, John. *Cellini*. Macmillan, 1985.

40 The performance of a renowned actor

Pierre de L'Estoile, *Journal entry describing the Gelosi*, 1577

Giuseppe Pavoni, *Diary of the Wedding Celebrations of Ferdinando de' Medici and Christine of Lorraine*, 1589

Tomaso Garzoni, *On actors and authors of comedies*, 1595

Gabriello Chiabrera, *Sonnet for Isabella Andreini*, 1601

The actor, poet, and playwright Isabella Andreini (1562–1604) belonged to a theater troupe known as the Compagnia dei Gelosi, with whom she performed a full spectrum of roles from boisterous comedy to high tragedy. The most celebrated Italian actor of her day, Andreini came to be recognized for the subtlety and intelligence of her performances, despite the general attitude at the time that women who exhibited themselves onstage were little better than prostitutes. Indeed, it is clear from the diary of Pierre de L'Estoile (1546–1611), who saw the Gelosi perform in Paris, that women's bodies were highly eroticized in these performances. Nevertheless, from their first appearance in the mid-sixteenth century, these professional Italian acting troupes included female members.[1] Literally translated as "comedy of the profession" or "guild," commedia dell'arte had its roots in improvised street theater, which was often bawdy and employed broad humor. However, Italian commedia dell'arte in the late sixteenth century was not the exclusively slapstick genre it is often identified with, as Isabella Andreini's career demonstrates. Andreini and the Gelosi toured Europe, performing for royalty, including the king of France, and in 1589 took part in the Florentine celebrations for the union of Grand Duke Ferdinando I de' Medici with Christine of Lorraine. The most lavish wedding festivities the Medici ever undertook, a year was spent in preparations for monthlong entertainments that accompanied the grand *entrata* (entry) of the royal bride into Tuscany; they included banquets, jousting, animal-baiting, parades, a public masquerade, a football game, and various spectacles including a mock naval battle at the Pitti Palace. At the theater in the Uffizi, over the course of a week, a series of dramatic performances known as the *intermedi* were performed. These avant-garde compositions based on ancient philosophical and mythological themes fused music, drama, and poetry and were accompanied by elaborate stage effects. One of the musicians involved was Jacopo Peri (1561–1633), who several years later would go on to compose *Dafne*, the first opera. Along with these exalted theatrical pieces, the Gelosi were hired to perform the play *La Pazzia* (*Madness*), written by and starring

DOI: 10.4324/9781003284284-44

Isabella Andreini. Well-known for her ingenious improvisations, Andreini's mad scene—by turns heartbreaking and hysterically funny—brought down the house, as recounted by an eyewitness, the Bolognese envoy Giuseppe Pavoni. Echoing Pavoni's admiration are the words of two contemporaries: the popular author of encyclopedic treatises, Tomaso Garzoni (1549–1589), and the poet Gabriello Chiabrera (1552–1638), both enthusiastic fans of Andreini.

Pierre de L'Estoile, *Journal entry describing the Gelosi in Paris*, 1577

The women . . . puff out their gilded, shining chests like soldiers showing off uniforms. Their chests are naked, and the breasts sway up and down, perpetually in motion . . . corresponding to the corruption of the age. . . . The Gelosi have been permitted to take the stage again, thus bringing honor on the heads of actors, buffoons, whores and pederasts.

Giuseppe Pavoni, *Diary of the Wedding Festivities of Ferdinando de' Medici with Christine of Lorraine*, 1589

Fooled by Flavio's treachery, knowing no remedy for her illness, she gave in completely to her pain. Vanquished by passion, overcome by rage, and completely beside herself, she ran like a madwoman throughout the city. She stopped everyone she met, speaking to passersby in Spanish, Greek, Italian, and many other languages, but always nonsensically. Among other things she performed, she began to speak French, and to sing certain songs (also in French), which gave so much pleasure to the Most Serene Bride, that words cannot express it. After that she started to imitate the dialects of all her fellow actors—Pantalone, Gratiano, Zanni, Pedrolino, Francatrippe, Burattino, Captain Cardone, and Franceschina[2]—and she did this so naturally and with so many absurdities, that words cannot describe the worthiness and virtue of this woman. Finally, by the fiction of Magic, she returned to her first self with the help of certain waters given her to drink. Then, in an elegant and learned style, explaining the passions and travails of love that all undergo who find themselves trapped in similar nets, she ended the Comedy, demonstrating in the performance of her Madness her healthy and learned intellect.

Tomaso Garzoni, *On actors and authors of comedies and tragedies*, 1595

The gracious Isabella, dignity of the scene, ornament of the stage, a superb spectacle no less of *virtù* than of beauty, has so illuminated the style of her profession, that while the world lasts, while the centuries endure, while times and seasons have life, every voice, every language, every cry, will echo the celebrated name of Isabella.

Gabriello Chiabrera, *Sonnet for Isabella Andreini*, 1601

The day on which, sublime in lowly cloaks,
Isabella imitated high madness;
And exalted with angelic features
Had greater glory from the wisdom of others;

Then, wise among the sound, wise among the songs,
She did not move a foot that did not bring forth Amore,
Nor lifted voice that did not create lovers,
Nor made a smile that did not delight a heart.

Whoever was that day to gaze happily,
For all else of this world desire ceased,
That his life forever was serene.

O! of the stage sweetest Siren,
O! of Italian theatres the Fenice,
O! among Thespians unsurpassable Clio.

Notes

1 "The earliest commedia contract dates from 1545, and the company of players it unites is all-male. However, in a contract recorded from Rome in 1564, a woman's name appears." McGill 61.
2 These are all stock characters in commedia dell' arte.

Sources

Pierre de L'Estoile, *Journal* in Kathryn Bosi, "Accolades for an Actress: On Some Literary and Musical Tributes for Isabella Andreini," *Recercare*, Vol. 15 (2003), 73–117, p. 77n.

Giuseppe Pavoni, *Diary of the 1589 Wedding Festivities* in Robert Henke, *Performance and Literature in the Commedia dell'Arte*, Cambridge UP, 2002, pp. 103–4.

Tomaso Garzoni. *On actors and authors* in *Piazza Universale di tutte le professioni del mondo*, Somasco, 1595, in Kathleen McGill, "Women and Performance: The Development of Improvisation by the Sixteenth-Century Commedia Dell'Arte." *Theatre Journal*, Vol. 43, No. 1 (1991), 59–69, p. 64.

Gabriello Chiabrera, *Sonnet* in Anne MacNeil, "The Divine Madness of Isabella Andreini," *Journal of the Royal Musical Association*, Vol. 120, No. 2 (1995), 195–215, p. 195.

References

Andrews, Richard. "Isabella Andreini and Others: Women on Stage in the Late Cinquecento," *Women in Italian Renaissance Culture and Society*, ed. Letizia Panizza, Legenda, 2000, pp. 316–33.

Clubb, Louise George. *Italian Drama in Shakespeare's Time*, Yale UP, 1989.

Macneil, Anne. *Music and Women of the Commedia dell'Arte in the Late Sixteenth Century*, Oxford University Press, 2003.

Saslow, James M. *The Medici Wedding of 1589: Florentine Festival as Theatrum Mundi*, Yale UP, 1996.

Part V

Loves, ideal and real

Figure 5.1 Correggio, *Io and Jupiter*, *c.*1530, Kunsthistorisches Museum, Vienna.

41 The notary who invented the love sonnet

Giacomo da Lentini, *Four Sonnets*, *c.*1240–50

"How do I love thee? Let me count the ways." So begins the forty-third of Elizabeth Barrett Browning's *Sonnets from the Portuguese* published in 1850. Since Shakespeare's time, the word "sonnet" has been linked with the love lyric. The English word comes from the Italian *sonetto*, which in turn derives from "little song" in Provençal, the language of the medieval wandering troubadours. The sonnet, however, was invented in Sicily by the poet Giacomo da Lentini (*c.*1210–*c.*1260).[1] He signed his poems "the Notary," indicating his official position at the court of Emperor Frederick II in Palermo, but little else is known about his life. Forty-one of the Notary's poems have come down to us, more than exist by any other poet of the so-called "Sicilian School." These poets were secretaries, judges, and notaries educated in law, who participated in the vibrant cultural life at the court of Frederick, himself an accomplished poet.[2] After the death of Frederick at mid-century, the sonnets written by these Sicilian lawyer–poets migrated to the Italian Peninsula, where they inspired a whole new group of mostly Tuscan poets. One of them was Dante, who gave a name to their style of poetry, calling it the *dolce stil novo* (the "sweet new style"), and he cast himself as the leader of this poetic revolution. While admiring the verses of Giacomo da Lentini, Dante felt that he and his fellow *stilnovisti* were reinvigorating the love lyric, expressing sentiments in language that was fresher—in Dante's own words, writing "in that fashion that love dictates."[3] For although sonnets may deal with other topics, it is love that is most closely associated with this poetic form. Love is the central focus of Dante's sonnets in his collection, the *Vita Nuova*, and Petrarch's 317 sonnets in his *Canzoniere*. Moreover, the love sonnets of Dante, Petrarch, and Giacomo da Lentini all have their roots in conventions of courtly love expressed in medieval troubadour poetry—most notably the feudal duty of the lover to serve his lady. In addition to professing his love and celebrating the rapture it brings, the poet inevitably complains as well, of the pain suffered from her cruelty.

DOI: 10.4324/9781003284284-46

Giacomo da Lentini, "*Si come il sol*"

Just like the sun that sends its rays
Through glass without fragmenting it,
Or ladies' mirrored images
Pass through the eyes and go beyond,

So Love will strike where he intends
And send his dart from where he stands:
It strikes the place that's least foreseen,
Goes through the eyes and cleaves the heart.

The place where Love's dart comes to rest
Flames up as soon as it is struck
And burns within, unseen without;

And it joins two hearts into one
And teaches them the art of love:[4]
Each loves the other equally.

Giacomo da Lentini, "*Si alta amanza*"

A love so noble seized my heart
That I despair of its success:
To choose to love a bird of prey[5]
May come from pride, but not from fault,

For Love will prod it and bestir
The fragrant flower, a gentle breeze
Will bend a lofty tree, soft tears
Will always cut the diamond's rough.

So, Lady, if my tears and plaint
Can crack the diamond's stoniness,
The pain of love that burdens me

Might moderate your arrogance,
Make you subdue your stoniness,
And, Lady, light the fire of love in you.

Giacomo da Lentini, "*Certo me par*"

It seems quite clear a noble lord should base
His rule at first on forcefulness,
So that he's feared by men of evil will
And those whose will is good may strengthen it.

In doing so he might achieve great fame
And bring a happy end to his regime,
For if he starts by acting ruthlessly,
He still can end his rule by being kind.

But, Love, in you I find the opposite,
Like someone who is full of perfidy,
Since at the start you don't at all seem rank,

Then down the road you bare your evil hand:
You're least endeared to those who serve you best,
So I declare you lord of treachery.

Giacomo da Lentini, "*Sì como 'l parpaglion*"

Just as the butterfly in nature's grasp
Does not recoil from rushing into fire,
You've forced me to react, my noble one,
And do not care if I catch fire and burn.

Approaching you, my heart is reassured
Believing such bright light is meant for play:
For like a child I overlook the heat,
But then I've never had good luck at all.

I mean the heart, not having what it wants,
Must die by burning in the lovely flame,
To end its life just as the phoenix does;

Then love by nature calls it back to life,
And beauty raining down provides it warmth,
Restoring it to life when all is done.

Source

Giacomo da Lentini, *The Complete Poetry*, trans. Richard Lansing, U Toronto P, 2018, pp. 113, 131, 135, 136.

References

Barolini, Teodolinda. "Dante and the Lyric Past," in *The Cambridge Companion to Dante*, ed. Rachel Jacoff, Cambridge UP, 1993, pp. 14–33.

Levin, Phillis, ed. *The Penguin Book of the Sonnet: 500 Years of a Classic Tradition in English*, Penguin Books, 2001.

Mallette, Karla. *The Kingdom of Sicily, 1100–1250: A Literary History*, U Pennsylvania P, 2005.

Notes

1 The Italian sonnet originally consisted of two rhymed quatrains followed by two rhymed tercets; over time, poets writing in various languages have introduced variations in the fourteen-line pattern, as well as the rhyme scheme.

2 For an intriguing discussion of the cultural context within which the sonnet form originated see Levin xl–xlvii.

3 Barolini 24, citing *Purgatory* 24: 52–4.

4 "*The art of love*: The phrase 'l'arte de l'amore' explicitly recalls the title of Ovid's *Ars amatoria* and Andreas Capellanus's *De arte honeste amandi*. Ovidian imagery pervades the sonnet." (RL)

5 "The *bird of prey* ('aguila') to which the lady is compared is the eagle." (RL) Falconry was a popular pastime at court; Frederick himself was the author of a treatise on the topic.

42 A mystic marriage with Christ

Raymond of Capua, *Life of St. Catherine of Siena*, 1395

Figure 5.2 Giovanni di Paolo, *St. Catherine's Mystic Marriage*, 1460s, Metropolitan Museum of Art. This painting is one of a series of ten small panels by Sienese painter Giovanni di Paolo (di Grazia, *c.*1399–1482) depicting scenes from the life of St. Catherine. It was once part of an altarpiece that the Sienese guild of Pizzicaiuoli (sellers of dry goods) commissioned to hang in their chapel in the church of the hospital of Santa Maria della Scala in Siena

DOI: 10.4324/9781003284284-47

Caterina di Iacopo di Benincasa was twelve years old when her parents began thinking of finding her a husband. They tried to persuade her, but Caterina refused, preferring to live chastely and devote herself to God. Some years later she did marry—she experienced a mystic vision of a wedding ceremony in which she was the bride and Christ the groom. This story became an essential element in the legend surrounding St. Catherine of Siena (**#24**). She told it to the Dominican friar who was her confessor, Raymond of Capua (Raimondo della Vigna, 1330–1399), and he recorded it in the *Life of St. Catherine* (*Legenda maior*). Though hers is a dramatic and colorful account, it is important to note that Catherine was not the first woman to experience such a mystic marriage. Famously, her namesake, St. Catherine of Alexandria, who was believed to have been born a thousand years before the Sienese saint, had a vision of a mystic marriage with Christ. Images of the marriages of both Catherines are represented repeatedly in Renaissance art; sometimes the bridegroom is represented as an adult, sometimes as an infant. And there were many other holy women who had a similar vision: St. Angela of Foligno (1248–1309), St. Teresa of Avila (1515–1582), St. Catherine de' Ricci (1522–1590), and St. Maria Maddalena de' Pazzi (1566–1607), to name a few. According to the *Catholic Encyclopedia,* "from the earliest times to the present, history has recorded seventy-seven mystical marriages."[1] Of course, nuns are all technically "brides of Christ," and during the Renaissance, their symbolic nuptials—the vestition, profession, and consecration ceremonies—closely reflected many of the customs observed in secular weddings. These included giving a dowry in the presence of a notary; placing a ring on the bride's finger; the wearing of a bridal crown; receiving a trousseau; and holding a banquet with invited guests. The similarity of the rituals intensified a nun's commitment to her heavenly spouse so vividly recounted in Catherine's vision. Catherine of Siena, however, never became a nun, instead she chose to be a Dominican tertiary rather than live enclosed in a convent.

Raymond of Capua, *Life of Saint Catherine of Siena*, 1395

Chapter XI: Of her marriage with our Lord, and of the miraculous ring that she received.

The soul of Catherine became daily more enriched with the grace of the Savior. She flew rather than walked in the paths of virtue, and she conceived the holy desire of arriving at so perfect a degree of faith that nothing would henceforth be capable of separating her from her divine Spouse, whom her heart aspired alone to please. She therefore besought God to augment her faith and render it sufficiently strong to resist any and every enemy. Our Blessed Lord answered her, "I will espouse you in faith." And each time Catherine renewed her prayer, Jesus Christ repeated the same answer.

One day, at the approach of the holy season of Lent, when Christians celebrate the Carnival . . . Catherine withdrew into her cell, there to enjoy her Spouse more intimately by fasting and prayer: she reiterated her petition with more fervor than ever, and our Lord answered her: "Because you have shunned the vanities of the world and forbidden [yourself] pleasure, and have fixed on me alone all the desires of your heart, I intend, while your family is rejoicing in profane feasts and festivals, to celebrate the wedding which is to unite me to your soul. I am going, according to my promise, to espouse you in faith."

Jesus Christ then spoke once more, when the Blessed Virgin appeared; and with his glorious Mother, St. John the Evangelist, the apostle St. Paul, St. Dominic, the founder of her Order, and with them, the prophet David who drew from his harp tones of heavenly sweetness. The Mother of God took in her holy hand, the right hand of Catherine, in order to and present it to her Son, asking Him to deign to espouse her in faith. The Savior consented to it with love, and offered her a golden ring, set with four precious stones, in the center of which blazed a magnificent diamond.[2] He placed it himself on Catherine's finger, saying to her: "I your Creator and Redeemer, espouse you in Faith and you shall preserve it pure, until we celebrate together in Heaven the eternal nuptials of the Lamb. Daughter, now act courageously; accomplish without fear the works that my Providence will confide to you; you are armed with Faith, you will triumph over all your enemies."

The vision disappeared, and the ring remained on the finger of Catherine. *She* saw it, but it was invisible to others! She acknowledged to me, while blushes mantled her cheek, that it never left her, and that she was never weary with admiring it. There was already one Catherine, queen and martyr, who, after baptism, espoused our Lord. We have here a second, who, after many victories won of the flesh and the devil, celebrated also her regal espousals with Jesus Christ.

Notes

1 Poulain, Augustin. "Mystical Marriage." *The Catholic Encyclopedia*. Vol. 9, Robert Appleton Company, 1910.

2 For a different version of Catherine's mystic marriage, with a fuller discussion of the ring, see Walker Bynum 174–5; 377 n.135.

Source

Raymond of Capua. *The Life of St. Catherine of Sienna*, trans. the Ladies of the Sacred Heart, P. J. Kennedy & Sons, 1862, pp. 75–76.

References

Bynum, Caroline Walker. *Holy Feast and Holy Fast: The Religious Significance of Food to Medieval Women*, U California P, 1987.

Christiansen, Keith, Laurence B. Kanter and Carl Brandon Strehlke. *Painting in Renaissance Siena, 1420–1500*, Abrams, 1988.

Kaftal, George. *St. Catherine in Tuscan Painting*, Blackfriars, 1949.

Klapisch-Zuber, Christiane. "Zaccharias, or the Ousted Father: Nuptial Rites in Tuscany between Giotto and the Council of Trent," in *Women, Family, and Ritual in Renaissance Italy*, U Chicago P, 1985, pp. 178–212.

Lowe, Kate. "Secular Brides and Convent Brides: Wedding Ceremonies in Italy During the Renaissance and Counter-Reformation," in *Marriage in Italy, 1300–1650*, ed. Trevor Dean and K.J.P. Lowe, Cambridge UP, 1998, pp. 41–65.

Poulain, Augustin. "Mystical Marriage," *The Catholic Encyclopedia*, vol. 9, Robert Appleton Company, 1910.

43 A record of life's loves and sorrows

Giovanni di Paolo Morelli, *Memoirs*, 1393–1411

Giovanni di Paolo Morelli (1371–1444) was born into a prominent Florentine merchant family; his father, the proprietor of a wool dying company, died in 1374, leaving behind a wife and four children. Along with his older brother and two sisters, the boy was raised in the home of his mother's second husband. Unlike his father, Giovanni was not involved in business, but lived off income from various investments and real estate holdings. Records from the 1427 Florentine Catasto (income tax) indicate that he was the 122nd richest person out of 10,000 heads of household. His first marriage was with Caterina Alberti, and the couple had seven children, four boys and three girls; however, only one child survived to adulthood and outlived them. After Caterina's death, Giovanni remarried in 1415, but it was not a happy match and the couple separated, leading to bitter legal battles. Throughout his life Morelli was active in the political sphere and a supporter of Cosimo de' Medici. He held many public offices, attaining the highest office in Florentine government, standardbearer of justice, in 1441. Morelli also served as captain of Pisa in 1427, and *podestà* of the town of Montepulciano in 1444, the year of his death. We know some of this information through official documents, but the extremely detailed information available to us about Morelli's personal life comes from his *ricordi* or memoirs. It was a common practice among Florentines at this time to record family and business information for future generations (see also Gregorio Dati, #73). Few of these memorialists were as expressive with their emotions as Morelli, however. In the following selections, Giovanni recalls the painful loss of three people he loved: his sister, Mea (short for Bartolomea); an unnamed woman to whom he had been engaged before marrying Caterina; and his eldest son, Alberto.

Giovanni di Paolo Morelli, *Memoirs*, 1393–1411

Bartolomea di Paolo Morelli

The first fruit of Paolo's marriage was a baby girl; she was born on Monday, June 23rd, at seven thirty, in the year of Our Lord 1365.[1] She was baptized in the Baptistry of San Giovanni the following Saturday morning the 28th of

DOI: 10.4324/9781003284284-48

that month. The names given to her were Giovanna and Bartolomea; Lione Lioni, Tommaso di Bese Busini, and the innkeeper Francesco Brunellini acted as her godfathers. She was always called Mea.

Mea was of normal height, with beautiful blond hair, a very fine figure, and so amiable that she dripped with charm. Her hands were like ivory, and so shapely that they seemed to have been painted by Giotto; they were long and soft, with tapering fingers and long, shapely nails, pink and clear. Her beauty was matched by her talents, for she could do any kind of women's work with her own hands; she was extremely adept in everything she did. Her speech was refined and pleasing, her actions pure and temperate, her words effectual. She was a spirited, frank woman with the mettle of a man, and abounded in every virtue. She could read and write as well as any man; she sang and danced perfectly, and could have served men or women at table as adroitly as any young man used to serving at wedding banquets or similar occasions. She was expert at running a household, without a hint of avariciousness or stinginess. But she made the most of everything, admonishing and guiding her household with good teachings and her own good example, living a joyful, happy life. She wisely set about making all of the various members of her household happy, allaying every trouble, anger, or sadness that she might see in any of them. She handled everything wisely and with benevolence, and, as you shall see, she had to deal with her husband's family, which was large and unruly.

The conservators of his family and hers arranged for Mea to be married to Antonio d'Agnolo Barucci; she had a dowry of one thousand five hundred florins. Antonio lived with his father and mother, who were quite old, but prosperous, and with a wretched brother of his, who also took a wife at the same time. They also had two sisters, both grown and married, and two nephews, good youths, by one of the sisters. I have told all this so that I might return to what I said before: that Mea, wise and discerning as she was, was loved by everyone, although there was little harmony among the other members of the family. Her goodness was the more commendable, for where there was great discord and scandal, she alone was loved by all. She managed to bring peace and harmony to many unpleasant situations among them.

Mea was married in 1380, and Antonio and his brother Francesco put on a great, joyful celebration. At that time the Barucci family lived in great state and had a fortune of twenty thousand florins; they were wool merchants, much loved by everyone, wise, pleasant, and very respectable. Mea had four children with Antonio, but none of them lived longer than two years; the last, a baby boy, was born on the 8th of February, 1387, and was named Agnolo. Mea had been unwell for about a week when she gave birth to this baby in the eighth month of her pregnancy; she never recovered, but died of that same illness on Saturday the 15th of February, at the eighth hour. The baby died the next day, so Mea left no offspring. She was buried in the church of Santa Croce, under the transept, on the left side of Agnolo Barucci's tomb.

As you enter under the transept of the church, there is a door that leads to a sort of vault on the right side, along the wall. I want to describe this very clearly, for seeing where her bones are buried should make us all think of her goodness. I especially entreat everyone who is descended from Paolo Morelli to go and see the place where Mea lies, at least on All Souls Day, and to pray to God for the well-being of her soul. For the true light and fruit of her soul are prayer and almsgiving; may God grant that they help her blessed soul.

Of the first woman whom Giovanni Morelli took to wife

On the fifteenth day of December 1395, I, Giovanni di Paolo Morelli, became betrothed to Caterina, the daughter of Alberto di Luigi degli Alberti; the middlemen were Messer Lotto Castellani and Agnolo Ricoveri. I got a dowry with her of a thousand florins (the document was drawn up by Ser Michele Aldobrandini, who lives in Porta Rossa). I married her on the 27th of January at our property near San Gaggio. I think that this marriage greatly diminished my honor and my prospects in the government; I would have done better if I had married into another family. I believe that God determines the day that the man and woman are born who are destined to marry. I say this because originally I had agreed to marry another woman, and in the hopes of being with her I lost out on the opportunity to make many advantageous connections that I could have made. The father of that woman betrayed me; he had promised me her hand in marriage, via an intermediary, and later he shook my hand in the church of Santa Croce, and I shook his. He did this because he believed that it would be to his advantage. I ended up suffering greatly because of this, because I loved the woman and had wanted to make her my wife from the time that she was very young. Later I came to realize that rather than a misfortune, this was a great boon from God and from St. Catherine—who, on account of the great devotion I have for her, I begged to bring about what was most advantageous for me and for my family and for my soul. And I truly believe that she heard my prayer, as unworthy as I am. So I am content with what she granted me, and I hope that I will continue to derive the benefit that one can hope for in this world; I believe that it all turned out for the best.

The illness of my eldest son Alberto

During these dark, unpleasant times for me, on account of the heavy, complicated burdens I have always had to bear, on Monday morning the 19th of May, 1406, my eldest son Alberto[2] was taken ill, with blood flowing out of his nose. He had had three nosebleeds the previous day and night, before we realized that he had a fever. On Monday morning while he was at school, the fever seized him, blood flowed out of his nose, and he lost control of his bowels. It pleased God for him to live sixteen days, in great pain and suffering, until Friday night June 5th, at the third hour. His illness took this course: he continuously had a fever, which would get higher every evening; he grew worse day after day. After two days, during which he hadn't been able to keep anything in his stomach, he got a pain below his liver, above where the thigh joins the body. The pain was horrifying and excruciating, and for sixteen days he got no relief, nor did those who were caring for him; he cried out in pain continuously. His body was swollen, and he seemed to be in a paroxysm of pain. There is no heart so hard that wouldn't have felt pity for him, seeing him in so much pain. He beseeched God and the Virgin Mary many times, asking that the painting of Our Lady be brought to him; he embraced it with innumerable supplications, prayers, and vows; no one could be so hard-hearted as not to be moved to great pity at the sight of him. He adjured his father, his mother, his relatives, and whoever was present, with such humility and such moving words that it was indescribable. At last he died; all the help we tried to give him, all our prayers and supplications and vows were of no avail; God wanted his life to come to an end!

May it please God to have brought to an end the strife, toil, and tribulation that to my mind followed my son from the time he was a little child. Of his own volition, at the age of four he wanted to come into my shop; at six, he knew the Psalms; at eight, the rudiments of Latin grammar. He knew how to write, and sent letters in his own hand to his cousins or mother when they were in the country. At nine years of age, he read the Latin authors and learned to read business letters. He had a good memory, spoke well, and could retain what he had learned; he had a pleasing appearance, and was gentle and well-mannered. He liked to take risks and was a little wild. The death of this child was an incalculable loss to me and his mother; it saddened his relatives and neighbors, his teacher, his fellow students, the peasants at our home in the country, our servants, and anyone who had ever known or seen him. His body was laid to rest on Friday, June 5, at the 11th hour, in the church of Santa Croce, in our family sepulcher, in the passage where the men are buried; it was not out of order to bestow this honor upon him. May God give his soul repose in Heaven, and may it please him to give life to Alberto's father, mother, brothers, and sisters, if that should be best for their souls; if not, may God do his holy will.

I could never have imagined that God taking my son from me, passing from this life to the next, could have been and continues to be such a knife in my heart. Many months have passed since the time of Alberto's death, and neither his mother nor I can forget. We continuously have his image before us—all his ways, the things he said and did—reminding us of him day and night, at breakfast, at supper, in the house, outside, sleeping, waking, in the country, in Florence. In any way we think about him, it keeps a knife in our hearts. And truly, this is not happening because we are obsessed with him; it's just the opposite. From the day he left us, we have tried to keep him out of our thoughts as much as possible, except when we are praying. After he died, we left the house and stayed away a month before any of us returned; and then for the entire summer no one slept in his room; and for more than a year after he died, I, Giovanni, didn't enter his room, for no other reason than overwhelming grief. May God grant that this shall not be a reason for hastening the end of our lives!

Notes

1 Giovanni's father was Paolo (Pagolo) di Bartolomeo Morelli; the baby girl mentioned here is Giovanni's older sister.
2 Morelli records the birth of Alberto earlier in his memoir as March 10, 1396, which is 1397 in modern dating. Hence, Alberto was nine years old when he became ill.

Source

Giovanni Morelli, *Memoirs* in *Merchant Writers: Florentine Memoirs from the Middle Ages and Renaissance*, ed. Vittore Branca, trans. Murtha Baca, U Toronto P, 2015, pp. 128–30, 182, 224–25.

References

Ciappelli, Giovanni. *Memory, Family, and Self: Tuscan Family Books and Other European Egodocuments (14th–18th century)*, Brill, 2014.
Herlihy, David and Christine Klapisch-Zuber. *Tuscans and Their Families: A Study of the Florentine Catasto*, Yale UP, 1985.
Ross, James Bruce. "The Middle Class Child in Urban Italy, Fourteenth to Early Sixteenth Century," in *The History of Childhood*, ed. Lloyd DeMause, Harper & Row, 1975, pp. 183–228.

44 Two extramarital encounters described

Aeneas Sylvius Piccolomini, *The Story of Two Lovers*, 1444

Aeneas Sylvius Piccolomini, *Letter to his father*, 1443

Before he became Pope Pius II, Enea Silvio Bartolomeo Piccolomini (Aeneas Sylvius Piccolomini, 1405–1464) was already well-known and recognized for his brilliant mind, eloquence, and literary skills. Enea Silvio was crowned poet laureate by Emperor Frederick III at the Imperial Diet of Frankfurt in 1442. Then, in addition to his many works of poetry and prose in Latin, in 1444 he wrote an erotic novella titled *De duobus amantibus historia* (*The Story of Two Lovers*). The tale of an adulterous love affair, similar to those in Boccaccio's *Decameron*, the book became wildly popular; by 1500 it was printed in Latin in thirty-seven editions and translated into a variety of languages. The story is set in the winter of 1432–33 when Emperor Sigismund passed through Siena on his way to Rome to be crowned by Pope Eugenius IV. At that time, Enea Silvio was employed as secretary to a cardinal, and he became acquainted with members of the official delegation. It is believed that the plot was inspired by the true story of the love affair of his friend Kaspar Schlick, the emperor's chancellor, with a married Sienese lady. Two years after writing this book, Piccolomini took holy orders. He was appointed bishop of Trieste in 1447, then bishop of Siena in 1450, and he became a cardinal in 1456. Fourteen years after writing *The Story of Two Lovers*, in 1458 Enea Silvio was elected Pope Pius II. Once he became pope, he downplayed much of his earlier profane writings, as well as many details of his past life—his motto as pope became: "reject Aeneas and remember Pius." As a young man, he had many love affairs, which produced at least two illegitimate children. In a 1443 letter, Enea Silvio describes one of these liaisons to his father.

Aeneas Sylvius Piccolomini, *The Story of Two Lovers*, 1444

[*The lovers have finally managed to arrange a tryst and Lucretia, by dropping a jewelry box from her window, gets her husband to open the door and Eurialus slips in, hiding himself in a closet.*]

DOI: 10.4324/9781003284284-49

Having closed the door, she said,

"Come out my Eurialus, come out my beloved, my supremest pleasure, come out, wellspring of my delights, honeycomb of my joy, come, my incomparable sweetness. Now we are safe, and the field lies open for us to talk freely; now it is safe for us to embrace. Fortune wanted to hinder our kisses, but the gods look with favor on our love and would not abandon such faithful lovers. Come now to my arms, there is nothing any longer to fear, my lily and crown of roses. Why do you stay there, what are you afraid of? I'm here, your Lucretia. Why do you hesitate to embrace Lucretia?"

Eurialus, once his terror had finally passed, collected himself and enfolding the woman in his arms, said,

"I have never been so afraid; however, for you such troubles are worth enduring. Without hardship no one deserves such sweet kisses and embraces as these. And to tell the truth, I have paid well for such a great reward. If after death I could return to life and enjoy you fully, I would wish to die a thousand times, if your embraces were to be bought at this price. O my happiness, o my beatitude, is this a vision I behold, or is it reality? Is it you in my arms or am I deceived by empty dreams? You are here for certain—I possess you!"

Lucretia was dressed in a filmy shift that clung smoothly to her limbs, neither her breasts nor backside were hidden, the lines of her body as completely on display as the brightest constellation in the sky [the Bear]. Her neck was white as the snow, the light of her eyes like the splendor of the Sun, her gaze merry, her face eager, her cheeks like lilies mixed with red roses, a sweet and modest smile upon her lips, her ample bosom, with breasts firm like two pomegranates that palpitated and aroused longing. Eurialus could hold back his excitement no longer, and forgetting his fear, threw off all restraint and clasping the woman, said,

"Now let us enjoy the fruits of love!"

And to these words, he matched the deeds. The woman made some resistance, saying she was worried about propriety and her reputation and that her love required no more than words and kisses. Smiling at these words, Eurialus said,

"Either it is known that I came here or it is not known. If it is known, there is no one who will not suspect all the rest and it's foolish to suffer shame without having committed the offence. And if it is not known, no one need know. This is a token of love and I will die before I am deprived of it."

"But it's a crime," said Lucretia.

"It would be a crime," replied Eurialus, "not to take advantage of good things when one can. Must I really lose such a sought-after, much desired opportunity that has been granted me?"

And removing Lucretia's garment, he effortlessly won over the woman who resisted, but who did not want to win. And Venus did not cause his hunger to be sated, as with Amnon once he had known Tamar,[1] but aroused even greater amorous thirst. Nevertheless, aware of the danger, after drinking some wine and eating a bit, Eurialus left, against Lucretia's wishes.

Aeneas Sylvius Piccolomini, *Letter to his father*, 1443

Aeneas Sylvius, poet, sends manifold greetings to his father, Silvio.

Father, you write that you are uncertain whether to rejoice or to mourn that the Lord has given me progeny. Although I see the cause for joy, I do not see one for sorrow. What is sweeter for a human being than to beget someone similar to himself, both to extend his bloodline and for you to have someone to leave behind? What is more blessed on earth than to see one's children's children? Truly, it is an enormous pleasure for me that my seed was fruitful and that, before I die, something of me remains. I give thanks, Father, to the Lord who prefigured a woman's childbearing in the sea, that a little Aeneas will play near you and my mother, and that the grandfather will supply the comfort that a father should supply. If my birth was a joy to you, Father, why should my son not be a joy to me? Will not an infant's face also give joy to you when you see my image in it? Will it not be a pleasure to you when a child hangs from your neck and utters childish words of coaxing?

But you say I should bewail my crime—that I begot my son in sin. I do not know what opinion you have of me. Certainly, you begot no son of stone or iron, being flesh yourself. You know what kind of rooster you were. I am no eunuch, nor one of the frigid. Nor am I a hypocrite, wishing to seem, rather than to be, good. I will admit my error freely because I am neither more holy than David, nor wiser than Solomon. This fault is ancient and entrenched, but I do not know anyone who lacks it. It is quite clear that this plague, if it is a plague to use nature's gifts—although I do not see why sexual intercourse ought to be condemned so much—is broadly compatible with nature, which does nothing wrongly. In all lovers it arouses this appetite so that the human race will be continued.

You say, I think, that there are certain limits within which this is permissible, nor should this appetite be indulged outside the legitimate bonds of matrimony. This fault rightly and often is admitted into the precincts of marriage. There also are certain limits to drinking, eating, and talking, but who observes them? Who is so just that he does not lapse seven times a day? The hypocrite talks and says that he knows of no fault in himself. I know there is no merit in me, and only divine compassion, which knows we are sinful and prone to lust, and which—as is obvious to all—closes not to us the font of indulgence, gives me hope of mercy. But enough of this.

Now, because you asked me for news, lest you nourish a stranger for me, I will expound in a few words how this came about. Two years have not elapsed since I was an envoy at Strasbourg.[2] It was Quinquagesima,[3] just before last year's Lent. When I was at leisure for many days, a woman came there from Britain, seeking my place of lodging in one of the buildings. I was attracted to her neither because of her beauty nor her age, but rather because she knew Italian very well and greeted me in Tuscan, which pleased me all the more for being so rare in that region. I delight in women's jests. She excelled in these, and soon I thought about the fluency of Cleopatra, who allured not only Antony but also Julius Caesar with eloquence. I said to myself, "Who would reprehend me if I, a little man,[4] were to do what great men have not spurned?" I took as examples sometimes Moses, sometimes Aristotle, sometimes Christians. What more? Desire triumphed; I grew heated. I undertook to enflame the woman with many flatteries, but, as a wave is driven back by the rough shores of a strait, she held my words in contempt and broke off contact for three days. A five-year-old was present whom Melincus, the father, had entrusted to our host and over whom the woman watched lest our host lose sight of the girl, and he gave her up to the woman as if to maternal care. Night came, on the day following which the woman was to leave. I feared my prey would escape. I asked that the latch of the door of her chamber not be fastened. I said I would come on that stormy night. She refused and offered me no hope. I persevered. She always offered the same response.

She went to her room. I said to myself, "Do I know whether she will do what I commanded?" I remembered Zima the Florentine.[5] I said, "Perhaps she will imitate his friend. Try it." Afterward, when I heard silence all around, I went up to the woman's bedchamber. The door was closed but not locked. I opened it, entered, and possessed the woman. There my son was begotten. The woman is called Elizabeth. Her pregnancy lasted from February 13 of last year to November 13, when she gave birth. The woman told me this when she was at Basel afterward. Although I gave her no money, but sent up earnest prayers, I thought this was a case of gold corrupting, as is the way of women. Nor did I make a pledge in words. Now, because I see her asserting this when she can hope for nothing from me, when name and time of conception combine to convince me of paternity, I think the boy mine, and I ask you, my father, to receive and nourish your grandson until, grown up, he should come to me and learn my disciplines. Do not think I wish to enrich the woman by lying about a son.

Now I turn to other things. You write, my father, that you and Mother have grown old; that, as you have attained these years, they ought to be a pleasure to you and to her, since what you sought as a youth now you can do freely and well, serving God, free from all the passions which alienate the minds of the young from God. Nor should you tell me that "age steals everything, even the soul,"[6] as if you think the soul, which is divine and immortal, can perish. The poet, however, wished to indicate that with the advance of age, the vigor of soul which is alight in youth flickers, but is inclined more to vices than to virtues. In older people, the soul is purified, seeking only honest things, which I hope is true of you and my mother—although she never clung to mundane desires—and that, by a certain heroic power, it will lead you, as one of the blessed, to serve God alone. This should serve to make your old age less sad. If you were young, I would fear for you more.

What you write of the children of my sister Laudomia certainly is pleasing to me. It is your obligation to take care that they learn letters which alone place some men above others. I, when I see my estate better established, will adopt one of them. Jacopo Tolomei,[7] if he should write to me, will not go unanswered. He should not expect more since I write many letters of necessity, leaving me no desire to write more. That he delivers ordinary lectures[8] and with a salary delights me, and I observe with pleasure the daily increase of his fame. I enclose a letter to Bartolomeo Guglielmi with this one, and I am never forgetful of his merits toward you and Mother, or that he loves Caterina, my sister, to an extraordinary degree. I commend Mother to you and to your trust, and I pray God that, when I come back to my fatherland, I may find both of you still alive. With joy we will hold a party, and whatever time remains to you we will pass as you wish. Nor will there be any disagreement between you and me. Greet Giovanni and Laudomia, his wife, for me. Receive my little son. And, whatever you do, answer me.

Farewell.

From Graz, September 20, 1443.

Notes

1 Biblical story in which Amnon rapes his half-sister Tamar and then drives her away. 2 Sam. 13:1–20.
2 "In the winter of 1442 Felix V had sent Aeneas, one of his secretaries, with Johann Passart, prior of Utrecht, to represent him before the city council of Strasbourg" *Reject Aeneas,* p.160.
3 One of the Sundays during Carnival preceding Ash Wednesday.
4 The name "Piccolomini" means literally "little men" in Italian.
5 A character from Boccaccio's *Decameron* III, 5.
6 A quote from Virgil's *Eclogues.*
7 A friend of Aeneas who taught law at the University of Siena.
8 "Ordinary lectures, offered early in the day, were the most important in the curriculum and brought the best pay" *Reject Aeneas*, p.162.

Sources

Enea Silvio Piccolomini. *Historia de duobus amantibus*, ed. Donato Pirovano. Edizioni dell'Orso, 2001, trans. Kaborycha with assistance from Dr Michael Beer.

Reject Aeneas, Accept Pius: Selected Letters of Aeneas Sylvius Piccolomini (Pope Pius II), introduced and translated by Thomas M. Izbicki, Gerald Christianson, and Philip Krey. Catholic University of America Press, 2006, pp. 159–62.

References

Piccolomini, Aeneas Sylvius (Pope Pius II). *Commentaries*, ed. Margaret Meserve and Marcello Simonetta, Harvard UP, 2003.

Piccolomini, Aeneas Sylvius (Pope Pius II). *The Two Lovers: The Goodly History of Lady Lucrece and Her Lover Eurialus*, ed. with introduction and notes by Emily O'Brien and Kenneth R. Bartlett, Dovehouse Editions, 1999.

45 Venus triumphs at the court in Ferrara

Petrarch, *Triumph of Love*, 1350–74

Figure 5.3 Francesco del Cossa, *Month of April*, 1469–71, detail, East wall of Hall of the Months, Palazzo Schifanoia, Ferrara.

Francesco del Cossa (*c.* 1435–1477) was one of a team of artists who were commissioned by Duke Borso d'Este (1413–1471) to decorate the walls of the Palazzo Schifanoia in Ferrara. Its name means "escape from cares," and this palace on the outskirts of town was used as a guesthouse and site for courtly entertainments. Thus, the paintings that covered the walls in its Hall of the Months celebrate the courtly pleasures enjoyed by the duke and his guests. It is one of the largest secular fresco cycles of the Renaissance, with bright paintings of the twelve months splashed across every surface in three broad horizontal bands. The lower band represents images of Borso and his court; the middle band contains references to the signs of the zodiac and astrological decans; and at the top, a pagan god from antiquity presides over each month. The Month of April is ruled by Venus, the goddess of love, and at her feet is a chained warrior. Usually identified with Mars, the god of war, who was in love with Venus, the image has also been said to represent Borso d'Este, and his wish to be perceived as a peaceable prince, subdued by love.[1] The scene

DOI: 10.4324/9781003284284-50

also celebrates the central place of music at the Este court, showing ladies holding lutes, recorders, and a rebec. The presence of lovers embracing and fondling one another, not to mention the abundance of rabbits, emphasizes the sexual act and its consequence—reproduction—and in this context, the musical instruments take on erotic overtones as well. Though there are many added details in the complex iconography of this painting,[2] fifteenth-century viewers would have instantly recognized references to Petrarch's *Triumph of Love*, one in a series of six vernacular poems on the themes of Love, Chastity, Death, Fame, Time, and Eternity. One of the most influential and widely read books during the fifteenth century, with more than three hundred extant manuscripts containing the *Trionfi* (*Triumphs*), it was more popular than Petrarch's love sonnets to Laura or even Dante's *Divine Comedy*.[3] And its popularity did not end with manuscript copies. Throughout the Renaissance, the theme was displayed frequently in the form of painted decorations on domestic furniture and tapestries. Moreover, with its origins in the ancient tradition of the victor parading his spoils of war on triumphal carts though the streets of Rome, similar civic pageants with floats bearing staged tableaux vivants were common in festivals during Petrarch's time and throughout the Renaissance. Petrarch's *Triumph of Love*—or, more properly, the triumph of Cupid— opens in Vaucluse (#3), in the springtime, and describes his vision of the victorious child-god leading his captives in a long procession. From the greatest ancient heroes and Olympian gods, down to the humblest mortals everywhere and throughout time, no one can be free of bondage to Cupid.

Petrarch, *Triumph of Love*, 1350–74

This is the land so pleasing to Venus,
and which to her was sacred in that time
when Truth lay hidden and yet unknown;
and still its value is so scant esteemed,
retaining much of its vile origins,
that sweet it seems to evil men, bitter to the good.
It was here this fine Lord came to triumph
over us and all the rest, bound in a snare
from the Indian Sea to Ultima Thule,
worries in our breasts, vanity in our arms.
Fleeting delights are there, and constant cares,
roses in winter, ice in midsummer.
Before us is uncertain hope and fleeting joy,
behind, penitence and sorrow,
known to the kingdoms of Rome and Troy.
And the valley all around echoed
with birdsong and babbling streams,

whose banks were white, green, vermilion,
deep purple, and yellow; surging from springs
brooks glide through tender grasses on hot days.
In deep thickets, the sweet summer breezes refresh.
[. . .]

Not only humans, but a large number of gods
fill the woods and myrtle groves.
You see fair Venus, and with her, Mars,
his feet, arms, and neck fettered in chains,
and Pluto and Persephone to one side.
You see jealous Juno and blond-haired Apollo,
once scornful of the youthful archer,
who dealt him such a defeat in Thessaly.[4]
What can I say? In short, in this place are
imprisoned all the gods named by Varro,[5]
and there, laden with innumerable bonds,
before the chariot is Jupiter enchained.

Notes

1 Rosenberg 45–6.
2 Rosenberg cites a variety of sources including Manilius, Albericus, and Boccaccio 45.
3 Ianucci, xi. Dario Del Puppo comments, "The *Trionfi* was a bestseller in the Quattrocento because Petrarch was the paragon for other poets and because his poem in *terza rima* portrays the pageantry and grandeur of Ancient Rome. To look at the hundreds of codices that have come down to us, the *Trionfi* was a 'must-have' work," "*Accessus ad auctores": studies in honor of Christopher Kleinhenz,* Arizona Center for Medieval and Renaissance Studies, 2011, p. 340.
4 In Thessaly, Apollo fell in love with the nymph Daphne, who rejected him, and escaped him by transforming into a tree.
5 Marcus Terentius Varro (116–27 BCE).

Sources

Petrarch. *Trionfi*, Rizzoli, 1957, IV, 106–27; I, 149–60, trans. Kaborycha.

References

Colantuono, Anthony. "Estense Patronage and the Construction of the Ferrarese Renaissance, *c.*1395–1596," in *The Court Cities of Northern Italy: Milan, Parma, Piacenza, Mantua, Ferrara, Bologna, Urbino, Pesaro, and Rimini*, ed. Charles M. Rosenberg, Cambridge UP, 2010.

Eisenbichler, Konrad and Amilcare A. Iannucci, eds. *Petrarch's Triumphs: Allegory and Spectacle*, Dovehouse Editions, 1990.

Lockwood, Lewis. *Music in Renaissance Ferrara, 1400–1505: The Creation of a Musical Center in the Fifteenth Century*, Oxford UP, 2009.
Petrarch. *Triumphs*, trans. Ernest Hatch Wilkins, U Chicago P, 1962.
Rosenberg, Charles M. "Borsian and Ferrarrese Imagery in the Heavenly Zone in the Salone dei Mesi," *Atlante di Schifanoia*, Vol. 5 (1989), pp. 43–49.
Shephard, Tim, Sanna Raninen, Serenella Sessini and Laura Ştefănescu. *Music in the Art of Renaissance Italy, 1420–1540*, Harvey Miller Publishers, 2020.
Winternitz, Emanuel. *Musical Instruments and Their Symbolism in Western Art: Studies in Musical Iconology*, Yale UP, 1979.

46 Philosophers' handbooks on love

Marsilio Ficino, *On Love*, 1474

Leone Ebreo (Judah ben Isaac Abravanel), *Dialogues of Love*, *c.*1501–11

Tullia d'Aragona, *On the Infinity of Love*, 1547

Why read a handbook on love written by a philosopher? What do philosophers know about it? As the first to produce a complete translation of Plato's dialogue about love, Marsilio Ficino (1433–1499) was considered an expert on the topic. A humanist scholar employed by the Medici, Ficino made an enduring impact on European culture with his Latin translations of Plato—regarded as standard over the next three hundred years—as well as with his interpretations of Platonic philosophy. On the request of Lorenzo de' Medici, in 1474 Ficino translated his Latin commentary on the *Symposium* into Italian for two of Lorenzo's friends, under the title *Sopra lo amore*. Although it did not come out in print until more than half a century later in 1544, when it appeared, the work became a highly influential *trattato d'amore*, or "treatise on love," a popular genre that flourished in Italy especially during the sixteenth century.[1] Written from a philosophical perspective by a respected authority, such a book provided advice on a subject of great interest to the general public. The setting for Ficino's popular treatise on love is a fictional banquet held for nine real Florentines, Ficino's friends and family, who gather to read Plato's *Symposium* together. Plato's work is set at a party—in ancient Greece, a symposium was a drinking party that took place following a banquet—during which the guests discuss the nature of love, desire, and beauty. Ficino emphasizes the point of view that sensual love, which springs from an individual's physical desire for a beautiful person, should not be an end in itself. Love inspired by the earthly beauty of the beloved ought rather to cause the lover to rise above desire of the body and strive to possess true beauty, which exists only in God. The idea of "Platonic love" as an attraction that is not sexually consummated fits neatly with Christian belief that the physical must be transcended—or entirely avoided—in order to reach union with God. This is not precisely what the ancient Greek philosopher had in mind; nevertheless, Ficino, drawing upon earlier Neoplatonist philosophers, found a persuasive way of reconciling Plato's thought with Christianity, and these ideas

DOI: 10.4324/9781003284284-51

were highly influential on sixteenth-century writers such as Baldassarre Castiglione (#56).

One Jewish Renaissance philosopher who also grappled with Plato's theory of love was Judah ben Isaac Abravanel (or Abrabanel, *c.*1460–*c.*1530), better known in Italian as Leone Ebreo. Born in Lisbon, Judah was a learned humanist trained as a doctor who served as royal physician at the Spanish court. In 1492, he had to leave the Iberian Peninsula to avoid conversion to Christianity, though his eldest son was taken from him and forced to convert. Afterward, Judah and the rest of his family took refuge in Italy, where once again they were compelled to move frequently from place to place. In 1501, he moved to Genoa, where he began writing his philosophical treatise on love. Judah died before the book was first printed in 1535 as *Dialoghi d'amore* (*Dialogues of Love*). The work went on to be immensely popular during the Renaissance: "between 1541 and 1607 it was republished no less than twenty-four times, and between 1551 and 1660 it was translated into French, Latin, Spanish, and Hebrew. More than just a bestseller, it exerted a deep influence over future generations, in the work of figures as diverse as Giordano Bruno, John Donne, Miguel de Cervantes, and Baruch Spinoza."[2] The two characters in Leone's dialogue are a man and a woman: Philo is the lover, and the object of his desire is Sophia, wisdom. Together, they are the yin and yang of "philo-sophy." Philo insistently expresses his longing for her, while Sophia wittily spars with him in this entertaining and complex synthesis of the ideas of both Plato and Aristotle. Moreover, Leone Ebreo also manages to merge Jewish scholarship with Ficino's Christian Neoplatonism, as well Renaissance aesthetic theory. His work was widely read and admired by, among others, the courtesan, philosopher, and poet Tullia d'Aragona (1510–1556). In her 1547 *On the Infinity of Love*, written in the form of a dialogue with her friend, the philosopher and historian Benedetto Varchi (1503–1565), Tullia draws on many of the ideas of Leone Ebreo. Referring to him as Filone, both Tullia and Varchi praise his writing on love as some of the finest ever written.

Marsilio Ficino, *On Love*, 1474

Plato on the primeval form of man: the fable of Aristophanes

Aristophanes said that Love [Eros], above all other gods is the generous guardian, teacher, and physician to the human race. To start with, it is necessary to relate what in the beginning was the form of humans and their passions. It was not then like now, but very different: to begin with there were three genders, not only male and female like now, but a third, composed of both. And every person was complete within themselves, composed of a rounded back and circular sides with four hands and four legs, and with two faces on a rounded neck in similar manner. The masculine gender was born of the Sun; the female of the Earth; the mixed gender from the Moon, hence they were proud in mind and robust in body. Therefore, they lifted their hands to fight the gods and wanted to rise up to Heaven. And this is why Jove sawed each one in half down the middle, making two from each, like someone who splits a hardboiled egg in half lengthwise with hair. Furthermore, he threatened that if they rose up pridefully against him again, that he would saw them another time in the same way. Ever since human nature was divided, each person has desired to be rejoined to their other half, and they ran about, throwing their arms around one another, embracing, craving to be restored once again to their former state. And they would certainly have perished from hunger and idleness if God had not found a way for them to copulate.

This is how mutual love originated in humans; Nature's ancient reconciler, striving to make one from two, cures the human condition. Each of us is one half of a person, like those fish known as "*orata*," which when a single one is sliced down the middle lengthwise, two live fish are left. Every human seeks their other half and whenever someone encounters another of whichever sex attracts them, they respond powerfully, filled with ardent love and cannot bear to be separated from them, even for a moment. And thus, the eager desire to be made whole again is called love. This, in the present day benefits us, rendering each of us most dear to their other half and offering highest hope for the future, that if we honor God, He will restore us to our ancient form, and thus healing us, make us blessed.

What lovers seek

But what are they seeking, when they love reciprocally? They seek beauty, because love is the desire to enjoy beauty, that is, physical comeliness. Beauty is a kind of splendor that ravishes the human spirit. Bodily beauty is nothing other than splendor in the adornments of colors and lines; beauty of the mind is the dazzling harmony between knowledge and moral behavior. It is the light of the body not known to the ears, nose, taste, or touch, but to the eye. If the eye alone recognizes it, only the eye can enjoy corporeal beauty. And since love is the desire to enjoy beauty, which is only experienced through the eye, the bodily lover is content with sight alone. Thus, the lust for touching is not a part of love, nor an expression of the affection of the lover, but a type of lewdness and agitation in a man who is servile. That light of the spirit we can only comprehend with our intellect.

Leone Ebreo, *Dialogues of Love*, *c.*1501–11

Dialogue I: Philo and Sophia on Love and Desire

Philo: My acquaintance with you, O Sophia, awakes in me love and desire.

Sophia: These effects of your acquaintance with me, O Philo, seem to be at variance; but perhaps it is passion which makes you speak thus.

Philo: At variance they are; but—with its effects in you, which are so far from any reciprocity.

Sophia: Nay, but they are at variance among themselves too: love and desire are incompatible affects of the will.

Philo: Why incompatible?

Sophia: Because: of the things by us reckoned good we love those which we have and possess,[3] and desire those we lack;[4] so that what we love we first desire, but when the desired object has been obtained, love supervenes and desire ceases.

Philo: On what is this opinion of yours based?

Sophia: Instances of things which we love or desire. Do you not see that we desire health when we have it not, yet we should scarcely say we love it; when we have gained it, we love it without desiring it. Wealth, legacies, gems, while unpossessed, are objects of desire, not of love: once acquired, however, they are desired no longer, but loved.

[. . .]

Philo: I will speak in more general terms. You know that love is of things which are good or are considered good, for whatever thing is good is worthy of love. And even as there are three sorts of goods, to wit: the profitable, the pleasurable and the virtuous,[5] so too there are three sorts of love: for one is of pleasure, another of profit, and a third of virtue. Virtue and profit, when once ours, must be loved at all times, whether before we have gained them or after. Pleasant things, however, we do not love after we have gained them, for whatever things delight our material senses are of such kind that their possession rather engenders loathing than love. On this reasoning you must needs confess that we love things before we possess them and likewise at the same time as we desire them; and as desire dies once they have been completely possessed, so our love of them usually dies too. Hence you will allow that love and desire can coexist.

Sophia: Your arguments do, in my opinion, validly establish that first thesis of yours, yet do not lessen the force or truth of mine. How, then, is it possible that any truth should conflict with truth itself? Solve me this uncertainty, which troubles me not a little.

Philo: I come, O Sophia, to ask of you a cure for my sufferings; and you ask me for a solution of your perplexities. Perhaps you do so to make me change a course that displeases you; or because you indeed dislike the concepts of my poor mind no less than the affections of my afflicted heart.

[. . .]

Dialogue III Philo and Sophia on the Origin of Love

Philo: In the *Symposium* Plato only discusses that love in men which has its final cause in the lover but not in the beloved; for this is principally called love, and that which has its end in the beloved is called friendship and beneficence. Plato defines correctly the former kind of love as the desire of beauty, and declares that it is not found in God, because he who desires beauty neither possesses it nor is beautiful himself, whereas God, who is supremely beautiful, has no lack of beauty, nor can He desire it. His love, therefore, cannot be of this first kind.

[. . .]

Sophia: What is beauty? Does it add anything else to the good besides its goodness?

Philo: To explain and to define beauty would require long converse; for many perceive and name it, yet they know not what it is.

Sophia: Who is there who cannot distinguish between the beautiful and the ugly?

Philo: Everyone recognizes the beautiful, but few know what it is which makes all beautiful things beautiful, and which we call beauty.

Sophia: I pray you, tell me what this is.

Philo: Beauty has been defined in various ways. . . . For the present I will only give you in brief its true and universal definition. Beauty is grace which delights the mind which recognizes it and moves it to love. And that good thing or person in which this grace is found is beautiful; but the good which is without it is neither beautiful nor ugly: it is not beautiful because it has not grace, and it is not ugly because it does not lack goodness. But that which lacks both these things, to wit, grace and goodness, not only is not beautiful, but is bad and ugly.

[. . .]

Sophia: This definition pleases me; but I would know why not every good thing has this grace.

Philo: Good, useful, temperate and pleasurable things are found amongst the objects of all external senses; but the grace which is called beauty and which delights and moves the soul to true love, is not found in the objects of the three material senses, taste, smell and touch, but only those of the two spiritual senses of sight and hearing. Pleasant and nourishing food and drink, soft perfumes, a healthy clime, the delights of modest lovers' intercourse, although the goodness, sweetness, gentleness, and utility of all these things is necessary for both human and animal existence, yet they are not beautiful. For in these material objects there is no grace or beauty, nor can these [qualities] be transmitted by the three gross material senses to delight our soul and prompt it to love of the beautiful. Beauty is only found in the objects of sight, such as beautiful forms and shapes and beautiful pictures, the perfect symmetry of the parts with the whole, well-proportioned limbs, beautiful colors and clear light, the Sun, Moon and stars, and the heavens in all their splendor. . . .

Sophia: Has man, perchance, another faculty, besides those of sight and hearing, with which he can apprehend the beautiful?

Philo: The cognitive faculties, which are more spiritual than sight and hearing, have an even greater knowledge of the beautiful.

Sophia: Which are these?

Philo: The imagination and fancy, which arranges, distinguishes and ponders the things of the senses, and discerns in many other sources grace and beauty, moving the soul to love and delight. And, indeed, we speak of a beautiful fancy, a beautiful thought, or a beautiful invention. The understanding has a far greater knowledge of the beautiful, for it apprehends universal, [in]corporeal and incorruptible grace and beauty in particular and corruptible bodies, which is far more potent in inspiring love and pleasure in the soul. Such are the laws and virtues and the learning and sciences of man, for study, law and science can all be called beautiful. The most exalted knowledge of man, however, is that of pure intellect, which, being absorbed in the science of the Divine and of things abstracted from matter, rejoices in and becomes enamored of the highest grace and beauty which is in the Creator and Artificer of all things; and it therein attains to its ultimate happiness.

[. . .]

[*Philo recounts the Fable of Aristophanes and Sophia responds.*]

Sophia: The story is full of charm and beauty, and it is impossible not to believe that it signifies some philosophical beauty, more especially since it was composed by Plato himself, in the *Symposium*, in the name of Aristophanes. Tell me, therefore, Philo, what is the allegory.

Philo: The myth was handed down by earlier writers than the Greeks—in the sacred writings of Moses, concerning the creation of the first human parents, Adam and Eve. . . . it was from [Moses] that Plato took his myth, amplifying and polishing it after Greek oratory, thus giving a confused account of the Hebrew version.

Tullia d'Aragona, *On the Infinity of Love* , 1547

Tullia: Honest love, which belongs properly to noble persons, that is those with refined and virtuous minds—whether they are rich or poor—is not generated by desire, like that other kind [of love] and has as its main object the transformation of the beloved into oneself, so that the two can become one, or four; of such a transformation have Messer Petrarch and the most reverend Cardinal Bembo[6] written so gracefully. This can only be accomplished in the realm of the spirit, hence in such a love, only "spiritual" senses can have a place: vision, hearing, and imagination [*fantasia*]. It is true that the lover, beyond desiring the spiritual, also seeks a bodily union, making themself as much as possible, one with the beloved. And because this cannot be achieved—that two bodies merge with each other, they will never fulfill this desire and arrive at its end. They cannot love in this finite way as I concluded above. Although much more could be said on this matter of the two kinds of love, it seems I have said enough to demonstrate my conclusion to be true.

Varchi: I like everything that you have said very much, and you have filled me with an ineffable sweetness. And although I have some doubts about things that you have said, they are only slight. Above all, I am pleased that you have not only read Filone [Leone Ebreo], but have understood him and kept him in your mind.

Tullia: Ah! Since you have mentioned Filone, out of the love you bear me, tell me your opinion and judgment of him.

. . . .

Varchi: Of all those [philosophers] that I have read, both ancient and modern, who have written about love, in any language, I like Filone better than the rest. And I feel that I have learned more from him, the more so because in my opinion, he discourses not only more generally, but with greater truth and perhaps doctrine.

Tullia: Have you read Plato and Marsilio Ficino's *Convivio* (symposium)?

Varchi: Yes, my lady, and they both seem wonderful to me, but I like Filone more. . . . Many have written of love, some in a learned manner, others more lightly, but I prefer Filone to all the others, even if in some things, especially when dealing with the Jewish faith, I would rather excuse than approve what he writes.

Notes

1 Jayne 2.

2 Pescatori 3.

3 "Love may be described generally as the everlasting possession of the good." Plato, *Symp* 206a.

4 "Every one who desires, desires that which he has not already . . . and which he does not possess." Plato, *Symp* 200e.
5 "Aristotle, *Nichomachean Ethics* 8.2.1155b. Leone is indebted to this passage throughout much of the present discussion." Perry 117.
6 Pietro Bembo (1536–1589), author of *Gli Asolani*, a treatise on love in dialogue form.

Sources

Marsilio Ficino, *Sopra lo amore, ovvero il convito di Platone*, ed. Giuseppe Rensi, Lanciano, Carabba, 1934, pp. 31–32, 40–42, trans. Kaborycha.

Leone Ebreo, *The Philosophy of Love*, trans. F. Friedeberg-Seeley and Jean H. Barnes; with an introduction by Cecil Roth, Soncino Press, 1937, pp. 3–5, 234–5, 264–7, 345.

Tullia d'Aragona, *Della infinità d'amore: dialogo*, Daelli, 1864, pp. 62–65, trans. Kaborycha.

References

d'Aragona, Tullia. *Dialogue on the Infinity of Love*, ed. and trans. Rinaldina Russell and Bruce Merry, U Chicago P, 1997.

Ficino, Marsilio. *Commentary on Plato's Symposium on Love*, trans. and ed. Sears Jayne, Spring Publications, 1985.

Giovannozzi, Delfina. "Leone Ebreo in Tullia d'Aragona's *Dialogo*. Between Varchi's Legacy and Philosophical Autonomy," *British Journal for the History of Philosophy*, Vol. 27, No. 4 (2019), pp. 702–17.

Hebreo, León. *Dialogues of Love*, trans. Cosmos Damian Bacich and Rossella Pescatori; introduction and notes by Rossella Pescatori, U Toronto P, 2009.

Howlett, Sophia. *Marsilio Ficino and His World*, Palgrave Macmillan, 2016.

Hughes, Aaron W. "Transforming the Maimonidean Imagination: Aesthetics in the Renaissance Thought of Judah Abravanel," *The Harvard Theological Review*, Vol. 97, No. 4 (October 2004), pp. 461–84.

Maggi, Armando. "On Kissing and Sighing: Renaissance Homoerotic Love from Ficino's *De Amore* and *Sopra Lo Amore* to Cesare Trevisani's *L'impresa* (1569)," in *Same-sex Desire and Love in Greco-Roman Antiquity and in the Classical Tradition of the West*, ed. Beert C. Verstraete and Vernon Provencal, Harrington Park Press, 2005.

Perry, T. Anthony. *Erotic Spirituality: The Integrative Tradition from Leone Ebreo to John Donne*, U Alabama P, 1980.

Plato. *Symposium*, trans. Benjamin Jowett, Oxford UP, 1892.

47 A spiritual and earthly object of desire

Angelo Poliziano, *Stanzas for Giuliano de' Medici*, 1478

Figure 5.4 Sandro Botticelli, *Birth of Venus*, 1484–6, Uffizi.

The goddess of love, entirely nude, stands gracefully poised, displaying a perfection of female beauty that embodies the Platonic concept of ideal form. With this work, and his other large-scale paintings on mythological themes, Sandro Botticelli (**#12**) broke new ground in Renaissance art. Though images of ancient gods and goddesses commonly adorned marriage chests and other domestic furnishings during the Renaissance, Botticelli was the first to take the subject matter "seriously." Botticelli's mythologies succeeded, in the words of Ernst Gombrich, in "opening up to secular art emotional spheres which had hitherto been the preserve of religious worship."[1] To begin with, in this painting the artist had to select which myth of the goddess's birth to

DOI: 10.4324/9781003284284-52

depict. Known as Venus in Latin and Aphrodite in Greek, the goddess of love had many names, and there were various myths regarding her origins. Plato made a distinction between the older primordial myth and a more recent one, and proposed that there were two separate goddesses, one representing spiritual love, the other physical love: "the elder one, having no mother, who is called the heavenly Aphrodite—she is the daughter of Uranus; the younger, who is the daughter of Zeus and Dione—her we call common."[2] It is the older legend, the birth of Venus Urania who emerged fully formed upon the waves, that Botticelli chose to portray in his celebrated canvas. And it is no coincidence that his friend Angelo Poliziano (#53) wrote verses describing that version of the legend of the birth of Venus in terms that are strikingly similar to visual elements in the painting. The two Florentines moved in the same circles, undoubtedly discussing artistic ideas and sharing insights. Both were employed by the Medici: Poliziano was tutor to their children, and Botticelli, in addition to producing works of art for their walls, was sometimes also called upon by his patrons to create ephemeral decorations for celebrations. When in January 1475 the Medici held a spectacular joust, the banner that Giuliano de' Medici (1453–1478) carried into the lists was decorated with an image of the goddess Pallas Athena in a white robe. Painted by Botticelli, it represented Giuliano's beloved, Simonetta Vespucci, recognized as one of the great beauties of the day. That painting no longer exists, but the poet Angelo Poliziano immortalized the event in a long allegorical poem titled *Stanzas for the Tournament of Giuliano de' Medici*, (begun in 1475 and left unfinished in 1478), and it is within this poem that the vignette describing the birth of Venus appears. Was Botticelli's *Birth of Venus* painted as a decoration for a Medici festivity? We will probably never know. It was certainly owned by the family; the *Birth of Venus*, as well as Botticelli's *Primavera* (*c.*1478), both originally hung in Medici residences. The latter painting in particular was commissioned for the marriage of Lorenzo di Pierfrancesco de' Medici (#75). In a letter to the young bridegroom, Marsilio Ficino (#46), echoes the Platonic notion that the beauty of Venus ought to lead Lorenzo di Pierfrancesco's soul to higher spiritual aspirations, identifying the goddess with *humanitas* (humanity), "a nymph of excellent comeliness, born of heaven and more than others beloved by God all highest." The philosopher goes on to compare Lorenzo's bride with the Platonic ideal: "Oh, what exquisite beauty! How beautiful to behold. My dear Lorenzo, a nymph of such nobility has been wholly given into your hands. If you were to unite with her in wedlock and claim her as yours, she would make all your years sweet."[3]

Angelo Poliziano, *Stanzas for Giuliano de' Medici*, 1478

[*The poet describes the Island of Cyprus, where the goddess Venus dwells, and her palace, which has the following scene sculpted on its gates.*]

In the tempestuous Aegean Sea, into the womb of Tethys[4]
the severed genitals are seen being received,[5]
and beneath the spinning of the various planets
they drift over the waves, enveloped in white sea-foam;
from within is born in lovely, graceful movements
a damsel of unearthly countenance,
urged and driven by the frolicking zephyr breezes,[6]
she sways atop a conch shell, and the heavens seem to stir with pleasure.

You would say the foam was real, and so was the sea,
and the conch shell and the blowing of the wind too;
you'd see the lightning flashing in the goddess's eyes as well,
the heavens and the elements laughing all around her;
the *Horae*[7] tread the sands in white garments,
the breeze curling the loose and waving hair;
their faces neither all alike, nor all different,
as is the case with sisters.

You'd swear that she'd just emerged from the waves,
that goddess pressing her long tresses with her right hand,
covering her sweet apple[8] with the other,
and imprinted by her sacred, divine foot,
the shore is clothed in grasses and flowers.

Notes

1 Gombrich 43.
2 *Symp*. 180d-e, Jowett trans. This distinction between the celestial (Aphrodite Urania) and the earthly (Aphrodite Pandemos) is discussed at length by Wind 138–40.
3 Gombrich, 16–17.
4 In Greek mythology, Tethys was the daughter of the gods Uranus and Gaia; she married her brother Oceanus and gave birth to many river gods and goddesses.
5 This account is based largely on the writings of Hesiod, a Greek poet from the eighth century BCE. In *Theogony* 175–85, Hesiod recounts how the Titan Cronos castrated his father, Uranus, whose testicles, falling into the sea led to the birth of Venus.
6 Zephyrus was the name for the god of the west wind, who appears also in Botticelli's *Primavera*, pursuing the nymph Chloris.
7 The *Horae* in Greek mythology were female personifications of the seasons. The single *Hora* depicted by Botticelli represents Spring, similar to the figure of Flora in his *Primavera*.
8 The word *pome* (*pomo*) means literally "apple" as well as "pommel." In the context of female anatomy, apple can refer to the breast; here it indicates the area of flesh covering the pubic bone, known as the "mons veneris."

Sources

Angelo Poliziano. *Stanze cominciate per la giostra del magnifico Giuliano di Piero de' Medici*, ed. Saverio Orlando, Rizzoli, 1983, Book I, 99–101, p. 34, trans. Kaborycha.

References

Dempsey, Charles. *The Portrayal of Love: Botticelli's 'Primavera' and Humanist Culture at the Time of Lorenzo the Magnificent*, Princeton UP, 1992.

Gombrich, Ernst H. "Botticelli's Mythologies: A Study in the Neoplatonic Symbolism of His Circle," *Journal of the Warburg and Courtauld Institutes*, Vol. 8 (1945), 7–60.

Poliziano, Angelo. *The Stanze*, trans. David Quint, U Massachusetts P, 1979.

Warburg, Aby. "Sandro Botticelli's *Birth of Venus* and *Spring*," in *The Renewal of Pagan Antiquity: Contributions to the Cultural History of the European Renaissance*, vol. I (1932), The Getty Research Publications, 1999.

Wind, Edgar. *Pagan Mysteries in the Renaissance*, Oxford UP, 1980.

48 A poet's amorous raptures and torments

Gaspara Stampa, *Four sonnets*, 1554

Gaspara Stampa (*c.*1523/25–1554) was a renowned *virtuosa*, a professional singer who performed at elegant Venetian social gatherings; she was also one of the most accomplished women poets of the Renaissance. Though originally from Padua where her father worked as jeweler, when Gaspara was seven or eight years old he died, and her mother moved the family to Venice. There the children were educated in literature, instrumental music, and singing; the two sisters, Cassandra and Gaspara, performed regularly in the family home, which became a kind of cultural salon attended by literary notables including Francesco Sansovino, Benedetto Varchi, Ortensio Lando, Girolamo Parabosco, and Sperone Speroni. Guests came to hear the girls play the lute, the viola da gamba, and to sing; Gaspara's talent in particular drew enthusiastic accolades. She wrote many madrigals and accompanied herself on the lute, while singing poems either by Petrarch or original verse of her own. Musical performances of this kind were common in Venice among courtesans, and though there is no certain proof, it is probable that Gaspara Stampa was a courtesan, given her high-profile artistic career and her unconventional lifestyle. She gave birth to two illegitimate children by a Venetian nobleman while in her early twenties and never married. In 1548, she met the man who would become the central focus of much of her poetry: Count Collaltino di Collalto, a nobleman from the March of Treviso and a professional soldier. Their love affair lasted several years, with lengthy periods of separation when Collalto went to fight in France and elsewhere. When the relationship eventually ended, she still continued composing poetry and refining her earlier work. After Gaspara died suddenly of a fever in 1544, Cassandra published the first edition of her sister's collected verse, the *Rime*, containing 310 poems, 280 of which are sonnets. In these, Gaspara voices the depth of her feeling for her lover, expressing herself in full-throated Petrarchan idiom: the poet burns and freezes; all of Nature echoes her torments and heightens her ecstasies. Just as Petrarch first sets eyes on Laura on a significant date—Easter—so Stampa meets Collalto on Christmas. And as Petrarch uses the name of his beloved to refer to the laurel tree and poetic laurels, so Stampa plays on the name Collalto, meaning "high mountain,"

DOI: 10.4324/9781003284284-53

in reference to his high social position or haughty manner. However, there are significant differences for Stampa as a woman writing in this vein. Rather than fantasizing about a cruel and unattainable object of her love, she writes about a man with whom she has had an actual physical relationship, which she makes clear in her poems, although never as explicitly as Venetian courtesan Veronica Franco (**#67**). Stampa "wrote with astonishing human passion, though with the consequence of being called courtesan or whore," a double standard that was applied to women's erotic poetry.[1] This is also why, although she does praise his beautiful face and eyes, Stampa dwells less on Collalto's specific physical appearance than a male poet might, when describing his female love object. Despite these gender constraints, or perhaps on account of them, Stampa's verse soars, expressing what is highest and most universal in the human experience of love.

Sonnet CIV

O night, to me brighter and more blessed
than the most blessed days and clearer;
night, worthy to be praised not only by myself,
but by the finest, most subtle minds.

You who have been the sole, faithful handmaid
of all my joys; all my life's bitterness
you have made sweet and dear,
returning to my arms the one who has bound me.

All I lacked was to be transformed
into fortunate Alcmene, for whom
Aurora held off longer than usual.[2]

Yet, I can never say enough
of you, candid night, that the subject
would not surpass my song.

Sonnet CXI

Place me where the wrathful sea moans and breaks,
or where the waters are stiller and more tranquil;
place me where the Sun burns and blazes strong,
or where the ice strangles and transfixes.

Place me in the frozen Don, the cold Ganges,
where manna drips from sweet dewdrops,

where unholy air glimmers with poison,
or where one laughs and weeps for Love.

Place me where the crude, wicked Scythian slashes,
or where the people are calm and peaceful,
where a human lives, and sooner or later, dies.

I will live as I have lived, and will be what I am,
so long as my two true, faithful stars
do not turn their accustomed light from me.

Sonnet CXXV

"Would you like to tell me a bit Love, about
what have I to do with these two sisters of yours,
Fear and Jealousy? And why it is that they
know no better place to lodge than in my heart?

You have thousands of other women who
burn, as I do, from your wicked little torches,
so send these sisters now to dwell with them;
do this so that one day they exit my own breast."

"I do have thousands," he replied,
"to whom I could send them, but none of these
has such reason to fear as you.

The lights you love are precisely those,
which to incite jealousy and passion
in all the world were selected by my mother."

Sonnet CXXVIII

If ever I were to say, my lord, that my ardor
for you should be extinguished, as I burn in a lively flame;
if ever I were to say I wanted to be deprived of love,
my heart unfettered from its handsome bond,

If ever I were to say that the beautiful face
—of which every hour I write and talk,
shunning all others—should never again
show its light, whether little or much, to my own,

If ever I were to say that, may both men and gods
kindle against me scornful Fortune's harm,
bringing my ultimate ruin.

But if I did not say this, and never did anything
to merit your disdain, then restore now
my life to me, as it was, happy and joyous.

Notes

1 Smarr 15.
2 In Greek mythology, Alcmene was the mother of Hercules, and lover of Zeus, who disguised himself as her husband in order to sleep with her. He had Aurora, the goddess of dawn, hold off the break of day so he could spend more time with Alcmene.

Source

Gaspara Stampa and Veronica Franco. *Rime*, ed. Abdelkader Salza, Bari, Laterza, 1913, trans. Kaborycha.

References

Bassanese, Fiora A. *Gaspara Stampa*, Twayne, 1982.
Braden, Gordon. "Gaspara Stampa and the Gender of Petrarchism," in *Texas Studies in Literature and Language*, Vol. 38, No. 2, Revising Renaissance Eroticism (Summer 1996), pp. 115–39.
Falkeid, Unn and Aileen A. Feng, eds. *Rethinking Gaspara Stampa in the Canon of Renaissance Poetry*, Ashgate, 2015.
Feldman, Martha. "The Courtesan's Voice," in *The Courtesan's Arts: Cross-cultural Perspectives*, ed. Martha Feldman and Bonnie Gordon, Oxford UP, 2006.
Moore, Mary B. "Body of Light, Body of Matter: Self-Reference as Self-Modeling in Gaspara Stampa," in *Desiring Voices: Women Sonneteers and Petrarchism*, Southern Illinois UP, 2000, pp. 58–93.
Smarr, Janet Levarie. "Substituting for Laura: Objects of Desire for Renaissance Women Poets," *Comparative Literature Studies*, Vol. 38, No. 1, Penn State UP (2001), pp. 1–30.
Stampa, Gaspara. *The Complete Poems: The 1554 Edition of the Rime, a Bilingual Edition*, ed. Troy Tower and Jane Tylus, trans. Jane Tylus, U Chicago P, 2010.

49 Love affairs of the Olympian gods

Ovid, "Io and Jupiter," *Metamorphoses*, *c.*1 CE

Lodovico Dolce, *Letter to Alessandro Contarini*, 1554

Wealthy and powerful Renaissance men liked to surround themselves with erotic images inspired by classical mythology—paintings such as Raphael's *Loggia of Psyche* for banker Agostino Chigi (1517–18, Villa Farnesina, Rome); Titian's *Mythologies* for Phillip II (1554–62, various museums[1]); and Annibale Carracci's *Loves of the Gods* for Cardinal Odoardo Farnese (1597–1601, Palazzo Farnese, Rome) are a few prominent examples. Increasingly sexually charged artistic treatments of mythological themes had begun to appear in the early sixteenth century, influenced by printed pornography. When Giovanni Jacopo Caraglio (*c.* 1505–1565) produced his 1526 engravings of *Loves of the Gods*, which featured the Olympian gods engaged in explicit sexual acts, he was directly inspired by a work known as *I Modi* (*The Positions*). Published in 1524, the book with Marcantonio Raimondi's (1480–1534) engravings of naked couples demonstrating coital positions accompanied by obscene verses written by Pietro Aretino created a scandal; all copies of the book were confiscated and destroyed. Raimondi had originally based his engravings on erotic drawings by Giulio Romano (1499–1546), a former member of Raphael's workshop in Rome. By 1524, Romano had become court artist for Federico Gonzaga in Mantua, and over the next two decades, he covered the walls and ceilings of Palazzo Te with images of the Olympian gods and goddesses cavorting with mortals.

Federico II Gonzaga (1500–1540) commissioned a series of mythological paintings on the theme of the *Loves of Jupiter* as a gift for the emperor, around the time Charles V raised Federico to become the first duke of Mantua.[2] Gonzaga's choice of Correggio (Antonio Allegri, 1489–1534) to paint four canvases on the stories of *Leda*, *Danaë*, *Ganymede*, and *Io* was particularly inspired (Figure 5.1). A "great poet of the body" is how Kenneth Clark has characterized Correggio, along with Titian, while contrasting "the robust eagerness of Titian with Correggio's delicate tremor of the flesh."[3] The greatest proponent of the school of Parma, Correggio is known for both his delicate chiaroscuro and refined sensual lyricism. *Poesia*, or visual poetry, was the term used to describe these evocative works of the two artists. The erotic mythologies of Titian and Correggio, especially scenes based on Ovid's *Metamorphoses*, exude sexual energy: Jupiter transforms into a shower of gold to

DOI: 10.4324/9781003284284-54

penetrate Danaë; a swan to couple with Leda; a bull to carry away Europa; and, in Correggio's unique depiction, the king of the gods assumes the form of a cloud to have sex with Io. As the name implies, *poesia* involves poetic license for the painter to interpret the scene; thus, Correggio's *Io and Jupiter* varies in significant ways from Ovid's original. The Latin poet describes the lustful Jupiter calling down a heavy cloud to conceal himself, as he chases Io into the forest, but the painter has the god transformed into an actual cloud. And whereas in Ovid, Jupiter rapes the girl; in the version Correggio painted for Gonzaga, Io willingly accepts the god's embrace. Io's pose, moreover, is designed as in other erotic mythologies "to enable the male viewer to imagine himself entering the scene and replacing the displaced lover."[4] This male response to a similar image is emphasized by the Venetian humanist scholar and art theorist Lodovico Dolce (1508–1568)—incidentally also the most well-known sixteenth-century Italian translator of the *Metamorphoses*—in a letter to Venetian notable Alessandro Contarini.

Ovid, "Io and Jupiter," *Metamorphoses*, c.1 CE

For Jove [Jupiter] not long before had seen her while
returning from her father's stream, and said;
"O virgin, worthy of immortal Jove—
although some happy mortal's chosen bride—
behold these shades of overhanging trees,
and seek their cool recesses while the Sun
is glowing in the height of middle skies."
And as he spoke he pointed out the groves:
"But should the dens of wild beasts frighten you,
with safety you may enter the deep woods,
conducted by a god—not with a god
of small repute, but in the care of him
who holds the heavenly scepter in his hand
and fulminates the trackless thunderbolts—
Forsake me not!" For while he spoke she fled,
and swiftly left behind the pasture-fields
of Lerna, and Lyrceia's arbors, where
the trees are planted thickly. But the god
called forth a heavy shadow which involved
the wide-extended Earth, and stopped her flight
and ravished in that cloud her chastity.

Meanwhile, the goddess Juno gazing down
on Earth's expanse, with wonder saw the clouds
as dark as night enfold those middle fields

while day was bright above. She was convinced
the clouds were none composed of river mist
nor raised from marshy fens. Suspicious now,
from oft-detected amours of her spouse,
she glanced around to find her absent lord,
and quite convinced that he was far from heaven,
she thus exclaimed: "This cloud deceives my mind,
or Jove has wronged me." From the dome of heaven
she glided down and stood upon the Earth,
and bade the clouds recede. But Jove had known
the coming of his queen. He had transformed
the lovely Io, so that she appeared
a milk-white heifer—formed so beautiful
and fair that envious, Juno gazed on her.

Lodovico Dolce, *Letter to Alessandro Contarini*, 1554

[*A description of Titian's painting* Venus and Adonis]
The Venus has her back turned, not for any artistic deficiency but to demonstrate double the art. Because in turning her face towards Adonis, straining with both her arms to retain him, and half-seated on a soft fabric of peacock-blue, she demonstrates in every way certain sweet and lively sentiments, and such that they cannot be seen except in her; the miraculous shrewdness of that divine spirit [Titian] is also revealed that in her intimate parts we recognize the creases on the flesh caused by her seated position. Why, it can in truth be said that every stroke of the brush is one of those strokes that nature executes with its own hand . . . I swear to you, sir, that there is no man so keen in sight or judgment, that seeing does not believe her alive; nor anyone made so cold by the years, or so hardened in his being, who does not feel a warming, a softening, a stirring of the blood in his veins. It is a real marvel; that if a marble statue could by the stimuli of its beauty so penetrate to the marrow of a young man, that he stained himself,[5] then, what must she do who is of flesh, who is beauty personified and appears to be breathing?

Notes

1 *Danaë*, *Venus and Adonis*, Prado, Madrid; *Perseus and Andromeda*, Wallace Collection, London; *Diana and Actaeon*, National Gallery of Scotland; *Rape of Europa*, Isabella Stewart Gardner Museum, Boston; *Diana and Callisto*, *Death of Actaeon*, National Gallery, London. The painting of *Venus and Adonis* is described in Dolce's letter to Contarini. See also **#38**.

2 Federico Gonzaga, who inherited the title of 5th marchese of Mantua, was elevated to duke of Mantua by Emperor Charles V on April 8, 1530. The emperor was his guest in Mantua from March 24 to April 19 of that year. See also **#59.**

3 Clark 125, 284.
4 See Barkan 218–19.
5 A legend in antiquity told of a statue of Venus so lovely that it aroused a young man who secretly went by night to have sex with it, staining the marble with his semen. Findlen 60.

Sources

Ovid. *Metamorphoses,* I, 587–621, Brookes More, Cornhill Publishing, 1922, pp. 28–33, ed. Kaborycha.

Ludovico Dolce, *Letter* in Carlo Ginzburg. "Titian, Ovid, and Erotic Illustration," in *Clues, Myths, and the Historical Method*, trans. John and Anne Tedeschi, Johns Hopkins UP, 1989, pp. 81–2.

References

Barkan, Leonard. *The Gods Made Flesh: Metamorphosis and the Pursuit of Paganism*, Yale UP, 1986.

Barolsky, Paul. *Ovid and the Metamorphoses of Modern Art from Botticelli to Picasso*, Yale UP, 2014.

Bull, Malcolm. *The Mirror of the Gods: How Renaissance Artists Rediscovered the Pagan Gods*, Oxford UP, 2005.

Clark, Kenneth. *The Nude: A Study of Ideal Art*, Harmondsworth, 1976.

Ekserdjian, David. *Correggio*, Yale UP, 1997.

Fabiański, Marcin. *Correggio's Erotic Poesie*, Jagiellonian University Institute of Art History, 1998.

Findlen, Paula. "Humanism, Politics, and Pornography," in *The Invention of Pornography: Obscenity and the Origins of Modernity, 1500–1800*, ed. Lynn Hunt, Zone Books; Distributed by MIT Press, 1993.

Nova, Alessandro. "Correggio's 'Lascivie'," in *Renaissance Love: Eros, Passion, and Friendship in Italian Art Around 1500*, ed. Jeanette Kohl, Marianne Koos and Adrian W.B. Randolph, Deutscher Kunstverlag, 2014.

Talvacchia, Bette. *Taking Positions: On the Erotic in Renaissance Culture*, Princeton UP, 1999.

Valladares, Hérica. "The Io in Correggio: Ovid and the Metamorphosis of a Renaissance Painter," in *The Afterlife of Ovid*, ed. Peter Mack and John North. Institute of Classical Studies, School of Advanced Study, U London P, 2015.

50 An artist's love for a younger man

Michelangelo Buonarroti, *Four Sonnets*, 1533

Universally regarded as the greatest sculptor, painter, and architect of his day, Michelangelo Buonarroti (1475–1564) was also recognized by contemporaries as an accomplished poet. He was sometimes referred to as "a new Apollo and a new Apelles," a comparison with both the Greek god of poetry and the greatest artist from antiquity. Michelangelo wrote more than 300 poems and was still working on these in his seventies, perhaps with the intention of publishing them. Though the volume of Michelangelo's *Rime* was printed posthumously in 1623, he had shared the poems with friends, and during his lifetime they were praised in humanist literary circles in Florence and Rome. He wrote intense and moving verse on a variety of topics—salvation, death, politics, art, and of course, love, which the artist expressed for both women and men.

Michelangelo wrote many of his finest love poems—forty-one sonnets—to a young man named Tommaso de' Cavalieri (*c.*1513–1587). The artist was fifty-seven years old and Tommaso was in his late teens when they first met in the fall of 1532. The two exchanged many letters, and Michelangelo made Tommaso gifts of some of his finest drawings, including the *Rape of Ganymede*, the *Punishment of Tityos*, the *Fall of Phaeton*, and the *Bacchanal of the Children.*[1] Descended from a very old, respected Roman family, the young nobleman was noted not only for his exceptional beauty but also for his "graceful decorum, excellent intelligence and graceful manners."[2] As befitted his education and social rank, Cavalieri was a prominent figure in Roman politics and held important public offices in Rome for four decades, rising eventually to the rank of *conservatore*, the highest civic office, in 1564 and 1571. In 1545 he married and later had two sons; one was Emilio de' Cavalieri, the composer and organist. Throughout his life, Tommaso was a patron of music and the arts, highly regarded as an art collector and arbiter of taste in Roman society, and frequently consulted on important projects by artists and patrons alike. He was appointed to oversee architectural projects in Rome, and he was able to use his influence to help Michelangelo carry out much of his work, including on the Campidoglio. The close bond between the two men lasted to the very end of Michelangelo's life, with Cavalieri present at the artist's deathbed.

DOI: 10.4324/9781003284284-55

Michelangelo Buonarroti, Sonnet *"Se nel volto per gli occhi"*

If the heart can be seen in the face through the eyes,
I have no other, more apparent sign
of my flame; so let these be enough,
my dear lord to petition for your mercy.

Perhaps your spirit, which sees, with greater credence
than I dare to believe, the virtuous fire
that burns me, will be quick to pity me,
like the grace that abounds for one who truly asks.

O happy that day, when this be sure to happen!
Let time and its hours stand still all at once,[3]
and the day, the sun in its ancient circuit,

so that I might have, even if it's not
on my own merits, my sweet and longed-for lord
in my unworthy yet ready arms forever.

Michelangelo Buonarroti, Sonnet *"Non so se s'è la desïata luce"*

I don't know if it is the longed-for light
of its first maker, which my soul feels;
or whether, from my memories[4] of people,
some other beauty shines forth in my heart;

or whether reports or dreams bring someone
before my eyes and present to my heart,
leaving behind something unknown and smarting
that is, perhaps, what now leads me to weep.

What I feel and seek, and who might guide me to it,
are not within me; nor can I see clearly
where I might find them, though others seem to show me.

This, lord, has happened to me since I saw you:
a bitter sweetness, a yes-and-no feeling moves me;
certainly it must have been your eyes.

Michelangelo Buonarroti, Sonnet *"Dal dolce pianto"*

From sweet weeping to a painful smile,
from an eternal to a briefer peace
have I fallen; for, where truth keeps silent,
the senses take over whoever's cut off from it.

And I don't know whether my heart or your face
deserves the blame for this pain, which hurts less
the more it grows, or if it's the burning torch
of your eyes, which are stolen from paradise.

Your beauty is not an earthly thing,
but made up in heaven as something divine among us;
thus, though deprived, I'm comforted by burning,

for near to you I cannot be otherwise.
Since heaven has ordained these weapons of my death,
who, if I die, could say you both[5] were wrong?

Michelangelo Buonarroti, Sonnet *"Felice spirito"*

O joyful spirit, who with eager burning
keep alive my old heart, near to death,
and, among your thousand other delights and blessings,
greet only me out of more noble people!

As you once did to my eyes, now to my mind
you come to console me for loss of others' time,
so that hope now seems to hold in check that sadness
which the soul feels no less than it feels desire.

Therefore, since he who speaks for me has found
grace for me from you amidst all your concerns,
he who writes to you thanks you for your grace.

What great, unseemly usury it would be,
presenting you with the most awful pictures[6]
to get in return beautiful, living people.

Notes

1 For these and other drawings by Michelangelo for Cavalieri, see Garrard, Mariangiu.
2 Benedetto Varchi, cited by Marongiu 287.
3 "Michelangelo echoes the traditional belief that the Sun and Moon would stand still and time stop on Judgment day." (JS)
4 "Michelangelo was in Florence at this time and thinking of Cavalieri. He wrote to Sebastiano del Piombo in Rome during August 1533 asking for news of Tommaso, adding that 'If he were to fade from my memory I think I should instantly die.'" (JS)
5 *you both*: "The final Italian verb is plural, presumably referring both to the addressee (otherwise addressed in the singular) and to God." (JS)
6 "Michelangelo had given Cavalieri several drawings on mythological and other themes. He seems here to express his surprised gratitude that such meager gifts have earned him Cavalieri's affection; perhaps also (given the conditional "would be") to be responding to some request from Cavalieri for more such gifts. Michelangelo expressed some reserve about naming the subjects of the drawings, which included the erotic myths of Ganymede and Tityos; thus the term *turpissime*, which can mean either "of low quality" or "shameful," may also indicate some ambivalence about the drawings' moral content." (JS)

Source

Michelangelo, *Sonnets* in James M. Saslow, *The Poetry of Michelangelo: An Annotated Translation*, Yale UP, 1991, pp. 181, 186, 189, 190–1.

References

Barkan, Leonard. *Michelangelo: A Life on Paper*, Princeton UP, 2011.

Buck, Stephanie, ed. with the assistance of Tatiana Bissolati. *Michelangelo's Dream*, Courtauld Gallery, Paul Holberton, 2010.

Clements, Robert J. *The Poetry of Michelangelo*, NYU Press, 1965.

Eisenbichler, Konrad. "The Religious Poetry of Michelangelo: The Mystical Sublimation," *Renaissance and Reformation*, New Series, Vol. 11, No. 1, Poetry and Religion 1545–1560 (February 1987), pp. 121–34.

Garrard, Mary D. "Michelangelo in Love: Decoding the *Children's Bacchanal*," *The Art Bulletin*, Vol. 96, No. 1 (March 2014), pp. 24–49.

Marongiu, Marcella. "Tommaso de' Cavalieri," in *Michelangelo: Divine Draftsman & Designer*, ed. Carmen C. Bambach, Metropolitan Museum of Art, Yale UP, 2017, pp. 287–89.

Ruvoldt, Maria. "Michelangelo's Open Secrets," in *Visual Cultures of Secrecy in Early Modern Europe*, ed. Timothy McCall, Sean Roberts and Giancarlo Fiorenza, Truman State UP, 2013, pp. 105–25.

Saslow, James M. *Ganymede in the Renaissance: Homosexuality in Art and Society*, Yale UP, 1986.

Part VI

Politics and statecraft

Figure 6.1 Paolo Veronese, *Apotheosis of Venice*, 1582, Sala del Maggior Consiglio, Palazzo Ducale, Venice.

51 The doge, embodiment of the state

Enrico Dandolo, *Promissione*, 1192

Geoffrey of Villehardouin, *Chronicle of the Fourth Crusade*, *c.*1207–13

William Wey, *Description of the death and election of a Doge*, 1462

One of the most distinctive features that set Venice apart from the other city–states on the Italian Peninsula throughout the Middle Ages and Renaissance was the office of the doge, the executive branch of the republic. When elected, each doge was required to pledge to adhere to the terms set out in a *promissione*, or oath of office. The earliest *promissione* that has been preserved is the one sworn by Enrico Dandolo when he was elected forty-first doge of the Venetian Republic on June 1, 1192. The text of this document indicates how the Venetian government was increasingly concerned with limiting the doge's autonomy in foreign affairs and insisting on his obedience to the will of the Senate, the Great Council, and various elected magistracies. Continually revised and refined with each doge, this contract inevitably became longer and more intricate, running to many pages and addressing in detail issues such as personal finances, conflicts of interest, and protection of national security. Paradoxically, as communal governments elsewhere in Italy began increasingly to give way to the unfettered rule of a *signore*, Venetians went in the opposite direction, ever more strictly limiting the powers of the doge who stood at the head of their government. Neither an autocrat nor a mere figurehead, the doge was accountable to the Senate and subject to severe punishment if he overstepped the limits of his authority, although certain individual doges—such as Dandolo himself—were extraordinarily vigorous and powerful leaders. Moreover, though the doge was made to rigorously abide by the law like any citizen, he was distinguished from all other Venetians by the elaborate rituals, pomp, and splendor that accompanied the office, giving him the external appearance of a monarch. The individual who held the office of doge literally embodied the state; he was "that likeness which represents the government of the Venetians," in the words of the Council of Ten.[1] And while the powers of his office became more circumscribed over time, the pageantry attached to his office increased; visitors to the city never failed to marvel at the public spectacles that surrounded the person of the doge. Both the French

DOI: 10.4324/9781003284284-57

chronicler Geoffrey of Villehardouin (*c.*1150–*c.*1218) in the thirteenth century and the English pilgrim William Wey (*c.*1407–1476) two centuries later are effusive in expressing their respect for the authority of the doge, awe for the ceremony that surrounds him, and admiration for the institution he embodies.

Enrico Dandolo, *Promissione*, 1192

These are the items that We, Enrico Dandolo, doge by the grace of God, are bound to observe as long as we live as doge.

1 We will assume administration of the country and we will watch over its government in good faith.

2 And we will be diligent as to equity and justice for all who seek it, and for those who have sought it, it will be produced in good faith without any delay and without fraud, unless it is stayed by a majority of the Council, or unless the matter falls under the jurisdiction . . . with regard to established laws and judgments passed by a decision of the judges, we will diligently bring it to completion in good faith and without fraud.

3 In the case of lawsuits that come before us, we will postpone nothing through any kind of fraud. If, perhaps, our judges appear at some time or other to disagree regarding a pronouncement of law, we then must decide the law, opting for the better faction [of judges], which seems to us to be in accord with custom. Where, in fact, custom fails us, we will, without fraud, render a decision according to our own conscience. We will accept no gift, nor will we allow such to be accepted either to aid or to harm any party or any person. And if for us anyone then accepts a gift on our behalf and informs us of it, we will have it returned in a timely fashion without fraud. We will also accept no gift nor will we allow one to be accepted for anyone . . . or on behalf of the commune of the Venetians.

[. . .]

5 Also all deliberations that we, along with the majority of the Council, command to be secret, we will keep secret, according to our understanding of the situation.

6 And if in our tenure any of the assets, possessions, or funds of the commune of the Venetians shall be given or promised to any person or persons, we will not hold firm that donation or promise unless it was first considered and confirmed by a majority of the Council.

[. . .]

11 We will not dispatch legations and letters to the Roman Pontiff, to emperors, or to kings without [the consent of] the majority of the Council.

12 We will not appoint judges in our palace without election.

13 We will not appoint notaries without [the consent of] a majority of the Council and the approval of the people.
14 We will not undertake any inquiry regarding any offense against us without a decision from the judges.

Geoffrey of Villehardouin, *Chronicle of the Fourth Crusade, c.*1207–13

[*The Frankish envoys ask Doge Enrico Dandolo to help them in their crusade by providing ships to transport them to the Holy Land.*]

"Signors," said the Doge, "we will tell you the conclusions at which we have arrived, if so be that we can induce our great council and the commons of the land to allow of them; and you, on your part, must consult and see if you can accept them and carry them through.

"We will build transports to carry four thousand five hundred horses, and nine thousand squires, and ships for four thousand five hundred knights, and twenty thousand sergeants of foot. And we will agree also to purvey food for these horses and people during nine months. This is what we undertake to do at the least, on condition that you pay us for each horse four marks, and for each man two marks.

"And the covenants we are now explaining to you, we undertake to keep, wheresoever we may be, for a year, reckoning from the day on which we sail from the port of Venice in the service of God and of Christendom. Now the sum total of the expenses above named amounts to 85,000 marks.

"And this will we do moreover. For the love of God, we will add to the fleet fifty armed galleys on condition that, so long as we act in company, of all conquests in land or money, whether at sea or on dry ground, we shall have the half, and you the other half. Now consult together to see if you, on your parts, can accept and fulfil these covenants."

The envoys then departed, and said that they would consult together and give their answer on the morrow. They consulted, and talked together that night, and agreed to accept the terms offered. So the next day they appeared before the Doge, and said: "Sire, we are ready to ratify this covenant." The Doge thereon said he would speak of the matter to his people, and, as he found them affected, so would he let the envoys know the issue.

On the morning of the third day, the Doge, who was very wise and valiant, assembled his great council, and the council was of forty men of the wisest that were in the land. And the Doge, by his wisdom and wit, that were very clear and very good, brought them to agreement and approval. Thus he wrought with them; and then with a hundred others, then two hundred, then a thousand, so that at last all consented and approved. Then he assembled well ten thousand of the people in the church of St. Mark, the most beautiful church that there is, and bade them hear a mass of the Holy Ghost, and pray to God for counsel on the request and messages that had been addressed to them. And the people did so right willingly.

[*The crusaders, having failed to come up with the money to pay the Venetians, agree to attack Zara, which they take, and next they prepare to attack the city of Constantinople.*]

Meanwhile the Doge of Venice had not forgotten to do his part, but had ranged his ships and transports and vessels in line, and that line was well three crossbow-shots in length; and the Venetians began to draw near to the part of the shore that lay under the walls and the towers. Then might you have seen the mangonels shooting from the ships and transports, and the crossbow bolts flying, and the bows letting fly their arrows deftly and well; and those within defending the walls and towers very fiercely; and the ladders on the ships coming so near that in many places swords and lances crossed; and the tumult and noise were so great that it seemed as if the very earth and sea were melting together. And be it known to you that the galleys did not dare to come to the shore.

Now may you hear of a strange deed of prowess; for the Doge of Venice, who was an old man, and saw nothing (as he was blind), stood, fully armed, on the prow of his galley, and had the standard of St. Mark before him; and he cried to his people to put him on land, or else that he would do justice upon their bodies with his hands. And so they did, for the galley was run aground, and they leapt therefrom, and bore the standard of St. Mark before him on to the land. And when the Venetians saw the standard of St. Mark on land, and the galley of their lord touching ground before them, each held himself for shamed, and they all got to the land; and those in the transports leapt forth, and landed; and those in the big ships got into barges, and made for the shore, each and all as best they could. Then might you have seen an assault, great and marvelous; and to this bears witness Geoffrey of Villehardouin, who makes this book.

William Wey, *Description of the funeral and election of a Doge*, 1462

On 3 May of that year [1462] the lord Pasquale Malpiero, the very illustrious Doge of Venice quitted this world,[2] and was laid out in his palace for three days. Then he was taken for burial. At his funeral first arrived all the confraternities, in religious dress with candles and scourges in their hands. Before them crosses and tapers were carried. Then came the parish clergy of Venice, the secular and regular clergy, and lastly the canons of St Mark's with a cross and tapers. Next came two noblemen carrying his arms. Then came his body laid out as follows: on his head he wore his biretta and his face was uncovered; under his head was placed a cushion of cloth of gold. His body was dressed in the golden robe of his office and a cloak. On his feet there were slippers, with golden spurs to one side; on the other side was placed his sword in a gilded scabbard. And with these accoutrements he was buried high up in the wall of the church of the Friars Preachers [Santi Giovanni e Paolo] in Venice.

After his death and burial, the Venetians met to elect a new Doge, summoned by the appointed Councillors. Called to the election were all the eminent nobles, who, on oath, were to choose from among the more noble of those lords firm in the Catholic faith. They themselves had to swear, on pain of losing all their worldly goods, to choose the man who was wisest, the best provided by circumstances, the staunchest in defense of the faith and the most experienced in the affairs of the world, to serve the city and its dominions. Those 100, with some notaries, were confined to a house from which they were not to emerge until they had elected forty of the more noble for this honorable task.[3] Then the forty took Communion so that they might elect him whom they believed would be most firm in upholding the Catholic faith and of the greatest benefit to the city of Venice. And the man acknowledged to have the majority of the votes they accepted as their Doge. They will not, on pain of death, reveal the name of the loser. Then he who has the majority and who is elected to the office of Doge is taken to his house. As he is taken by the water, the Venetians come up to him saying, "All your possessions are now ours"; and he says, "I know that well, but I beseech you to accept between you 100 ducats, and that will content you." And he gives them the money, and scatters coins as he goes, to clear a way home. And, after he has settled his domestic affairs, he is led by the lords of the city to the Ducal Palace. They make him a knight, and they robe him in the vestments of his office and place a biretta covered in precious stones on his head. And the following Sunday he comes to the church of St Mark, and before him process all the confraternities, one of which puts on a pageant for him. Then come the religious in procession with relics, torches, crosses and canopies. Among them are many children dressed as angels; they sing *Te Deum laudamus*, etc. And thus he leaves the church of St Mark with a great procession, and a multitude of the people. Coming to the Ducal Palace, he stands on the threshold, turning to face the people. Then all the lords climb towards him in reverence to pay their respects. Once all this is over he dines in his Palace, where he will remain for the rest of his life. After his election, ambassadors from the various subject provinces attend him bearing gifts, heartily congratulating him on his elevation to such dignity.

Notes

1 This phrase of the Council of Ten from 1447 is cited by Romano, who further explains that "the doge was understood to embody or make visible the spirit or essence of the Republic." Romano xxi.

2 "The Doge actually died on 5 May 1462. William Wey (*c.*1407–1476), a Fellow of Eton College, was making his second pilgrimage to Jerusalem; he is inaccurate on dates as on many other particulars." (JL)

3 "Wey telescopes the complicated procedural stages of the election; the ultimate electoral college numbered forty-one. He seems not to have known that the election took place within the Ducal Palace." (JL)

Sources

Enrico Dandolo, *Promissione* in Thomas F. Madden, *Enrico Dandolo & the Rise of Venice*, Johns Hopkins UP, 2003, pp. 96–8.

Geoffrey of Villehardouin, *Chronicle of the Fourth Crusade* in *Memoirs of the Crusades*, trans. Frank T. Marzials, J.M. Dent, 1908, pp. 6–7, 42–3, ed. Kaborycha.

Wey, *Description* in "Death and election of a Doge noted by a visiting pilgrim," ed. and trans. John Law, in Chambers, David and Brian Pullan, with Jennifer Fletcher. *Venice: A Documentary History, 1450–1630*, Blackwell, 1992, pp. 45–6.

References

Brennan, Michael G. *English Travelers to Venice, 1450–1600*, Routledge, for the Hakluyt Society, 2022.

Romano, Dennis. *The Likeness of Venice: A Life of Doge Francesco Foscari 1373–1457*, Yale UP, 2007.

Szépe, Helena Katalin. *Venice Illuminated: Power and Painting in Renaissance Manuscripts*, Yale UP, 2018.

52 Political discord in communal Italy

Dante Alighieri, *Inferno X*, 1314

Thomas Aquinas, *On Kingship*, 1260–5

Dante Alighieri, *Monarchy*, *c.*1316

"Man is a political animal," wrote Aristotle in the fourth century BCE, referring to the natural human instinct to participate in the life of the "polis," or city–state. Dante Alighieri (1265–1321) was without a doubt just such a political animal, passionate about how his own city–state of Florence was governed. In addition to being a scholar and poet, Dante also held public office, serving as one of the seven priors of the Florentine Republic. Such involvement in politics was risky, given that the Florentine commune was torn apart by violent hostilities between rival parties. At the time his party fell out of power, Dante was on a diplomatic mission in Rome, and he was exiled from Florence. Forbidden to return under pain of death, he wrote the entire *Comedy* while in exile. In the tenth canto of the *Inferno,* Dante addresses the internecine strife in Italy, as well as his own exile, in an imagined exchange of rancorous barbs with a famed leader of the opposing political party.

A generation before Dante, also emerging from the contentious world of communal era politics, was Dominican friar and theologian St. Thomas Aquinas (Tommaso d'Aquino, 1225–1274). Born in Roccasecca, a town south of Rome, Aquinas rose to become a prominent professor at the University of Paris, where he threw himself into the study of Aristotle, many of whose writings had recently become available in Latin. Aquinas used the philosophy in Aristotle's *Ethics* and *Politics* to develop a theory of government applicable to his own time. Although in the passage cited below, he asserts that monarchy is the best system of government, Aquinas also recognizes its potential flaws. He condemns tyrannical abuse of power, although he stops short of advocating the murder of tyrants; elsewhere in his writings, Aquinas embraces the possibility of a just system of collective government. Dante was very familiar with the thinking of both Aquinas and Aristotle on politics, as is evident in his treatise *Monarchy*. By the time he wrote this, Dante had come to believe that the embattled Italian city–states would never be at peace unless unified by a monarch. In this scholarly work written in Latin, Dante, too, looks to the ancient world for answers, though it is not the Greek polis, but the Roman Empire that inspires him. Here, the exiled Florentine citizen expresses his disillusionment with communal politics and

DOI: 10.4324/9781003284284-58

advocates the rule of an emperor as the only viable political solution for his tumultuous times.

Dante Alighieri, *Inferno X*, 1314

[*Dante and his guide Virgil are wandering through the sixth circle of Hell, where heretics are punished, when a figure rises up and directly addresses the poet.*]

"O Tuscan, you who through the fiery city, 22
    a living man, walk and speak so fittingly,
    please rest awhile in this place.
By your speech it is clear 25
    that you are from that noble native land
    which I treated perhaps too harshly."
So suddenly this sound had burst 28
    from one of the tombs, that fearful,
    I drew a bit nearer to my guide.
He told me: "Turn around! What are you doing? 31
    Over there you can see Farinata[1] has risen;
    you can see all of him from the waist up."
I had already been staring at him, 34
    and he held himself erect
    as if he had great disdain for Hell.
The brave and ready hand of my guide 37
    urged me toward the sepulcher toward him,
    saying: "Your words must be well-considered."
When I came up to the foot of his tomb, 40
    he took one look at me, and then almost scornful,
    asked: "Who were your ancestors?"
Since I was desirous to obey, 43
    I did not hide it, but revealed all to him.
    at which, his brows lifted slightly.
Then he said: "They were fiercely opposed 46
    to me, to my family, and to my party,
    so that twice I had to scatter them."[2]
"If they were driven away," I replied, 49
    "at least each time they returned,
    but yours never mastered that art."[3]

[*The conversation is interrupted when Dante meets the father of his good friend Guido Cavalcanti and speaks with him, then Farinata addresses him again.*]

And continuing from before, he said: 76
"If they had poorly learned that art,
that torments me more than this bed.
Yet the face of the lady who reigns here[4] 79
will not have fifty times rekindled, before
you yourself will know the weight of that art.
And as you wish to return to the sweet world, 82
tell me why that populace is so cruelly
set against my family in all their laws?"
To which I replied: "The anguish and slaughter 85
that colored the Arbia[5] red
gave rise to such prayers in our temple."
Then sighing, he shook his head. 88
"I was not alone," he said, "nor certainly
without reason did I act along with the others.
But when the rest would have 91
allowed Florence to be eradicated,
there, did I alone outright defend her."[6]

Thomas Aquinas, *On Kingship*, 1260–5

Book I, Chapter VI

HOW PROVISION MIGHT BE MADE THAT THE KING MAY NOT FALL INTO TYRANNY

Since the rule of one man, which is the best, is to be preferred, and since it may happen that it be changed into a tyranny, which is the worst . . . a scheme should be carefully worked out which would prevent the multitude ruled by a king from falling into the hands of a tyrant. . . . Then, once the king is established, the government of the kingdom must be so arranged that opportunity to tyrannize is removed. At the same time his power should be so tempered that he cannot easily fall into tyranny. How these things may be done we must consider in what follows.

Finally, provision must be made for facing the situation should the king stray into tyranny.

Indeed, if there be not an excess of tyranny it is more expedient to tolerate the milder tyranny for a while than, by acting against the tyrant, to become involved in many perils more grievous than the tyranny itself. For it may happen that those who act against the tyrant are unable to prevail and the tyrant then will rage the more. But should one be able to prevail against the tyrant, from this fact itself very grave dissensions among the people frequently ensue: the multitude may be broken up into factions either during their revolt against the tyrant, or in the process of the organization of the government, after the tyrant has been overthrown.

Dante Alighieri, *Monarchy*, *c.*1316

Book I, vi

If we consider a small community, whose purpose is neighborly support in relation both to people and to goods, there must be one person who guides the others, either appointed by someone from outside or emerging as leader from among their number with the agreement of the others; otherwise not only will they fail to achieve that neighborly collaboration, but sometimes, if a number of people contest the leadership, the whole community is destroyed. If we consider a city, whose purpose is to be self-sufficient in living the good life,[7] there must be one ruling body, and this is so not only in just government, but in perverted forms of government as well; if this should not be the case, not only is the purpose of social life thwarted, but the city itself ceases to be what it was. Lastly, if we consider an individual kingdom—and the purpose of a kingdom is the same as that of a city, but with greater confidence that peace can be maintained—there must be one king who rules and governs; otherwise not only do those who live in the kingdom not achieve that purpose, but the kingdom itself falls to ruin, in accordance with those words of the infallible Truth: "Every kingdom divided against itself shall be laid waste."[8] If this holds true in these cases and in individuals who are ordered to one particular goal . . . there must therefore be one person who directs and rules mankind, and he is properly called "Monarch" or "Emperor."

Book I, xv

All concord depends on the unity which is in wills; mankind in its ideal state represents a kind of concord; for just as one man in his ideal state spiritually and physically is a kind of concord (and the same holds true of a household, a city, and a kingdom), so is the whole of mankind; thus the whole of mankind in its ideal state depends on the unity which is in men's wills.[9] But this cannot be unless there is one will which controls and directs all others towards one goal, since the wills of mortals require guidance on account of the seductive pleasures of youth, as Aristotle teaches at the end of the *Ethics*.[10] Nor can such a single will exist, unless there is one ruler who rules over everybody, whose will can control and guide all the other wills. . . . For mankind to be in its ideal state there must be a monarch in the world, and consequently the well-being of the world requires a monarchy.

Book I, xvi

O human race, how many storms and misfortunes and shipwrecks must toss you about while, transformed into a many-headed beast,[11] you strive after conflicting things. You are sick in your intellects, both of them,[12] and in your affections; you do not nurture your higher intellect with inviolable principles, nor your lower intellect with the lessons of experience, nor your affections with the sweetness of divine counsel, when it is breathed into you by the trumpet of the holy spirit: "Behold how good and how pleasant it is for brethren to dwell together in unity."[13]

Notes

1 Farinata degli Uberti (d.1264), who belonged to one of the most distinguished noble Florentine families was a powerful leader of the Ghibillines. He is in this circle of Inferno because after his death, he was declared a heretic by his enemies.
2 After their victory in 1248, the Ghibellines exiled their enemies, the Guelfs—the party Dante's family belonged to—and when the Guelfs returned ten years later, they retaliated by exiling the Ghibellines. The Ghibellines regrouped in Siena, with Farinata as their leader and with the help of Sienese allies they launched an attack on the Florentines, defeating them again at the Battle of Montaperti on September 4, 1260.
3 On June 11, 1289, the Guelfs definitively crushed the Ghibellines at the Battle of Campaldino. Dante, a member of the Guelf party, likely fought in that battle.
4 The lady is Persephone, wife of Pluto, the lord of the underworld in Greek mythology. She is associated with the Moon, so Farinata tells Dante that not fifty months will go by before he too will know the sorrow of exile. Dante was exiled from Florence in 1302.
5 The Arbia is a river that flows near the village of Montaperti, not far from Siena.
6 After the Battle of Montaperti, at the Council of Empoli when the rest of the Ghibellines wanted to completely destroy Florence, Farinata opposed them.
7 "This definition is Aristotelian; see *Politics* 3, 9 128ob 29–34. To live the 'good life' is to live as a human being in the fullest sense, to live the life of a rational creature who applies reason to making discriminations of right and wrong, good and evil; a community achieves the 'good life' when it provides the conditions which enable its citizens to fulfil themselves in this way." (PS)
8 Matt. 12:25; Luke 11:17
9 "Aquinas *In Eth.* devotes Lecture VI on Book IX to a discussion of concord in these terms." (PS)
10 *Ethics* 10, 9 1179b 32f.
11 Rev. 12:3 and 17:9
12 "That is, theoretical and practical." (PS)
13 Ps. 133:1

Sources

Dante Alighieri. *Inferno*, ed. Natalino Sapegno, La Nuova Italia, 1976, trans. Kaborycha.
Thomas Aquinas. *On Kingship*, trans. Gerald B. Phelan, Hyperion, 1949, pp. 23–5.
Dante Alighieri. *Monarchy*, trans. and ed. Prue Shaw, Cambridge UP, 1996, pp. 10–11; 27; 28–9.

References

Bigongiari, Dino, ed. *The Political Ideas of St. Thomas Aquinas*, Hafner, 1969.
Davis, Charles Till. "Dante and the Empire," in *The Cambridge Companion to Dante*, Cambridge UP, 1993.
Durling, Robert M. "Canto X: Farinata and Cavalcante," in *Inferno: A Canto-by-Canto Commentary*, UC Press, 1998.
Najemy, John. "Dante and Florence," in *The Cambridge Companion to Dante*, Cambridge UP, 1993.

53 A deadly attack on the Medici family

Angelo Poliziano, *On the Pazzi Conspiracy*, 1478

Figures 6.2a and 6.2b Bertoldo di Giovanni, *The Pazzi Conspiracy Medal*, 1478, Metropolitan Museum of Art, NYC Left: The obverse of the medal depicts a bust of Lorenzo de' Medici above a depiction of his attackers; the Latin inscription reads: "LAURENTIUS MEDICES SALUS PUBLICA" ("Lorenzo de' Medici Public Salvation"). Right: The reverse side shows a bust of Giuliano de' Medici above a depiction of Giuliano attacked and fallen to the ground; it reads "IULIANVS MEDICES LUCTVS PUBLICUS" ("Giuliano de' Medici Public Mourning").

"I do not believe that Florence had ever experienced a day of such travail," wrote Francesco Guicciardini, describing the violent climax of the Pazzi Conspiracy on April 26, 1478.[1] Though the historian was only a child when the assault on Lorenzo and Giuliano de' Medici took place, when he wrote these words decades after the fact, the traumatic impact of that bloody day still resonated. Of the various versions that have come down to us, one of the most dramatic is the eyewitness account of Angelo Poliziano (Angelo Ambrogini, 1454–1494), recorded very soon after the event at which he was physically present alongside the Medici brothers. A member of Lorenzo's inner circle of friends and associates, Poliziano's attachment to the family

DOI: 10.4324/9781003284284-59

went back to his childhood. Angelo Poliziano was a humanist scholar and poet who took on the name of his birthplace, the Tuscan hill town of Montepulciano, where his father was murdered when the boy was not yet ten years old. Angelo was sent to Florence, where he learned first Latin and then Greek at the Florentine Studio. When he was only fifteen years old, his Latin verse translation of Homer's *Iliad* brought him to the attention of Lorenzo. The ruler of Florence befriended the young scholar and invited him to make use of the Medici library. Poliziano came to live in the Medici household, becoming in time tutor to Lorenzo's children. Thus, as an ally of the family, in his moving account *Coniurationis commentarium* (*Commentary on the Pazzi Conspiracy*), the humanist is primarily concerned with defending his patrons. He portrays the Medici as the innocent victims of the Pazzi, depicting the rival clan and their associates as evil men motivated by envy, arrogance, and greed. Poliziano concentrates on immediate events rather than providing a full account of the unfolding of events leading up to that day, which involved underhanded political maneuvering on both sides. This text was part of a barrage of pro-Medici propaganda meant to influence public opinion and to rally support behind Lorenzo. Produced in the immediate wake of the disaster, such propaganda included public ceremonies of mourning for Giuliano and thanksgiving for Lorenzo, written invectives against the pope and other enemies of the Medici, and a variety of visual images condemning the assassins. A loyal Medici supporter who provided the latter was Bertoldo di Giovanni (*c.*1440–1491), a sculptor who had studied with Donatello. Though relatively little is known about Bertoldo's origins, he is well documented as an intimate member of Lorenzo's household. The sculptor had his own room in the Palazzo Medici and even accompanied Lorenzo to the baths at Bagno di Morba when he needed a treatment for gout. Very soon after the attack in the cathedral, Bertoldo produced a bronze medal for Lorenzo that visually represented the scenes in the choir described by Poliziano (Figures 6.2a, 6.2b). It was the custom for sculptors to make medals with portraits of important individuals, often to commemorate significant events, and these were done in conscious imitation of classical coins and medals. Lorenzo de' Medici himself had an immense collection of ancient cameos, coins, and medals; he possessed 1,866 bronze medals alone. When Renaissance rulers commissioned such medals, they were having themselves and their deeds deliberately cast in the image of the Caesars.

Angelo Poliziano, *On the Pazzi Conspiracy*, 1478

The Medici family was generally in all things most splendid and magnificent, above all in welcoming distinguished guests. No famous man could come to Florence or enter the Florentine countryside without being treated in this magnificent way. And so, when it happened that Cardinal Raffaello Riario, son of the sister of Count Girolamo, went to Jacopo Pazzi's country villa, where we have said the plot had been organized, the conspirators seized this opportunity to carry out their crime. In the name of the cardinal, they asked the two brothers to receive him in their villa outside the city in Fiesole. I myself went there with Lorenzo and little Piero, his son. Giuliano, prevented by an illness, stayed home, and this was what caused them to postpone the deed to the day that we have mentioned. Then they let Lorenzo know in a casual way, that the cardinal would like to be invited to a banquet at the [Medici] home in Florence to see its adornments—the carpets, tapestries, gemstones, silver, and all the priceless furnishings. The two excellent young men, unsuspecting any deceit, prepared the house, had all the decorations and hangings brought out, the fine silver, statues, and vases placed in full view, with the gems displayed on a sideboard; a magnificent banquet was prepared.

And then, when the time came, a handful of the conspirators wanted to know, "Where is Lorenzo? Where is Giuliano?" When they learned that they were both in Santa Reparata [the Duomo], they headed over there. The cardinal was led to the choir platform, as is the custom, and while the Mass was being celebrated, the archbishop, Jacopo Bracciolini, Jacopo Salviati, and several companions went to the Palazzo della Signoria to throw the rulers of Florence out and to occupy the palace themselves. The others remained in the church to carry out their crime. Giovanni Battista, assigned to the murder of Lorenzo, had refused; instead, they chose Antonio da Volterra and Stefano to do it,[2] while the rest were to attack Giuliano.

As soon as the priest had taken Communion, the signal was given and Bernardo Bandini, Francesco Pazzi, and other conspirators formed a circle around Giuliano. The first was Bandini, who stabbed the young man in the chest with a sword, driving it all the way through. Dying, he took a few steps, trying to flee; they followed him. The youth, gasping his last, fell to the ground, and as he was lying there Francesco stabbed him repeatedly with a dagger. Thus did they kill the honored youth. Giuliano's servant, frozen with terror, had shamefully hidden himself in a corner.

In the meantime, the designated assassins attacked Lorenzo, first Antonio da Volterra, who grabbed him by the left shoulder and tried to strike him in the neck. Undaunted, Lorenzo freed himself from his cloak, wrapped it around his left arm, and simultaneously drew his sword; however, as he made that movement, he was slashed in the neck. Yet, that vigorous, courageous man, grasping his sword, looking about him, watching on all sides, kept up his defenses. He went toward the assassins, who fled, terrified. Coming forcefully to his defense were Andrea and Lorenzo Cavalcanti, who flanked him: Lorenzo was wounded in the arm; Andrea was unscathed.

You could see the populace in turmoil: men and women, priests, children who were fleeing here and there, wherever their feet could carry them. Cries and weeping echoed all around, but no distinct words could be made out; some thought the church was collapsing. Bernardo Bandini, not content with having slaughtered Giuliano, made his way toward Lorenzo, who had taken refuge with a few of his supporters in the sacristy. On his way, Bandini struck and killed with a sword thrust to the stomach Francesco Nori, a wise man, a merchant and ally of the Medici family. His body, as he died, was taken inside the same sacristy in which Lorenzo had retreated. Then I, who had joined the others inside that place, closed the bronze sacristy doors. In this way, we averted the danger posed by Bandini. As we kept guard over the doors, others inside were anxious, worried about Lorenzo's wound. Then, Antonio Ridolfi, Jacopo's son and a worthy man, began to suck the wound.[3] Lorenzo did not give a thought to his own injury, but continually asked about Giuliano, from time to time, full of indignation, threatening and lamenting that such men had sought to kill him.

At this same time, a group of young men, faithful to the Medici family, was gathering at the doors of the sacristy, weapons in hand. Together they shouted that they were friends and relations: "Come out, come out Lorenzo, before the enemy forces take control!" Those of us who were inside were afraid, not knowing whether they were friends or foes; nevertheless, we asked them whether Giuliano had been saved. To this they did not answer. At this point, Sigismondo Della Stufa, an eminent young man, who had shared an exceptional friendship and an incredible affection with Lorenzo since childhood, mounted the stairs and went rapidly to peer out from the little window that looked out over the church from the organ loft, and seeing Giuliano's cadaver stretched on the ground, understood immediately the crime that had been committed. He recognized the friends standing at the door and ordered it to be opened. As they rushed in, they gathered around Lorenzo, enclosing him in a circle of armed guards and brought him home, taking pains so he would not encounter Giuliano's body. I headed straight home, passing Giuliano's body piteously lying there pierced by many wounds, defiled and bloody. Trembling, and hardly in possession of my faculties, before such an immensity of grief, supported by several friends I was led away toward home.

Notes

1 *The History of Florence*, trans. Domandi 34–5.
2 Giovanni Battista da Montesecco (c.1450–1478) was a *condottiero*, a professional soldier, and when he withdrew from his part in the conspiracy he was replaced by these men, both priests. Machiavelli, in his *History of Florence* describes the two as "entirely unsuited to the task," and blames the failure of the plot largely on them.
3 This was a precaution in case the dagger that penetrated the skin had been poisoned.

Source

Angelo Poliziano, *Coniurationis commentarium = Commentario della congiura dei Pazzi*, ed. Leandro Perini, traduzione di Sara Donegà, Firenze University Press, 2012, trans. Kaborycha.

References

Budd, Denise M. "Leonardo, Medici Ephemera, and the Art of the Pazzi Conspiracy," in *Watching Art: Writings in Honor of James Beck*, ed. Lynn Catterson and Mark Zucker, Ediart, 2006.

Celati, Marta. *Conspiracy Literature in Early Renaissance Italy: Historiography and Princely Ideology*, Oxford UP, 2021, pp. 157–90.

Draper, James David. *Bertoldo di Giovanni, Sculptor of the Medici Household*, U Missouri P, 1992.

Guicciardini, Francesco. *The History of Florence*, trans. Mario Domandi, Harper & Row, 1970.

Hook, Judith. *Lorenzo de' Medici: An Historical Biography*, H. Hamilton, 1984.

Martines, Lauro. *April Blood: Florence and the Plot Against the Medici*, Oxford UP, 2003.

Nethersole, Scott. *Art and Violence in Early Renaissance Florence*, Yale UP, 2018.

Poliziano, Angelo, *The Pazzi Conspiracy*, in *The Earthly Republic: Italian Humanists on Government and Society*, ed. Kohl and Witt, U Pennsylvania P, 1978, 293–322, trans. Elizabeth B. Welles.

Pollard, Graham. "The Italian Renaissance Medal: Collecting and Connoisseurship," *Studies in the History of Art*, vol. 21, Symposium Papers VIII: Italian Medals (1987), pp. 161–9.

Scher, Stephen K. *The Currency of Fame: Portrait Medals of the Renaissance*, photography John Bigelow Taylor. Thames and Hudson in association with the Frick Collection, 1994.

54 A sermon on Florentine political reform

Girolamo Savonarola, *Sermon XIII on Haggai*, Dec. 14, 1494

Luca Landucci, *Diary*, Dec. 14, 1494

The Observant Dominican friar Girolamo Savonarola (1452–1498) held sway over the Florentine people through his prophecies and fiery oratory during the years 1494 through 1498. In addition to urging spiritual repentance and religious reform, Savonarola used his authority to encourage political reform. Following the exile of the Medici in 1494, the friar actively influenced the reshaping of the government of the republic through a series of powerful sermons he delivered late that year. Soon after Piero di Lorenzo de' Medici (1472–1503) was driven out of Florence on November 16, the friar began to openly accuse the former regime of having subverted the Florentine Republic. A *parlamento* (general assembly of citizens) met on December 2 to institute changes in electoral practices that the Medici had undermined. Meanwhile, as Medici supporters jockeyed for power in the new government, Savonarola's political rhetoric became more direct. In a sermon on December 7, he urged civic renewal and spoke of the need for Florence to become a "new city," with a "new government," and to find "new ways to live." He warned Florentines: "The first thing you must do is this: you must make such laws that never in the future will anyone be able to make himself ruler [*capo*] over you, otherwise you will have laid foundations on sand."[1] Then, preaching to a vast audience from the pulpit of Florence's cathedral the next week on December 14, 1494, Savonarola delivered his most forceful sermon on politics. It was the third Sunday in Advent, and the friar's topic was Haggai, an Old Testament prophet who urged the rebuilding of the Temple. The influence of the political theories of Dominican theologian Thomas Aquinas, as well as that of Aristotle (#52), are evident in his sermon. Going beyond mere theory, in this sermon Savonarola makes concrete suggestions for a much broader political representation than Florentines had ever previously known. He calls for a large legislative body on the model of the Venetian Great Council, which was composed of 2,000 members, and further advises that groups of citizens from every neighborhood submit proposals of their own. Over the course of the next two weeks, these proposals were given to the Signoria—the governing body of the Florentine Republic, composed of eight priors and the standardbearer of justice. After reviewing these proposals, the

DOI: 10.4324/9781003284284-60

establishment of a Great Council was put to a vote on December 22 before two hundred representatives of the Florentine populace; it passed by an overwhelming majority and, on December 23, the Great Council was voted into law. In his diary entries made over the course of that month, the apothecary Luca Landucci (1437–1516) captures the tumultuous mood of those final weeks of December 1494. Four years later, Savonarola echoed many of the political ideas expressed in his December 14 sermon in a vernacular work titled *A Tract on the Constitution and Government of the City of Florence*. Published in 1498 only a few weeks before his death, in it he tells Florentines that once people "are liberated from servitude to a tyrant they will live in true freedom, which is more precious than gold and silver."

Girolamo Savonarola, *Sermon XIII on Haggai*, Dec. 14, 1494

As man is a social animal who does not know how to live alone, and is incapable of it, it was necessary for men to gather and congregate in cities, castles, or villages to create associations with one another for their common needs. And nature found the way for them to understand one another in these gatherings, by giving them power of speech and language so each could express ideas to each other, according to their necessities. Thus, every group of men gathered together is organized with a purpose—which can be arrived at by various paths—and needs to have someone to direct and rule the others. People everywhere, who tend toward their own natural good, need governing, and these governments are distinct from one another and differ in various ways. Some are ruled by one leader, some by more than one; some are ruled by the entire population together. Rule by one leader is good; it is the best, better than all others, more easily brought together and united. And the reason is that it is more difficult to bring many into agreement than a few—where valor [*virtù*] is more united it is stronger and it is easier to concentrate this in one person than in many. Though the best government is that of one over many when that one person is good, when the ruler is bad it is the very worst government. Nonetheless, as men are everywhere different, there are diverse modes of governments to be found in various countries.

In hot parts of this hemisphere, people are more weak-hearted than in other places, because they lack blood,[2] so in those places men easily let themselves be ruled by one leader; they obey simply, and willingly make themselves subject to him. In the cold, northerly zones, where there is much blood and little inventiveness [*ingegno*], similarly they stay put and remain subject to one lord and ruler over them. But in the middle areas like Italy where there is plenty of blood and inventiveness [*ingegno*] together, men do not patiently remain subject to a single ruler, but each of them wants to be the leader to govern and rule the others, to command and not to be commanded.

And from this are born all the dissension and discord among citizens in a city where one person wants to make himself great and dominate the others. Experience has demonstrated this often enough, both in ancient Roman times, as well as today in Italian cities where every day one sees examples of it. And in your city [Florence] have you seen it and experienced it as well, and in our own time. Moreover, it is the counsel of theologians that in these regions, where men, by nature, will not tolerate having a superior [rule over them], that it is better to have rule by many, rather than by one. And this can be said to apply most of all to the city of Florence, where men's natures abound in blood and inventiveness.

[. . .]

Your proverb is false, you who said that states are not to be governed with prayers and virtuous living.[3] And so, Florence, if you want your government to be stable, strong and long-lasting, you must turn to God and to living righteously, otherwise you will ruin yourself.

Furthermore, your magnificent Signoria must order all things that are contrary to divine law removed. First of all, to order that the clergy be good, for priests have to be the mirror for the people, so that everyone can look at them and learn how to live the right way. Bad priests and other bad religious are to be banned. I do not say you are to do this on your own, nor that you deprive them of their benefices, but with the authority of the Supreme Pontiff, you shall see to it that the clergy and other religious in your city are good. And they ought not to enrich themselves so much with possessions, but for God's sake give to the poor and abandon all excess; and in this way they shall attain Paradise.

It is necessary, I say, to make sure that the clergy is good and that everything be reformed. Likewise, it is necessary that the Signoria makes a law against that accursed vice of sodomy, for which Florence is infamous throughout all of Italy. And this evil reputation is born perhaps because you talk and prattle about it so much, so that perhaps there is not as much of it as reputed. Make a law against it, say I, without mercy, that is, so that such persons are stoned and burned. You also need to rid yourself of poetry, games, and taverns, and women's evil habits of dress.[4] Everything that is harmful to the soul's health must be eliminated, so that each lives not for the sake of worldly things, but for God, in simplicity and charity.

[. . .]

It is also necessary in a well-ordered city that those who govern see to it that the taxes that are paid to the city and its territories are justly apportioned according to one's goods, and not arbitrary, as has been done at times, so that men can strive for the universal good. Furthermore, take care that the taxes on goods are moderate so that the taxes are not higher than the income from the goods, and similarly, the *gabelles* [customs duties] so that public and private each has its place.[5] Indeed, it is necessary to remove every trace of tyranny and corruption. It would be a good thing to pass certain measures to bring dowries under control, since lineages and families are impoverished when dowries are excessive. For example, the largest dowries ought not to exceed 500 ducats, and those of artisans, no more than around 300, as determined by those whose duty it is to deal with such things. And no individual ought to be able to ruin the *Monte* dowry fund,[6] which is a common good that everyone partakes in.

Most of all, you must be careful that no one makes himself ruler, nor dominates over the others in the city.

[. . .]

They say that a populace under a tyrant is like a river that is restrained and held back by force, and as soon as it finds an opening to escape, it breaks forth impetuously destroying everything. And thus, divine justice will have it because such tyrants are visited on a populace for their sins, as Scripture says: "I gave thee a king in mine anger." [Hosea 13:11] And when punishment has been meted out—for as God is merciful, it cannot last forever—the tyrant is sent away, and all the populace rises up against him. But when God wishes to show mercy, he expels the tyrant. Thus, take care that no one raises himself as ruler in your city, and watch over the common good. And how you ought to do this, I will explain, as God inspires me.

I have told you these past days that when people naturally want to do a thing, the main consideration is the form it takes; therefore, I told you that you must select a good form for this new government of yours, and above all that no one ought to think of making himself ruler if you want to live in freedom. The form you have begun cannot last unless you reorganize it better. I believe that there is no better [example] than that of the Venetians and that you should take your example from them, cutting out, however, anything that is not appropriate nor needed by you, such as having a doge (**#51**).

[. . .]

You have in your city sixteen companies of standardbearers [*gonfalonieri di compagnia*] as you call them, who are in charge of all the citizens throughout the city. Gathering the citizens together, each in his *gonfalone*,[7] let them all be consulted and examined about which form seems best for your government. Let each *gonfalone* select for itself and thus there will be sixteen forms. Then all the standardbearers shall meet and choose four of the suggestions that seem best and most stable to them, and then let them bring those before the magnificent Signoria. After the Mass of the Holy Spirit is chanted in their hall, they shall elect one of those four. You may be certain that the government thus chosen will be God's own choice. And I believe, as I said above, that the form of government of the Venetians is very good and you should not deem it shameful to learn from others, because the form they have was given to them by God and since they adopted it there has never been civil discord among them. And know this, Florence, that God has been established as your *medico* [physician][8] and if you observe what I've told you, you need not fear your enemies because you will always be more powerful than they are, and God will defend you.

Luca Landucci, *Diary*, 1494

14th December (Sunday).

The same day Fra Girolamo did his utmost in the pulpit to persuade Florence to adopt a good form of government; he preached in Santa Maria del Fiore [the Duomo] every day, and today, which was a Sunday, he wished that there should be no women, but only men; he wished that only the *Gonfaloniere* and one of the *Signori* should remain in the *Palagio* [Palazzo Vecchio], and that all the offices of Florence should be there; and he preached much about State matters, and that we ought to love and fear God, and love the commonweal; and no one must set himself up proudly above the rest. He always favored the people and he insisted that no one ought to be put to death, but there must be other forms of punishment; and he continued to preach in this manner every morning. Many forms were drawn up, and there was much controversy among the citizens, so that every day it was expected that the bell would be rung for a *parlamento*.

[. . .]

16th December (Tuesday).

Nothing but the sermons of the said *Frate* [Savonarola].

19th December (Friday).

Many schemes of government were taken to the *Palagio*. Each *Gonfaloniere* made a scheme, as the *Frate* had proposed.

21st December (Sunday).

He preached again; and still he did not wish any women to come; he went on discoursing about State matters, and great fear was felt lest the citizens should not agree. *Chi la voleva lessa e chi arrosto* [One wished it boiled and another roast: i.e. everyone had a different opinion] one agreed with the *Frate*, and another was against him; and if it had not been for him there would have been bloodshed.

[. . .]

22nd December (Monday).

This day many things were voted in the *Palagio*: Anyone who slew a man could not return to Florence; and a law as follows against the unmentionable vice [sodomy]: the first time, the offender to be punished with the *gogna*,[9] the second time, to be fastened to a pillar, and the third time, to be burnt; and many other laws, all recommended by the *Frate*.

[. . .]

28th December (Sunday).

Fra Girolamo preached, and again wished no women to be present. There was a great crowd; it was judged that there were always 13 to 14 thousand people at his sermons. Everyone felt very distrustful, fearing some trouble in the beginning of this new government.

29th December.

The new *Signori* were drawn by lot, which is a fresh way of choosing them. The First *Gonfaloniere* is one of the Corbizi, this news being received joyfully, seeming to promise a popular and more impartial government.

Notes

1 Note the similarity of the proverb cited by Machiavelli in *The Prince,* chapter 9: "He who lays foundations on the people lays foundations on mud." Furthermore, in Sermon XIII below, Savonarola uses the term *virtù* in a sense similar to that of Machiavelli; he also employs the metaphor of a torrential river.

2 A reference to humoral theory in medicine that was current at the time. According to ancient Galenic medicine, there were four humors that determined a person's personality and affected their health: blood, choler, black bile, and yellow bile. Having much blood indicated a sanguine temperament, characterized by an energetic, social disposition. Girolamo Savonarola's grandfather was Michele Savonarola (*c.*1385–1464), a renowned Ferrarese physician, author of a number of influential medical texts.

3 This is a reference to Cosimo de' Medici's often quoted saying that "states cannot be ruled by paternosters."

4 "It was largely due to Savonarola's authority that the new regime waged probably the most concentrated and effective attack on sodomy ever known in Florence. But the attempt to impose a monastic-like rule in the city did not go uncontested. Alongside the struggle during these years over the political character of the new regime, conflict raged over the severe moral regimen that Savonarola championed." Rocke 204.

5 See **#63** on the Florentine Catasto for various kinds of taxation in quattrocento Florence.

6 For the *Monte delle doti* see p. 332.

7 For *gonfaloni*, see **#63** on the Florentine Catasto.

8 Savonarola has deliberately chosen the term "*medico*" (physician) as a reference to the Medici family. God will take the place of the Medici, he implies, and heal the Florentine people.

9 "*Alla gogna* was when a prisoner was exposed on the outer wall of the prison of the Bargello, with his hands bound behind him to one of the iron rings, bareheaded, with his hat at his feet to receive *soldi*, and a placard on his breast upon which his crime was written. He had to remain there an hour, during which time the old bell of the prison was rung." (ARJ)

Sources

Girolamo Savonarola, *Sermon*, in *Prediche sopra Aggeo, con il Trattato circa il reggimento e governo della citta di Firenze*, ed. Luigi Firpo, Belardetti, 1965, trans. Kaborycha.

Luca Landucci, *A Florentine Diary from 1450 to 1516*, trans. Alice de Rosen Jervis, J.M. Dent & Sons Ltd.; E. P. Dutton & Company, 1927, pp. 76–8, ed. Kaborycha.

References

Polizzotto, Lorenzo. *The Elect Nation: The Savonarolan Movement in Florence, 1494–1545*, Oxford UP, 1994.

Rocke, Michael. *Forbidden Friendships: Homosexuality and Male Culture in Renaissance Florence*, Oxford UP, 1996, esp. ch. 6 "Politics and Sodomy in the Late Fifteenth Ceutury: the Medici, Savonarola, and the Abolition of the Night Officers."

Rubinstein, Nicolai and Sarah-Louise Raillard. "The Early Years of Florence's Grand Council (1494–1499)," *Revue française de science politique* (English Edition), Vol. 64, No. 6, Florence (1200–1530): Reinvention of Politics (2014), pp. 99–127.

Savonarola, Girolamo. *Selected Writings of Girolamo Savonarola: Religion and Politics, 1490–1498*, trans. and ed. Anne Borelli and Maria Pastore, Yale UP, 2006.

Savonarola, Girolamo. *Treatise on the Constitution and Government of the City of Florence*, in *Humanism & Liberty: Writings on Freedom from Fifteenth-century Florence*, trans. and ed. Renee Neu Watkins, U South Carolina P, 1978.

Weinstein, Donald. *Savonarola and Florence: Prophecy and Patriotism in the Renaissance*, Princeton UP, 1970.

55 Cesare Borgia's assassinations

Niccolò Machiavelli, *Letters to the Council of Ten*, Dec. 23; Dec. 26, 1502

Niccolò Machiavelli, *The Prince*, Chapter VII, 1513

Niccolò Machiavelli, *How Duke Valentino Killed the Generals Who Conspired Against Him*

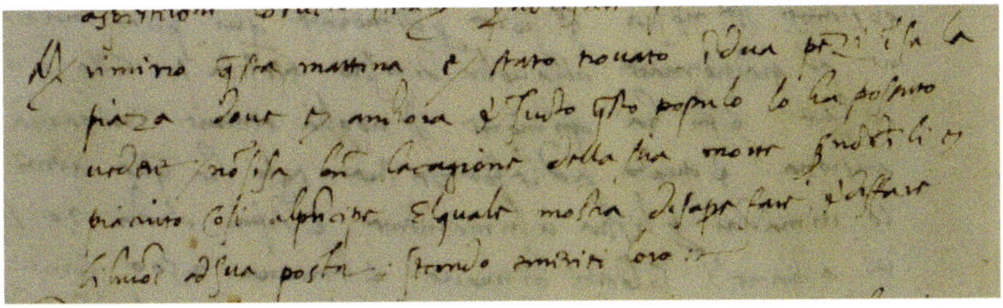

Figure 6.3 Niccolò Machiavelli, *Letter to the Council of Ten*, December 26, 1502, Florence State Archive, Dieci di Balia, Cart. Resp. 119, fol. 43v. The passage from this dispatch in Machiavelli's handwriting reads: "*Messer Rimirro questa mattina è stato trovato in dua pezi in su la piaza dove è anchora; et tucto questo populo lo ha possuto vedere; non si sa bene la cagione della sua morte, se non che li è piaciuto così al Principe, el quale mostra di sapere fare et disfare li huomini ad sua posta, secondo e'meriti loro.*" English translation below.

At the opening of the sixteenth century, Cesare Borgia, Duke Valentino (1475–1507), was one of the most formidable military leaders on the Italian Peninsula. In 1502, Cesare, son of Pope Alexander VI, was engaged in military conquest of territories claimed by the papacy in large swathes of the Romagna region and posed a substantial threat to Florence. Niccolò Machiavelli had unique opportunities to get to know the duke firsthand, as he was sent to Borgia on three official missions on behalf of the Florentine Republic (**#19**). It was Machiavelli's duty as envoy to send back official reports in

DOI: 10.4324/9781003284284-61

which he recorded his observations of Cesare Borgia's character, intentions, and impending actions. Among Machiavelli's detailed dispatches from the town of Cesena in late December of 1502 were those concerning the fate of Remirro de Orco (also known by his Spanish name Ramiro de Lorqua or Lorca), one of the duke's henchmen. When he came to write *The Prince*, having had more than a decade to reflect on the event, Machiavelli used the episode to illustrate the effectiveness of Cesare Borgia's strategies for ruling territories that he had conquered. In *The Prince* he plainly states, "I could not give better advice for a new prince, than to follow the example of his [Cesare's] actions." Machiavelli returned to the theme of tactical use of violence in describing further events that took place in the town of Senigallia on December 31, 1502, when Duke Valentino killed a group of his military captains who had plotted against him. Once again, Machiavelli was an eyewitness to events; these he recorded succinctly in *The Prince* and at some length in a separate work on *How Duke Valentino Killed the Generals Who Conspired Against Him*. Taken together, these accounts of Borgia's deliberate brutality paint a vivid picture of the actual political tactics as used by a Renaissance prince "on the ground."

Niccolò Machiavelli, *Letter to the Council of Ten*, December 23, 1502

Messer Remirro, who was this Lord's [Cesare Borgia, Duke Valentino] top man [*il primo huomo*] returned yesterday from Pesaro and has been placed in the bottom of a tower by him. It is unlikely that he won't be sacrificed to these people, who much desire it. . . . From Cesena December 23, 1502

Niccolò Machiavelli, *Letter to the Council of Ten*, December 26, 1502

Messer Remirro was found this morning in two pieces in the piazza,[1] where he still is; and the whole populace was able to view it. The precise reason for his death is not known, besides that thus it pleased the prince [Cesare Borgia], who shows that he knows how to make and unmake men at his will, according to their merits. . . . From Cesena December 26, 1502

Niccolò Machiavelli, *The Prince*, Chapter VII, 1513

Having taken the Romagna, the duke [Cesare Borgia] found it to be controlled by weak lords who had despoiled their subjects rather than ruling them, and who had given the people reason for disunity rather than unity, to the point that the entire region was full of thievery, fighting, and every kind of outrage. He judged it necessary to render it peaceful and obedient to royal authority and to give it good governance, so he put in charge Remirro de Orco, a cruel and efficient man to whom he gave fullest power. In a very short time that man pacified the region, winning very great renown. Afterward, the Duke decided that such excessive authority was not appropriate because he suspected it was becoming hateful; and he installed a civil court in the center of the province, with an excellent president, where every city had a representative. And because he knew that the severe measures imposed had given rise to hatred, in order to purge the people's minds and to win them over entirely, he wanted to demonstrate that if any cruelty had occurred, it had not come from him, but from the harsh nature of his agent. And he seized the opportunity one morning in Cesena to have Remirro's body [that had been cut] in two pieces placed in the public piazza with a block of wood and a bloody knife beside it. The ferocity of that spectacle left the people both satisfied and stupefied.

Niccolò Machiavelli, *How Duke Valentino Killed the Generals Who Conspired Against Him*[2]

> [*While Cesare Borgia was elsewhere, his generals gathered secretly at a castle belonging to Cardinal Orsini in Magione, near Perugia.*]

They called a meeting in Perugia—the Diet of Magione. Present were Cardinal Giambattista Orsini, Signor Paolo Orsini, Duke Francesco Orsini of Gravina, Vitellozzo Vitelli, Liverotto da Fermo, Giampaolo Baglioni, the tyrant of Perugia, and Antonio da Venafro, who had been sent by Pandolfo Petrucci, the ruler of Siena. They discussed Duke Valentino's power and spirit, and how vital it was for them to check his hunger for supremacy before he ruined them all. They decided to stand by the Bolognese tyrant, Giovanni Bentivoglio, against Duke Valentino, and to seek to win over the Florentines. They sent emissaries to both Bologna and Florence, promising to help Bentivoglio and entreating the Florentines to join them in the fight against Duke Valentino, their common enemy.

[. . .]

But the Florentines, because of their hatred for the Vitelli and the Orsini, not only declined an allegiance but sent their minister Niccolò Machiavelli to offer duke Valentino shelter and aid against his new enemies. The Duke, in Imola, was in the grip of fear, for in a single stroke and against all expectations his former generals had become his enemies, and he found himself with a war on his doorstep. But he took courage from the Florentines' offer, and decided to forestall the war through peace negotiations, and in the meantime to marshal some help. He sent to the King of France for additional men, and hired all the cavalrymen he could find and anyone who had anything to do with horses.

Despite Duke Valentino's efforts his enemies advanced, reaching Fossombrone, where they encountered some of his soldiers, whom the Vitelli and Orsini routed. As a result of this, the duke put all his resources into trying to stop this trouble through peace negotiations. As he was a great dissembler, he did not neglect to give every indication that the conspirators had taken up weapons against a man who had agreed to let them keep whatever territories they had acquired, and announced that he would be happy enough to keep the title of prince while they ruled the principality. Duke Valentino was so successful in his persuasion that the conspirators laid down their arms and sent Signor Paolo Orsini to him to negotiate a truce. In the meantime, Duke Valentino had continued building up his army, diligently strengthening his cavalry and infantry, and he distributed his men throughout the Romagna so that these preparations would not be noticed.

In the meantime, five hundred French lancers had also arrived, and though Duke Valentino was now strong enough to attack his enemies in open war, he nevertheless calculated that it would be safer and more useful to deceive them, so he continued his peace negotiations, orchestrating them so diligently that a truce was successfully concluded. He gave the conspirators back the old mercenary positions they had held in his army, made them a present of four thousand ducats, promised not to harm the Bentivoglio family, and even arranged an alliance through marriage with Giovanni Bentivoglio.[3] He also promised to order them into his presence only as often as they would allow. For their part, they promised to give him back the Duchy of Urbino and all the other territories they had occupied, to serve in all his campaigns, and not to make war on anyone or hire themselves out to anyone without his permission.

[*Cesare Borgia arranges to meet with the conspirators in the fortified town of Senigallia.*]

Duke Valentino approached Senigallia. When the vanguard of his cavalry arrived at the bridge, it did not cross, but stopped and formed two lines, one along the river, the other along the open country, leaving a path in the middle for the foot soldiers, who then marched straight into the town. Vitellozzo, Pagolo [Paolo], and Duke Orsini of Gravina rode toward Duke Valentino on mules, accompanied by a handful of horsemen. Vitellozzo, unarmed and wearing a cape lined in green, seemed quite afflicted, as if he were aware of his impending death, which, in view of the prowess of the man and his former fortune,[4] caused some amazement. And it is said that when he parted from his soldiers to go to Senigallia to meet the duke, it was as if he were saying a final farewell. He told his generals that he left his house and its fortunes in their hands, and cautioned his nephews that they should not remember the fortunes of their house, but the prowess of their fathers and uncles. When the three men arrived before the duke and greeted him with courtesy, they were received by him in a friendly manner and immediately escorted by the men who had been charged to keep an eye on them. The duke, however, saw that Liverotto was missing. He had remained back with his men in Senigallia and was waiting on the square in front of his quarters by the river, keeping them in order and exercising them. The duke winked at Don Michele, whom he had entrusted with the care of Liverotto, signaling that he see to it that Liverotto did not escape, at which Don Michele rode off to Liverotto and told him that this was not the time to have his men gathered outside their quarters, as they were to be occupied by the duke's men. He encouraged him to have them return to their quarters and come with him to meet the duke. Liverotto followed Duke Valentino's order and rode out to meet him, and the duke, seeing him, called out to him. Liverotto made his obeisance and joined the others.

They all rode into Senigallia and to the duke's quarters, where he led them into a secret chamber and had them taken prisoner. He then immediately mounted his horse and ordered that the soldiers of Liverotto and the Orsini be stripped of their arms and belongings. Liverotto's men were immediately plundered, as they were right there in Senigallia, but the men of the Orsini and the Vitelli, being at some distance and having a premonition of their masters' fate, had enough time to gather together, and, remembering the prowess and discipline of the House of Vitelli, stood their ground against the local people and the enemy soldiers, and saved themselves. But the soldiers of Duke Valentino, not content with merely plundering Liverotto da Fermo's men, began sacking Senigallia. And had the duke not put a stop to their audacity by putting many of them to death, they would have looted the town entirely.

When night came and the turmoil stopped, the duke felt that the time had come to kill Vitellozzo and Liverotto. He had them taken to a place together and strangled. Neither of them uttered any words worthy of their previous life: Vitellozzo begged that he might throw himself on the pope's mercy and plead for a full indulgence for his sins, while Liverotto, weeping, heaped all the blame for the harm done to Duke Valentino on Vitellozzo. The duke left Paolo Orsini and Duke Orsini of Gravina alive until he heard from Rome that the pope [Alexander VI, Cesare's father] had seized Cardinal Orsino, Archbishop of Florence, and Messer Iacopo da Santa Croce. At this news, on the eighteenth of January, 1502, they too were strangled in the same fashion at the Castle of Pieve.

Notes

1 "The 'two pieces' were Remirro's head and trunk. According to a local chronicler of the event, which Machiavelli also witnessed, ' . . . on the 25th, the night of the Christmas Feast, in the piazza of Cesena, [Remirro's] head was cut off with a butcher's falchion, and [the body] lay there on a mat all day . . . '" Connell 62.

2 It is uncertain precisely when Machiavelli wrote this account, which was published posthumously in 1533 under the title *Il modo che tenne il duca Valentino per ammazar Vitellozzo, Oliverotto da Fermo, il signor Pagolo et il duca di Gravina Orsini in Senigaglia* (*The Manner in Which Duke Valentino Killed Vitellozzo, Oliverotto da Fermo, Signor Pagolo, and Duke Orsini of Gravina in Senigaglia*).

3 "Cesare Borgia and Giovanni Bentivoglio agreed to the future marriage of Costanzo, Giovanni's nephew, with Angela Borgia-Lanzol, Borgia's niece. The wedding, however, never took place." (PC)

4 In this sentence, and in the one that follows, Machiavelli repeatedly employs the words *virtù* and *fortuna*, here translated as "prowess" and "fortune."

Sources

Machiavelli, *Two Letters*, in *Legazioni, commissarie, scritti di governo*, ed. Fredi Chiappelli, Laterza, Roma-Bari, 1973, pp. 363–66, trans. Kaborycha.

Machiavelli, *The Prince*, Chapter VII, Mondadori, 1994, 29–36, p. 33, trans. Kaborycha.

Machiavelli, *How Duke Valentino Killed the Generals Who Conspired Against Him*, in *The Essential Writings of Machiavelli*, ed. and trans. Peter Constantine, Modern Library, 2007, pp. 365–72.

References

Black, Robert. "Machiavelli in the Chancery," in *The Cambridge Companion to Machiavelli*, ed. John M. Najemy, Cambridge UP, 2010.

De Silva, Jennifer Mara, ed. *The Borgia Family: Rumor and Representation*, Routledge, 2020.

Machiavelli, Niccolò. *The Prince: With Related Documents*, 2nd ed., trans. ed. and with an Introduction by William J. Connell, Bedford/St. Martin's, 2016.

Mallett, Michael. *The Borgias, the Rise and Fall of a Renaissance Dynasty*, Academy Chicago Publishers, 1987.

Najemy, John M. "Machiavelli and Cesare Borgia: A Reconsideration of Chapter 7 of *The Prince*," *The Review of Politics*, Vol. 75, No. 4 (Fall 2013), pp. 539–56.

56 How the courtier ought to serve his prince

Baldassarre Castiglione, *The Courtier*, 1528

The Courtyer, English title page and prefatory sonnet, 1561

Not even forty years had passed since Baldassarre Castiglione (1478–1529) first published *Il Cortegiano* in 1528; by the time Thomas Hoby first translated the work into English in 1561, people everywhere were reading *The Courtier*. Contributing to the popularity of the work was its lively dialogue form: the characters are a group of witty men and women discussing court life. All readers, regardless of whether or not they lived at a court, were interested in the information the book had to offer on urbane manners and etiquette, as well as how to appear fashionably sophisticated, with detailed tips on how to dress, dance, and tell jokes. Judging by the way the book caught on, it appears the author successfully addressed people's general desire to acquire more genteel manners, a sign of rising social aspirations at this time. Moreover, in addition to the superficial advice on manners, the humanist Castiglione (**#18**) also captured more serious Renaissance concerns. The world was changing. In Italy, self-governing republics had been giving way to despotic signories; across the continent, formerly independent local lords were losing power in favor of centralized, increasingly absolutist monarchies; and everywhere aristocrats were having to learn to play a relatively servile role at royal courts. This involved being flexible; developing the capacity for hiding one's own nature, tastes, and inclinations; and adapting to those of the ruler. And Renaissance rulers, as was well known, could be petty, vain, selfish, or even cruel. Serving such a lord could lead to the loss of courtier's moral compass, which Castiglione only partially addresses by suggesting the courtier adopt the classical virtue of self-restraint. He invokes the *aurea mediocritas* or "golden mean" made famous by the ancient Roman poet Horace (Quintus Horatius Flaccus, 65–8 BCE) in a passage from one of his *Odes*. Under the conditions of life at a Renaissance court, Castiglione suggests it is necessary for an individual to walk a fine line between extreme behaviors in order to maintain their integrity. These virtues of moderation, temperance, and restraint may seem bland in comparison to the spirited concept of *virtù*, or manly prowess, that Niccolò Machiavelli, his contemporary, praises in *The Prince*; nonetheless, there are marked

DOI: 10.4324/9781003284284-62

similarities between these two. The advice that Castiglione gives the courtier—to disguise or subvert their own nature in the interests of the state—is surprisingly similar to Machiavelli's advice to the would-be prince. Unlike Machiavelli, Castiglione does not condone the use of treachery or violence to further the interests of the state. Both authors, however, emphasize adaptation to changing circumstances, and when necessary, concealment of one's true character as essential skills for political survival during complex, uncertain times.

Baldassarre Castiglione, *The Courtier*, 1528

Book II chapters 18–23

> [*After a discussion of various skills that a courtier needs to cultivate, one of the characters, Federico Fregoso, addresses how the courtier ought to speak with his lord.*]

"I consider that the conversation the courtier must be most studiously concerned to make pleasant is the conversation he has with his prince. And though the word 'converse' implies a certain equality, which seemingly cannot occur between a lord and his servant, for the time being we will use this term. I would desire then, that the courtier—in addition to always displaying the qualities that we have already discussed—should turn all his thoughts and the force of his mind to loving, almost adoring the prince whom he serves, above all other things. He ought to direct his behavior, wishes, and all his means toward pleasing the prince."

At that, Pietro da Napoli promptly spoke up:

"There are plenty of courtiers like this around nowadays, since it seems to me that what you have just sketched for us is a noble flatterer."

"You are greatly mistaken," replied Federico, "because flatterers love neither their lords nor their friends. What I am telling you that I want most from our courtier is that he supports the one he serves, gratifying all his wishes, without being a sycophant, because I am referring to wishes that are reasonable and honorable, or rather, are in themselves neither good nor bad, such as playing a game or devoting oneself to some activity or another. In this I would like the courtier to be accommodating—even if it is foreign to his nature—so that whenever the lord sees him, he expects to hear words that are pleasant. This will happen if he has the good judgment to known what pleases the prince, the wit and prudence to know how to adapt and to deliberately will himself to like a thing that by nature might perhaps be unpleasant to him. And taking care to do this, he will never be reluctant to appear before his prince, or be melancholic, or taciturn like so many who seem to hold grudges against their masters, something that is really odious. They should not spread malicious gossip, especially about their lords."

[*After a discussion of courtiers' behavior in foreign courts, Fregoso continues.*]

"I can hardly deny that there are many Spaniards who are arrogant; though the ones who are held in the highest regard are mostly extremely modest. Others can be found who are so cold as to go to excessive lengths to avoid contact with others and surpass a certain mean [*mediocrità*], making themselves esteemed too shy or too proud.[1] Such men I would never praise—modesty should never be so dry and arid so as to become rudeness. May the courtier be eloquent, when it is fitting to him, prudent and wise in his discourse about the state, and may he possess such judgment that he knows how to adapt himself to the customs of nations in which he finds himself, and then in the most trivial matters let him be entertaining and know how to converse well on every topic.[2] But above all he should always be inclined towards what is good—not envious or slanderous, nor ever seeking grace or favor in dishonest ways or by evil means."

Calmeta then said,

"I assure you that all other ways are more dubious and take longer than these you criticize, because these days—I repeat myself again—rulers only love those who follow that path."

"Don't say that," Federico replied, "because that would be too clear an argument that rulers these days are all corrupt and evil, which is not true, since some good ones are to be found. But if our courtier by chance should find himself in the service of one who is corrupt and evil, as soon as he realizes it, he should leave, so that he does not suffer as do all good men who serve evil ones.

"He must pray to God," said Calmeta, "to give him good ones, because once he's got them, they must be endured. Once he has begun to serve a master, there are infinite considerations that keep a gentleman from leaving him. The misfortune was there from the beginning: a courtier is like an ill-omened bird born in an unhappy place."

"It seems to me," said Federico, "that moral considerations ought to come before all others—as long as a gentleman doesn't abandon his master during a war or some kind of adversity, so that people might believe he did it to follow fortune, or that he thought he had lost the means of deriving advantages for himself—at all other times I believe he ought to quit the kind of service that makes him feel ashamed in the company of good men, since everyone assumes that he who serves a good man is good, and he who serves an evil one is evil."

Then Ludovico Pio said,

"I would like you to clarify one doubt I have in my mind. It is this: is a gentleman, while serving a prince, required to obey him in everything he commands, even if these things are dishonorable and vile?"

"In dishonorable things we are never required to obey anyone," answered Federico.

"And what if," said Ludovico, "I am in the service of a prince who treats me well, and relies on me to do all I can for him. Say he commands me to murder someone, or to perform any other deed of the kind: should I refuse to do it?"

"You must obey your lord in all things that are useful to him and honorable, not those that are shameful and do harm. But if he asks you to commit treachery, not only are you not obligated to do it, but you are obligated *not* to do it, both for your own sake, and so as not to be the agent of your lord's shame. It is true that many things that appear at first sight to be good are evil, and many appear evil, that are actually good. Thus, it is sometimes permitted in the service of one's rulers, to kill not just one man, but ten thousand, and to do many other things that to someone who doesn't consider matters correctly would seem evil, and yet they are not."

To this Gaspar Pallavicino replied,

"Ah then, by your faith, explain this a bit and teach us how to distinguish between those things that are really good from those that only appear to be good."

"Pardon me," said Federico, "I do not want to enter into this, as there would be too much to say, but I leave it up to your own discretion."

The Courtyer, English title page and prefatory sonnet, 1561

THE COURTYER

OF

COUNT BALDESSAR CASTILIO

DIVIDED INTO FOURE BOOKES.

VERY NECESSARY AND PROFITABLE

FOR YONGE GENTILMEN AND

GENTILWOMEN ABIDING IN COURT,

PALAICE OR PLACE,

DONE INTO ENGLYSHE BY

THOMAS HOBY

1561

Thomas Sackevylle in commendation of the worke.[3]

To the reader

These royall kinges, that reare up to the skye
Their Palaice tops, and decke them all with gold:
With rare and curious woorkes they feed the eye:
And showe what riches here great Princes hold.
A rarer work and richer far in worth,
Castilios hand presenteth here to thee.
No proud ne golden Court doth he set furth
But what in Court a Courtier ought to be.
The Prince he raiseth houge and mightie walles,
Castilio frames a wight of noble fame:
The kinge with gorgeous Tyssue claddes his halles,
The Count with golden vertue deckes the same,
Whos passing skill lo Hobbies pen displaise
To Brittain folk, a work of worthy praise.

Notes

1 "Licinius, life makes better sense /lived neither pushing farther and farther/to sea, nor always hugging the dangerous/shore, shaking at the thought of storms. /Cherish a golden mean and stay/exempt from a filthy hovel/and exempt from the envy/a mansion excites." Horace, *Ode II,10*, 1–8 in *The Essential Horace: Odes, Epodes, Satires, and Epistles*, trans. Burton Raffel, North Point Press, 1983, p. 44.
2 Throughout his lifetime Castiglione himself served as ambassador to both Italian and foreign courts.
3 This prefatory sonnet was written by Thomas Sackville (1536–1608).

Sources

Baldassarre Castiglione. *Il libro del Cortegiano*, Le Monnier, 1854, trans. Kaborycha.
The Courtyer of Count Baldessar Castilio Done into English by Thomas Hoby Anno 1561, David Nutt, 1900.

References

Castiglione, Baldassarre. *The Book of the Courtier: The Singleton Translation: An Authoritative Text, Criticism*, ed. Daniel Javitch, Norton Critical Edition, 2002.
Cox, Virginia. "Castiglione's *Cortegiano*: The Dialogue as a Drama of Doubt," in *The Renaissance Dialogue: Literary Dialogue in its Social and Political Contexts, Castiglione to Galileo*, Cambridge UP, 1992, pp. 51–8.
Falvo, Joseph D. *The Economy of Human Relations: Castiglione's "Libro del cortegiano"*, P. Lang, 1992.
Javitch, Daniel. "*Il Cortegiano* and the Constraints of Despotism," in *Castiglione: The Ideal and the Real*, ed. Robert H. Hanning and David Rosand, Yale UP, 1983, pp. 17–28.

Lovett, Frank. "The Path of the Courtier: Castiglione, Machiavelli, and the Loss of Republican Liberty," *The Review of Politics*, Vol. 74, No. 4 (Fall 2012), pp. 589–605.

Partridge, Mary. "Thomas Hoby's English Translation of Castiglione's 'Book of the Courtier'," *The Historical Journal*, Vol. 50, No. 4 (December 2007), pp. 769–786.

57 Praise for the Venetian constitution

Gasparo Contarini, *The Commonwealth and Government of Venice*, *c.*1530

Gasparo Contarini (1483–1542) was a Venetian nobleman whose family, it is said, descended from the first doge. Though the family was one of the most powerful in the city, occupying more seats in the Great Council than any other, the branch that Gasparo was born into was no longer wealthy. Nevertheless, as a boy he studied with the finest humanist teachers in Venice, including Giorgio Valla, Marcantonio Sabellico, and Antonio Giustinian; at the age of eighteen, Contarini went to the University of Padua where he remained for eight years, studying the liberal arts. Apart from a short period when he joined a monastery, Contarini led an active public life: he was a member of the Great Council and traveled widely as an ambassador of Venice. Later he was appointed cardinal and participated prominently in both the Council of Trent and the Diet of Regensburg, where he attempted to introduce reforms. The author of books covering a wide variety of disciplines, Contarini is best known for his work describing the structure of the Venetian Republic, in Latin titled *De magistratibus et republica venetorum*. First published in Paris in 1543, the book was highly influential abroad, especially in England, where Lewis Lewkenor, a contemporary of Shakespeare, translated it into English and published it in 1599. Venetian government institutions were scrutinized in England over the course of the seventeenth century during its Civil War and the debate over the respective powers of king and parliament. Describing the so-called "mixed" constitution of Venice, Contarini outlines a three-part structure of government, which consists of the monarch, the aristocracy, and the people. Venice, he claims blends the best of three systems of government: monarchy (the Doge), aristocratic oligarchy (the Senate, the Council of Ten, and the *Savi*), and democracy (the Great Council). To drive home his argument, in true humanist style, Contarini makes ample use of examples from classical antiquity. He also emphasizes how "natural" this way of government is and invokes Platonic and Pythagorean images of harmony of the spheres to demonstrate how, in this most imperfect of worlds, Venetian citizens alone enjoy perfect social harmony. And perhaps the most persuasive argument of all, to the English—as well as other readers of Contarini's work—was the durability of the Venetian Republic. In politically volatile

DOI: 10.4324/9781003284284-63

times, a republic whose institutions had lasted more than a thousand years was—and still is—an exceptional model to be admired.

Gasparo Contarini, *The Commonwealth and Government of Venice*, *c.*1530

The first book of the magistrates and commonwealth of the Venetians

Being therefore determined to write of this our commonwealth, to the end that everyone may know whether the same be well or ill disposed, I think it best to take my beginning from hence. That man is by nature made a civil creature, but alone by himself, neither able to live well, nor to live at all, which every day's necessity, and the manner of victualing and clothing approves: and for this cause even from the beginning did men enter into civil society, and therein continued to the end, that so they might live happily and commodiously, which is, that with mutual help and diligence they might obtain the chief good incident to men, so long as the course of this their mortal life endures, whereunto the whole reason of civil institution pertains, that by the easiest way possible the citizens may be made possessors of a happy life. But a life happy and blessed is so termed of great philosophers, the which contains in itself the use of virtue, which they do approve with most assured reasons and undeniable arguments. Now the use of virtue appears as well in the offices of war, as in the functions of peace: which notwithstanding though the praise of war, and the manner of discipline thereunto belonging, be necessary to a city, for the preservation of the liberty and defense of the confines, and contains in itself great dignity and goodliness: yet the common sense of men does not allow these offices of war (by which the ruin and slaughter of mankind is procured) to be for themselves desired, and that all other civil offices should be thereunto referred: for it were the token of an uncivil disposition, or rather of a man hating humanity to wish for wars, slaughters, and burnings, for this only cause that he might be famous in matters of war, and add thereunto (if it please you) that he might be honored with the name of a great captain: wherefore all philosophers of greatest mark have in this one point agreed, that war is to be desired for the cause of peace, and that the whole function of military virtue, and the commendation thereof ought to be referred to the offices of peace: wherefore that governor of a commonwealth that would be accounted worthy of praise, and (as the saying is) a man perfectly accomplished, ought to use that temperature, and to maintain that order, that the whole commonwealth may seem accommodated to virtue, and withall, that it be rather thought to attend to the exercises of peace, than to the offices of war, yet in the meantime not condemning such things as pertain to the discipline of wars; because many times the military virtue (so that the same be used without injury) is necessary to defend and to enlarge the confines. But things being once ordered as we have said, it is wont then to be doubted of, whether it be better that one or few have the government of the whole city, or rather the whole multitude, as many do describe the estate of that, which ought properly to be called a commonwealth.

The second book of Venetian commonwealth and magistrates

The exterior show of the prince [doge] in the city of Venice delivers to the eyes of the beholders the person of a king, and the very resemblance of a monarchy: Therefore it shall not in my opinion be amiss, if having described that assembly of citizens, which represents the form of a popular estate (though for the dignity of the matter insufficiently, yet considering the slenderness of our forces not altogether undiligently) if we now take upon us to express the first reason that moved our wise & virtuous ancestors to place one man only at the helm of their commonwealth, and also when and what was the beginning of this royal and princely institution. [. . .]

This monarchal government was therefore established in this commonwealth of ours with singular wisdom and judgment, and withall the same so curbed & restrained with laws, that all dangerous inconveniences, whereby the commonwealth might sustain harm, are thereby removed, and those commodities jointly embraced that proceed from a kingly and royal government: so that there seems nothing to remain which we could wish for, having a commonwealth unenthralled, enjoying a true liberty and freedom, and yet nevertheless, as it were a king for our governor. A prince therefore is chosen, who is entitled with the dignity of a duke [doge], retaining the government of the commonwealth while the time of his life endures, and chiefly and above all other things, having care of the common good.

The third book of the magistrates and commonwealth of the Venetians

Every institution and government of man, the nearer it aspire to the praise of perfection and goodness, the nearer should it imitate nature, the best mother of all things: for so has she disposed the order of the whole world, that those things that are devoid of sense and understanding should be ruled by those that have sense and knowledge. And therefore, in this assembly of men, (which of us is called city) old men ought to be preferred before the younger sort as those that are less subject to the perturbations of the mind, and withal having been of longer life, must needs be of greater experience in the affairs of the world. Therefore Aristotle, in his *Politics* most wisely says, that in every commonwealth which would emulate and follow the wisdom and policy of nature, old men should be placed at the helm . . . neither is the name of Senate from elsewhere derived, than from old men who in the Latin tongue are called *senes*.

[. . .]

With this reason therefore was the Senate ordained and established in this commonwealth of ours, and likewise the Council of the Ten, who in the city of Venice in whose commonwealth (as I said) there is a mixture of these governments royal, popular, and noble, do represent the state of the nobility and are (as it were) the mean or middle, which reconciles and binds together the two extremes, that is the popular estate represented in the Great Council, and the prince, bearing a show of royalty. So says Plato are the extreme elements, the earth and the fire, joined and bound together with the middle elements, as in a well-tuned diapason [the octave] the extreme voices are concorded together by the middle tunes of the diatesseron [perfect fourth] and the diapente [the perfect fifth].

Source

Gasparo Contarini, *The Commonwealth and Government of Venice*, trans. Lewis Lewkenor, London, 1599, ed. Kaborycha.

References

Contarini, Gasparo. *The Republic of Venice: De magistratibus et republica Venetorum*, ed. and intro. Filippo Sabetti, U Toronto P, 2020.

Gleason, Elisabeth G. *Gasparo Contarini: Venice, Rome, and Reform*, U California P, 1993.

McPherson, David. "Lewkenor's Venice and its Sources," *Renaissance Quarterly*, Vol. 41, No. 3 (Autumn 1988), pp. 459–66.

Pocock, J.G.A. "Gianotti and Contarini: Venice as Concept and as Myth," in *The Machiavellian Moment: Florentine Political Thought and the Atlantic Republican Tradition*, Princeton UP, 1975, pp. 272–330.

58 Envisioning a queenly republic

Marin Sanudo, *Praise of the City of Venice*, 1493

James Howell, *Upon the Citty and Signorie of Venice*, 1651

When the English tourist Thomas Coryat visited the Ducal Palace and looked up at Paolo Veronese's (Paolo Cagliari, 1528–1588) magnificent *Apotheosis of Venice* on the ceiling of the Sala del Maggior Consiglio (Figure 6.1), he was sure he was looking at a sacred image; Coryat described the painting in his 1611 travel memoir as representing the crowning of the Virgin Mary, Queen of Heaven. Certainly, there was a tradition of blurring the sacred and the secular in Venetian art that had been duly condemned by religious authorities, with Veronese identified as one of the prime offenders (**#29**). The divinity, however, is not the Virgin, but regal Venice herself. Also known by the title of *Pax Veneta*, this image was intended to inspire admiration and awe for the Venetian Republic and for its dignitaries who met in that hall. Though there are other paintings that praise the government of individual Renaissance states, projecting images of civic harmony—one example is Ambrogio Lorenzetti's *Effects of Good Government* (1338–40, Palazzo Pubblico, Siena)—Veronese's work stands out as "magniloquent political propaganda at its best."[1] This enormous canvas hangs over the throne of the doge, and at the top, it represents Venice, whose nickname was La Serenissma (her most serene highness). Thus, Venice is personified as a queen,[2] dressed in opulent gold robes, ermine cape, and pearls, being crowned by a winged figure of Victory as Fame sounds a trumpet above her. On either side of her are the towers of Venice's Arsenal. Behind her is a classically inspired triumphal arch with twisted columns representing Solomon's Temple. There are six allegorical figures at her feet; from left to right: a man crowned with laurel who wears a golden breastplate and toga represents Honor; a woman holding an olive branch symbolizes Peace; Security is a woman with a crown in one hand and a caduceus in the other; Felicity lolls back on her elbow beside the naked figure of Ceres sitting near a large bushel of grain indicating Abundance; the woman with the red cap, the *pileus* worn by citizens in ancient Greece and Rome, represents Liberty.[3] Below the top level is a crowd of citizens—men and women, young and old—of varied social rank and from diverse regions. Jostling one another behind a

DOI: 10.4324/9781003284284-64

balustrade, they are all celebrating joyfully, and at the base of the painting are soldiers and prisoners. Figures of young men representing the four seasons cling to the columns. The program for this entire painting was devised by a group of officials of the Venetian government, and aside from a few elements apparently added by Veronese, such as the statues of Hercules and Mercury at the top of the arch and the lion of St. Mark lurking behind the soldiers, the painter strictly adhered to the official guidelines. The imagery in this painting contributes to what has become known as the "myth of Venice." Venetians and foreigners alike were susceptible to this myth, as demonstrated by Marin Sanudo (1466–1536), a proud Venetian citizen who in his diary effusively describes the unique foundations of his city, both historical and physical, and Welsh-born traveler James Howell (1594–1666). Howell's book about Venice opens with his poem in praise of the city, in which he compares Venice not only to a queen, but to Venus, goddess of love. This analogy was not uncommon, as like the mythical goddess born from sea-foam (#47), Venice arose from the waters of the Adriatic.

Marin Sanudo, *Praise of the City of Venice*, 1493

This city of Venice is a free city, a common home to all men, and it has never been subjugated by anyone, as have been all other cities. It was built by Christians, not voluntarily but out of fear, not by deliberate decision but from necessity. Moreover it was founded not by shepherds as Rome was, but by powerful and rich people, such as have ever been since that time, with their faith in Christ, an obstacle to barbarians and attackers. And, having described its origin, with God's grace I will describe its site and things worthy of record.

This city, amidst the billowing waves of the sea, stands on the crest of the main, almost like a queen restraining its force. It is situated in salt water and built there, because before there were just lagoons, and then, wanting to expand, firm ground was needed for the building of palaces and houses. These are being constructed all the time; they are built above the water by a very ingenious method of driving piles, so that the foundations are in water. Every day the tide rises and falls, but the city remains dry. At times of very low tides, it is difficult to go by boat to wherever one wants. The city is about 7 miles in circumference; it has no surrounding walls, no gates which are locked at night, no sentry keeping watch as other cities have for fear of enemies; it is so very safe at present, that no one can attack or frighten it. As another writer has said, its name has achieved such dignity and renown that it is fair to say that Venice merits the title "Pillar of Italy", "deservedly it may be called the bosom of all Christendom". For it takes pride of place before all others, if I may say so, in prudence, fortitude, magnificence, benignity and clemency; everyone throughout the world testifies to this. To conclude, this city was built more by divine than human will. . . .

And the order with which this holy Republic is governed is a wonder to behold; there is no sedition from the non-nobles (*popolo*), no discord among the patricians, but all work together to [the Republic's] increase. Moreover, according to what wise men say, it will last forever, as appears from this epigram found in the *Supplementum chronicarum*:

> So long as the sea contains dolphins, so long as clear skies contain stars; so long as the moist ground gives forth her pleasant fruits; so long as the human race carries on its generations upon the Earth, the splendor of the Venetians will be celebrated for all eternity.

James Howell, *Upon the Citty and Signorie of Venice*, 1651

Could any State on Earth Immortall be,
Venice by Her rare Goverment is She;
Venice Great Neptunes Minion, still a Mayd,
Though by the warrlikst Potentats assayd;
Yet She retaines Her Virgin-waters pure,
Nor any Forren mixtures can endure;
Though, Syren-like on Shore and Sea, Her Face
Enchants all those whom once She doth embrace;
Nor is ther any can Her bewty prize
But he who hath beheld Her with his Eyes;

These following Leaves display, if well observd,
How She so long Her Maydenhead preservd,
How for sound prudence She still bore the Bell;
Whence may be drawn this high-fetchd parallel,

Venus and Venice are great Queens in their degree,
Venus is Queen of Love, Venice of Policie.

Notes

1 Humfrey 257–8. *Pax veneta* (Venetian peace) draws the implicit parallel with the Roman Empire and the so-called *pax romana* it imposed on subject territories. Another title that is often given to this painting is *Triumph of Venice*.
2 Rosand also suggests that she represents the queen of the Olympian gods, Juno.

3 The *pileus* is similar to the so-called "Phrygian cap" worn during the French Revolution as a symbol of liberty.

Sources

Marin Sanudo, *Praise of the City of Venice* in *Venice: A Documentary History, 1450–1630*, ed. Chambers, David and Brian Pullan, with Jennifer Fletcher, Blackwell, 1992, 4–21, pp. 4–5, 21.

James Howell, *Upon the Citty and Signorie of Venice* in *S.P.Q.V. A Survey of the Signorie of Venice, of Her Admired Policy, and Method of Government, etc.*, Richard Lowndes, 1651.

References

Finlay, Robert. "Politics and History in the Diary of Marino Sanuto," *Renaissance Quarterly*, Vol. 33, No. 4 (Winter 1980), pp. 585–98.

Humfrey, Peter. *Painting in Renaissance Venice*, Yale UP, 1995.

Muir, Edward. "Images of Power: Art and Pageantry in Renaissance Venice," *The American Historical Review*, Vol. 84, No. 1 (February 1979), pp. 16–52.

Rosand, David. *Myths of Venice: The Figuration of a State*, U North Carolina P, 2001.

Sinding-Larson, Staale. *Christ in the Council Hall: Studies in the Religious Iconography of the Venetian Republic*, L'Erma di Bretschneider, 1974.

Starn, Randolph and Loren Partridge. *Arts of Power: Three Halls of State in Italy, 1300–1600*, UC Press, 1992.

59 Emperor Charles V in Italy

Luigi Gonzaga, *Account of the Emperor Charles V's Italian Sojourn and Coronation in Bologna*, 1530

Charles V, *Political Testament to Philip II*, 1548

He had already been crowned Holy Roman Emperor in 1520 in Aachen, Germany, site of Charlemagne's court, but Charles V (Habsburg, 1500–1558) decided to have a second coronation. The event was predicted by Francesco Guicciardini in a 1528 letter to Pope Clement VII: "He will want to come to Rome for the imperial crown: it would be foolish not to expect it. . . . because with this trip he will double his power and reputation."[1] And Charles did go; however, the coronation did not take place in Rome, but in Bologna. Rome was still reeling from the 1527 Sack by imperial troops (**#26**), so it was judged more prudent to hold the event in Bologna, a key city in the Papal States and also the farthest north, thus along the way to Austria and Germany. A vivid eyewitness account of the emperor's ceremonial entry into the city on November 5, 1529, is provided by Luigi Gonzaga, a member of the powerful ruling family of Mantua. During the Renaissance, such ceremonial entries were customarily held for princes, popes, visiting heads of state, and royal brides and bridegrooms. These elaborate festivities involved processions through streets adorned with ephemeral decorations, endless banquets, races, jousting, and theatrical spectacles that could go on for days or weeks. Charles V remained in Bologna for four months, his visit there culminating with the coronation by Pope Clement VII on February 24, 1530. During the nine months that he remained in Italy, Charles not only consolidated his power on the peninsula by personally meeting with rulers of local states who were subject to him, but he also established connections with Italian artists, notably Titian (**#38**). As predicted by Guicciardini, the emperor's visit to Italy greatly enhanced his prestige there; furthermore, exposure to the art and architecture in Italian courts enabled Charles V to expand his patronage networks, thereby adding to his own image of imperial magnificence.[2]

The first thirty years of his reign were characterized by a series of military and political successes, and during his last active years as emperor, Charles V governed his immense empire from Germany and the Low Countries, before retiring to a monastery in Spain in 1557. He had groomed his son for power from an early age, and Philip II (1527–1598) was eighteen years old when in 1543 he was appointed regent of the Spanish kingdoms.

DOI: 10.4324/9781003284284-65

After five years in this role, he was summoned to the imperial court in Brussels by his father, who arranged for Philip to travel through the territories of northern Italy. The young heir apparent arrived in Genoa where he made a triumphal entry and was lavishly hosted by Andrea Doria. He then went on to Milan, where he was to be made duke in 1550, and then to Mantua with the Gonzaga family. It was an opportunity for the many rulers of dependent Italian states to pay tribute to the future King of Spain (see Lorenzo Pagni's *Letter*, #60). Charles had wanted to leave his son all the territories he controlled, including the German lands and title of emperor, but he was ultimately overruled by the German electors who voted instead for Charles's brother Ferdinand. It turned out to be a blessing in disguise, by directing Philip's attention and resources elsewhere: he was left to rule "only" Spain, Flanders, Italy, and, more importantly, the American possessions, which filled the royal coffers with immense wealth. Even without the German portion, Philip inherited what at the time was the largest empire the world had ever known. Thus, to guide his son in this gargantuan task, before he abdicated, Charles left detailed instructions in his so-called *Political Testament*, dated January 18, 1548.

Luigi Gonzaga, *Account of Charles V's Italian Sojourn and Coronation in Bologna*, 1530

5 November, 1529

Friday, the fifth of November, was set for the entry of His Majesty into Bologna, to honor as highly as possible such an emperor, and done in a way as never seen before by Christians, which was carried out as follows:

First, the Holy Father and the Lords of Bologna had all the roads, from the Porta del Reno to San Petronio and the Palace [the Palazzo dei Signori] covered with hangings of different sorts of cloths, with five or six most beautiful triumphal arches constructed in different styles and manners according to the ancient Roman custom, which made a splendid spectacle, with all the streets decorated with arches of all kinds of greenery and infinite numbers of coats of arms of the Holy Father, those of the emperor, and of the city of Bologna. In addition to this they had built an enormous platform of wood, hung with draperies so large that they covered the entire façade of San Petronio, as high as the top of the entry stairs, and broad as almost half the piazza, and on the side of the Palace it was so large that it arrived all the way to the door of the Palace, with stairs wide enough to ascend and descend with ease, and it did not block anything; there was enough room for carts to pass beneath. This platform was built for the ceremony of the meeting of the emperor and the pope, and so had to be large enough to accommodate many people, as happens at such events.

24 February 1530

His Holiness Pope Clement VII had first ordered the Church of San Petronio adorned with the finest gold and silk tapestries, and then had a beautifully designed wooden stand erected, which was so large that it filled the entire central area of the church leading right up to the main altar. On the right-hand side [of the altar] a seat was prepared, entirely covered in cloth of gold on a crimson background, which reached the ground, for His Holiness, and another on the left. . . .

Afterwards, a wooden bridge was constructed that was so long that it began at the door of the Palace and went all the way to San Petronio, with room for horses and carriages to pass beneath. This bridge was covered in the finest carpets; guarding it were four hundred of His Majesty's landsknecht soldiers and guarding the piazza were 2,000 Spanish infantry with arquebuses and pikes and ten pieces of heavy artillery blocking the openings of the streets. The city gates were thus shut, drawbridges raised, and at every gate were two hundred foot soldiers, Spanish and German, who stood guard throughout the coronation ceremony. These preparations having been made, the best streets of Bologna were decorated with banners, and noble ladies were arrayed at the windows facing the streets where His Holiness and His Majesty were to pass. It was a splendid sight to see, with the whole populace of Bologna turned out in so orderly a fashion.

> [*There follows an extended description of the arrival of dignitaries of the Church, ambassadors, Italian and foreign nobility, the emperor accompanied by his court. After the Mass and coronation ceremony, the exit procession is described.*]

[The emperor] accompanied by his high treasurer with a silver vase full of gold and silver coins went along tossing money to the people. . . . you heard nothing but shouts of "Caesar! Caesar! Long live Emperor Charles!"

Emperor Charles V, *Political Testament to his Son Philip II*, 1548

Seeing that human affairs are beset with doubt, I can give you no general rules save to trust in Almighty God. You will show this best by defending the faith. After all our trouble and labor in bringing back the German heretics, I have come to the conclusion that a general council is the only way. Even the German Estates have agreed to submit to it. Have a care, therefore, that the council [of Trent] continues, in all reverence to the Holy See. But proceed cautiously against the abuses of the Vatican when they affect your own lands. Make choice of worthy and learned men for parishes and benefices, for the greater glory of the Church and the quiet of your own conscience; choose such as will stay in their cure [parish] and perform their duties. Preserve peace and avoid war, unless you are forced to it in your own defense, for warfare is a heavy burden on our hereditary lands, which I have left to you not diminished in anything, but increased. Unhappily I have from time to time been forced to cede certain of the privileges of the Crown; you can try to regain them.

Peace will depend not so much on your actions as on those of others. It will be a difficult task for you to preserve it, seeing that God has bestowed so many great kingdoms and principalities on you. I therefore suggest the following things for your consideration. You yourself know how unreliable Pope Paul III is in all his treaties, how sadly he lacks all zeal for Christendom, and how ill he has acted in this affair of the council above all. Nevertheless, honor his position. The Pope is old; therefore, take careful heed to the instructions which I have given my ambassador in Rome in case of an election. There will always be trouble with the Pope, in Naples, in Sicily, and in Castile on account of the Pragmatica.[3] Look to it. Keep a good understanding with the Venetians. I have done much for the Duke of Florence and he is grateful; he is also our kinsman since he married into the family of Toledo.[4] The Duke of Ferrara leans to France: handle him cautiously. The Duke of Mantua is to be trusted: cherish him for he has suffered much in the wars. Genoa is the most important of all to us. Act shrewdly and skillfully in your dealings with it. Siena and Lucca, let us hope, will remain under the protection of the King of the Romans.[5] . . . Defend Milan with good artillery, Naples with a good fleet. . . . The Neapolitans are much given to revolt; let them be constantly reminded of how the French sacked their town. Apart from this, treat them with moderation. You can never manage without Spanish troops in Italy.

Notes

1 Dandelet 93.
2 See Dandelet chapter 2 "The Hybrid Empire of Charles V," esp. 97–9.
3 "The Spanish government had issued a *Pragmatica* forbidding any foreigner to hold a benefice in Spain." Brandi 496.
4 Eleonora of Toledo, daughter of the Spanish viceroy of Naples, married Cosimo I de'Medici in 1539.
5 The official title of Charles's brother was Ferdinand, king of the Romans (r.1531–64), until he became Emperor Ferdinand I von Habsburg (r.1556–64).

Sources

Luigi Gonzaga, *Account of Charles V's Italian Sojourn* in *Cronaca del soggiorno di Carlo V in Italia (dal 26 luglio 1529 al 25 aprile 1530)*, ed. Giacinto Romano, Hoepli, 1892, pp. 113–14, 208–9, 222, trans. Kaborycha.

Charles V, *Political Testament* in Karl Brandi, *The Emperor Charles V: The Growth and Destiny of a Man and of a World-Empire*, trans. C.V. Wedgwood, Jonathan Cape, 1939, pp. 582–7, ed. Kaborycha.

References

Clarke, Georgia. "The Emperor's Hat: City, Space, and Identity in Contemporary Accounts of Charles V's Entry into Bologna in 1529," *I Tatti Studies in the Italian Renaissance*, Vol. 16, No. 1/2 (September 2013), pp. 197–220.

Dandelet, Thomas James. *The Renaissance of Empire in Early Modern Europe*, Cambridge UP, 2014.

Dandelet, Thomas James and John A. Marino, eds. *Spain in Italy: Politics, Society, and Religion 1500–1700*, Brill, 2007.

Eisenbichler, Konrad. "Charles V in Bologna: The Self-fashioning of a Man and a City," *Renaissance Studies*, Vol. 13, No. 4, Special Issue: Civic Self- Fashioning in Renaissance Bologna: Historical and Scholarly Contexts (December 1999), pp. 430–9.

Mitchell, Bonner. *The Majesty of the State: Triumphal Progresses of Foreign Sovereigns in Renaissance Italy, 1494–1600*, Olshcki, 1986.

Pagden, Anthony. *Lords of All the World: Ideologies of Empire in Spain, Britain and France c. 1500–c. 1800*, Yale UP, 1995.

Parker, Geoffrey. *Emperor: A New Life of Charles V*, Yale UP, 2019.

60 Art, luxury, and gifts in diplomacy

Niccolò de' Carissimi da Parma, *Letter to Francesco Sforza*, 1459

Lorenzo de' Medici, *Letter to Bianca Maria and Galeazzo Maria Sforza*, 1466

Antonio Montecatini, *Letter to Ercole d'Este*, 1480

Lorenzo Pagni, *Letter to Pierfrancesco Riccio*, 1550

In 1459, the fifteen-year-old Galeazzo Maria Sforza (1444–1476) was sent by his father, the duke of Milan, to pay a visit to their Medici allies in Florence. The Milanese alliance was critical; thus, it was important to establish good relations between the Medici family and Galeazzo who, as the eldest son, would succeed Duke Francesco Sforza (1401–1466). The Palazzo Medici had only recently been completed; sparkling new and a showplace for art, it was designed not just to delight the owners but also to dazzle guests. Judging by the description in a letter written by Niccolò de' Carissimi da Parma, a counsellor to Galeazzo, the Medici home abundantly achieved its goal. Adding to the festivities, Cosimo's ten-year-old grandson Lorenzo di Piero (the Magnificent, 1449–1492) presided at an opulent joust in the Milanese guest's honor. Moreover, the bond between the two families was permanently enshrined in a portrait of the youthful Sforza prince astride a white horse in the foreground of Benozzo Gozzoli's *Journey of the Magi* painted that same year on the walls of the chapel in the Medici Palace. On such occasions, it was also customary to exchange sumptuous gifts, including clothing. Seven years later, the teenaged Lorenzo received a velvet tunic as a gift from the duke and dowager duchess of Milan. His letter of thanks demonstrates Lorenzo's awareness from an early age of the diplomatic function of gift exchange. And beyond these kinds of gifts that were constantly being exchanged, the art collections and abundant trappings of luxury in the palace had powerful political functions as well, increasing the prestige and power of the ruler. Not only the wealth but also the taste of the patron was on show, their knowledge and appreciation of art, as well as their ability to attract the finest talent and to commission major works of art. Lorenzo was known to lead his guests through the palace, eliciting awed responses at the family's vast collection of precious treasures.[1] One of these occasions was recorded in the letter of Andrea Montecatini, ambassador to Duke Ercole d'Este in 1480,

DOI: 10.4324/9781003284284-66

after the Ferrarese ambassador and Cardinal Giovanni d'Aragona were taken on a tour by Lorenzo personally.[2]

A century later, a descendent from another branch of the family, Cosimo I de' Medici (1519–1574), seized control of the government to become hereditary ruler—first as duke of Florence, later grand duke of Tuscany. He and his wife Eleonora di Toledo (1522–1562) were exacting patrons of the arts. Concerning one of Eleonora's artistic commissions, Vasari wrote to Vincenzo Borghini in May 1562: "If I have succeeded in satisfying the Duchess, it will be no small thing."[3] When a state portrait was to be painted of the couple's eight-year-old son and heir, Francesco (1541–1587), it was decided that he should be portrayed in the same garments he wore when he was officially presented the year before to the future King Philip II in Genoa (**#59**). The painting was to be a reminder of that diplomatic event, as Eleonora makes clear by insisting that Agnolo Bronzino (**#69**) accurately reproduce the fabric.[4] It is no mere coincidence that Bronzino, court painter for the Medici, was unmatched in his exquisite depiction of luxury textiles. Multiple copies were made of Bronzino's Medici family portraits, which were sent as gifts to courts across Europe, simultaneously promoting the dynasty's political agenda and its reputation as patrons and connoisseurs of fine art.

Niccolò de' Carissimi da Parma, *Letter to Francesco Sforza*, Apr. 17, 1459

In the meantime the aforesaid count,[5] together with the company, went on a tour of this palace, and especially of its noblest parts, such as some of the studies, chapels, salons, chambers, and garden, all of which are constructed and decorated with admirable mastery, decorated on every side with gold and fine marbles, with carvings and sculptures in relief, with pictures and inlays done in perspective by the most accomplished and perfect of masters, even to the very benches and floors of the house; tapestries and household ornaments of gold and silk; silverware and bookcases that are endless and without number; then the vaults or rather ceilings of the chambers and salons, which are for the most part done in fine gold with diverse and various forms; then a garden done in the finest of polished marbles with diverse plants, which seems a thing not natural, but painted. And among other things there is an adder in the form of the device of Your Excellency,[6] and beside it there is the shield with the arms of the aforementioned Cosimo. This adder and arms are of new-planted grass in a piece of ground so that, the more the grass grows, the more the device will grow. I am not saying these things distinctly, for it would not be possible, since they are things which can not only be expressed, but also imagined. And whoever sees them judges that they are celestial rather than earthly things, and everyone is agreed that this house is the most finished and ornate that the world has ever had or may have now, and that it is without comparison. In sum, it is believed by all that there is no other earthly paradise in the world than this. If Your Lordship were to see it, I take it for certain that it would cost you a good sum of money, because with the magnanimity and greatness of mind that you have, you too would want to do something worthy—and not only equal this but surpass it if it were possible. To me it seems like being in a new world, and I am of the opinion that in my days I shall never see anything worthier than this which I have seen and am first seeing. And not only I hold this opinion, but all the company here, who do nothing else but discuss it.

Lorenzo de' Medici, *Letter to Bianca Maria Sforza and Galeazzo Maria Sforza*, Jun. 9, 1466

I do not know how I can begin to thank Your Most Illustrious and Excellent Lordships[7] for such a worthy and elegant gift, with which Your Most Illustrious and Excellent Lordships have now honored me by your immense mercies. And if I had one hundred tongues and all the paper in Fabriano,[8] and all the quills that one could possibly find, my soul would still not be able to offer a hundred thousandths of the thanks I owe you. May God most high, giver of grace and all good things, favor you and show you my thanks. The tunic (*giornea*),[9] brought to me, your most faithful servant, by your messenger, reached me in time,[10] and I do not know what could possibly be more useful and dear to me. Eternally, as long as I live and no matter who follows me, with respect to Your Illustrious Lordships, we will wear your insignias and devices, not on our shoulders, but sculpted and infixed in the center of our heart. I thank you once again, as much as I can and know how to do, for such an excellent and magnificent gift, and into perpetuity I dedicate myself and understand myself to be your most faithful servant. May God on high protect Your Excellencies as you wish for all time, you to whom I always devote myself.

Antonio Montecatini, *Letter to Duke Ercole d'Este*, Aug. 21, 1480

Then he entered the *studio*, the chamber that had belonged to Piero, and there he examined the said studio with copious quantities of books, all worthy, written with a pen—a stupendous thing. Then we returned to the little loggia opening off the study. And there on the table he had brought his jewels . . . vases, cups, hard-stone coffers mounted with gold, of various stones, jasper and others. There was a crystal beaker mounted with a lid and a silver foot, which was studded with pearls, rubies, diamonds, and other stones. [He also showed] a dish carved inside with diverse figures, which was a worthy thing, reputed to be worth 4,000 ducats. Then he had brought two large bowls full of ancient coins, one of gold coins and the other full of silver, then a little case with many jewels, rings and engraved stones . . . then Monsignor went to see San Marco and the library (#33), and then Lorenzo's garden there.

Lorenzo Pagni, *Letter to Pierfrancesco Riccio*, Jan. 20, 1550

Speaking with Our Lady Duchess [Eleonora di Toledo] as Your Lordship ordered me in writing this morning,[11] concerning the red velvet tunic to be worn by Prince Francesco and Her Excellency's satin gown of the same color to send them to Bronzino, I received the following response from her in these, or similar words: "*Come puede il Bronzino hazer el retratto di Franzischillo, sin haverlo adelante?*"[12] I responded that all I knew was that Your Lordship asked that the portraits be finished, which were being requested with much insistence by Monsignor d'Arras.[13] Then Her Excellency added that I ought to write to Your Lordship to inform Bronzino that as to Prince Francesco's tunic, he is to depict the red brocade as beautifully as he knows how, but that he accompany it with a cape lined with marten or ermine, as it is not fitting that his lordship by depicted only in a tunic, but with a cape like the one he wore in Genoa.[14] And as to the question of Her Excellency's gown, she told me the same as about Prince Francesco's tunic, that Bronzino should paint it in his own way in that color. I wanted to relate all this so that you would be informed. And having written all that I had to say three hours ago and sent it with the court dispatch, I have nothing else to report on, except the well-being of Their Illustrious Lordships. I kiss your hands and pray Our Lord preserve you many years in good health and contentment according to your desires.

Notes

1 We have detailed information about the individual items and their values from the 1492 inventory of goods; the value came to a total of 79,618 gold florins. "The value of a florin should be understood in terms of its buying power. In 1480 one estimate of the cost of living stated that an annual income of seventy florins was sufficient to support a worker, his wife, and three or four children for one year." Stapleford 14.

2 For another mention of Lorenzo showing the Medici treasures to a guest see p.269 on Cardinal Raffaello Riario's visit.

3 Edelstein 234.

4 For the meeting with Philip, the concern had been to choose "appropriate clothing for Francesco—no doubt to demonstrate not only the luxury of the Florentine court but also the continued high quality of the products of its textile industry." Edelstein 227.

5 Galeazzo Maria Sforza's title was count of Pavia.

6 A viper, or adder, was on the coat of arms of the dukes of Milan.

7 Francesco Sforza died in March of 1466; thus, his son Galeazzo Maria was the new duke of Milan. Bianca Maria was Galeazzo's mother and widow of the late duke.

8 Fabriano was famous for paper production; see Marco Polo, #72.

9 "Men's *giornee* were typically tunics worn over tightly buttoned doublets; the garment's origins can be traced to military attire, though they could be quite lavish. . . . In the Medici armory, upper body garments were outfitted with silk, damask, and colored velvets." (TM, SR)

10 Lorenzo had requested a tunic with the Sforza coat of arms to be worn in a joust that he had planned.
11 Lorenzo Pagni was secretary to Duke Cosimo I; he writes to Pierfrancesco Riccio, the duke's majordomo.
12 "How can Bronzino paint a portrait of little Francesco without having it before him?" Eleonora, daughter of the Spanish viceroy of Naples, seems to have spoken in her native Spanish, which the court secretary has attempted to capture.
13 Antoine Perrenot de Granvelle was an extremely influential statesman in the service of Emperor Charles V, and later, of his son Philip II.
14 Genoa was where Francesco's meeting with future King Philip II had taken place.

Sources

Niccolò de' Carissimi da Parma, *Letter* in Rab Hatfield, "Some Unknown Descriptions of the Medici Palace in 1459," *The Art Bulletin*, Vol. 52, No. 3 (September 1970), 232–49, pp. 232–33.

Lorenzo de' Medici, *Letter* in Timothy McCall and Sean Roberts, "Art and the Material Culture of Diplomacy," in *Italian Renaissance Diplomacy: A Sourcebook*, ed. Monica Azzolini and Isabella Lazzarini, Pontifical Institute of Mediaeval Studies/ (Durham Medieval and Renaissance Texts and Translations; 6). 2017, 214–33, pp. 227–8.

Antonio Montecatini, *Letter* in Luke Syson and Dora Thorton. *Objects of Virtue: Art in Renaissance Italy*, Getty Museum, 2001, pp. 81–2.

Lorenzo Pagni, *Letter*, transcribed in Italian by Edelstein p. 245; and ASF MdP 1176 ins 13 doc 1 "20 gennaio 1550", The Medici Archive Project Doc ID 3243; trans. Kaborycha.

References

Edelstein, Bruce. "Bronzino in the Service of Eleonora di Toledo and Cosimo I de' Medici: Conjugal Patronage and the Painter-Courtier." In *Beyond Isabella: Secular Women Patrons of Art in Renaissance Italy*, ed. Sheryl E. Reiss and David G. Wilkins, Truman State UP, 2001, pp. 225–61.

Fusco, Laurie and Gino Corti. *Lorenzo de' Medici: Collector and Antiquarian*, Cambridge UP, 2006.

Jardine, Lisa. *Worldly Goods: A New History of the Renaissance*, Macmillian, 1996.

Kent, Dale. *Cosimo de' Medici and the Florentine Renaissance: The Patron's Oeuvre*, Yale UP, 2000.

Kent, Francis W. *Lorenzo de' Medici and the Art of Magnificence*. Johns Hopkins University Press, 2004.

Stapleford, Richard, ed. and trans. *Lorenzo de' Medici at Home: The Inventory of the Palazzo Medici in 1492*, Pennsylvania State UP, 2013.

Syson, Luke. "The Medici Study," in *At Home in Renaissance Italy*, ed. Marta Ajmar-Wollheim and Flora Dennis; summary catalogue ed. Elizabeth Miller. V & A; distributed in North America by Harry N. Abrams, 2006, pp. 288–93.

Part VII

Domestic life, family, society

Figure 7.1 Sano di Pietro, *St. Bernardino Preaching in the Piazza del Campo*, c.1445, Museo dell'Opera del Duomo, Siena. The Sienese artist Sano di Pietro (1406–1481) portrays men and women attending a sermon in the Campo, the central piazza of the city, with its city hall, the Palazzo Pubblico, as the backdrop. The artist captures the mood of rapt attention as they strain to catch every word uttered by the renowned local preacher. This work was painted the year after Bernardino died as part of a campaign for his canonization.

61 A merchant criticized by his wife

Margherita Datini, *Letter to Francesco Datini*, 1386

Margherita Bandini (1360–1423), the youngest of five children, was the daughter of a formerly wealthy and influential Florentine family. She met Francesco di Marco Datini (*c.*1335–1410), her future husband, in Avignon. Her mother, of the Gherardini magnate clan, had taken the family to Avignon after Margherita's father was executed for being involved in a conspiracy against the Florentine government, and all the family's property was confiscated. Unlike Margherita, Francesco Datini was from a modest social background, born in the town of Prato and orphaned at a young age. He was an energetic businessman, drawn like many Tuscan merchants to Avignon because that city, as the seat of the papacy at the time, was a rich source of income (**#23**). Francesco had raised himself to great wealth by running a variety of successful business enterprises in southern France. The couple married in 1376 when Margherita was sixteen years old and Francesco was around forty. When they returned to Tuscany in 1383, they set up a household in Francesco's hometown of Prato, establishing two trading companies, one in Pisa and another in Florence. Over the following years, the Datini business grew to include a wool company and dye-works in Prato, a trading company in Genoa, with branches in Spain and the Balearic Islands, as well as a bank in Florence.

The couple divided their time largely between Florence and Prato and, of necessity, were often separated, with Margherita managing a large portion of the business affairs in Francesco's absence. Out of a need to keep him updated when they were apart, Margherita continually wrote letters to her husband—she had taught herself to write for this purpose—and her letters are a rich source of information about the inner workings of the business, household, and marriage of this late fourteenth-century power couple. Unable to have children herself, Margherita raised as her own daughter an illegitimate child named Ginevra who Francesco had fathered with an enslaved domestic servant. Margherita outlived her husband by a dozen years, administered his legacy, served on the board of his charitable foundation, the Ceppo, and also created her own bequest for the Hospital of Santa Maria Nuova in Florence.

DOI: 10.4324/9781003284284-68

She lived most of her final years in Florence and chose to be buried there in the church of Santa Maria Novella near her ancestors.

Margherita Datini, *Letter to Francesco Datini*, 1386

In the name of God, amen. On the 20th of January 1385 [1386]

Today I received your letter, written on the 19th of this month and I will respond here as necessary.

You say about one of the letters that I sent you that it was very nicely composed. I don't know if you are saying that in jest, but if you meant it, I am pleased.

In my opinion it appears that Boninsegna and I have not advised you well, as you've never wanted to do what he tells you. I do not speak of myself, since I'm a woman and a man doesn't let himself be ruled by women's advice.

Concerning your arrival here, I am pleased. I ask you to make an effort and do me a big favor: I am begging you to avoid having gout this Carnival season. It would be very bad for you, with all you have to do right now. You should not always be having troubled thoughts, and don't go around saying that I make fun of all your suffering. I don't mind if you tell me face to face, but don't write these things.

You left a warehouse here to be managed by two people who might be said to be worth less than half a person. You know how your friend goes away as he pleases. One day the bell sounds at vespers; some days it doesn't ring at all; and on Saturday when there is most need it doesn't ring. Think how your affairs are being managed! You send us letters constantly, and between having them carried over there where he is and having the others sent, the warehouse is closed half the time. A lot of people come looking for you and find the door shut; it seems like a business run by children. I would advise you if you have another leaky boat around, send him here, because you seem to like that. You can stay up late writing long letters of four or five pages, but it means nothing to the friend you send it to, since he has two lady-tutors who help him read: his mother and his daughter. They and all the other women at the warehouse read your letters. That's how much sense he has: this way you will never need to tell others about all your business. I don't know what need there is to write your friend telling him about all your cares and every single matter. You might say to me: "What do you know about what I write to him?" I know nothing except what I can imagine, knowing what you are like. Simone tells me you write him letters that are three or four pages long; I can't believe these bibles you send day after day are all about business. This must be a way you have of unloading your soul of worries that you have, but I would not trust him more than the others. The reason is that, aside from Boninsegna and Tieri, there is no one who doesn't cheat you a dozen times a day. You have seen it yourself and know whether or not I am speaking the truth and you ought to guard yourself against that one man most of all. He knows better how to do it than all the others, since he's had practice. I wish to God that these were outright lies about him, although it's rare that the things I tell you aren't true. If you were as highly honored as you have been disrespected it would be a good thing for you, since a hundred people wish you harm, although they didn't use to. I am telling you this because these things I hear people saying weigh on me and your shame seems like my own. I trust in God that you will recognize this one as you recognized the others. On this matter I will say no more. I pray you do not handle this like you do other matters; these are things that create too much hatred and could ruin your whole business. I pray you that you handle yourself calmly with him and with the others until you are somewhat relieved from these worries of yours and can deal with them as they deserve. For God's sake don't let yourself get carried away by this wickedness, since it would ruin you. Give them your word and many promises until you achieve what you want, as a man kisses the hand that he wishes to have chopped off.

I understood a lot of things from your other letter and it troubles me that it is written with much melancholy and that you are full of it. As you do not want to reveal anything to me, I believe it is for the best and I appreciate it. I wish you would do the same with others—you would be more praised than you are. It weighs on me that when you return, your health might be worse and this is the greatest worry I have, since for so many reasons, you gave me the worst day of my life, (even if perhaps I thought it was worse than it was.) Think of living in a manner so that all your affairs will go well. They will succeed if you will it. I do not want to say any more about this. I am asking you to burn this letter after you read it; do this service for me, I pray you. Lapa and all the other women send a hundred thousand greetings. May God protect you always.

From your Margherita, who commends herself to you, from Florence

Source

Margherita Datini, *Letter* in Lisa Kaborycha, trans. and ed. *A Corresponding Renaissance: Letters Written by Italian Women, 1375–1650*, Oxford UP, 2016, pp. 102–04.

References

Bryce, Judith. "'Les Livres des Florentines': Reconsidering Women's Literacy in Quattrocento Florence," in *At the Margins: Minority Groups in Premodern Italy*, ed. Stephen Milner, U Minnesota P, 2005, pp. 133–61.

Crabb, Ann. *The Merchant of Prato's Wife: Margherita Datini and Her World, 1360–1423*, U Michigan P, 2015.

Datini, Margherita. *Letters to Francesco Datini*, trans. Carolyn James and Antonio Pagliaro, Iter Inc.: Centre for Reformation and Renaissance Studies, 2012.

Nigro, Giampiero, ed. *Francesco di Marco Datini: The Man, the Merchant*, U Florence P, 2010.

Origo, Iris. *The Merchant of Prato: Francesco di Marco Datini*, Penguin, 1992 [1957].

62 A Venetian noble's marriage advice

Francesco Barbaro, *On Wifely Duties*, 1415

Twenty-five years old when he wrote his treatise on marriage, Francesco Barbaro (1390–1454) was a learned humanist who had studied Greek and Latin with some of the finest scholars of his day and three years earlier had earned doctorates in civil and canon law at the University of Padua. As a Venetian aristocrat, Barbaro over the course of his life held office as a senator and was governor of various *terraferma* cities—Vicenza in 1423, Bergamo in 1430, Verona in 1434, Brescia in 1437, and Padua in 1445. Like many eloquent humanists, Barbaro frequently served as ambassador, representing the Venetian Republic at the Council of Florence, at the court of the Holy Roman Emperor in Bohemia, and he was sent on official embassies to Mantua, Ferrara, and Milan. Barbaro was known as a collector of manuscripts; he commissioned translations from the classics and made many translations of his own. Barbaro's Latin treatise *On Wifely Duties* (*De re uxoria*) is similar to *On the Family* (*I libri della famiglia*), a vernacular work written a dozen years later by Florentine humanist Leon Battista Alberti (**#12**). Both draw on classical texts for inspiration—works by ancient authors such as Xenophon, Plutarch, Cicero, and Valerius Maximus—and both similarly codify contemporary patrician family values, emphasizing the supremacy of the father within the household. In his book, Alberti famously compares the role of the father to that of a vigilant spider, who is "so alert and watchful that if there is a touch on the finest and most distant thread he feels it instantly, instantly appears, and instantly takes care of the situation."[1] Like the spider, the father of the family rules over an elaborate web of household affairs performed by others, but is ready to leap in when necessary. While in his treatise Alberti advocates delegating important domestic responsibilities to the wife, as Margaret King points out, Barbaro's work goes further toward empowering women: "It is revolutionary because it identifies the mother—a woman, not a man; an interloper in the household, not its patriarch—as the critical figure for the rearing of the young and consequently, for the social and cultural reproduction of the noble family."[2] The connection between the noble Venetian Barbaro and another elite Florentine family was the motivation for writing this book. During the summer of 1415, Barbaro had been

DOI: 10.4324/9781003284284-69

a houseguest of the Medici family and became friends with the two sons of Giovanni di Bicci de' Medici—Cosimo (1389–1464) and Lorenzo (*c.*1395–1440)—who were both close to him in age. He composed this work later that year as a wedding gift to Lorenzo on the occasion of his marriage to Ginevra Cavalcanti in May, 1416. A bachelor at the time he wrote this, Barbaro himself would marry the Venetian noblewoman Maria Loredan four years later, and the couple had five children.

Francesco Barbaro, *On Wifely Duties*, 1415

On household management

I am of the opinion, which you Lorenzo, I am sure will approve, that a wife's concern for household management brings not inconsiderable usefulness. Indeed, that most prudent man Augustus Caesar aptly commented that if Alexander had been able to keep and preserve all that he had won through fortune and his great deeds he would have received more rewards and praise. For that reason, women ought not to be cheated of their glory if they succeed in administering all the goods gathered in the home, as is their duty. They ought thus to take pains to govern their households as Pericles daily managed the affairs of Athens and they ought to continually examine themselves, so they do not fall short in their care, devotion, and diligence in domestic matters. It greatly helps in things pertaining to the household if they become accustomed to staying at home and looking after everything. Here the example of the very prudent stableman comes to mind, who when he was asked what chiefly caused a horse to grow sleek, replied, "His master's eye." To commend a wife's duties to posterity, attached to the bronze statue of Gaia Caecilia, daughter of Tarquinius, were a household shoe, a distaff, and spindle so that women in the future might assiduously imitate her diligence. What negligent estate manager can hope to have hardworking peasants? What sleepy general can make his soldiers vigilant for the republic? If a housewife, therefore, wants her maids to serve well at home, she must not instruct them with words alone, but indicate, demonstrate, and through her actions show them the way to do it. Nothing is really more excellent in household affairs than when everything has its place and is kept there. Certainly nothing is more beautiful or useful than order, which is always of the utmost importance. We consider that a chorus or an army, unless order is properly preserved, can be called neither a chorus nor an army. I would have wives imitate queen bees, who know, receive, and keep safe until needed, whatever is brought into their hives. They are always there to preside over their honeycombs so that they will be diligently constructed and mature well. Housewives may send their maids and manservants out [on chores] if they learn of some future profit to be made, but if the servants are needed at home, they should be urged to stay, ordered what to do, and directed. They should also consider it their duty to make sure no misfortune comes to their husbands' food pantries, wine cellars, or oil cellars. Just as generals review the number of their soldiers regularly, so wives should frequently and accurately inspect the number of provisions stored at home, so that they will not discover to their great detriment that what should have lasted for years is barely sufficient for a month.

On the education of children

Once their children have passed infancy, mothers must devote great ingenuity, care, and effort so that they will excel in endowments of mind and body. First, they should teach them duty toward God Eternal, their fatherland, and their parents, so that they will become accustomed from earliest years to those virtues that are the foundations of all others. Only those children who fear God, obey the laws, honor their parents, respect their superiors, are good-natured with their peers, and polite [*humani*] toward their inferiors give any cause for hope. Let these children then, meet everyone with kindness in their features, upon their brows, and with their words, enjoying familiarity, however, with only the best people. Let them learn to be temperate in food and drink, so that the foundation for self-control later in life will be laid down. Let them be reminded to avoid pleasures that are disgraceful and turn their attention and studies to matters that will be fitting, useful, and agreeable when they are older. If mothers can instruct their children in these things, they will be much better prepared for the benefits of education. We often see how the tasks and rewards from princes are willingly accepted, while those issued by ordinary people are unwelcome. Who does not know what great authority that even the slightest bland words of a parent have over their children? And thus, we know the wise Cato the Elder diligently taught his children reading and writing, among other things, so as not to be lacking in his duties as a father.[3] Even that rough foreigner Euridice is to be deemed worthy of no small praise, for when she was already an adult she acquired the knowledge of literature, that monument of virtue and learning. So that, having given her children life, she was also able to show them the rules for living well and happily, using the rich seasonings of the humanities. Mothers should keep children from excessive laughter and not let them use words uttered rashly, for one is a proof of stupidity, the other of rage. And they should warn them that anything which is indecent to do is indecent even to speak about. Accordingly, they need to be kept from using filthy or rude language, and if they say something foul or licentious, they should receive not a smile or a kiss, but [a lash of] the whip. Now and then they should teach them not to mock anyone for their poverty, their humble birth, or other misfortunes, because such behavior will kindle fierce enmities and will form habits of arrogance. They should instruct their children in sports in which they willingly learn to exert themselves, so that if the need arises, they will be able to bear even greater hardships. I would have mothers condemned for showing anger, greed, or sexual passion in the presence of their children, for these vices weaken virtue.

Notes

1 Alberti 206.
2 King 1.
3 "As soon as the boy showed signs of understanding, his father took him under his own charge and taught him to read, although he had an accomplished slave, Chilo by name, who was a school-teacher, and taught many boys. Still, Cato thought it not right, as he tells us himself, that his son should be scolded by a slave, or have his ears tweaked when he was slow to learn, still less that he should be indebted to his slave for such a priceless thing as education. He was therefore himself not only the boy's reading-teacher, but his tutor in law, and his athletic trainer, and he taught his son not merely to hurl the javelin and fight in armour and ride the horse, but also to box, to endure heat and cold, and to swim lustily through the eddies and billows of the Tiber." Plutarch, *Lives*, trans. Perrin, Vol 2, Loeb, 1914, p. 363.

Source

Francesco Barbaro, *On Wifely Duties* in *De re uxoria a cura di Claudio Griggio e Chiara Kravina*, ed. Leo S. Olschki, MMXXI, pp. 272–75, 286–89, trans. Kaborycha.

References

Alberti, Leon Battista. *The Family in Renaissance Florence*, trans. Renée Neu Watkins, U South Carolina P, 1969.

Barbaro, Francesco. *On Wifely Duties*, trans. Benjamin G. Kohl in *The Earthly Republic: Italian Humanists on Government and Society*, U Pennsylvania P, 1978, pp. 179–228.

Barbaro, Francesco. *The Wealth of Wives: A Fifteenth-century Marriage Manual*, ed. and trans. Margaret L. King, Iter Academic Press; Arizona Center for Medieval and Renaissance Studies, 2015.

Bell, Rudolph M. *How to Do It: Guides to Good Living for Renaissance Italians*, U Chicago P, 1999.

Chojnacki, Stanley. *Women and Men in Renaissance Venice: Twelve Essays on Patrician Society*, Johns Hopkins UP, 2000.

Frick, Carole Collier. "Francesco Barbaro's *De re uxoria*: A Silent Dialogue for a Young Medici Bride," in *Printed Voices: The Renaissance Culture of Dialogue*, U Toronto P, 2004, pp. 193–205.

63 A saint's stepmother files her taxes

Sandra di Nuccio di Ser Cione, *Catasto declaration*, 1427

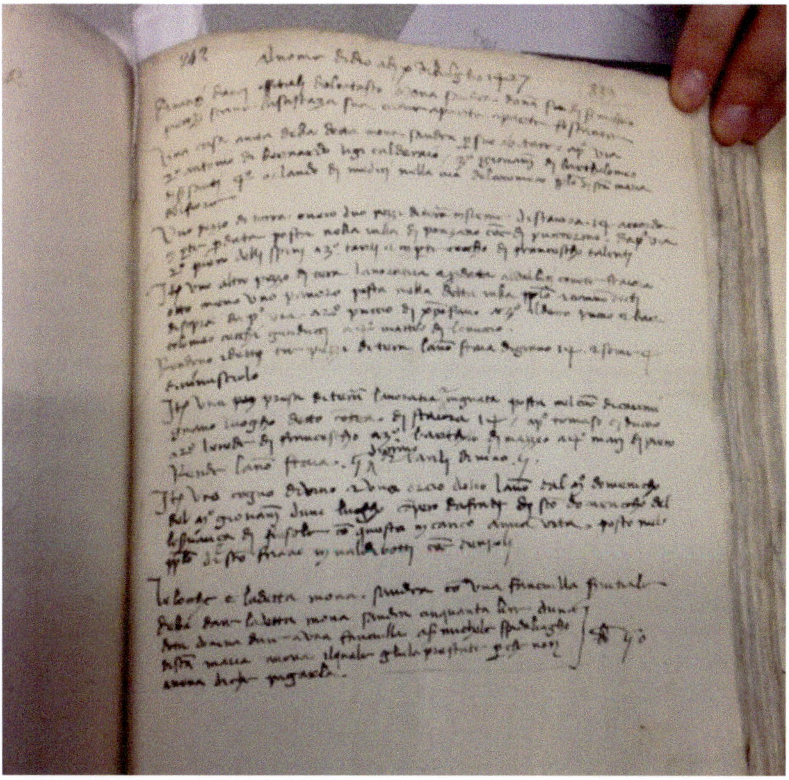

Figure 7.2 Catasto 55 fol. 839r Archivio di Stato di Firenze. This is a page of a Florentine citizen's 1427 tax declaration. The city was divided into four *quartieri* (quarters) and each *quartiere* further subdivided into four neighborhoods called *gonfaloni*. Taxpayers' submissions were organized according to the region of the city in which they resided. The sheets of paper were bound together into different volumes. This volume contains tax declarations from the *quartiere* of San Giovanni, the *gonfalone* of the Drago.

DOI: 10.4324/9781003284284-70

Like every other head of household in Florence in 1427, Sandra, the widow of Ser Niccolò Pierozzi, was required to file her tax declaration.[1] The Florentine Republic was driven to initiate this radical new income tax by social and political pressures: the dramatic demographic decline caused by the Black Death and subsequent waves of the disease had reduced the population of Florence from around 120,000 in the year 1300 to less than 40,000 a century later. This meant that, in order to pay for the city's infrastructure and especially for its defenses—mercenary armies needed to be paid—the Florentine government needed to come up with a more effective system of taxation. Moreover, in the wake of social turbulence due to the 1378 uprising of the Ciompi wool workers, it was imperative that assets were determined in a manner acceptable to all citizens. Of the three existing systems, two weighed especially on the average Florentine: the indirect taxes known as the *gabelles*, customs duties levied on goods entering the city, and *prestanze*, or "forced loans." The latter, especially in times of war, were imposed on all citizens, although only the wealthy could afford to pay in full—and thus be paid back with interest—whereas the others paid what they could and were not reimbursed. The third means of taxation, which was disliked by the wealthy landowning class, was the *estimo*, which assessed payments based on taxpayers' signed statements estimating the value of their property. The solution arrived at in 1427 was the Catasto, a combined income and property tax for which every household was obliged to submit a signed return. Apart from the granular detail of economic conditions in fifteenth-century Florence it reveals—for example, in 1427, eighty-two percent of households paid less than a florin in taxes or owed nothing whatsoever, and 2,924 were entirely destitute[2] — the Catasto provides a vast amount of other information. Gene Brucker has observed that "the thousand-odd volumes of the Florentine Catasto constitute the richest source for the social and economic history of any European community prior to the French Revolution."[3] Historians have mined the Catasto for information about the lives of artists, merchants, humanists, and other prominent Florentines, as well as individuals who otherwise would have been unknown to us.

Sandra di Nuccio di Ser Cione had been widowed for a decade, and her only natural son, Jacopo, had died young. From her Catasto return we learn that in 1427 Sandra was living alone in via del Cocomero (today's via Ricasoli), attended only by a serving girl. Though she was not well-off, Sandra was by no means as poor as many Florentine widows.[4] She lived off earnings from the sale of grain from several small pieces of land that she owned in the countryside near Pontormo and Carmignano, as well as wine and olive oil from some property purchased from the friars of San Domenico in Fiesole—this last possibly arranged through her stepson's connections. For although next to nothing is known about Sandra, her stepson Antonino Pierozzi (1389–1459) is famous. Antonino's father, Niccolò, was a successful notary who married three times and had a total of seven children. Antonino's mother died when he was six years old, and his father married a third wife, Sandra, in 1395. The young man joined the observant branch of the Dominican order when he was sixteen years old, and he went on to became prior of the Convent of Fiesole. Then, in 1437, he became prior of San Marco and in 1446, archbishop of Florence. Beyond his many learned theological writings, including his masterpiece, the *Summa Theologica*, Antonino was a reformer, and he preached what has been termed a "civic theology" for the way he addressed many of the social concerns of the day.[5] He was an immensely popular religious figure, especially among the poor of Florence. When he died in 1459, ordinary Florentines thronged his funeral; he was canonized as St. Antoninus in 1523.

Sandra's Catasto reveals that her home was located close to the via Larga where Giovanni di Bicci, father of Cosimo the Elder, lived. Indeed, one of her neighbors was a Medici. The wealthiest Florentine in 1427 was Palla di Nofri Strozzi, with 103,306 florins in taxable assets.[6] St. Antoninus's stepmother was assessed at 165 florins. The same year that Sandra filed this tax report, Antonino, who was already a prominent public figure, delivered his influential Florentine Lenten sermons.[7]

Sandra di Nuccio di Ser Cione, *Catasto declaration*, 1427

In the name of God, on the 10th day of July 1427

Before the officials of the Catasto, Mona Sandra, widow of Ser Niccolò Pierozzi, declares her property:

A house owned by the said Mona Sandra, used for her own residence [bounded] on the 1st side by the street; on the 2nd by Antonio, son of Bernardo the coppersmith; on the 3rd by Giovanni, son of Bartolomeo, son of Ser Santi; on the 4th by Orlando de' Medici[8] in via del Cocomero in the parish of Santa Maria del Fiore.

A piece of land, or rather, two pieces of land together, 14 *staiora*;[9] one of the aforesaid parts located in the village of Ponzano within the town of Pontormo [bounded] on the 1st side by the road; on the 2nd by Piero delli Spini; on the 3rd side in part by Cecco di Francesco Talenti.

Item. Another piece of tillable land connected to the aforementioned location, 8 *staiora*, less one *panoro*, located in the aforesaid village mentioned above, [bounded] on the 1st side by the road; on the 2nd by Puccio, son of Cristofano; on the 3rd by the same Puccio and Bartolomeo Cecchi Guiducci; and on the 4th by Matteo, son of Bonuccio.

The three aforementioned pieces of land yield 14 bushels of grain per year and 4 *some*[10] of wine.

Item. Some tillable land and a small vineyard located within the town of Carmignano in a place called Contea of 14 *staiora*, [bounded] on the 1st side by Tommaso, son of Duccio; on the 2nd by the heir of Francesco; on the 3rd by Bartolo di Mazzeo; on the 4th Mari, son of Piero. The annual yield is 4 bushels of grain and 4 barrels of wine.

Item. A *cogno*[11] of wine and an *orcio*[12] of oil per year from Domenico, son of Giovanni, from a place bought from the observant friars of San Domenico in Fiesole, for my use during my lifetime, located in the community of San Francesco in Val di Botte, town of Empoli.

The mouths to feed in the household: the aforesaid Mona Sandra with a serving girl. Said Mona Sandra owes fifty lire for a girl's dowry that she had to give to Ser Michele, rector of the hospital of Santa Maria Nuova, which money he had lent her because she didn't have the means to pay it.

Notes

1 In 1427, around 60,000 households in the cities, towns, and rural areas subject to the Florentine Republic filed taxes, of these around 10,000 were in the city of Florence.
2 De Roover 30.
3 Brucker 11.
4 There are many Catasto declarations filed by widows, as "in Florence, one adult woman in four was a widow in 1427." The majority were extremely poor, yet all had to file their taxes: "The miserable were exempt from taxes, but not from the obligation to file a return. This category gathered in the infirm, the aged, minor orphans, and, above all, widows." Herlihy and Klapisch-Zuber 216–17.
5 Howard 199–202.
6 "In 1427 the Medici were not yet the richest family in Florence. Giovanni di Bicci was only third on the list." De Roover 28. The 1457 Catasto record reveals the household of Cosimo de' Medici on the via Larga as the wealthiest in Florence.
7 Howard 140.
8 Orlando di Guccio de' Medici was head of a household of seven and declared 4,193 florins in assets. He is buried in a tomb carved by Bernardo Rosselino in the Church of the Santissima Annunziata in Florence.
9 A measurement of land: one *staioro* = 525 square meters; the *staioro* was divided into 12 *panora*.
10 A *soma* equaled 2 barrels; a barrel contained about 46 liters.
11 A *cogno* equaled 10 barrels.
12 An *orcio* contained about 33 liters.

Source

Catasto 55 fol. 839r Archivio di Stato di Firenze, trans. Kaborycha.

References

Brucker, Gene. "Florentine Voices from the Catasto, 1427–1480," *I Tatti Studies in the Italian Renaissance*, Vol. 5 (1993), pp. 11–32.

de Roover, Raymond. *The Rise and Decline of the Medici Bank, 1397–1494*, Harvard UP, 1963.

Herlihy, David and Christiane Klapisch-Zuber. *Tuscans and Their Families: A Study of the Florentine Catasto of 1427*, Yale UP, 1985.

Howard, Peter Francis. *Beyond the Written Word: Preaching and Theology in the Florence of Archbishop Antoninus, 1427–1459*, Olschki, 1995.

Peterson, David Spenser. "Archbishop Antoninus: Florence and the Church in the Earlier Fifteenth Century," (PhD Dissertation, Cornell University, 1985).

64 A friar preaches civic and domestic peace

St. Bernardino of Siena, *Vernacular Sermons in the Campo of Siena*, 1427

Bernardino of Siena (Bernardino degli Albizzeschi, 1380–1444), born to a noble Sienese family, lost both of his parents when he was six years old. As a young man he studied canon law, but when in 1400 a violent wave of plague washed over Siena, he volunteered in the city's hospital, Santa Maria della Scala. Bernardino himself caught the disease, and after he recovered, he considered becoming a hermit. At the age of twenty-two, Bernardino instead chose to become a friar in one of the most rigorous and austere orders, the Franciscan Observants, who were dedicated to St. Francis's original goal of "rejecting the world for themselves yet embracing it as preachers and social activists."[1] Within three years the young friar was busy preaching in the city of Siena and its surrounding countryside. Bernardino roved beyond his native Tuscany; during the course of his life he preached throughout Italy in the regions of Piedmont, Lombardy, Veneto, Liguria, Emilia-Romagna, Umbria, and the Marche. He eventually became so famous that there was not enough space in cathedrals and basilicas to hold the audiences, so he delivered sermons in the open air in public piazzas. This was especially true for the important sermon cycles held during the seasons of Lent and Advent, like the one depicted in the painting by Sano di Pietro (Figure 7.1). A sign of his extreme popularity was Bernardino's canonization in 1450, less than twenty years after his death. Like Catherine of Siena (**#24**), the most famous Sienese saint before him, Bernardino played a prominent role in the city's politics, but unlike Catherine, Bernardino was not known as a mystic. As David Herlihy writes: "Bernardino was a saint of a different sort. He did not shift his gaze repeatedly from heaven above to the world below. There is no report in his biographies of impassioned conversations with God. His chief attention was given to the conduct of his contemporaries, and to its social and religious implications. Bernardino radically transformed the art of preaching in Italy, in both its content and its style."[2] However, like Catherine, who died the same year he was born, Bernardino was concerned with keeping the peace in Siena. Although politics had changed since the Trecento, the potential for violence in Tuscany was ever present; indeed, both the pope and the Sienese government had invited the friar to preach in the city in order to reduce hostilities between political

DOI: 10.4324/9781003284284-71

factions.[3] In these sermons, the Sienese saint did not consider politics in a narrow sense though. Rather, Bernardino reached out to people by drawing a parallel between relations within the family and relations between citizens in the city–state. His audience could identify with the many descriptions of domestic situations—the relations between parents, children, husbands, wives, and widows—while, on a grander scale, he was able to connect the microcosm of private life with the macrocosm of the public sphere. This was a central theme in the cycle of forty-five vernacular sermons that Bernardino delivered over the course of three months in 1427, beginning on August 15 and ending on October 5. His words were diligently transcribed by a man in the crowd named Benedetto di maestro Bartolomeo who was by trade a cloth cutter.

Bernardino of Siena, *Sermon 17*, September 1, 1427

On the governing of states

O city of Siena, believe me, do as I say, in praise of God. If an evildoer comes into your hands, punish him. And if a good man presents himself, praise him, even as you praise God, for everything comes back to God. Listen to the words of Paul in Romans, Chapter VIII: "*Diligentibus Deum, omnia cooperantur in bonum*—all things work together for good to them that love God." That widow who had perfect faith spoke to Elias, and she asked, praising God, that her son be restored to life. And he, in praise of God, begged God's grace, and the miracle was done, through [her] faith and the intervention of that holy prophet, thus the mother received the grace that she asked for. And just as I have taught men how they ought to rule the city and its town hall, so I also want to instruct women what they ought to do in their homes. . . .

If you cannot pass your time in contemplation, at least say what [prayers] you can and God will show you his grace; and another will step up and do so in your place, for Jesus Christ saw that everyone was not fit for rising to the contemplative life.

[. . .]

The Lord said, "Mary hath chosen that good part" and yet you know that Martha, who led the active life, did not chose a bad part, rather it was an excellent part.[4] I would also like to say this: that I commend the mixed life. Are there those of you women here who serve God both in this life and the next, loving Him and loving your neighbor both? You do well. Do you have a sick person in your house?—"Yes." Do you not know what good you do by caring for him? Do not leave him in order to come to a sermon! Do you have a husband and children who need to be cared for?—"Yes." Do not neglect those who need you, to attend a sermon. First take care of your home and all the things that are needful there, and then come to the sermon, otherwise I would not praise your coming.

Bernardino of Siena, *Sermon 18*, September 2, 1427

On how one should love one's neighbor

The person who truly loves, and loves from the heart, needs to get along in agreement with everyone. He shouldn't behave like the donkey: when you push the donkey it pushes back, and when you pull it, it pulls away. Don't act like this when you see that your neighbor is in need; be sure to help them, always. God didn't want humankind to have any other principle but one—that's the mystery! It was only so we together should be joined in union with each other.

First, you see that God created Adam alone; not Adam and Eve together, but first Adam and then Eve. He didn't do this with the beasts and wild animals, which he created two by two. And also look at the place from which he created Eve: not from the head of man, nor from his feet, but from his mid-section, also a mystery, to signify that she should not be the boss over man. O how badly it goes for her when she is in charge over the man! Also take note, that he chose not to create her from man's foot. This indicates that a man should not degrade his wife: he ought to treat her as a woman and not as a slave. Moreover, I say that he took her from the middle part of Adam so that the two would be equal. . . .

Another similarity with God—who is unified in the Trinity, three in one, and could never have within himself any division, for if he were divided in any manner he would not be God—is that just as there can be no division in him, similarly, we ought to be in harmony. As the Prophet David said of them, "*Deus qui inhabitare facit unius moris in domo*—God, who causes those to inhabit together those who are of one custom, of one mind, without any arguing."[5] That is, the father with his wife, children, and his brothers, all in an orderly manner, agree to live well, in peace and harmony. Likewise, it can be applied to a city, and the citizens who live there, great and small, rich and poor, all with the intention to live well. O how blessed that city, which can be so well-ordered according to the glory of God! Thus it is said, "*In tribus congratulator cor meum, etc.*—My heart rejoices in three things: one is the unity of citizens; another is the love and harmony between brothers; another is the love between man and wife."[6]

Bernardino of Siena, *Sermon 19*, September 3, 1427

On how the husband ought to love his wife, and the wife her husband

I am speaking this morning about the true friendship that a wife and husband ought to have for one another. The wise woman will have brought her daughter with her to this morning's sermon: she who is not as good, will have left her in bed. Oh, you would have done much better to have brought her to hear these truths!

[*Bernardino describes men's various motives for choosing wives, including their expectations of receiving large dowries*]

And furthermore, I'm saying to you, woman, don't ever take a husband who loves your money more than he loves you. Listen! I want to give you an example from St. Gregory, who says there was once a rich woman who was widowed, and for a long time she lived like that. She was wise, young, good, beautiful, and wealthy. When she was asked, "For goodness' sake, why don't you get yourself a husband?" She replied, "I can't find anyone who doesn't love my property more than they love me, and I don't want to give myself to that type of person. But if I were to marry, it would never be to someone who loves me just to have my possessions; and this is the only reason that I haven't remarried." Now you see how it works, when a woman marries a man who only wants her things. . . . Soon afterwards, there will be no true friendship between them, so that when she becomes a little faded, he won't like her so much anymore. If a woman has possessions, and has beauty, and good sense, so much stronger the friendship. If, added to that she is rich, wise, good, God-fearing, and bears children, behaves well with her mother-in-law and father-law, bringing love to everyone in the household, giving charity and praying in honor of God, she will inspire love in everyone who deals with her. If she has all these qualities even the stones will speak well of her. Oh! To such persons as these is true friendship shown. It is not a big dowry alone that makes a woman well-liked, not even a huge dowry, or beauty, but only goodness will make her really loved. And so, women, if you have daughters to marry off, make sure that they have the dowry of virtue if you want them to be loved by their husbands.

O you who use love charms so your daughter's husband will care for her, do you know what God in his judgment will do? He will make sure the good times won't last, and so you'll never be content, and neither will he or she. O men, have you understood me? Believe me now, and remain firm, since everything I've told you is true, because whenever there is but little virtue, friendship can be neither great nor bountiful. If there is a go-between [*mezzana*],[7] that go-between is friendship; the greater the virtues, the greater and more bountiful the friendship.

Notes

1 Polecritti 7.
2 Herlihy 174–5.

3 Polecritti 183–5.
4 A reference to the episode in Luke 10:38–42 that tells of the two sisters, Mary and Martha, who receive a visit from Christ: Martha complains because while she has been scurrying around serving the guests, Mary was sitting at Jesus's feet quietly listening. Jesus reprimands Martha saying, "Martha, Martha, thou art careful and troubled about many things: But one thing is needful: and Mary hath chosen that good part, which shall not be taken away from her." This biblical passage has traditionally been interpreted as praise of the contemplative, over the active life.
5 Ps. 67:7. This passage from the Vulgate is here translated from Bernardino's Italian.
6 Eccles. 25:1: "In three things I was beautified, and stood up beautiful both before God and men: the unity of brethren, the love of neighbours, a man and a wife that agree together." KJV.
7 The *mezzana* or matchmaker, was a person who helped introduce couples and arrange marriages. Throughout this passage, Bernardino refers to various popular customs practiced at the time including dowries, love charms, and matchmakers.

Source

Bernardino da Siena, *Sermons* in *Prediche volgari sul Campo di Siena 1427*, ed. Carlo Delcorno, Vol. I, Rusconi, 1989, pp. 499–501, 509–11, 539, 543–45, trans. Kaborycha.

References

Bornstein, Daniel and Roberto Rusconi, eds, Margery J. Schneider, trans. *Women and Religion in Medieval and Renaissance Italy*, ed. U Chicago P, 1996.

Debby, Nirit Ben-Aryeh. *Renaissance Florence in the Rhetoric of Two Popular Preachers: Giovanni Dominici (1356–1419) and Bernardino da Siena (1380–1444)*, Brepols, 2001.

Herlihy, David. "Santa Caterina e San Bernardino: Their Teachings on the Family," in *Women, Family, and Society in Medieval Europe: Historical Essays, 1978–1991*, Berghahn Books, 1995, pp. 174–92.

Mormando, Franco. *The Preacher's Demons: Bernardino of Siena and the Social Underworld of Early Renaissance Italy*, U Chicago P, 1999.

Origo, Iris. *The World of San Bernardino*, Harcourt, Brace & World, 1962.

Polecritti, Cynthia L. *Preaching Peace in Renaissance Italy: Bernardino of Siena and His Audience*, Catholic U America P, 2000.

Randolph, Adrian. "Regarding Women in Sacred Space," in *Picturing Women in Renaissance and Baroque Italy*, ed. Geraldine A. Johnson and Sara F. Matthews Grieco, Cambridge UP, 1997, pp. 17–41.

Strehlke, Carl Brandon. "Art and Culture in Renaissance Siena," in *Painting in Renaissance Siena, 1420–1500*, Abrams, 1988, pp. 33–43.

65 Managing matters of life, death, dowry

Alessandra Macinghi Strozzi, *Letter to Filippo Strozzi*, 1449

Alessandra Macinghi (*c.*1408–1471) was in her teens when she married Matteo Strozzi, then twenty-five. Though the Strozzi was a highly respected, elite Florentine clan, when they fell out of political favor with the Medici, they were banned from Florence. Alessandra joined her husband in exile in Pesaro, where he died shortly afterward in 1435 in a brutal epidemic of the plague. This epidemic also took the lives of three of the couple's eight children. Although she was not yet thirty when she was widowed, Alessandra never remarried. Her sons spent many years in exile, but because female members of the family were exempted from the ban, she and her daughters remained in Florence. From her home there, Alessandra tirelessly looked after the Strozzi's interests: she managed business and property transactions, and she worked on improving ties with the Medici family so one day her family could be reunited. In this letter, one of seventy-three that have survived, Alessandra writes to her eldest son Filippo Strozzi (1428–1491) giving him news of family and friends. She also informs him of two important financial decisions that need to be made: the first involves purchase of property adjoining their own in order to enlarge the Strozzi home, and the second concerns her daughter Caterina's pregnancy. Alessandra argues that there is an urgent need to take out life insurance in the eventuality of Caterina's death.

Alessandra Macinghi Strozzi, *Letter to Filippo Strozzi*, 1449

In the name of God on the 26th day of December 1449

I have received several of your letters since August, but didn't answer any of them; the reason for this was first of all my illness, which began on the 9th of September. Then, on the 26th when the plague began to appear near us in Quaracchi, I sent Matteo to stay with Caterina and Marco in the Mugello, where he's been for more than two months.[1] So I didn't respond to your letters, because I couldn't, especially without Matteo. I will write to you myself in the future if it pleases God.[2]

DOI: 10.4324/9781003284284-72

Since I was sick with dysentery it was Marco who warned me that I ought to take refuge in his house in the Mugello, as the plague was nearing Quaracchi, but I was too sick to leave.[3] And while I was ill, people began dying of it [the plague] here, as I said above. And as I was not feeling any better, my brother Zanobi sent word to tell me to get out of here and to go stay with him in Antella where it was healthy and he had a safe place.[4] So I went, although I was in such a state that it was very difficult getting me there, where by the grace of God I recovered. And finding myself well off there—being the beginning of winter and near Florence—I judged that things would improve, as they in fact did. And having also heard that Niccolò wanted to pass through here, I did not leave. I stayed there until the 16th of this month, as they returned to Florence for Niccolò's visit. I would have stayed two more months, it was so completely clear [of disease] that no one was dying anymore there with signs of plague, at a time when four or five, or even six a day were dying elsewhere. Indeed, in these eight days no more than one per day passed away. And because it's happened like this other times in the past, we cannot be sure [enough] about our family. May God free us completely from this pestilence.

I was told by you, and before that by Soldo degli Strozzi and Matteo di Giorgio[5] of the death of our Filippo, and I was very saddened by this, considering the damage it causes to us, in the first place, and then to our whole family. His virtue was such that he gave us all a good reputation. It is not possible to recover from such a death as this; we must bear it with patience and trust in God's will. F[rancesco] della Luna[6] also died, which was a great blow. And here Antonangiolo Macinghi died and many other of our Strozzi relations. And during these past days Margherita di Pippo Manetti[7] died, with her two children, so this time it touches us very close to home. May God in His mercy put an end to this. And regarding Filippo's death, I have letters from you and from Iacopo telling how he and Niccolò got together in Barcelona, may God grant them a good voyage. I have been informed that Niccolò[8] will be stopping by our house and I am to show him great hospitality, and that he will be taking Matteo to Barcelona, so I should be getting him ready. So I have done this and I await him gladly, as I have a great desire to see him. I will do my utmost to show him every possible honor. I know I am incapable of doing as much as he deserves, but I will be excused as long as I do everything I can and I do it willingly, just let God bring him here safely. Yesterday I heard he was in Rome; I guess he will leave there after the holidays are over, and he is expected here on the fourth or fifth of January.

I sent two large balls, a pair of penknives, and a dozen quills along with Soldo, seeing as Matteo wasn't going. I had ordered a pair of friar's clogs, some towels, and handkerchiefs sent to you, all for Matteo, now

I must send for some more. Let me know if any wagoners arrive over there. I would also send you some fennel, if you want some.

[. . .]

Nothing at all is happening in the house of Donato Rucellai, on account of this plague, as he has not been in Florence. I want to let you know that it's mine to buy and that he can't have it without my permission.[9] I will not run out of time as I have many years in which to buy it; I am only waiting for the five hundred florins of Caterina's dowry to come to term, which as you know will be in April of 1450. Then I will be able to act on our behalf and they will see what I mean to do when I have the money in hand.

I believe Marco must have told you that Caterina is pregnant and is due to give birth in mid-February. It seems to me that given her state, we ought to take out insurance so that we do not lose the five hundred florins invested in the *Monte*;[10] we would lose the money and the person at the same time if God had other plans for her and we were to lose her before April.[11] I have discussed this with Antonio Strozzi; in any case he thinks we could spend 12 florins in order to insure her those three months, namely: January, February, and March. I will wait to hear from Niccolò and I will do as he says, but then we must take swift action. Marco doesn't believe we should do it; he says she is in good health and he does not want to throw away so many florins. I think it's better to throw them away and be on the safe side. However, don't write to him, he might take it amiss, and it's our own business. I pray God that He does not take her away before her time—that she remains sound and healthy in both mind and body is my greatest wish.

I am thinking, God willing, to go to Rome for the Jubilee[12] in April; if there were any way you could come there, so I could see you before I die, it would be a great comfort to me. As you see, I have nothing else in this world besides you three sons of mine, and for your own good I have let you go, one by one, with no care for my own happiness and now I have so much sorrow at letting go of this last one[13] that I do not know how I will be able to live without him. The sorrow is too great and I love him too much, as he resembles his father. He has become a handsome boy during this time that he has been in the country, seeing him before and seeing him now, he has completely changed. May God grant that he gives me comfort. And so I pray you, since I will be left so dejected, to give me a little comfort when I go to Rome; may God give me enough life to see you all again as I desire.

I had letters in October from Lorenzo,[14] who is well; write him often, as it is good for him. I received the power of attorney you sent me; when I need more documents, I will let you know. Nothing else for now. God keep you safe from harm.

From your Alessandra, in Florence.

Notes

1 Caterina was Alessandra's older daughter (b.1431) and Marco Parenti was her husband. Matteo, named after Alessandra's husband, was her youngest son, born in 1436 soon after his father's death. Quaracchi is a small town on the western outskirts of Florence, about 10 kilometers from the center of Florence. The Mugello is a rural, hilly region to the north of Florence where many Florentines had country homes, most notably, the Medici family.
2 Alessandra preferred to have her son Matteo act as her scribe.
3 Dysentery, before the advent of antibiotics, was frequently fatal. It was an especially common cause of infant mortality.
4 Antella is a small town in the countryside, about 14 kilometers south of Florence.
5 Heather Gregory: "Formerly a business partner of Alessandra's husband, he now worked for Niccolò Strozzi and his brothers." *Selected Letters* 225.
6 Heather Gregory: "Husband of Alessandra di Messer Filippo Strozzi, who was an aunt of the Filippo Strozzi whose death has just been mentioned." *Selected Letters* 225.
7 Heather Gregory: "A first cousin of Alessandra's husband." *Selected Letters* 225.
8 Niccolò di Lionardo Strozzi, first cousin to Matteo Strozzi, was a successful banker who helped Alessandra's sons by giving them work abroad. Unlike other male members of the Strozzi clan, Niccolò was not under the ban of exile and could come and go through Florence.
9 In an earlier letter Alessandra had discussed wanting very much to purchase this house. By law, because it adjoined her own, she had the first right to buy it. She writes to Filippo on November 8, 1448: "I am not saying this for me, as I have only a short time to live, but for you, and your descendants, who will not always be in such hardship; as that house adjoins this one, it would make ours the most beautiful house in this neighborhood." Guasti 39. Years later, when Filippo returned from exile, one of the wealthiest men in Florence, he would indeed buy that adjoining house as his mother advised, then go on to build the Palazzo Strozzi, the most impressive private home in Renaissance Florence.
10 The *Monte delle doti* was a dowry investment fund initiated by the Florentine state in 1425. When a baby girl was born, parents invested money in the fund, which came to term when the girl reached marriage age. If the girl died, the money reverted to the state.
11 "About one-fifth of the deaths of married women in Florence seem to have been associated with childbearing." Herlihy and Klapsich-Zuber 277.
12 The Papal Jubilee began on Christmas Day in 1449.
13 Alessandra's youngest son, Matteo, born 1436, who went to join his brother in Naples the following year when he was fourteen years old, and died in August 1459, aged 23.
14 This is Filippo's younger brother Lorenzo (b.1432). Heather Gregory notes that in 1453 he was in Bruges working for Jacopo Strozzi. *Selected Letters* 65.

Source

Alessandra Macinghi Strozzi, *Lett*er in Lisa Kaborycha, trans. and ed. *A Corresponding Renaissance: Letters Written by Italian Women, 1375–1650*, Oxford UP, 2016, pp. 132–35.

References

Crabb, Ann. *The Strozzi of Florence: Widowhood and Family Solidarity in the Renaissance*, U Michigan P, 2000.
Goldthwaite, Richard A. "The Strozzi in the Fifteenth Century," in *Private Wealth in Renaissance Florence: A Study of Four Families*, Princeton UP, 1968, pp. 31–73.

Gregory, Heather. "The Return of the Native: Filippo Strozzi and Medicean Politics," *Renaissance Quarterly*, Vol. 38, No. 1 (Spring 1985), pp. 1–21.

Herlihy, David and Christiane Klapsich-Zuber. *Tuscans and Their Families: A Study of the Florentine Catasto of 1427*, Yale UP, 1978.

Kirshner, Julius and Anthony Molho. "The Dowry Fund and the Marriage Market in Early Quattrocento Florence," *The Journal of Modern History*, Vol. 50, No. 3 (September 1978), pp. 403–38.

Macinghi Strozzi, Alessandra. *Letters to Her Sons, 1447–1470*, ed. and trans. Judith Bryce, Iter Academic Press: Arizona Center for Medieval and Renaissance Studies, 2016.

Macinghi Strozzi, Alessandra. *Selected Letters*, trans. with an introduction and notes by Heather Gregory, UC Press, 1997.

Phillips, Mark. *The Memoir of Marco Parenti: A Life in Medici Florence*, Princeton UP, 1987.

66 A playwright stages scenes from life

Antonia Tanini Pulci, *St. Guglielma*, *c.*1483

Antonia Tanini Pulci, *St. Theodora*, *c.*1500

"Possibly the first woman in Western Europe to see her own writings through the printing press,"[1] Antonia Tanini (1452–1501) was the author of several popular Florentine sacred dramas (*sacre rappresentazioni*). Daughter of the merchant Francesco Tanini and a Roman woman named Jacopa,[2] the dramatist is often known by the surname Pulci, from her husband, the poet Bernardo Pulci (1438–1488). Antonia wrote in elegant vernacular Florentine and was skilled at capturing the rhythm of everyday speech and portraying social realities that resonated with her audience. Hers is a rare example of an authentic "female voice" in Renaissance theater that represented conditions of everyday women's lives, even when the heroines in her dramas were royal saints or virgin martyrs. For instance, in one play the English princess Guglielma against her will is pressured by her family to marry. When she repels her brother-in-law's sexual advances, he slanders her. Yet, Guglielma decides to remain silent rather than publicly denounce him—a choice undoubtedly made by real women under similar situations. Moreover, as many of these dramas were performed in convents, with nuns as actors, sometimes we get a peek at what life must have been like within the cloister—the friendships, rivalries, and domestic concerns are revealed in the dialogue of such plays. The drama of *St. Theodora* opens with a *frottola* (comic scene) in which a pair of nuns complain about the costumes they have been assigned to wear in the play. In her own experience, Antonia Tanini had known both marriage and life within a religious community. Though her early married life was marked by financial hardships, Antonia was comfortably well-off by the time of her husband's death in 1487. Despite her brother's pressure for her to remarry, she decided instead to buy a home to live together with other women as a third-order Augustinian sister.[3]

DOI: 10.4324/9781003284284-73

Antonia Tanini, *St. Guglielma, c.*1483

[*The queen is alone, the king's brother having left the room after threatening her.*]

GUGLIELMA:

I will remain silent, woe, what a great offense
has been attempted upon the queen,
defiling the king's great majesty!
If I speak out my court will be thrown into turmoil—
O God, you are my guide and my defender.
Susanna[4] I know, was saved by you;
I don't know what I should do or say;
I will keep quiet until the king returns.
[. . .]
Oh my father, it was at your request alone,
and against my every wish that I took a spouse;
I always intended to live pure and chaste.
To me were burdensome those worldly spoils,
for which now I must bear such weighty grief.
I end my life in tears and sorrows;
Woe is me because you wanted to follow
the ways of the world, filled alas, with suffering.

Antonia Tanini, *St. Theodora, c.*1500[5]

Here begins the comedy, or rather tragedy of SAINT THEODORA, Virgin and Martyr, and first, two nuns enter: SISTER ANGELA *and* SISTER HIPPOLYTA.

SISTER ANGELA: In the end, it's really true that a stuck-up person always gets everything she wants; this is what she's done, as if the entire convent belonged just to her. But I have a craving to do something that she won't like very much.

SISTER HIPPOLYTA: Oh, take a look at us, we're a pair of trouble-makers! I'm so overflowing with fury and outrage, that I must pour it out someplace: I want to rip up these lines; they're completely senseless.

SISTER ANGELA: You're so right, a thousand times over; there are seven or eight of us who have lines to say, and they only want to dress three or four in nice clothes. You and I have to do without them, and we'll be mocked by the whole convent.

SISTER HIPPOLYTA: If I continue to feel as I do now, it's I who will mock them; they'll have to stay and watch and it'll give me pleasure to bend their noses out of shape—I want to make fun of them all!

SISTER ANGELA: I'm not so sure; I'm a little afraid the prior will be angry.

SISTER HIPPOLYTA: Don't get worked up Angela. Personally, I don't take much account of him. The old man will stay put by the fire and won't trouble his brain over it, whatever we do.

SISTER ANGELA: Alright, just as you wish; we've decided not to say our lines in this play and they'll just be wasting their time if they try to give us grief over it. All they'll get from it is our contempt. But now I see your sister coming our way.

SISTER HIPPOLYTA: Let her come, if she wants to. I won't change my mind; I'll never give in to her.

Enter SISTER DANIELA: Well now, aren't you coming? You seem confused: can't you see that it's already evening and all the people are gathered in the hall?

SISTER ANGELA: Go ahead and put on your show. We don't want to come, so don't waste your time talking to us. Go perform it yourself.

SISTER DANIELA: O my dear sisters, why are you doing this? If you stay here it will certainly put everyone out. Don't delay getting dressed: it will be said that you're being obstinate.

SISTER HIPPOLYTA: They've treated us so well in sharing around the costumes! They've tricked us a thousand times, taking the best for themselves: the golden chains, necklaces and rings, all the fancy hats and wigs. They've taken everything, leaving nothing for us but a sack full of rags.

And they say I should hurry to get dressed! I'd have to be pretty thick to obey this order. It would only be by mistake, if I ever wore this stuff that they found in the trash! I'm not afraid of anyone, and I'm not going to get dressed. You're just wearing yourself out for nothing talking to me.

SISTER DANIELA: O my little Polly, there's no shortage here of clothes and jewelry.

SISTER ANGELA: For dressing old hags, there's plenty. And we'll appear like servants, and the rest of you like grand ladies. What will people say when they see us looking so ugly?

SISTER HIPPOLYTA: They'll blame all our teachers who were not capable of providing better for us.

SISTER ANGELA: I've been given rags and leftover scraps—O how lovely I will be!

SISTER HIPPOLYTA: In short, Sister Daniela, we don't want to come.

Enter SISTER COSTANZA: Alas! What is this I hear: have you two gone crazy? Everyone is already gathered in the hall.

SISTER ANGELA: The blabbermouth, that's all we needed! Go away, Sister Costanza; you've said enough. Don't give us more of your sermons, we don't think them any good. Go preach to yourself; you're not the abbess or the prioress, either.

SISTER COSTANZA: Get up, there's still time, tell me the reason you're so angry. You know I've always loved you like sisters. I beg you, don't be the ones to ruin a party. Don't be stubborn, you can be in charge, and I know that if you wish it all will go well.

SISTER MASSIMA: I'm in such pain that I feel my heart will burst: it's getting late and we're not dressed. And still you will not come!

SISTER HIPPOLYTA: Massima, don't try to beg us and to annoy the two of us at once.

SISTER COSTANZA: These two are so hard-headed that they are convinced that the costumes have been divided up in such a way that the best ones and the brightest colors have been taken by us.

SISTER MASSIMA: Oh the two of you are so wrong! I want both of you to come now and take anything you like. So long as we can be in peace, we don't care about anything else, just let us go now and start the show.

SISTER ANGELA: If this is what you want to do, we will fly like the wind, and I truly repent what I said.

SISTER COSTANZA: It's only a little sin, let's say nothing more of it. We'll say that as a lark, we were joking amongst ourselves. But I pray you, let's go or we'll be late.

SISTER HIPPOLYTA: Can I have that cloak?

SISTER MASSIMA: Yes, and a golden cap as well. But I see the others coming out already dressed, let's walk briskly, or the play will have begun.

[*They go inside to get dressed, and the woman who introduces the play begins to speak*.]

Notes

1 Newbigin 2016, 337.
2 For biographical details derived largely from Florentine Catasto records, see Weaver 2010, 1–33.
3 On the tertiary orders, see note on p.347.
4 See #70 on the biblical story of Susanna and the Elders.
5 For more information on the authorship and possible dating of this play, see Cook 1996, 28–32.

Sources

Antonia Pulci, *The Play of St. Guglielma*, in *Rappresentazione di santa Guglielma*, Bartolomeo de' Libri, 1495, fols. 3v-4r, trans. Kaborycha.

Antonia Pulci, *The Play of St. Theodora* in *Sacre rappresentazioni dei secoli xiv, xv, e xvi*, ed. Alessandro D'Ancona, 1872, vol. 2, 323–47, pp. 324–28, trans. Kaborycha.

References

Cook, James Wyatt, trans. and Barbara Collier Cook, eds. *Florentine Drama for Convent and Festival: Seven Sacred Plays*, ann. and trans. U Chicago P, 1996.

Newbigin, Nerida. "Antonia Pulci and the First Anthology of Sacre Rappresentazioni (1483?)," *La Bibliofilía*, Vol. 118, No. 3 (settembre–dicembre 2016), pp. 337–62.

Newbigin, Nerida. *Making a Play for God: The Sacre Rappresentazioni of Renaissance Florence*, Centre for Renaissance and Reformation Studies, 2021.

Pulci, Antonia. *Saints' Lives and Bible Stories for the Stage*, ed. Elissa B. Weaver, trans. James Wyatt Cook, Iter Inc.: Centre for Reformation and Renaissance Studies, 2010.

Weaver, Elissa B. *Convent Theatre in Early Modern Italy: Spiritual Fun and Learning for Women*, Cambridge UP, 2002, pp. 97–104.

67 The professional life of a courtesan

Veronica Franco, *Poem on the pleasures of love*, 1575

Veronica Franco *Letter to a woman who would have her daughter trained as a courtesan*, 1580

In 1574 when Henry III paid a state visit to Venice, Veronica Franco (1546–1591), the most celebrated courtesan of her day, was officially selected to entertain the king of France. A gifted poet who was both learned and beautiful, Franco was what was known as an "honest courtesan," one of a highly sought-after class of sex workers in Renaissance Venice who catered to the nobility. These glamorous women participated in the vibrant artistic, musical, and literary scene. It has been noted that it is no coincidence that Venetian painters specialized in depicting alluring female nudes, considering Venice had such a plentiful supply of courtesans willing to model for them. Indeed, in one of her letters, Franco thanks the painter Jacopo Tintoretto for painting an especially flattering portrait of her, writing, "I swear to you that when I saw my portrait, the work of your divine hand, I wondered for a while whether it was a painting or an apparition set before me by some trickery of the devil."[1] Posing for a portrait by Tintoretto was one way to augment her reputation, of course; another was to have her literary works printed. Franco published her *Poems in Terza Rima* in 1575, of which the *capitolo*[2] below is an example. She wrote this exaltation of her own sexual skills in response to a love poem by her patron, the wealthy literary connoisseur Domenico Venier. In 1580, Franco had a collection of fifty of her letters printed under the title *Lettere familiari a diversi*. These letters, including the one to Tintoretto, cover a variety of topics; in one of them she reprimands a woman who wants her daughter to become a courtesan. In the letter, she describes the dangers and humiliations involved in the life of a courtesan—Franco herself died in poverty at the age of forty-five.

Veronica Franco, *Capitolo* 2, 1575

And my beauty, such as it is,
which you never tire of praising,
I'll then employ for your contentment;
sweetly lying at your left side,
I will make you taste the delights of love

DOI: 10.4324/9781003284284-74

when they have been expertly learned;
  And doing this, I could give you such pleasure
that you could say you were fully content,
and at once fall more deeply in love.
  So sweet and delicious do I become,
when I am in bed with a man
who, I sense, loves and enjoys me,
  that the pleasure I bring excels all delight,
so the knot of love, however tight
it seemed before, is tied tighter still.
Phoebus,[3] who serves the goddess of love,
and obtains from her as a sweet reward
what blesses him far more than being a god,
  comes from her to reveal to my mind
the positions that Venus assumes with him
when she holds him in sweet embraces;
  so that I, well taught in such matters,
know how to perform so well in bed
that this art far exceeds Apollo's by far,
  and my singing and writing are both forgotten
by the man who experiences me this way,
which Venus reveals to those who serve her.

Veronica Franco, *Letter to a woman who would have her daughter trained as a courtesan*, 1580

I did not want to fail to write you these few lines, urging and warning you once more about your situation. Do not, in a single blow, kill both your soul and your honor along with that of your daughter, who, just considering her physically, is so lacking in beauty—not to mention other traits, as my eyes do not deceive me—and possesses so little grace and spirit in conversation, that you would break her neck trying to make her successful in the profession of a courtesan. To succeed in this is very hard work for a woman who possesses beauty, style, and judgment, and who has cultivated many skills, let alone a young person who is completely lacking in many of these and little above mediocrity in the others. And as you obstinately persist in your error, you would say to me that it is a matter of luck, but first I must respond, saying that one cannot do worse in this world than give oneself over to the whims of fate, which can so easily administer evil as well as good. A person of good sense builds hope upon the solid foundation of what is within oneself and what one can do.

But I will add this: supposing fortune were to be favorable and benevolent to you in everything, this kind of life always results in misery. It leads to such wretchedness, going against the grain of human feeling, forcing both body and mind to such servitude that it is frightening only to think of it. To give oneself as prey to so many men, with the risk of being stripped, robbed or killed, that in one single day everything you have acquired over so much time may be taken from you, with so many other perils of injuries and horrible contagious diseases; to drink with another's mouth, sleep with another's eyes, move according to another's desires, always running the clear risk of shipwreck of one's faculties and life, what could be a greater misery?[4] What riches, what comforts, what delights could be worth such a heavy price? Believe me, of all worldly misfortunes, this is the most extreme, and then if to the concerns of the world we add those of the soul, what could be more certain of perdition and damnation than this?

Pay attention to what is being said and in matters that pertain to life and salvation of the soul do not follow others' examples. Do not permit your wretched daughter's flesh to be cut to pieces and sold, you yourself acting as butcher. Consider how all this will end; and if you wish, look at all the examples: observe what you come across every day in the multitude of women who exercise this profession. But if reason, and all these worldly arguments ought to move you, even more so should those of Heaven replace them and draw you away from this grievously mistaken course. Turn your hopes to God and avail yourself of your friends' offers of help.

Notes

1 Jones and Rosenthal 37. There is no consensus among art historians as to which painting by Jacopo Tintoretto this might be, if it still exists, although the portrait in the Worcester Art Museum is often cited.
2 The *capitolo* is a form of interlocking verse that resembles the *terza rima* pattern used by Dante in the *Commedia*.
3 Phoebus Apollo, the god of poetry in ancient Greek and Roman mythology.
4 In Franco's Capitolo 24, "To a man who has insulted a woman," she refers to the ritual disfigurement of courtesans known as *dare la sfregia* (to give the scar), writing, "you threatened her mightily and swore that you would slash her face." Franco, *Poems and Selected Letters*, trans Jones and Rosenthal 245. Gang rape, known as *trentuno* (thirty-one), was a punishment meant to humiliate a courtesan. This was carried out, for instance, against Angela Zaffetta, who was raped by 80 men, instigated by an aggrieved former lover. The event was celebrated in verse by Lorenzo Venier in 1531. Rosenthal, *Honest Courtesan* 37–8.

Sources

Veronica Franco, *Capitolo 2* in *Poems and Selected Letters*, ed. and trans. A.R. Jones and M.F. Rosenthal, U Chicago P, 1998, 61–71, p. 69.

Veronica Franco, *Letter* in *A Corresponding Renaissance: Letters Written by Italian Women, 1375–1650*, Oxford UP, trans. and ed. Lisa Kaborycha, 2016, pp. 144–48.

References

Bassanese, Fiora A. "Private Lives and Public Lies: Texts by Courtesans of the Italian Renaissance," *Texas Studies in Literature and Language*, vol. 30, no. 3, Renaissance Culture, Literature, and Genres (Fall 1988), pp. 295–319.

Clarke, Paula C. "The Business of Prostitution in Early Renaissance Venice," *Renaissance Quarterly*, Vol. 68, No. 2 (Summer 2015), pp. 419–64.

Lawner, Lynn. *Lives of the Courtesans: Portraits of the Renaissance*, Rizzoli, 1987.

Rosenthal, Margaret F. *The Honest Courtesan: Veronica Franco, Citizen and Writer in Sixteenth Century Venice*, U Chicago P, 1992.

Ruggiero, Guido. *The Boundaries of Eros: Sex Crime and Sexuality in Renaissance Venice*, Oxford UP, 1985.

68 Venetian ladies discuss marriage

Moderata Fonte, *The Worth of Women*, 1592

Figure 7.3 In his *Portrait of a Widow*, *c.*1550–5, Gemäldegalerie, Dresden, Venetian artist Jacopo Tintoretto (Jacopo Robusti, 1518–1594) portrays a dignified woman dressed in mourning gazing over her shoulder, away from the viewer. Elsewhere in *The Worth of Women* Moderata Fonte praises the "stupendous" talent of Tintoretto's daughter Marietta, a painter.

DOI: 10.4324/9781003284284-75

Modesta dal Pozzo, who wrote under the pseudonym Moderata Fonte (1555–1592), was born in Venice into a family of wealthy *cittadini originari*, her father a lawyer.[1] Only one year old when both her parents died of plague, Modesta was raised in a convent until she was nine. There she was often presented to visitors and impressed them with her exceptional memory and spirited intelligence. Later she went to live with relatives and was educated along with a stepsister of her mother. When the stepsister married the attorney Nicolò Doglioni, Modesta went to live with them. She grew up in a cultivated environment, where she studied Latin, learned to draw, sing, and play the lute and harpsichord. Wanting to nurture Modesta's literary gifts, her uncle gave her full access to his library and encouraged her composition of poetry. She published a number of works in verse—a chivalric romance, the libretto for a cantata, sacred Easter narratives, and possibly other works that have been lost. The most famous work by Moderata Fonte is her prose dialogue *The Worth of Women Wherein Is Clearly Revealed Their Nobility and Their Superiority to Men*. It is set as a fictional discussion that takes place among a group of seven women friends, calling to mind the seven liberal arts so often represented in art with female allegorical figures. The number is also the same as the number of female narrators in Boccaccio's *Decameron*, and many of their names are those of heroines from antiquity who are mentioned in Boccaccio's *Famous Women* and elsewhere. The cast of characters is Adriana, an older widow; Virginia, her naïve, unmarried daughter; Elena, a young newlywed; Leonora, a young widow; Lucrezia, an older married woman; Cornelia, a younger married woman; and Corinna, who is young and determined to remain unmarried, dedicated to her studies.[2] The spirited arguments that Moderata Fonte placed in these speakers' mouths were highly influential in the *querelle des femmes*, often referred to in English as the "woman question," the ongoing debate over women's rightful place in society. It sparked Giuseppe Passi's 1599 misogynist tract *The Defects of Women* (*Dei donneschi diffetti*) and inspired Lucrezia Marinella (1571–1653) the following year to dash off a furious rebuttal titled *The Nobility and Excellence of Women, and the Defects and Vices of Men* (*Nobiltà et l'eccellenza delle donne, co' difetti et mancamenti degli uomini*).

Moderata Fonte's *The Worth of Women* was first published posthumously by her uncle in 1600. According to his biography of his niece, which he included at the beginning of the volume, she completed writing the book the day before she died in childbirth. Doglioni also notes with regret that she was unable to achieve more in her life, limited by "the misguided belief current in this city that women should excel in nothing but the running of their households."[3] And indeed, as emerges from the lively discussion in this dialogue, many women felt their freedom constrained by the strict gender roles in sixteenth-century Venetian society.

Moderata Fonte, *The Worth of Women*, 1592

They conducted her [Elena, the new bride] into the room and all sat down together with her, never ceasing to admire her. Virginia asked her how she had been all this time and if she was well. But Leonora, who was a very clever young woman, did not wait for Elena's response:

"How can you ask such a thing Virginia my dear, for we all know that according to common opinion, a new bride can only be well."

"Indeed," added Lucrezia, "don't say 'well,' but 'as well as can be expected.'"

"I can't say yet whether I'm doing well or badly," answered Elena, "because my husband keeps me pretty good company. Though there is one thing that displeases me: he does not want me to leave the house. I want to do nothing else but go to all the weddings and parties that I'm invited to, not only because this is a special time for me, but also out of a sense of my husband's honor, and my own as well. I wouldn't want people to think I wasn't dressed like a lady and nicely turned out, as I am."

"May it please God," said Cornelia, "that he will always treat you this way and worse does not follow— you do not know that the wedding cake is eaten quickly."

"The new wife still has her doubts," said Lucrezia, "her ideas are shifting back and forth, and she's right, because in the beginning everything is rosy."

"In fact, you should say that as long as things are new, everything seems fine," said Leonora.

"As far as that goes," answered Lucrezia, "I suppose it is much as it seems, because I would say, for example, that if some food that I like seems good to me, even if it's not good, it's as if it were."

"You make me laugh," said Leonora. "It's no wonder that the baker woman, who from standing all day in front of the oven, bursting with heat, runs home barefoot to her children out playing in the fresh air and strips them naked, as it seems to her that they are suffering from the heat, even though it's the middle of winter."

Laughing, Cornelia replied,

"Praise God that we can tell jokes and laugh about such things amongst ourselves and do as we please here, where there's no one to watch or correct us."

"Exactly," said Leonora, "if by chance some man were to hear us and to recount such pleasantries, how he would mock us! We would never be able to live with it."

"If we were to be honest," said Lucrezia, "we'd say that we're never well off unless we women are alone. Truly blessed is the woman who can live without any man's company."

"It seems to me," added Leonora, "that I live peacefully and experience the greatest of happiness without a man, considering what a lovely thing freedom is."

"It's possible that not all men are so bad," said Elena.

"If only they weren't," answered Cornelia, "and God willing you will not soon learn to prove the others right."

"Who knows? Maybe she will be lucky," said Virginia.

"It could be," answered Lucrezia. "Put your mind at rest."

"With all the bad things you are saying," said Elena, "I don't think Virginia would want to find out what it's like to have a husband."

"If it were up to me," said Virginia, "I know I would never choose to get married, but I have to obey my elders."

"As regards this, my daughter, I would feel the same way as you," added Adriana. "but your uncles have decided that you will be married. This is on account of the large amount of property you have inherited, which needs to be protected on your behalf; and I myself can't think of any better arrangement for you. Take heart, and don't worry, all men are not the same. Perhaps, who knows, you will have one who is better than the others [have gotten]."

"Oh, that's little comfort to all those who are drowned," said Leonora. "And this vain hope, that rarely comes true, spells certain ruin for many poor girls."

"Boundless hope may kill other people," said Corinna, "but this hope of yours doesn't fool me. I would rather die than submit myself to any man. The life I lead is too blissful, without having to fear some bearded fellow ordering me around."

"Oh happy Corinna!" said Lucrezia, "And what other woman in the world could compare to you? Surely, no one: not a widow, since she cannot be proud of having suffered a long time; not the married woman since she still endures hardship; nor the maiden who awaits a husband, because trouble is in store for her, as the proverb goes: 'Husbands and hardship are always at hand.' Happy and blessed then are you and whoever follows your example, and even more so since God has given you such a lofty mind that you delight in the exercise of virtuous actions and employ your deep thoughts in the valuable study of letters, so human, and yet so divine. You set out upon a heavenly life, while still living amidst the travails and dangers of this world, which you reject, refusing to deal with deceitful men and dedicating yourself to the virtues that will make you immortal. Certainly, with your sublime intellect you ought to write a volume on this topic, for pity's sake, in order to persuade wretched girls, who do not know how to tell good from evil, what is best for them. Thus, you will receive double glory by doing service both to God and to the world in full measure."

"This would be a very good deed," replied Corinna, "and I thank you for making me mindful of it. Perhaps one of these days I will write it."

Notes

1 Beneath the Venetian aristocratic class, respected "original" Venetian citizens were those who could prove their residence in the city for several generations; many were highly educated professionals who accounted for much of the administration of the republic. Veronica Franco's family were also *cittadini originari*.

2 Corinna perhaps belongs to a so-called "tertiary" or "third order" of women religious, who were affiliated with a traditional monastic order, taking certain vows similar to nuns, but not required to live enclosed within a convent. In addition to the traditional Catholic definition of tertiary orders, Gabriella Zarri suggests yet another meaning: "In some sixteenth-century sources, the term "third status" connotes a female condition presented as a third possibility for women's lives in addition to the traditional alternatives of marriage or the convent—that is, voluntary celibacy. "The Third Status" 197–8.

3 Cox 2.

Source

Moderata Fonte. *Il merito delle donne: ove chiaramente si scuopre quanto siano elle degne e più perfette de gli uomini*, ed. Adriana Chemello, Eidos, 1988, pp. 16–18, trans. Kaborycha.

References

Chojnacka, Monica. *Working Women of Early Modern Venice*, Johns Hopkins UP, 2001.

Ferraro, Joanne M. *Marriage Wars in Late Renaissance Venice*, Oxford UP, 2001.

Fonte, Moderata. *The Worth of Women Wherein is Clearly Revealed Their Nobility and Their Superiority to Men*, ed and trans. Virginia Cox, U Chicago P, 1997.

Labalme, Patricia H. "Women's Roles in Early Modern Venice: An Exceptional Case," in *Beyond Their Sex: Learned Women of the European Past*, New York UP, 1984.

Marinella, Lucrezia. *The Nobility and Excellence of Women, and the Defects and Vices of Men*, ed. and trans. Anne Dunhill, intro. Letizia Panizza, U Chicago P, 1999.

Price, Paola Malpezzi. *Moderata Fonte: Women and Life in Sixteenth-century Venice*, Fairleigh Dickinson: Associated University Presses, 2003.

Zarri, Gabriela. "The Third Status," in *Time, Space, & Women's Lives in Early Modern Europe*, Truman State UP, 2001, pp. 181–99.

69 A lovely child remembered

Selections from Medici court correspondence, 1540–2

Figure 7.4 Agnolo Bronzino, *Portrait of Bia de' Medici*, *c.*1542, Uffizi. The child is portrayed wearing a medallion around her neck with a portrait of Cosimo I de' Medici, identifying her as the duke's daughter. The artist Agnolo Bronzino (1503–1572) created many stunning portraits of the Medici family, including Duke Cosimo I, the Duchess Eleonora di Toledo, and their children. Bronzino's workshop produced multiple copies of these, which were sent as gifts to royal courts across Europe (**#60**). The portrait of Bia is unique; unlike the official portraits of the legitimate offspring of Cosimo, it was not intended to represent the dynastic aspirations of the Medici.

DOI: 10.4324/9781003284284-76

Extremely high child mortality was commonplace during the Renaissance, and it has been estimated that approximately half of all Florentine children died before their tenth birthday through illnesses like worms, diarrhea, infections, and a variety of transmissible diseases, including plague.[1] Death of children was not limited to the poor; the prosperous Florentine merchant Goro Dati (#73) recorded in his secret book over the course of the years 1393–1431 the births of twenty-six legitimate children, of whom only seven were still alive in 1431. No matter how wealthy or powerful, every family was afflicted, including the Medici. Duke Cosimo I de' Medici and his wife, the Duchess Eleonora di Toledo, had eleven children. Only eight survived infancy, and just four outlived their mother who died in 1562. Some scholars have speculated that since so many children died, parents in earlier times did not recognize the very young ones as fully developed human beings and, as a result, withheld their affection.[2] One child who singlehandedly appears to disprove such a theory is Bia de' Medici. The child of Cosimo and a "Florentine gentlewoman" whose identity is unknown, Bia was born in 1536/37. When the duke married Eleonora in 1539, the duchess did not hesitate to accept the child.[3] Bia was raised by her grandmother, Maria Salviati, mostly in the suburban Medici Villa di Castello. The girl also spent time at court with her father, Cosimo—along with his legitimate children, Maria and Francesco, as well as Giulia, the daughter of the deceased Duke Alessandro. The child seems to have charmed everyone, and there are frequent mentions of Bia, particularly after she fell ill with a fever in early February 1542, when a flurry of increasingly alarming letters were exchanged by highly placed members of the Medici court reporting on her deteriorating health. Bia died on March 1, 1542; a plaster death mask was made of her face, and she was buried in the Medici family chapel in San Lorenzo. Little else is known of the child.

Maria Salviati, *Letter from Florence to Ugolino Grifoni in Arezzo*, 1540

July 22 . . . It is not surprising that Signorina Bia is the joy of that court although she is not often there. She is so loveable, that we long to see her, but to please His Excellency we comply with his wish, and all the more willingly, as she is healthy and in a good mood. We are amazed that the discomforts of the road did not make her unwell. May God protect her as we desire.

Pierfrancesco Riccio, *Letters from Florence to the court in Pisa*, 1542

January 21 Bia is a little weak; may God restore her health. . . .

January 22 Bia is improving. . . .

January 23	Bia has a slight fever and the poor little thing says she is cold. . . .
January 24	Bia is doing better. . . .
January 25	Bia has a little fever every day, but it comes and goes; she has become rather thin. . . .
January 27	Bia's face is a little drawn. . . .
February 4	Signora Maria [Salviati] is with the duke's children . . . she is in good spirits; Bia has that slight fever of hers . . . .
February 7	Bia still has her fever and every day she gets thinner. . . .
February 23	Bia is gravely ill and the Signora [Maria Salviati] is distressed as Your Lordship can imagine. May God provide for that little girl and return her to health, since beyond the contentment it would give their Excellencies [the duke and duchess] and the Signora, all the city would rejoice, since everyone is pained by her illness. . . .
February 24	This morning Bia is a little weaker than yesterday; and though the fever seemed high today, still it appears to be lessening, which is no small thing. Today three physicians have seen her: Messer Niccolò di Messer Luca, Ripa, and Pasquali, and tomorrow they will arrive at some decision about the case.
February 25	[*in the morning*] Bia rested well last night and gives us reason to hope for her health, God willing. . . .
February 25	[*later in the day*] I am sorry not to be able to follow up with news of any improvement in Bia's health; the fever today has done the opposite to what I had hoped, and has turned on her. May God keep her in his holy hands.

Ugolino Grifoni, *Letter from Florence to the court in Pisa*, 1542

February 25	This is Bia's condition: this morning she had some bad episodes that give us cause for worry. Just now she has taken some porridge, although with great difficulty, as the catarrh never leaves her and her throat is rather swollen. Tomorrow will be the saddest day.

Averardo di Antonio Serristori, *Letter from Rome to Grifoni in Florence*, 1542

March 10	. . . I have learned of the death of Signorina Bia, although this happened some days ago, and it has upset me greatly; however, God arranges everything and we must have patience.

Notes

1 Carmichael 41. See also Orme 113 for similar statistics for England during the same period.
2 "Nobody thought, as we ordinarily think today, that every child already contained a man's personality. Too many of them died." Ariès 39.
3 It was not uncommon for illegitimate children to be raised along with the rest of the family. Goro Dati records the birth of an illegitimate son, Tommaso (**#73**); Francesco di Marco Datini and his wife, Margherita, adopted his illegitimate daughter, Ginevra (**#61**). The Florentine Catasto includes mention of numerous "bastard" children in households; taxpayers received deductions for every dependent child.

Sources

Maria Salviati, *Letter* in Conti, Cosimo. *La prima reggia di Cosimo I de' Medici nel Palazzo già della signoria di Firenze*, Giuseppe Pellas, 1893, pp. 118–22, trans. Kaborycha.

Pierfrancesco Riccio, *Letters* in Gaetano Pieraccini. *La stirpe de' Medici di Cafaggiolo*, vol. 2, Vallechi, 1924–1925, pp. 78–80, trans. Kaborycha.

Ugolino Griffone, *Letter* in Gaetano Pieraccini. *La stirpe de' Medici di Cafaggiolo*, vol. 2, Vallechi, 1924–1925, p. 80, trans. Kaborycha.

Averardo Serristori, *Letter* in *The Medici Archive Project* MAP Doc ID# 20181, MdP 3264 fol. 183, trans. Kaborycha.

References

Ariès, Philippe. *Centuries of Childhood: A Social History of Family Life*, Alfred A. Knopf, 1962.

Carmichael, Ann G. *Plague and the Poor in Renaissance Florence*, Cambridge UP, 1986.

Falciani, Carlo and Antonio Natali, eds. *Bronzino, Artist and Poet at the Court of the Medici*, Mandragora, 2010.

Langdon, Gabrielle. *Medici Women: Portraits of Power, Love and Betrayal from the Court of Duke Cosimo I*, U Toronto P, 2006.

Orme, Nicholas. *Medieval Children*, Yale UP, 2001.

Reed, Laurel. "Art, Life, Charm and Titian's Portrait of Clarissa Strozzi," in *Childhood in the Middle Ages and the Renaissance: The Results of a Paradigm Shift in the History of Mentality*, ed. Albrecht Classen, Walter de Gruyter, 2005.

70 Sexual abuse in art and in life

Arcangela Tarabotti, *Paternal Tyranny*, *c.*1650

Figure 7.5 Artemisia Gentileschi, *Susanna and the Elders*, 1610, Schloss Weißenstein, Pommersfelden, Bavaria.

DOI: 10.4324/9781003284284-77

Artemisia Gentileschi (1593–*c.*1656) was one of the most expressive and innovative painters of the generation that followed Caravaggio (1571–1610). She grew up in Rome, and when she was eighteen years old, her father (painter Orazio Gentileschi, 1563–1639) arranged for Artemisia to study perspective with his friend, the painter Agostino Tassi (1578–1644). Tassi subsequently raped his young student, as documented in detail in the lawsuit that followed. Though the event was real and traumatic, the sexual assault has tended to overshadow modern interpretations of almost all her paintings, including *Susanna and the Elders*. This is the artist's earliest known work, signed and dated 1610, when Artemisia was seventeen years old. As pointed out by Patricia Simons, "The canvas is often treated as a biographical response to her rape and intimidation but her testimony at the trial dates the beginning of the harassment to early May 1611."[1] Thus, this painting cannot be interpreted as a representation of Tassi's sexual abuse, rather, it must be considered as the adolescent artist's rendering of the subject matter prior to that event. The legend is taken from the Book of Daniel in the Old Testament and was represented frequently in Renaissance art. It tells of two elderly men who spy on Susanna while she is bathing; they demand she has sex with them, threatening to falsely accuse her of adultery with a certain young man if she refuses. The crime of adultery would not have carried serious consequences for a man, but for a woman the biblical punishment was death. The double standard in this Old Testament tale persisted in Renaissance Italy, when women were expected to be virgins before marriage and, once married, to remain faithful to their husbands. In Renaissance paintings of the scene, Susanna's nudity was normally represented seductively, her pose meant to excite the male viewer. Artemisia Gentileschi's portrayal of the scene tells a different story, as the female heroine violently resists their intended assault. Moreover, the fact that one of the men is younger and not physically repulsive, as often represented, suggests a more nuanced approach to representing female sexuality. Mary Garrard comments, "Artemisia's Susanna brings us closer to the world of flesh and blood women who might need to say no, yet are not immune to sexual attraction . . . she is not simply defending her honor as a flat moral absolute, she is also resisting potential sexual temptation. Her rejection is a test of her willpower."[2] Another feminist interpretation of the tale is that of Venetian nun Arcangela Tarabotti (1604–1652) whose polemical book *Paternal Tyranny* (*La Semplicità ingannata*, published posthumously in 1654) condemns the patriarchal structure of society and the many injustices perpetrated against women, including coercive sexual relations.

Arcangela Tarabotti, *Paternal Tyranny*, c.1650[3]

Women are seduced and then punished by men

Why on earth publish lying fictions just when you dedicate yourselves to assaulting the Fortress of Chastity as Cupid's disciples? You preach a sheltered life for women, digging up evidence from the tale of Bathsheba: while bathing in an open place she made even King David lie—that holy prophet whose heart was in tune with God's. Ask yourselves, witless ones, who was the true cause of her fall, and then deny it if you can. It was nothing else but the king's lust. Uriah's wife was at home, minding her own affairs bathing—whether for enjoyment or necessity, it matters little—but David eyed her too. Her beauty inflamed him, and his eyes were the gateway to his heart; by various ruses he obtained the satisfaction his sensuality demanded. What blame can one possibly attribute to that innocent woman, overwhelmed by the splendor of the king's majesty? She is more worthy of pardon than the royal harp player: she allowed herself to be overcome by a force from on high, as it were; he succumbed to the pull of flesh doomed soon to rot and darts from two eyes that pierce only those wanting to be wounded.[4]

Whoever paid attention to your stories would believe that Dina's curiosity—she was the patriarch Jacob's daughter—to see the city of Salem was the reason for the slaughter of so many men. But if you look at the facts, you would realize that it was Prince Sichem's unbridled lust, coupled with his violation of the girl, that brought about the catastrophe.[5] You don't mention at all chaste Susanna, her honor threatened by the lust of two old men within the privacy of her own garden: then her life was threatened as well, had she not been delivered at a single stroke from shame and death by God.

There is no lack of examples of betrayed and violated women. Lucretia was raped by King Tarquin the Proud; by slaying herself with her own hand she provided ample testimony of our sex's chaste will and the betrayal, cruelty, perverse lust, and treachery of men. One could weave story upon story about deceived, raped, and abandoned women who would rather die than live once they were dishonored. Decent people confirm that the proper abode of chastity is a woman's breast and its companion shame is a shield against your proven perfidy. So when women refuse to listen to your version of these myths, fables, and histories, they preserve their honor intact. Just think, how many young virgins allowed their flesh to be lacerated by iron rakes, tormented by barbs, pulled limb from limb on the wheel rather than yield to man's lust?[6] In resisting, these pure doves won for themselves the palm of victorious martyrdom. They truly deserve the virgin's crown, for even against the whole world they would have stood firm. How many more willingly drowned themselves at sea, how many slayed themselves with their own hands to escape your infamous desires?

Notes

1 Simons 41.
2 Garrard 76. Garrard also cites a portion of the Tarabotti passage that follows.
3 Tarabotti worked on this book, her most famous, probably over the course of many years. Despairing of having it published in Italy, toward the end of 1650 she arranged to have it published in France.

4 2 Sam. 11.
5 Gen. 34.
6 Examples of such virgin martyrs are St. Catherine of Alexandria, St. Agatha, and St. Lucy, among others.

Source

Arcangela Tarabotti. *Paternal Tyranny*, trans. Leitizia Panizza, U Chicago P, 2004, pp. 115–16.

References

Garrard, Mary D. *Artemisia Gentileschi and Feminism in Early Modern Europe*, Reaktion Books, 2020.

Simons, Patricia. "Artemisia Gentileschi's Susanna and the Elders (1610) in the Context of Counter-Reformation Rome," in *Artemisia Gentileschi in a Changing Light*, ed. Sheila Barker, Harvey Miller, 2017, pp. 41–57.

Weaver, Elissa B. "'With Truthful Tongue and Faithful Pen': Arcangela Tarabotti Against Paternal Tyranny," *Annali d'Italianistica*, vol. 34, Speaking Truth to Power From Medieval to Modern Italy (2016), pp. 281–96.

Part VIII

Travel, curiosity, and wonder

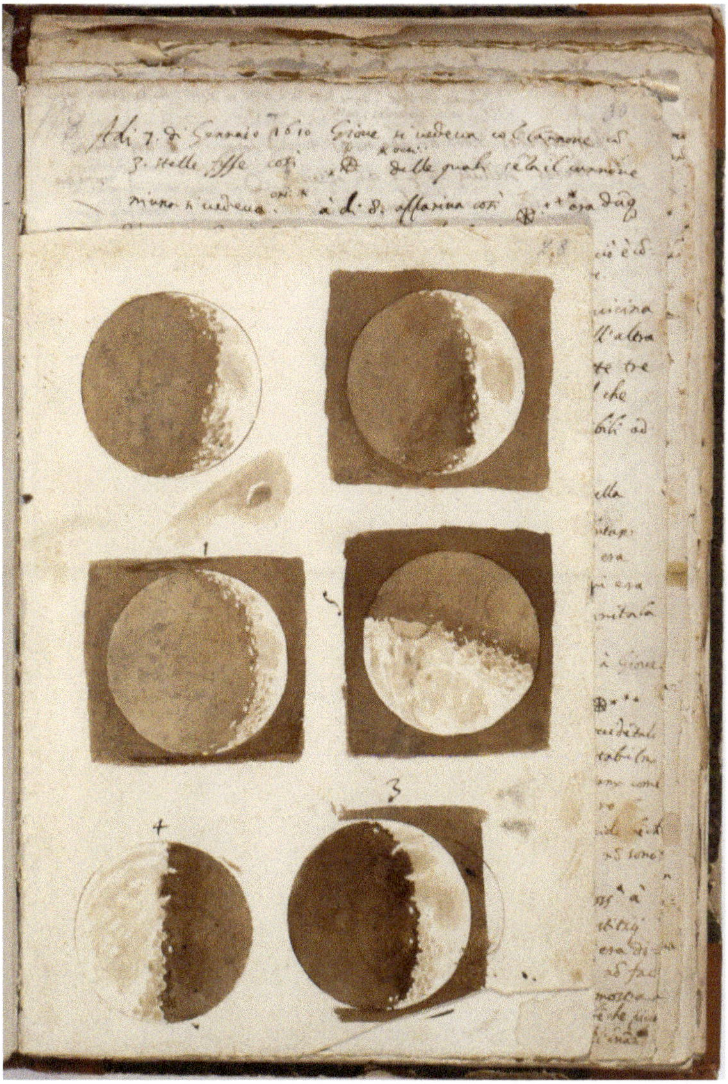

Figure 8.1 Galileo Galilei, *Ink and wash drawing of the Moon*, 1609, Florence, Biblioteca Nazionale Centrale, Ms. Gal. 48, f. 28r, in a folder containing the scientist's notes.

71 A medieval Jewish traveler in Italy

Benjamin of Tudela, *Book of Travels*, *c.*1165–73

Benjamin of Tudela (Benjamin ben Jonah, *c.*1130–1173) was born in the city then known as Tutela or Tuteila in the Navarre region of Spain. Practically nothing else is known about him beyond the information recorded in the roughly forty pages of his travel journal that have come down to us today. Writing in Hebrew, Benjamin described his travels throughout the Mediterranean, Middle East, and North Africa between the years 1165 and 1173.[1] The account is filled with descriptions of local folklore and history, with a focus in particular on documenting the Jewish communities in all the places he travelled, providing names of rabbis and local leaders, while recording the size of the Jewish populations. In his journey through the Italian Peninsula, after some brief notes about the city–states of Genoa, Pisa, and Lucca, Benjamin provides especially detailed information about the city of Rome, told from a Jewish perspective. He describes the long-established Roman community of Jews, who had resided there continuously since at least the first century BCE.[2] He paints a vibrant picture of the cities of the south, especially Salerno, the great center for study of medicine at the time, and the thriving mercantile community there. Benjamin reserves his highest praise for the parks and palaces of Palermo, the principal city in Sicily. Dating back at least to the late Roman Empire in the fourth century CE and remaining under successive Ostrogothic, Byzantine, and Arab rulers, the Jewish community in Sicily continued to flourish under the Norman kings, becoming the largest in Italy by the time of Benjamin's visit there around the year 1170.[3] The Jews Benjamin encountered in multicultural Palermo lived alongside Christians and Muslims. Jews were permitted to own land, and like Muslims, had their own legal courts.[4] This mostly peaceful coexistence of the various faiths in the region came to an end in the late fifteenth century and coincided with the culmination of the Spanish Reconquista. Forced to wear identifying badges and subjected to outbreaks of violence, the Jewish community, which by then accounted for a fifth of Palermo's population, was expelled from Sicily in 1492.[5]

DOI: 10.4324/9781003284284-79

Benjamin of Tudela, *Book of Travels*, *c.*1165–73

Description of cities on the Italian Peninsula and the Island of Sicily

From Marseilles one can take ship and in four days reach Genoa, which is also upon the sea. Here live two Jews, R. Samuel, son of Salim, and his brother, from the city of Ceuta, both of them good men. The city is surrounded by a wall, and the inhabitants are not governed by any king, but by judges whom they appoint at their pleasure. Each householder has a tower to his house, and at times of strife they fight from the tops of the towers with each other. They have command of the sea. They build ships which they call galleys, and make predatory attacks upon Edom and Ishmael[6] and the land of Greece as far as Sicily, and they bring back to Genoa spoils from all these places. They are constantly at war with the men of Pisa. Between them and the Pisans there is a distance of two days' journey.

Pisa is a very great city, with about 10,000 turreted houses for battle at times of strife. All its inhabitants are mighty men. They possess neither king nor prince to govern them, but only the judges appointed by themselves. In this city are about twenty Jews, at their head being R. Moses, R. Chayim, and R. Joseph. The city is not surrounded by a wall. It is about six miles from the sea; the river which flows through the city provides it with ingress and egress for ships.

From Pisa it is four parasangs[7] to the city of Lucca, which is the beginning of the frontier of Lombardy. In the city of Lucca are about forty Jews. It is a large place, and at the head of the Jews are R. David, R. Samuel, and R. Jacob.

Thence it is six days' journey to the great city of Rome. Rome is the head of the kingdoms of Christendom, and contains about 200 Jews, who occupy an honorable position and pay no tribute, and amongst them are officials of the Pope Alexander, the spiritual head of all Christendom. Great scholars reside here, at the head of them being R. Daniel, the chief rabbi, and R. Jechiel. He is a handsome young man of intelligence and wisdom, and he has the entry of the Pope's palace; for he is the steward of his house and of all that he has. He is a grandson of R. Nathan, who composed the Aruch[8] and its commentaries. Other scholars are R. Joab, son of the chief rabbi R. Solomon, R. Menachem, head of the academy, R. Jechiel, who lives in Trastevere, and R. Benjamin, son of R. Shabbethai of blessed memory. Rome is divided into two parts by the River Tiber. In the one part is the great church which they call St. Peter's of Rome. The great Palace of Julius Caesar was also in Rome. There are many wonderful structures in the city, different from any others in the world. Including both its inhabited and ruined parts, Rome is about twenty-four miles in circumference. In the midst thereof there are eighty palaces belonging to eighty kings who lived there, each called Imperator, commencing from King Tarquinius down to Nero and Tiberius, who lived at the time of Jesus the Nazarene, ending with Pepin, who freed the land of Sepharad from Islam, and was father of Charlemagne.

There is a palace outside Rome (said to be of Titus). The Consul and his 300 Senators treated him with disfavor, because he failed to take Jerusalem till after three years, though they had bidden him to capture it within two. In Rome is also the palace of Vespasianus, a great and very strong building; also the Colosseum, in which edifice there are 365 sections.[9] . . . In Rome there is a cave which runs underground, and catacombs of King Tarmal Galsin and his royal consort who are to be found there, seated upon their thrones, and with them about a hundred royal personages. They are all embalmed and preserved to this day. In the church of St. John in the Lateran there are two bronze columns taken from the Temple, the handiwork of King Solomon, each column being engraved "Solomon the son of David." The Jews of Rome told me that every year upon the 9th of Ab they found the columns exuding moisture like water.[10] There also is the cave where Titus the son of Vespasianus stored the Temple vessels which he brought from Jerusalem. There is also a cave in a hill on one bank of the River Tiber where are the graves of the ten martyrs. In front of St. John in the Lateran there are statues of Samson in marble, with a spear in his hand, and of Absalom the son of King David, and another of Constantinus the Great, who built Constantinople and after whom it was called. The last-named statue is of bronze, the horse being overlaid with gold.[11] Many other edifices are there, and remarkable sights beyond enumeration.

From Rome it is four days to Capua, the large town which King Capys built. It is a fine city, but its water is bad, and the country is fever-stricken. About 300 Jews live there, among them great scholars and esteemed persons, at their heads being R. Conso, his brother R. Israel, R. Zaken and the chief rabbi R. David, since deceased. They call this district the Principality. From there one goes to Pozzuoli which is called Sorrento the Great, built by Zur, son of Hadadezer, when he fled in fear of David the king. . . . A spring issues forth from beneath the ground containing the oil which is called petroleum. People collect it from the surface of the water and use it medicinally. There are also hot-water springs to the number of about twenty, which issue from the ground and are situated near the sea, and every man who has any disease can go and bathe in them and get cured. All the afflicted of Lombardy visit it in the summer-time for that purpose.

From this place a man can travel fifteen miles along a road under the mountains, a work executed by King Romulus who built the city of Rome. He was prompted to this by fear of King David and Joab his general. He built fortifications both upon the mountains and below the mountains reaching as far as the city of Naples. Naples is a very strong city, lying upon the sea-board, and was founded by the Greeks. About 500 Jews live here, amongst them R. Hezekiah, R. Shallum, R. Elijah Hacohen and R. Isaac of Har Napus, the chief rabbi of blessed memory.

Thence one proceeds by sea to the city of Salerno, where the Christians have a school of medicine. About 600 Jews dwell there. Among the scholars are R. Judah, son of R. Isaac, the son of Melchizedek, the great Rabbi, who came from the city of Siponto; also R. Solomon (the Cohen), R. Elijah the Greek, R. Abraham Narboni, and R. Hamon. It is a city with walls upon the land side, the other side bordering on the sea, and there is a very strong castle on the summit of the hill. Thence it is half a day's journey to Amalfi, where there are about twenty Jews, amongst them R. Hananel, the physician, R. Elisha, and Abu-al-gir, the prince. The inhabitants of the place are merchants engaged in trade, who do not sow or reap, because they dwell upon high hills and lofty crags, but buy everything for money. Nevertheless, they have an abundance of fruit, for it is a land of vineyards and olives, of gardens and plantations, and no one can go to war with them.

Thence it is a day's journey to Benevento, which is a city situated between the sea-coast and a mountain, and possessing a community of about 200 Jews. At their head are R. Kalonymus, R. Zarach, and R. Abraham. From there it is two days' journey to Melfi in the country of Apulia, which is the land of Pul, where about 200 Jews reside, at their head being R. Achimaaz, R. Nathan, and R. Isaac. From Melfi it is about a day's journey to Ascoli, where there are about forty Jews, at their head being R. Consoli, R. Zemach, his son-in-law, and R. Joseph. From there it takes two days to Trani on the sea, where all the pilgrims gather to go to Jerusalem; for the port is a convenient one. A community of about 200 Israelites is there, at their head being R. Elijah, R. Nathan, the expounder, and R. Jacob. It is a great and beautiful city.

From there it is a day's journey to Colo di Bari, which is the great city which King William of Sicily destroyed.[12] Neither Jews nor Gentiles live there at the present day in consequence of its destruction. Thence it is a day and a half to Taranto, which is under the government of Calabria, the inhabitants of which are Greek. It is a large city, and contains about 300 Jews, some of them men of learning, and at their head are R. Meir, R. Nathan, and R. Israel.

From Taranto it is a day's journey to Brindisi, which is on the sea coast. About ten Jews, who are dyers, reside here. It is two days' journey to Otranto, which is on the coast of the Greek sea. Here are about 50 Jews, at the head of them being R. Menachem, R. Caleb, R. Meir, and R. Mali.

[*Description of travels through the Middle East to China and back through North Africa to Sicily*]

[From Egypt] it takes twenty days by sea to Messina, which is the commencement of Sicily and is situated on the arm of the sea that is called Lipar, which divides it from Calabria. Here about 200 Jews dwell. It is a land full of everything good, with gardens and plantations. Here most of the pilgrims assemble to cross over to Jerusalem, as this is the best crossing. Thence it is about two days' journey to Palermo, which is a large city. Here is the palace of King William. Palermo contains about 1,500 Jews and a large number of Christians and Mohammedans.[13] It is in a district abounding in springs and brooks of water, a land of wheat and barley, likewise of gardens and plantations, and there is not the like thereof in the whole island of Sicily.

Here is the domain and garden of the king, which is called Al Harbina (Al Hacina),[14] containing all sorts of fruit-trees. And in it is a large fountain. The garden is encompassed by a wall. And a reservoir has been made there which is called Al Buheira,[15] and in it are many sorts of fish. Ships overlaid with silver and gold are there, belonging to the king, who takes pleasure-trips in them with his women.[16] In the park there is also a great palace, the walls of which are painted, and overlaid with gold and silver; the paving of the floors is of marble, picked out in gold and silver in all manner of designs. There is no building like this anywhere. And this island, the commencement of which is Messina, contains all the pleasant things of this world. It embraces Syracuse, Marsala, Catania, Petralia, and Trapani, the circumference of the island being six days' journey. In Trapani coral is found, which is called Al Murgan.

Notes

1 Benjamin was the first European in the Middle Ages to describe China and India, although scholars do not believe that he personally journeyed to the Far East, but gained his information from traders he met.
2 See Roth Chapter 1, "The Classical Period."
3 Simonsohn 105–6.
4 "This is illustrated, among others, by the declaration by the bishop of Catania in 1168 that Latins, Greeks, Jews and Saracens were to be judged in accordance with their law." Simonsohn 112.
5 "In the second half of the 15th century the Jews of Palermo would seem to have accounted for 1/5 of the city's population, which then had around 25,000 inhabitants." Mandalà 462.
6 "The meaning of course is that the Genoese pillage Christian and Mohammedan places alike." (NA)
7 "*Parsah*, from Persian *farsang*, an ancient Persian distance unit corresponding to around 5.6 km. One day of traveling appears to have been equivalent to 6 1/2 parasangs." Jacoby 144.
8 "The great work alluded to is the *Talmudical Dictionary,* completed in 1101." (NA)
9 "Having regard to the various readings, it is possible that the Thermae of Diocletian or more probably the Flavian amphitheatre, which early in the Middle Ages began to be called the Colosseum, is here referred to." (NA)
10 "For centuries the Jews have refused to walk under [the Arch of] Titus, the destroyer of Jerusalem. Consequently, Benjamin most likely did not walk under the arch while he visited Rome and he purposefully does not directly allude to it in his travelogue, but clearly describes instead the details that evoke the arch itself as well as the dishonor it represents for the Jews as a day of ignominy since it marks . . . the first and second destruction of the Temple of Jerusalem." Piera 74.
11 "This is the statue of Marcus Aurelius now before the Capitol." (NA)
12 "This city was destroyed by William the Bad in 1156. It was ordered to be restored by William the Good in 1168, so that Benjamin must have visited Bari before that date." (NA)

13 "Edribi, who wrote his *Geography* in Sicily in 1154 at the request of King Roger II, calls the island a pearl, and cannot find words sufficient in praise of its climate, beauty, and fertility. He is especially enthusiastic concerning Palermo." (NA)
14 "*Hacina* is the Arabic for a fortified or enclosed place." (NA)
15 "*Buheira* is the Arabic word for a lake. The unrivalled hunting grounds of William II are well worth visiting, being situated between the little town called Parco and the magnificent cathedral of Monreale, which the king erected later on." (NA)
16 "King William II, surnamed 'the Good,' was sixteen years old when Benjamin visited Sicily in 1170. During the king's minority the Archbishop was the vice-regent. He was expelled in 1169 on account of his unpopularity." (NA)

Source

Benjamin of Tudela, *Travels in Italy* in *The Itinerary of Benjamin of Tudela: Critical Text, Translation and Commentary*, ed. and trans. Marcus Nathan Adler, Phillip Feldheim, Inc., 1907, pp. 5–15, 108–09.

References

Benjamin, Sandra, ed. *The World of Benjamin of Tudela: A Medieval Mediterranean Travelogue*, Fairleigh Dickinson UP; Associated University Presses, 1995.

Jacoby, David. "Benjamin of Tudela and His Book of Travels," in *Venezia incrocio di culture*, ed. Klaus Herbers and Felicitas Schmieder, Edizioni di storia e letteratura, 2008, pp. 135–64.

Mandalà, Giuseppe. "The Jews of Palermo from late Antiquity to the Expulsion (598–1492–93)," in *A Companion to Medieval Palermo: The History of a Mediterranean City from 600 to 1500*, ed. Annliese Nef; French and Italian texts trans. Martin Thom, Brill, 2013.

Piera, Montserrat. "Vulnerable Medieval Iberian Travellers: Benjamin of Tudela's *Sefer ha-massa'ot*, Pero Tafur's *Andaás e viajes*, and Ahmad al-Wazzan's *Libro de la cosmogrophia et geographia de Africa*," in *Remapping Travel Narratives (1000–1700): To the East and Back Again*, Arc Humanities Press, 2018.

Roth, Cecil. *The History of the Jews of Italy*, The Jewish Publication Society of America, 1946.

Shalev, Zur. "Benjamin of Tudela, Spanish Explorer," *Mediterranean Historical Review*, Vol. 25, No. 1 (2010), pp. 17–33.

Simonsohn, Shlomo. "Sicily: A Milennium of Convivenza (or Almost)," in *The Jews of Europe in the Middle Ages (Tenth to Fifteenth Centuries): Proceedings of the International Symposium Held at Speyer, 20–25 October 2002*, ed. Christoph Cluse, Brepols, 2004.

72 Marco Polo marvels at paper money

Marco Polo, *Description of the World*, *c*.1298

Marco Polo (1254–1324) was a newborn when his father, Nicolò, and uncle, Matteo, left for Constantinople. Venetian merchants, the brothers had a trading base in Crimea, and around 1260, it was from there that they ventured east to the court of Kublai Khan (1215–1294). By the time they returned to Venice, Marco was fifteen years old, and when they left on their second journey to the Mongol court, Marco went with them. The young man quickly learned the language and customs of the Mongols and became a trusted agent of the Great Khan, serving on many official commercial and diplomatic missions, travelling in particular to India and Ceylon. On his return to Italy twenty-four years later, Marco was captured in a naval battle by the Genoese. In prison, a fellow captive named Rustichello of Pisa, an author of romances, acted as his ghost writer. Written in an Italianate medieval French, the book's original title is *Le divisament dou monde* (*The Description of the World*), also known as *Le Livre de Merveilles* (*The Book of Marvels*). The book became immensely popular throughout Europe; there are today around one hundred fifty surviving manuscripts in a dozen languages that were copied during the Middle Ages and Renaissance. Readers were astounded by the narrative, which encompassed details about strange customs, extraordinary monuments, and natural wonders, not to mention the vast expanse of the continent. "Never before or since has one man given such an immense body of new geographical knowledge to the West," writes John Larner.[1] Though Arab merchants had ventured to China and described the Far East, their writings were not widely known to Christian readers in the Middle Ages.[2] Europeans had been interested in Asia from the time of the Crusades and grew increasingly alarmed in the early 1200s by reports of the conquests of Genghis Khan, who "in spite of the primitive means at his disposal, it is possible [. . .] succeeded in destroying a larger part of the human race than any expert in modern technology."[3] In the mid-thirteenth century, undeterred by fear of the "Golden Horde," missionaries determined to convert them to Christianity reached the Mongol capital and afterward produced written accounts of the peoples and places they encountered; these included the writings of Giovanni da Pian del Carpine and William of Rubruck. The Polo family of merchants, however, proved even more intrepid than the friars, and none of the missionaries' accounts circulated as

DOI: 10.4324/9781003284284-80

widely as that of Marco Polo nor made so great an impact on the European mind. Aside from tall tales of fantastical peoples and monsters, possibly suggested by Rustichello's imagination, what the Venetian supplied was an incisive and panoramic view of a rich, flourishing civilization that outshined anything that existed at the time in Western Europe. Like the Jesuit missionary Matteo Ricci (1552–1610) three centuries later, who would write that "of the grandeur of China, it is for certain that nothing in the world is greater,"[4] Marco Polo displays the greatest admiration, even awe for aspects of Chinese culture—an example is their use of paper money. The technology of making paper had been introduced to the West from China via Arabs in Andalusia and paper was being produced by 1264 in Fabriano, Italy. In his report on his mission to the Mongols in 1255, Franciscan friar William of Rubruck also made a brief mention of the use of paper money in China,[5] but Marco Polo's description is much more detailed. Scholars have at times cast doubt on the authenticity of the text of *The Description of the World*, questioning whether Marco Polo ever went to China. This description of paper money, in particular, has been used to conclusively disprove such suggestions.[6] There were doubters in Marco Polo's own day as well. One of his contemporaries, Iacopo da Acqui, wrote, "because there are many great and strange things in that book, which are reckoned past all credence, he was asked by his friends on his death-bed to correct the book by removing everything that went beyond the facts. To which his reply was that he had not told *one-half* of what he had really seen!"[7]

Marco Polo, *The Description of the World*, c.1298

How the Great Khan causes the bark of trees, made into something like paper, to pass for money all over his country

Now that I have told you in detail of the splendor of this city of the emperor's, I shall proceed to tell you of the mint which he has in the same city, in the which he has his money coined and struck, as I shall relate to you. And in doing so I shall make manifest to you how it is that the Great Lord may well be able to accomplish even much more than I have told you, or am going to tell you, in this book. For, tell it how I might, you never would be satisfied that I was keeping within truth and reason!

The emperor's mint then is in this same city of Cambaluc,[8] and the way it is wrought is such that you might say he has the secret of alchemy in perfection, and you would be right! For he makes his money after this fashion.

He makes them take of the bark of a certain tree, in fact of the mulberry tree, the leaves of which are the food of the silkworms—these trees being so numerous that whole districts are full of them. What they take is a certain fine white bast or skin which lies between the wood of the tree and the thick outer bark, and this they make into something resembling sheets of paper, but black. When these sheets have been prepared they are cut up into pieces of different sizes. The smallest of these sizes is worth a half tornesel; the next, a little larger, one tornesel; one, a little larger still, is worth half a silver groat of Venice; another a whole groat; others yet two groats, five groats, and ten groats. There is also a kind worth one bezant of gold, and others of three bezants, and so up to ten. All these pieces of paper are issued with as much solemnity and authority as if they were of pure gold or silver; and on every piece a variety of officials, whose duty it is, have to write their names, and to put their seals. And when all is prepared duly, the chief officer deputed by the Khan smears the seal entrusted to him with vermilion, and impresses it on the paper, so that the form of the seal remains printed upon it in red; the money is then authentic. Any one forging it would be punished with death. And the Khan causes every year to be made such a vast quantity of this money, which costs him nothing, that it must equal in amount all the treasure in the world.

With these pieces of paper, made as I have described, he causes all payments on his own account to be made; and he makes them to pass current universally over all his kingdoms and provinces and territories, and everywhere his power and sovereignty extends. And nobody, however important he may think himself, dares to refuse them on pain of death. And indeed everybody takes them readily, for wherever a person may go throughout the Great Khan's dominions he shall find these pieces of paper current, and shall be able to transact all sales and purchases of goods by means of them just as well as if they were coins of pure gold. And all the while they are so light that ten bezants' worth does not weigh one golden bezant.

Furthermore all merchants arriving from India or other countries, and bringing with them gold or silver or gems and pearls, are prohibited from selling to anyone but the emperor. He has twelve experts chosen for this business, men of shrewdness and experience in such affairs; these appraise the articles, and the emperor then pays a liberal price for them in those pieces of paper. The merchants accept his price readily, for in the first place they would not get such a good one from anybody else, and secondly they are paid without any delay. And with this paper-money they can buy what they like anywhere over the empire, whilst it is also vastly lighter to carry about on their journeys. And it is a truth that the merchants will several times in the year bring wares to the amount of 400,000 bezants, and the grand sire pays for all in that paper. So he buys such a quantity of those precious things every year that his treasure is endless, whilst all the time the money he pays away costs him nothing at all. Moreover, several times in the year proclamation is made through the city that anyone who may have gold or silver or gems or pearls, by taking them to the mint shall get a handsome price for them. And the owners are glad to do this, because they would find no other purchaser give so large a price. Thus the quantity they bring in is marvelous, though those who do not choose to do so may let it alone. Still, in this way, nearly all the valuables in the country come into the Khan's possession.

When any of those pieces of paper are spoilt—not that they are so very flimsy neither—the owner carries them to the mint, and by paying three per cent, on the value he gets new pieces in exchange. And if any baron, or anyone else, has need of gold or silver or gems or pearls, in order to make plate, or girdles, or the like, he goes to the mint and buys as much as he likes, paying in this paper money.

Now you have heard the ways and means whereby the Great Khan may have, and in fact *has*, more treasure than all the kings in the world; and you know all about it and the reason why. And now I will tell you of the great dignitaries which act in this city on behalf of the Emperor.

Notes

1 Larner 97.
2 For instance, the work of cartographer al-Idrisi (Abu or Abdallah Muhammad ibn Muhammad ibn Abdallah ibn Idris, al-Sharif al-Idrisi, *c.*1100–65) for Roger II in Palermo in 1154. Benjamin of Tudela (**#71**) also provided credible information about China, although it is unlikely that he personally went there.
3 Dawson xii.
4 Hsia 73.
5 Dawson 171.
6 Vogel 126–9. For a summary of the opposing argument, see Frances Wood, *Did Marco Polo Go to China?* Secker & Warburg, 1995.
7 Yule-Cordier 54.
8 Khanbalikh (Beijing).

Source

Marco Polo, *Travels*, trans. Henry Yule, revised by Henri Cordier, John Murray, 1920, pp. 424–26, ed. Kaborycha.

References

Dawson, Christopher. *Mission to Asia*, U Toronto P, 1980.
Hsia, R. Po-chia. *A Jesuit in the Forbidden City: Matteo Ricci 1552–1610*, Oxford UP, 2010.
Jackson, Peter. "Marco Polo and His *Travels*," *Bulletin of the School of Oriental and African Studies, University of London*, Vol. 61, No. 1 (1998), pp. 82–101.
Kurlansky, Mark. *Paper: Paging Through History*, Norton, 2017.
Larner, John. *Marco Polo and the Discovery of the World*, Yale UP, 1999.
Polo, Marco. *Travels*, trans. with introduction and notes by Nigel Cliff, Penguin, 2015.
Vogel, Hans Ulrich. *Marco Polo Was in China: New Evidence from Currencies, Salts and Revenues*, Brill, 2013.
Zhang, Longxi. "Marco Polo, Chinese Cultural Identity, and an Alternative Model of East-West Encounter," in *Marco Polo and the Encounter of East and West*, ed. Suzanne Conklin Akbari, Amilcare Iannucci and John Tulk, U Toronto P, 2008.

73 A merchant's literal and literary voyages

Goro Dati, *Diary* (*Libro segreto*), 1431

Domenico di Neri di Miniato Del Sera, *Inscription in a manuscript of Dati's* Sfera, 1480

Figure 8.2 Anonymous, illustrated manuscript pages from Dati's *Sfera*, *c.*1450, New York Public Library, MA 109 ff.15v-16r. The images surrounding the text from left to right represent the regions of Tartary, with the Caspian and Black Sea cities of Tana and Kaffa and the land mass of Asia Minor; while across the page are Syria, with depictions of the cities of Jerusalem, Cairo, and Mecca, with the Jordan, Tigris, and Euphrates rivers and indications of Egypt and Ethiopia on the far right. At the center, bridging the two pages, is a depiction of an enormous mountain, on top of which is a boat and two doves flying to it. The text beside it explains that this is where Noah's Ark came to rest after the Flood.

DOI: 10.4324/9781003284284-81

When his father died in 1374, Goro Dati (Gregorio di Anastagio Dati, 1362–1435) went to work for a silk merchant; ten years later, he matriculated in the Silk Guild and went on to become consul of the guild. Eventually, Dati held a variety of government offices in Florence, including the highest position of all, that of standardbearer of justice in 1429. Goro married four times, fathering twenty-eight children, as well as at least one illegitimate son by an enslaved woman during one of his business voyages. This, and more, is known about him, as Dati recorded details of his business and personal life in his *Diary* (*Libro segreto* or secret ledger). The custom of writing down family memoirs was common during this period; Florentines had various ways of referring to their record books, today often grouped under the general category *libri di famiglia* (family books).[1]

In addition to his private records, meant only for the eyes of his family, Goro also authored two books that circulated widely in Florence: *Istoria di Firenze dal 1380 al 1405* (*History of Florence*) and the cosmo-geographical vernacular poem in eight-line stanzas *La Sfera* (*The Sphere*).[2] In this text, the Florentine merchant describes the heavenly and earthly spheres as they were understood in his day from the writings of early thirteenth-century scholar Johannes de Sacrobosco, as well as the ancient authors Aristotle and Ptolemy. He further provides descriptions of exotic locations illustrated with maps that draw on traditions of medieval *mappaemundi*, maps of the Holy Land, and navigators' charts. The overlap between merchant routes during Dati's day and the contents of his didactic poem are notable. Equally remarkable are the intersections of ancient knowledge and recent cartographical depictions of coastlines. Dati would likely have been familiar with mariners' maps—known as portolan charts—from his travels across the Mediterranean; he incorporated many of these practical images in the margins of his text, along with legendary locations mentioned in the Bible. Renaissance readers found this information highly practical, and it was frequently copied—around one hundred fifty manuscript copies survive today. The inscription made by a member of the Florentine Wine Merchants' Guild, Domenico Del Sera, in his copy of the manuscript in 1480 provides an idea of how this text was being read by merchants at the time. For today's readers, like his *Diary*, which gives a glimpse of Dati's life, *La Sfera* provides a snapshot of the early Quattrocento Florentine merchant's worldview. Commentator Dario Del Puppo writes, "Like his contemporaries, Dati lived on the cusp of a major shift when empirical knowledge, technology, and science were challenging existing beliefs and when commercial practices threatened the dominant religious ideology."[3]

Gregorio Dati, *Diary (Libro segreto)*, 1431

In the name of God, his Mother and all the Saints of Paradise, I shall begin this book wherein I shall set forth an account of our activities so as to have a record of them, and wherein having once more and always invoked the name of God, I shall record the secret affairs of our company and their progress from year to year. This ledger belongs to Goro [Gregorio], son of Stagio Dati, and I shall call it the secret ledger. In the name of God, Father, Son, and Holy Ghost, I shall here record some particular things known to myself. God grant they meet with the approval of whoever learns of them when I am gone.

I learn from old registers that Dato and Pero di Bencivenni[4] were purse-vendors on the Ponte Vecchio next to the fishmongers, and that their shop was destroyed by the flood of 1333.[5] It appears from there that Dato had many sons, the eldest of whom, Stagio,[6] was born on 9 March 1317. His mother's name was Monna Filippa. According to Stagio's registers he married our mother, Monna[7] Ghita, in the year . . . ,[8] giving her the ring on 5 August and celebrating the wedding on 4 November.[9]

I find that Stagio went into partnership with Vanni di Ser Lotto [Castellani]. The company was set up on 1 January 1353 with a capital of one thousand gold florins. This appears on page 3 of Register A.

I was born on 15 April 1362. This is recorded in a register marked with an asterisk on page 85 where the seventeen children he had by Mona Ghita are listed in order of age.

Our father Stagio left this world for a better one on 11 September 1374, when he was a Consul of the Wool Guild and Treasurer of the Commission on the Salt Tax and Forced Loans. He had been ill for several days before his death and, several days earlier, while still in health, had made a will. He received all the sacraments of the church as befits a devout Christian, and by the mercy of God passed on to eternal life in a state of grace.

On 15 April 1375, when I had learned enough arithmetic, I went to work in the silk merchant's shop belonging to Giovanni di Giano and his partners. I was thirteen years old and I won their esteem.

We gave Madalena [Goro's sister] in marriage in June 1380. This is recorded in register E, page 84.

I left Giovanni di Giano on 2 October 1380, spent fifteen months with the Wool Guild and returned to him on 1 January 1382.

[. . .]

Memoranda, 1393

In God's name, I shall continue this record of my activities, which it is well to have in writing so as to recollect them, and which I began back on page 1. My beloved wife, Bandecca, went to Paradise after a nine-month illness started by a miscarriage in the fifth month of pregnancy.[10] It was eleven o'clock at night on Friday, 15 July 1390, when she peacefully returned her soul to her Creator in Buonaccorso Berardi's house. The next day I had her buried in S. Brancazio; she had received the last sacraments.

I went to Valencia on 1 September 1390, taking Bernardo with me. I came back on 30 November 1392, having suffered much hardship during my stay, both in mind and body. We were still owed 4,000 Barcelona pounds by Giovanni di Stefano, who acknowledged this debt in a notarized deed which I brought back with me to Florence. In Valencia I had an illegitimate male child by Margherita, a Tartar slave whom I had bought. He was born on 21 December 1391, in Valencia on St. Thomas's Day and I named him after that saint. I sent him to Florence in March on Felice del Pace's ship. God grant that he turn out well.

On the expiration of our partnership, on 1 January 1393, Michele di Ser Parente withdrew. Later, I made an agreement with him whereby he made over to me his share in Giovanni di Stefani's debt and a few other items which are entered on page 6.

I married my second wife, Isabetta, the daughter of Mari Vilanuzzi on Sunday, 22 June, as is recorded on the other side of this page.

On 10 September 1393, I left Florence for Catalonia and, while we were at sea in a small galley a little beyond Portovenere, a galley from Briganzone came after us, held us up, and robbed us and took our goods to Baldo Spinoli at Briganzone. We got some of them back later, although with great difficulty and at great expense. I came back here on 14 December. On 20 April, I went to Valencia on Felice's ship. I visited Majorca and Barcelona where Simone joined me, after which we both went to Valencia where I left him. I returned home by land and reached Florence on 24 January 1395. Thanks be to God. Our partnership expired on 1 February 1395, and that year I did business of my own and was very successful. Thanks be to God. I went into partnership once more with Michele di Ser Parente on 1 January 1396, and the terms and clauses are entered on page 6.

Our Simone, who had been in Valencia since December 1394, wanted to come to Florence. He arrived on 12 December 1396, and left to go back there on 3 January 1397. However, while he was at sea, a Neapolitan galley overtook him just outside Pisa and took him as a prisoner to Naples. On 3 April, he was released for ransom at Gaeta, from whence he made his way back to Valencia.

Domenico di Neri di Miniato Del Sera, *Inscription in a manuscript of La Sfera*, 1480

I remember that Neri di Miniato Del Sera died in 1468, in August on the eve of the Feast of St. Lawrence, and he left this book to Domenico di Neri di Miniato his son, because he delighted in sea voyages and wanted to know many things about the world, having sought out many countries by land and by sea, and seen everything in the world. Thus, he wished that anyone who read this book would want to see the beauties of the world travelling by sea, and to become a good, experienced merchant, trading in all kinds of things, whether from Tuscany, the East, or the West. And that person will become experienced if he follows this book and wants to know good countries for doing business. Let him follow these seas that make men industrious navigators and good merchants, and he will leave a good account of himself. March 1480.

Notes

1 Alternately referred to as *ricordanze*, *ricordi*, *diari*, these are described by Ciappelli 26. See also Morelli's *Memoirs* (#43). Here the term "diary" is used for Dati's record book, following Martines's translation.
2 It was long believed that the Dominican friar Leonardo Dati was its author; today, *La Sfera* is generally accepted as the work of Goro.
3 Del Puppo 326.
4 Dato would have been Goro's grandfather and Pero his grand-uncle.
5 The Ponte Vecchio was washed away in the 1333 flooding of the Arno River.
6 Goro's father was Stagio (short for Anastagio), thus the name Goro di Stagio means "Goro, the son of Stagio." It was the practice to add the patronymic to Christian names.
7 *Monna* is a shortened form of Madonna, just as "Mrs." in English is an abbreviation for "mistress." A variant form is *mona*, as in Mona Lisa.
8 The year was left blank by Goro, who was presumably hoping to find the exact date at some point to fill it in.
9 For details on marriage customs in Florence during this period, see Klapisch-Zuber, *Women and Family*.
10 Dati wedded Bandecca di Buonaccorso Berardi, the daughter of his business partner, in 1388. He married a total of four times; all but his last wife predeceased him.

Sources

Goro Dati, *Diary* in *Two Memoirs of Renaissance Florence: The Diaries of Buonaccorso Pitti and Gregorio Dati*, trans. Julia Martines, ed. Gene Brucker, Harper & Row, 1967, pp. 107–8, 112–13.

Domenico di Neri di Miniato, *Manuscript inscription* in Del Puppo, Dario. "Literary Imagination and Mercantile Pragmatism in Goro Dati's *Sfera*," in *"Accessus ad auctores": Studies in Honor of Christopher Kleinhenz*, Arizona Center for Medieval and Renaissance Studies, 2011, pp. 343–44, trans. Kaborycha.

References

Baker, Nicholas Scott. "'*Tutto il mondo è paese*' Locating Florence in Premodern Eurasian Commerce," in *Florence in the Early Modern World: New Perspectives*, ed. Nicholas Scott Baker and Brian Jeffrey Maxson, Routledge, 2020.

Botana, Federico. "The Cosmos in Goro Dati's *Sfera*," in *Learning Through Images in the Italian Renaissance: Illustrated Manuscripts and Education in Quattrocento Florence*, Cambridge UP, 2020.

Branca, Vittore, ed. and Murtha Baca, trans. *Merchant Writers: Florentine Memoirs from the Middle Ages and Renaissance*, U Toronto P, 2015.

Ciappelli, Giovanni and Patricia Lee Rubin, eds. *Art, Memory, and Family in Renaissance Florence*, Cambridge UP, 2000.

Clemens, Raymond. "Medieval Maps in a Renaissance Context: Gregorio Dati and the Teaching of Geography in Fifteenth-Century Florence," in *Cartography in Antiquity and the Middle Ages, Vol. 10 of Technology and Change in History*, Brill, 2008, pp. 237–56.

Epurescu-Pascovici, Ionuț. "Gregorio Dati (1362–1435) and the Limits of Individual Agency," *Medieval History Journal*, Vol. 9 (2006), pp. 297–325.

74 Claiming and renaming a wondrous land

Cristoforo Colombo, *Letter to Luis de Santángel*, 1493

Bartolomé de las Casas, *A Brief Description of the Destruction of the Indies*, 1542

Bernardino de Sahagún, *The Florentine Codex*, 1577

Cristoforo Colombo (1451–1506) came from an extremely humble social background—his father was a wool carder and weaver in Genoa. Becoming a sailor in his early teens, Columbus went to join the well-established Genoese community on the Iberian Peninsula. The Genoese were famed as cartographers and navigators, and Genoa, since the twelfth century, had a vast commercial network stretching beyond the Mediterranean to the Aegean and the Black Sea. Along with fellow countrymen, Columbus served the Portuguese, frequently navigating the Atlantic from Guinea on the West African coast, north to the Azores, up to Ireland, and possibly to Iceland. Though he had little or no formal schooling, Columbus taught himself some Latin, and filled with curiosity, he read widely, especially works dealing with travel and cosmography. The many books collected by Columbus over the course of his lifetime included Marco Polo's *Travels* (#72), as well as two works that suggested the existence of an undiscovered land on the other side of the globe called the Antipodes. These books were Pierre d'Ailly's *Imago mundi* and the *Historia rerum* by Enea Silvio Piccolomini (Pius II, #44). In the latter volume, a note is attached in Columbus's handwriting about Florentine cosmographer Paolo dal Pozzo Toscanelli (1397–1482). Columbus was familiar with the Florentine's theory that the Atlantic Ocean was smaller than generally believed and that Asia could be reached by sailing westward. With his experience navigating the waters of the Atlantic, and his firm conviction that by crossing it he could arrive in China, Columbus repeatedly attempted to persuade the rulers of either Portugal or Spain to fund his voyage. When at last the king and queen of Spain agreed, Columbus set sail in August of 1492, and in his letter to the royal treasurer Luis de Santángel dated February 15, 1493, he described when land was first sighted on October 12, 1492. In this letter, Columbus declared that he had arrived at "the Indies," and throughout his life, he continually asserted that it was part of Asia, despite the undeniable newness of everything he and his crew encountered. From almost the moment his ships arrived, his reaction to the land and its peoples was one of wonderment, in

DOI: 10.4324/9781003284284-82

the letter repeatedly using the words "marvel" and "marvelous" to describe what he found. All throughout his subsequent voyages to the New World—Columbus eventually made a total of four— and for the rest of his life, he insisted it was Asia, rather than a new continent, he had sailed to. It is odd though: if Columbus actually believed he had reached the lands of China or India with their ancient civilizations, enormous cities, and famous monuments described by travelers before him, why was his first act to plant a flag and lay claim to these lands on behalf of the Spanish crown? And why did he rename all the places? Stephen Greenblatt views the urge to take possession of the strange and wondrous land as a characteristically Renaissance response, referring to this act as "the colonizing of the marvelous."[1]

While dazzled by accounts of marvels coming from the New World, Europeans were not unaware of the dark side of this colonization—the massacre, rape, and enslavement of the native Taíno peoples of the Caribbean carried out by Columbus and his men. Notably, Bartolomé de las Casas (1484–1566), a Spanish Dominican friar, witnessed the devastation in conquered territories. He recorded the atrocities against the indigenous peoples in his *Brevísima relación de la destrucción de las India*s (*A Brief Account of the Destruction of the Indies*), written in 1542, and within decades it had been translated into Dutch, French, English, and German. News of Columbus's voyages had by this time spread everywhere; indeed, the letter to Santángel was published in Barcelona almost immediately after it was written in 1493, translated into Latin in May, then printed everywhere in Europe.[2] In the same year, the first illustrated account of Columbus was published in Italian in Florence, while from Venice, the great center of Renaissance printing, many works on cartography and cosmography were produced and disseminated across Europe.[3] And in addition to intense curiosity about such matters as its geography, flora, and fauna, many were interested in the ethnography of the peoples in this new land. One of these was Ferdinando de' Medici, the future Grand Duke Ferdinando I (#30), who as a cardinal in Rome had purchased a manuscript in three volumes compiled by Franciscan friar Bernardino de Sahagún (*c.*1499–1590). Unlike the Taínos who left no record, this book, illustrated with many images, contains accounts in the native Nahuatl language of the culture and history as told by Aztecs themselves. Written in 1577, the work was banned in Spain, but the precious original was preserved by the grand duke in the Medici collection in Florence. The so-called *Florentine Codex* "remains the most important history of New Spain, recording the lives of the natives before, during, and just following the conquest."[4]

Cristoforo Colombo, *Letter to Luis de Santángel*, February 15, 1493

Sir:

As I know you will be rejoiced at the glorious success that our Lord has given me in my voyage, I write this to tell you how in thirty-three days I sailed to the Indies with the fleet that the illustrious King and Queen, our Sovereigns, gave me, where I discovered a great many islands, inhabited by numberless people; and of all I have taken possession for their Highnesses by proclamation and display of the Royal Standard without opposition. To the first island I discovered I gave the name of San Salvador, in commemoration of His Divine Majesty, who has wonderfully granted all this. The Indians call it Guanaham. The second I named the Island of Santa Maria de Concepcion; the third, Fernandina; the fourth, Isabella; the fifth, Juana; and thus to each one I gave a new name.

When I came to Juana, I followed the coast of that isle toward the west, and found it so extensive that I thought it might be the mainland, the province of Cathay; and as I found no towns nor villages on the sea-coast, except a few small settlements, where it was impossible to speak to the people, because they fled at once, I continued the said route, thinking I could not fail to see some great cities or towns; and finding at the end of many leagues that nothing new appeared, and that the coast led northward, contrary to my wish, because the winter had already set in, I decided to make for the south, and as the wind also was against my proceeding, I determined not to wait there longer, and turned back to a certain harbor whence I sent two men to find out whether there was any king or large city. They explored for three days, and found countless small communities and people, without number, but with no kind of government, so they returned.

I heard from other Indians I had already taken that this land was an island, and thus followed the eastern coast for one hundred and seven leagues, until I came to the end of it. From that point I saw another isle to the eastward, at eighteen leagues' distance, to which I gave the name of Hispaniola. I went thither and followed its northern coast to the east, as I had done in Juana, one hundred and seventy-eight leagues eastward, as in Juana. This island, like all the others, is most extensive. It has many ports along the sea-coast excelling any in Christendom—and many fine, large, flowing rivers. The land there is elevated, with many mountains and peaks incomparably higher than in the center isle. They are most beautiful, of a thousand varied forms, accessible, and full of trees of endless varieties, so high that they seem to touch the sky, and I have been told that they never lose their foliage. I saw them as green and lovely as trees are in Spain in the month of May. Some of them were covered with blossoms, some with fruit, and some in other conditions, according to their kind. The nightingale and other small birds of a thousand kinds were singing in the month of November when I was there. There were palm trees of six or eight varieties, the graceful peculiarities of each one of them being worthy of admiration as are the other trees, fruits and grasses. There are wonderful pine woods, and very extensive ranges of meadow land. There is honey, and there are many kinds of birds, and a great variety of fruits. Inland there are numerous mines of metals and innumerable people. Hispaniola is a marvel. Its hills and mountains, fine plains and open country, are rich and fertile for planting and for pasturage, and for building towns and villages. The seaports there are incredibly fine, as also the magnificent rivers, most of which bear gold. The trees, fruits and grasses differ widely from those in Juana. There are many spices and vast mines of gold and other metals in this island. They have no iron, nor steel, nor weapons, nor are they fit for them, because although they are well-made men of commanding stature, they appear extraordinarily timid. The only arms they have are sticks of cane, cut when in seed, with a sharpened stick at the end, and they are afraid to use these. Often I have sent two or three men ashore to some town to converse with them, and the natives came out in great numbers, and as soon as they saw our men arrive, fled without a moment's delay although I protected them from all injury.

At every point where I landed, and succeeded in talking to them, I gave them some of everything I had—cloth and many other things—without receiving anything in return, but they are a hopelessly timid people. It is true that since they have gained more confidence and are losing this fear, they are so unsuspicious and so generous with what they possess, that no one who had not seen it would believe it. They never refuse anything that is asked for. They even offer it themselves, and show so much love that they would give their very hearts. Whether it be anything of great or small value, with any trifle of whatever kind, they are satisfied. I forbade worthless things being given to them, such as bits of broken bowls, pieces of glass, and old straps, although they were as much pleased to get them as if they were the finest jewels in the world. . . . Then all, both men and women, as soon as they were reassured about us, came, both small and great, all bringing something to eat and to drink, which they presented with marvelous kindness.

Bartolomé de las Casas, *A Brief Description of the Destruction of the Indies*, 1542[5]

The Spaniards first assaulted the innocent Sheep, so qualified by the Almighty, as is premention'd, like most cruel Tygers, Wolves and Lions hunger-starv'd, studying nothing, for the space of Forty Years, after their first landing, but the Massacre of these Wretches, whom they have so inhumanely and barbarously butcher'd and harass'd with several kinds of Torments, never before known, or heard (of which you shall have some account in the following Discourse) that of Three Millions of Persons, which lived in Hispaniola itself, there is at present but the inconsiderable remnant of scarce Three Hundred. Nay the Isle of Cuba, which extends as far, as Valledolid in Spain is distant from Rome, lies now uncultivated, like a Desert, and intomb'd in its own Ruins. You may also find the Isles of St. John, and Jamaica, both large and fruitful places, unpeopled and desolate. The Lucayan Islands on the North Side, adjacent to Hispaniola and Cuba, which are Sixty in number, or thereabout, together with those, vulgarly known by the name of the Gigantic Isles, and others, the most infertile whereof, exceeds the Royal Garden of Sevil in fruitfulness, a most Healthful and pleasant Climat, is now laid waste and uninhabited; and whereas, when the Spaniards first arriv'd here, about Five Hundred Thousand Men dwelt in it, they are now cut off, some by slaughter, and others ravished away by Force and Violence, to work in the Mines of Hispaniola, which was destitute of Native Inhabitants: For a certain Vessel, sailing to this Isle, to the end, that the Harvest being over (some good Christian, moved with Piety and Pity, undertook this dangerous Voyage, to convert Souls to Christianity) the remaining gleanings might be gathered up, there were only found Eleven Persons, which I saw with my own Eyes. There are other Islands Thirty in number, and upward bordering upon the Isle of St. John, totally unpeopled; all which are above Two Thousand miles in Length, and yet remain without Inhabitants, Native, or People.

Bernardino de Sahagún, *The Florentine Codex*, 1577

Chapter 29. Of the pestilence of smallpox that broke out among the Indians after the Spaniards left Mexico

Large bumps spread on the people; some were entirely covered. They spread everywhere, on the face, the head, the chest, etc. [The disease] brought great desolation: a great many died of it. They could no longer walk about, but lay in their dwellings and sleeping places, no longer able to move or stir. They were unable to change position, to stretch out on their sides or face down, or raise their heads. And when they made a motion, they called out loudly. The pustules that covered people caused great desolation; very many people died of them, and many just starved to death; starvation reigned, and no one took care of others any longer. On some people, the pustules appeared only far apart, and they did not suffer greatly, nor did many of them die of it. But many people's faces were spoiled by it, their faces were made rough. Some lost an eye or were blinded.

Notes

1 pp. 24–5. "Why did Columbus, who was carrying a passport and royal letters, think to take possession of anything, if he actually believed that he had reached the outlying regions of the Indies? It did not, after all, occur to Marco Polo in the late thirteenth century to claim for the Venetians any territorial rights in the East or to rename any of the countries; nor in the fourteenth century did John Mandeville unfurl a banner on behalf of a European monarch." Greenblatt, p. 53.

2 Like much else concerning Columbus, this document is subject to controversy. The actual letter in Columbus's hand no longer exists, nor do two earlier drafts that he allegedly wrote. For a full discussion of the letter's authenticity, see Zamora, Introduction.
3 Markey 9; on Venice see Horodowich.
4 Markey 96.
5 This English edition was published in 1689; the first English edition was in 1583.

Sources

Columbus. "Letter to Luis de Sant Angel," in *American History Leaflets, Colonial and Constitutional*, ed. Professors Hart & Channing, January, 1892, pp. 1–8.

Bartolomé de las Casas. *A Brief Account of the Destruction of the Indies*, R. Hewson at the Crown in Cornhil, Near the Stocks-Market, 1689.

Bernardino de Sahagún, *Florentine Codex* in James Lockhart, *We People Here: Nahuatl Accounts of the Conquest of Mexico*, UC Press, 1993, pp. 181–5.

References

Bartolomé de las Casas. *A Brief Account of the Destruction of the Indies*, ed and trans. Nigel Griffen, with an introduction by Anthony Pagden, Penguin, 1992.

Delaney, Carol. "Columbus's Ultimate Goal: Jerusalem," *Comparative Studies in Society and History*, Vol. 48, No. 2 (April 2006), pp. 260–92.

Epstein, Steven A. *Genoa and the Genoese, 958–1528*, U North Carolina P, 1996.

Fernández-Armesto, Felipe. *Columbus*, Oxford UP, 1991.

Gorse, George L. "Christopher Columbus and Andrea Doria: The Two Worlds of Renaissance Genoa," *Mediterranean Studies*, Vol. 16 (2007), pp. 120–42.

Greenblatt, Stephen. *Marvelous Possessions: The Wonder of the New World*, U Chicago P, 1992.

Horodowich, Elizabeth. *The Venetian Discovery of America: Geographic Imagination and Print Culture in the Age of Encounters*, Cambridge UP, 2018.

Markey, Lia. *Imagining the Americas in Medici Florence*, Pennsylvania State UP, 2016.

Phillips, William D. and Carla Rahn Phillips. *The Worlds of Christopher Columbus*, Cambridge UP, 1992.

Zamora, Margarita. *Reading Columbus*, UC Press, 1993.

75 A Florentine invents America

Amerigo Vespucci, "*Mundus novus*" *letter, c.*1502

Figure 8.3 The *Allegory of America* is a preliminary drawing by Medici court artist Giovanni Stradano (Jan van der Straet, 1523–1605) for the series of engravings produced in the late 1580s entitled *Nova Reperta* ("New Discoveries"). America is represented as a semi-naked woman, awakened from a nap on a hammock in the midst of vegetation and exotic animals, with cannibals feasting in the background. The well-dressed man standing before her holding an astrolabe in one hand and banner topped with a crucifix in the other is Amerigo Vespucci. The caption under the finished engraving reads: "Amerigo rediscovers America, he called her but once and thenceforth she was always awake."[1]

The continents of North and South America were named after the Florentine Amerigo Vespucci (1454–1512), a contemporary of Botticelli and Machiavelli. The son of a prosperous Florentine notary, Amerigo received

DOI: 10.4324/9781003284284-83

a humanist education and also studied the mathematical and scientific disciplines for which Florence was renowned at the time, which included cartography and cosmography. In 1478 in the role of secretary, the young man accompanied a family member on a diplomatic mission to France on behalf of the Medici. Later he served as administrator for the household of Lorenzo di Pierfrancesco de' Medici (1463–1503), cousin of Lorenzo the Magnificent. In 1492, he went to work in Seville for the Medici bank at the branch which took part in financing Columbus's first expedition. Eventually, between 1497 and 1504, Vespucci, too, sailed on Spanish and Portuguese transatlantic voyages; though, unlike Columbus who was a skilled navigator and commanded a fleet, the Florentine served as pilot, making use of his background in astronomy and cartography. He participated in expeditions along the coast of South America, although the precise dates and number of his trips have been debated. After one of these voyages, Amerigo wrote a letter from Lisbon to his patron, Lorenzo di Pierfrancesco de' Medici in Florence, and this letter, known as the *Mundus Novus* (*New World*), made the name Amerigo Vespucci familiar across all of Europe.[2] The letter circulated as a pamphlet, was published in sixty separate editions, and by 1529 had been translated into eight languages. Importantly, based on the text of this letter, Vespucci is credited with being the first to recognize that the territory "discovered" by Columbus was not Asia, but a land mass previously unknown to Europeans. It was for this reason that, in 1507, the German cartographer Martin Waldseemüller (*c.*1470–1520) named the continent after Amerigo when he labeled the corresponding region on his world map "America." Though others had arrived before him in this unfamiliar land, it was Amerigo Vespucci who in a sense "invented" the concept of the New World. Learned people across Europe relied on ancient works of geography, especially those of Strabo (*c.*64 BCE–*c.*24 CE) and Ptolemy of Alexandria (*c.*100 CE–*c.*170 CE), for their knowledge of the world. Vespucci himself had studied these authors; yet in the first sentence of his letter, Vespucci asserts that "our ancestors had no knowledge" of these regions, shattering with one stroke the absolute authority of the ancient Greeks and Romans. Whereas Columbus went about naming the strange lands of the "Indies" after Jesus and the Virgin Mary (San Salvador, Santa María de la Concepcíon) and the Spanish monarchs (Fernandina, Isabella), Amerigo simply called it the "New World." The "invention of America" opened the path to new ideas and innovations, but it was also profoundly destabilizing, challenging Europeans' certainties about their world. As Tommaso Campanella (#80) would write nearly one hundred years later, "It is natural for men to study the works of God, to voyage across the world, searching for knowledge everywhere, to experience everything . . . but when they learn about something that is not to be found in [their books] they are scandalized and disturbed, as they are now, having only just learned about Galileo's observations, and previously, that Columbus had discovered a new hemisphere."[3]

Amerigo Vespucci, *"Mundus Novus" letter, c.*1502

Amerigo Vespucci to Lorenzo di Pierfrancesco de' Medici with many salutations,

In the past I have written to you in rather ample detail about my return from those new regions which we searched for and discovered with the fleet, at the expense and orders of His Most Serene Highness the King of Portugal [Manuel I 1495–1521], and which can be called a new world, since our ancestors had no knowledge of them and they are entirely new matter to those who hear about them. Indeed, it surpasses the opinion of our ancient authorities, since most of them assert that there is no continent south of the equator, but merely that sea which they called the Atlantic; furthermore, if any of them did affirm that a continent was there, they gave many arguments to deny that it was habitable land. But this last voyage of mine has demonstrated that this opinion of theirs is false and contradicts all truth, since I have discovered a continent in those southern regions that is inhabited by more numerous peoples and animals than in our Europe, or Asia or Africa, and in addition I found a more temperate and pleasant climate than in any other region known to us, as you will learn from what follows, where we shall briefly write only of the main points of the matter, and of those things more worthy of note and record, which I either saw or heard in this new world, as will be evident below.

We set out from Lisbon under favorable conditions on 14 May 1501 by order of the aforesaid king, with three ships, to go in quest of new regions to the south, and we sailed steadily for twenty months, and the route was as follows. We sailed to what were formerly called the Fortunate Islands and are now the Grand Canary Islands, which are in the third climate and at the bounds of the inhabited West. From there, we travelled on the Ocean Sea[4] along the entire African coast and part of the Ethiopian, as far as the Ethiopian promontory, as Ptolemy called it, which is now called Cape Verde by our people, and Bezeguiche[5] by the Ethiopians. . . . we sailed for two months and three days before sighting any land. What we suffered in that vast expanse of sea, what dangers of shipwreck, what physical discomforts we endured, what anxieties beset our spirits, I leave to the understanding of those who have learned well and from much experience what it means to quest after uncertain things, things they have dared to investigate without prior knowledge of them. And that I might condense the whole story into one sentence, know that out of the sixty-seven days we sailed, we had forty-four continuous days of rain, thunder, and lightning, so dark that we never saw sunlight in the day, nor clear sky at night. Fear so overwhelmed us that we had almost abandoned all hope of survival. However, in those frequent, terrible tempests of sea and sky, it pleased the Most High to show us a nearby continent, and new regions and an unknown world. Sighting them, we were filled with joy, which, as one can well imagine, seizes those who have found safety after calamities and misfortunes. Thus, on 7 August 1501, we dropped anchor off the shores of those regions, thanking our God with solemn prayer and the singing of a Mass. There we learned that the land was not an island but a continent, both because it extends over very long, straight shorelines, and because it is filled with countless inhabitants. For in it we encountered innumerable peoples and tribes, and all kinds of sylvan animals not found in our regions, and many other things we have never seen before, which would take too long to describe individually.

[. . .]

First, then, the people. We found such a great multitude of people in those regions that no one could count their number (as one reads in the book of the *Apocalypse*); a gentle, tractable people. Everyone of both sexes goes about naked, covering no part of the body, and just as they issued from their mothers' wombs so they go about until their dying day. They have big, solid, well-formed and well-proportioned bodies, and their complexions tend toward red, which happens, I suppose, because in going about naked they are colored by the Sun. They also have long black hair. They are nimble in gait and in their games, and have open, pleasant faces, which they themselves, however, disfigure. They pierce their own cheeks, lips, noses, and ears, and you must not imagine that these holes are small or that they have but one of them: indeed I saw several people who had seven holes in a single face, each big enough to hold a plum. They fill these holes with beautiful stones, cerulean, marblelike, crystalline, or alabaster, or with very white bones and other things artfully wrought in their fashion. . . . They have another custom that is appalling and passes belief. Their women, being very lustful, make their husbands' members swell to such thickness that they look ugly and misshapen; this they accomplish with a certain device they have and by bites from certain poisonous animals. Because of this, many men lose their members, which rot through neglect, and they are left eunuchs. They have no cloth of wool, linen, or cotton, since they need none. Nor have they private property, but own everything in common: they live together without a king and without authorities, each man his own master. They take as many wives as they wish, and son may couple with mother, brother with sister, cousin with cousin, and in general men with women as they chance to meet. They dissolve marriage as often as they please, observing no order in any of these matters. Moreover, they have no temple and no religion, nor do they worship idols. What more can I say? They live according to nature, and might be called Epicureans rather than Stoics. There are no merchants among them, nor is there any commerce. The peoples make war among themselves without art or order. The elders deliver orations to the young to sway their will, urging them on to wars in which they kill each other cruelly, and they take captives and keep them, not to spare them, but to eat them for food. . . .

The land of those regions is very fertile and pleasant, abundant in hills and mountains, countless valleys and huge rivers, watered by healthful springs, and filled with broad, dense, barely penetrable forests and all sorts of wild beasts. Great trees grow there without cultivation, and many of them produce fruits delicious to taste and beneficial to the human body, though several indeed are the opposite, and none of the fruits there are like our own. Numberless kinds of herbs and roots grow there as well, from which the people make bread and excellent foods. They also have many seeds, totally different from ours. There are no kinds of metal there except gold, in which those regions abound, although we did not bring any back with us on our first voyage. The inhabitants apprised us of it, and told us that in the interior there is great abundance of gold, which they do not at all value or consider precious. They are rich in pearls, as I wrote elsewhere. If I wanted to mention separately all the things which are there, and to write about the numerous kinds of animals and their great numbers, I would grow too prolix with a matter so vast; and I certainly believe that our Pliny did not come within a thousandth part of those types of parrots and other birds and animals which are in those regions, with such great diversity of forms and colors that even Polycletus,[6] master of painting in all its perfection, would have failed to depict them adequately. . . .

Sky and air are clear for most of the year and free from dense vapors. The rains there fall delicately and last three or four hours, then vanish like mist. The sky is adorned with very beautiful signs and figures, in which I noticed twenty stars as bright as we sometimes see Venus or Jupiter. I considered their movements and orbits and measured their circumferences and diameters with geometric methods, and determined that they are of great magnitude. I saw three Canopi[7] in the sky, two of which are bright indeed, and the third dim. The Antarctic Pole has no Ursa Major and Ursa Minor, as appear in our Arctic Pole, nor is any bright star seen near it; of the stars which are carried around it in smaller orbit, there are three which form the figure of an orthogonal triangle, of which half the circumference, or the diameter, is 9 ½ degrees. . . .

I encountered many other beautiful stars during this voyage of mine, and I notated their movements carefully and have described them beautifully and graphically in a booklet of mine. His Most Serene Highness the King has it at present, and I hope that he will return it to me. In that hemisphere I saw things which do not agree with the arguments of the philosophers: a white rainbow was seen twice around midnight, not only by me, but also by all the sailors. Likewise, several times we saw a new moon on the day when it was in conjunction with the Sun. Every night in that part of the sky, innumerable vapors and bright flares streak across. A bit earlier I spoke of the hemisphere, although, properly speaking, it is not fully a hemisphere with respect to ours; but since it approaches the shape of one, it is permissible to call it so.

Therefore, as I said, from Lisbon, our point of departure, 39 ½ degrees from the equator, we sailed fifty degrees beyond the equator, which together make about ninety degrees, and since this sum makes a quarter of the great circle, according to the true reasoning of measurement passed on to us by the ancients, it is clear that we sailed around a quarter of the world. . . .

The interpreter Giocondo[8] has translated this letter from Italian to Latin, so that all Latins may understand how many marvelous things are being discovered every day, and to curb the audacity of people who wish to study the heavens and their majesty and to know more than they are permitted to know, for, ever since the world began, the Earth's vastness and all things contained in it have been unknown.

Praise to God.

Notes

1 Markey 423.
2 The original letter has been lost. For arguments contesting its authorship, see Fernández-Armesto 117–23. For an opposing view, see Lehmann.
3 *Opere di Tommaso Campanella*, ed. D'Ancona 1854, 288, trans. Kaborycha.
4 The "Ocean Sea" was a name for the Atlantic Ocean used since ancient times. Deriving from the Titan Oceanus, it was believed to be a river that flowed around the Earth. After his voyage to the New World, Columbus was referred to as "Admiral of the Ocean Sea." Another name the ancients had for the body of water was "Atlanticus," which was derived from another Titan, Atlas.
5 "Bezeguiche is present-day Gorée, near Cape Verde." (LF)
6 "But 'Polycletus' was a sculptor; his name is being confused here with 'Polygnotus.'" (LF)
7 "The *Canopus* is a star of the first magnitude, originally one of the Constellation of Argo." (LF)
8 Traditionally identified with the Veronese Dominican Fra Giovanni del Giocondo (1433–1515), an architect and humanist who had in this era gone to Paris for the building of the Pont de Notre-Dame. (LF)

Source

Amerigo Vespucci, *Letters from a New World: Amerigo Vespucci's Discovery of America*, ed. Luciano Formisano, trans. David Jacobson, Marsilio, 1992, pp. 45–56.

References

Fernández-Armesto, Felipe. *Amerigo: The Man Who Gave His Name to America*, Random House, 2007.

Hough, Samuel J. *The Italians and the Creation of America*, Brown UP, 1980.

Johnson, Christine R. "Renaissance German Cosmographers and the Naming of America," *Past & Present*, No. 191 (May 2006), pp. 3–43.

Lehmann, Martin. "Amerigo Vespucci and His Alleged Awareness of America as a Separate Land Mass," *Imago Mundi*, Vol. 65, No. 1 (2013), pp. 15–24.

Markey, Lia. "Stradano's Allegorical Invention of the Americas in Late Sixteenth-Century Florence," *Renaissance Quarterly*, Vol. 65, No. 2 (Summer 2012), pp. 385–442.

O'Gorman, Edmundo. *The Invention of America. An Inquiry into the Historical Nature of the New World and the Meaning of Its History*, Indiana UP, 1961.

Waldseemüller, Martin. *The Naming of America: Martin Waldseemuller's 1507 World Map and the Cosmographiae introductio*, a new translation and commentary by John W. Hessler, GILES: Distributed by Antique Collectors' Club Limited, 2008.

76 Poet, artist, and scientist explore the Moon

Ludovico Ariosto, *Orlando furioso*, 1516

Figure 8.4 Lodovico Cigoli, *The Virgin of the Immaculate Conception*, detail, 1612, Pauline Chapel, Santa Maria Maggiore, Rome.

The artist known as Cigoli (Lodovico Cardi, 1559–1613) was a highly influential painter and architect in seventeenth-century Florence. He was also a good friend of Galileo, the two having met in their youth as students of perspective with mathemetician Ostilio Ricci. Both accomplished lutenists,

DOI: 10.4324/9781003284284-84

the two men shared many intellectual and artistic interests. Galileo regarded painting and science as related endeavors, which involved attentive observation of nature (**#10**), and was himself a master draftsman. They were members of the Accademia Fiorentina, the learned academy where discussions of science, literature, music, and art often overlapped. An example of this overlap is in Cigoli's painting of *The Virgin of the Immaculate Conception* (Figure 8.4). When Cigoli was commissioned to decorate a chapel in the Basilica of Santa Maria Maggiore in Rome with this theme, it was specified that Mary should be depicted with "the Moon under her feet."[1] Like the ancient goddess Diana (Artemis), by legend a virgin huntress, the Virgin Mary was also associated with the Moon, which was considered immaculate— literally "unspotted." The painter chose, however, to represent the lunar surface not according to legend, but as viewed through his friend's telescope. Throughout November and December of 1609, Galileo had gazed at the Moon through his device; the ink and sepia-wash drawings he made from those observations were the first realistic depictions showing the uneven lunar surface pitted with craters (Figure 8.1). The following year, Galileo published his findings in a book titled *Sidereus nuncius* (*The Starry Messenger*, 1610). There was great curiosity in Rome about his discoveries, and Cigoli in essence visually "published" Galileo's findings with this realistic painting of the Moon. Despite Aristotle and others who had described the Moon as a perfect sphere with a flawless surface, observations made with the naked eye since antiquity had led people to wonder about the "man in the Moon" patterns on its surface. In his notebooks, Leonardo da Vinci made detailed drawings of the Moon and speculated that its spots might be lunar seas.[2]

While many pictured to themselves a fanciful man in the Moon, Ludovico Ariosto (1474–1533) imagined what it might be like for a man to be *on* the Moon. In his exuberantly fantastical epic poem *Orlando furioso*, there is an episode in which Orlando's friend Astolfo goes on a lunar mission to find his friend's lost wits—since ancient times it was believed that lunacy was related to the phases of the Moon. Astolfo flies up to the Moon on Elijah's chariot with St. John the Evangelist, and there is a lengthy whimsical description of what he finds as he explores its surface. As it happens, Ariosto was one of Galileo's favorite authors. According to his biographer Vincenzo Viviani, Galileo knew the entire *Orlando furioso*—nearly forty thousand lines—by heart. In 1590, when he was around twenty-six years old, Galileo wrote an extended series of notes on literary criticism titled *Considerazioni al Tasso*, in which he compared the poetry of Torquato Tasso (1544–1595) unfavorably with that of Ariosto, in one place writing, "Ariosto never demonstrated such lazy imagination when he had Bradamante arrive at Merlin's tomb, Ruggiero to [the palace of] Logistilla, Astolfo to the Inferno, Earthly Paradise, or to the orb of the Moon."[3]

Ludovico Ariosto, *Orlando furioso*, 1516

Chapter XXXIV Astolfo's flight to the Moon in Elijah's chariot

When the Sun had sunk beneath the sea
and the Moon had raised her horn,
a chariot was prepared, which was used
for dashing through the heavens:
it was the same one that had lifted Elijah
above mortal eyes in the mountains of Judaea.

69
The holy Evangelist harnessed the team,
four steeds, redder than flame,
then he settled beside Astolfo,
took the reins, and headed for the sky.
The chariot revolved as it lifted into the air
and at once it arrived in the midst of the eternal flame,
though the old man miraculously
made them pass through without burning.[4]

70
They crossed the entire fiery sphere
and from there went to the lunar realm.
The Moon looked to them
smooth and spotless as a steel blade;
its size they found similar to this globe,
this lowly globe of Earth,
with its encircling sea,
though perhaps slightly smaller.

71
Astolfo was doubly astonished there:
Up close, that place was so large,
which seems only a small circle
gazed at by us from below;
and he had to squint with both eyes
to catch sight of Earth and the seas stretching round it;
since it made little light of its own
the image did not carry far.

72
Other rivers, other lakes, other plains,
other valleys, and other mountains are up there;
they are not like those among us.

There were cities and towns
with the grandest houses that the knight had ever seen
or ever would again.
And there were vast, lonely forests
where nymphs continually hunted wild beasts.

73
Astolfo did not stay to explore everything;
he had not come up there for that.
By the holy Apostle he was led
to a valley, confined by two mountains
where wondrously everything that has been lost
either from our carelessness,
or through the fault of time or Fortune,
all that has been lost on Earth is kept up there.

74
I do not speak only of kingdoms and riches,
the work of the goddess's fickle wheel,
but that which Fortune has not
in her power to give or take away:
Up there are many reputations that over time
are slowly devoured as if by termites down here.
Up there are infinite prayers and vows
that we sinners make to God.

75
The tears and sighs of lovers,
wasted time lost in gambling,
ignorant men's lengthy idleness,
useless plans that never work,
and many, many vain desires
mostly clutter that place:
In short, all the things you ever lost,
Can be found again if you go up there.

76
As the knight passed those heaps,
he asked his guide about this or that object.
He noticed a pile of swollen sacks
from which seemed to issue tumult and cries
and learned that they were the ancient crowns
of the Assyrians, of the Lydian lands,
of the Persians and Greeks, who once had been
glorious, and now their names are almost forgotten.

[. . .]

79
Ruins of cities and castles
with great treasures were jumbled in confusion.
These, he was told, were treaties
that had failed and badly-concealed plots.
He saw serpents with maidens' faces,
the work of counterfeiters and thieves;
then many kinds of pottery shards
that had been used to serve at petty courts.

80
A huge amount of spilled soup
he saw and asked his teacher about it.
"It is charity," he said, "left by people
to be given out after their death."
They passed a great mound of various flowers
once perfumed, now stinking.
That was the Donation (if one could call it that)
of Constantine to good Pope Sylvester.[5]

81
He saw a lot of birdlime for snaring,
which were, ladies, your charms.
It would take too long to list
all the things he was shown there:
a thousand verses would not suffice.
Up there are all the things we need.
Only folly do we have, and plenty of it;
folly stays here on Earth and never disappears.

82
Astolfo asked for some of his days and deeds
that he had once lost; their forms had changed
so that if his guide hadn't been there,
he would not have recognized them.
Then he came upon that which seems such a part of us
that vows would never be made to God for it.
I speak of brains: there was a mountain of them there,
many more than all the other things I've recounted.

83
The wits were like a light, elusive liquor,
that easily evaporated if not kept sealed;

and these were gathered in various vials,
some more, some less capacious, as was suitable.
The largest of them all was the one that held
the good senses of crazed Orlando;
and it was distinguished from the others
with a label that read: "Orlando's wits."

Notes

1 Ostrow 219.
2 Reaves and Pedretti 55–8; Zubov 151.
3 *Considerazioni* 176.
4 According to ancient/medieval cosmography, there was a ring of fire between Earth and the Moon.
5 See **#13** on the *Donation of Constantine*.

Sources

Galileo Galilei. *Considerazioni al Tasso*, Venice, 1793, trans. Kaborycha.
Ludovico Ariosto. *Orlando furioso*, ed. Santorre Debenedetti, Laterza, 1928, trans. Kaborycha.

References

Chappell, Miles. "Cigoli, Galileo, and Invidia," *The Art Bulletin*, Vol. 57, No. 1 (March 1975), pp. 91–8.
Cressy, David. "Early Modern Space Travel and the English Man in the Moon," *The American Historical Review*, Vol. 111, No. 4 (October 2006), pp. 961–82.
Mac Carthy, Ita. "Ariosto the Lunar Traveller," *Modern Language Review*, Vol. 104 (2009), pp. 71–82.
Ozstrow, Steven F. "Cigoli's Immacolata and Galileo's Moon: Astronomy and the Virgin in Early Seicento Rome," *The Art Bulletin*, Vol. 78, No. 2 (June 1996), pp. 218–35.
Reaves, Gibson and Carlo Pedretti. "Leonardo da Vinci's Drawings of the Surface Features of the Moon," *Journal for the History of Astronomy*, Vol. XVIII (1987), pp. 55–8.
Reeves, Eileen. *Painting the Heavens: Art and Science in the Age of Galileo*, Princeton UP, 1997.
Winkler, Mary G. and Albert Van Helden. "Representing the Heavens: Galileo and Visual Astronomy," *Isis*, Vol. 83, No. 2 (June 1992), pp. 195–217.
Zubov, V.P. *Leonardo da Vinci*, translated from the Russian by David H. Kraus, Harvard UP, 1968, 2014 De Gruyter online edition.

77 Belief in witches or in a new world?

Gianfrancesco Pico della Mirandola, *The Witch*, 1524

Renowned humanist Gianfrancesco Pico della Mirandola (1469–1533) was the nephew of an even more famous humanist by a very similar name: Giovanni Pico della Mirandola (1463–1494, **#16**). Giovanni Pico is celebrated as the author of a philosophical oration concerned with locating universal truths within widely diverging religious texts across world cultures and attempting to reconcile pagan philosophies with Christian doctrine. Gianfrancesco Pico is best known as the author of a popular book on the evils of witchcraft. Not limiting himself to theory, in 1522 he carried out a witch hunt in his small principality of Mirandola, working alongside the Dominican inquisitor Leandro Alberti (1479–1552). Gianfrancesco was actively involved in the trials and executions of seven men and three women for witchcraft. These events coincided with a peak in the witch craze in the Italian Peninsula, though many people, especially scholars, were skeptical about the existence of witches. In order to convince others of the reality of these satanic forces, Gianfrancesco wrote *Strix* (*The Witch*) in 1523, which was translated the following year by Leandro Alberti from Latin into Italian as *Strega*. The first book on witchcraft to be printed in vernacular Italian, by 1556 it appeared in four editions, demonstrating its outstanding popularity. As Tamar Herzig has pointed out, Gianfrancesco "was aware that the scholastic style in which Kramer wrote the *Malleus* [*maleficarum*] made it unattractive to many learned Italians. *Strix* was directed to precisely these educated readers who doubted the existence of witches. Pico—who argued that the *Malleus* is very important for understanding Italian witchcraft—used his classical erudition and adopted the literary form of a dialogue to make its content more palatable to contemporary readership."[1] It is important to note that being a humanist did not preclude belief in the occult; indeed both Gianfrancesco's uncle and Marsilio Ficino endorsed aspects of magical theory.[2] Furthermore, this dialogue raises even deeper questions that fall into the area of philosophical inquiry known as epistemology, which asks, "How do we know what we know?" Gianfrancesco Pico employs the four protagonists in his dialogue—an illiterate peasant woman called Strega (meaning "Witch"), an inquisitor named Dicaste, the skeptic Apistio, and the learned Fronimo—to enact and debate the most urgently topical Renaissance concerns. He stages a drama in which faith is

DOI: 10.4324/9781003284284-85

pitted against evidence of the senses, and the consensus of learned authorities is arrayed against an individual's own judgment. Finally, set against the backdrop of the disorientation caused by discovery of the New World, this dialogue underscores the limitations of ancient Greek and/or Roman sources in helping contemporaries understand the world around them.

Gianfrancesco Pico della Mirandola, *The Witch*, 1524

Book II

Apistio: Tell me everything, one bit at a time.

Strega: On holy days when I was in church, and the priest recited Mass as usual, he [the demon lover] ordered me to whisper, "It's not true, you're lying through your teeth." And when he [the priest] raised the Host over his head to show it to the congregation so they could worship it, he ordered me to turn my gaze away and to cross my fingers under my clothes as you see me doing now. Then he told me not to recount anything about our love affair to the priest. . . . And when after approaching the altar, the Host—the consecrated body of Christ—was placed in my mouth, he had me carefully take it out, pretending to wipe my mouth, and put it in a linen handkerchief so we could use it for our games and desecrate it as I told you before.

[She confesses to hiding the consecrated Host in her robe, then stamping on it and throwing it in her chamber pot.]

Apistio: And you obeyed this accursed order?

Strega: Woe is me, alas yes, I obeyed him. And I will tell you something horrible and terrifying if you will hear it: when I struck the Host with a stick in that filth, I saw blood flow from it.[3]

Fronimo: What do I hear today? Can this be? I believe that my ears will never again hear such wicked and impious villainy as this!

Apistio: Neither will I ever hear of such sacrilege and horrendous deeds.

Fronimo: For love of God, let us leave this place and go meet Dicaste. If you are agreeable, he will return with us.

Apistio: I would like that very much. Let's go.

Dicaste: So how is it going, are you satisfied? Is there anything else you want to know?

Fronimo: Ah, Dicaste, I'll tell you, we've heard such things that we are nauseated and don't want lunch. We've had enough of this.

Dicaste: Let's go a little farther off toward the garden and perhaps by walking and strolling around your appetite will return. You, over there, take the witch back to prison!

Apistio: I never imagined that such villainous deeds as those I've heard today from the witch, could be thought of, much less committed. Before, I would have easily pardoned this kind of man or woman, thinking them led frivolously or thoughtlessly into these errors; I believed that these male and female witches were deceived by the Demon's visions, illusions, and fictions. And even now—I'm giving you my opinion—I couldn't swear that they're not. But now, as the good and faithful Christian I am, believing that which all true Christians ought to believe, I could never agree to excuse or pardon such wicked villains, malicious despisers and defilers of our most Holy Faith.

Dicaste: If I can demonstrate to you that it is part of Christian religion to believe that such evil deeds are in reality carried out by these wicked persons, and if I bring forth so many witnesses that you will be unable to doubt that such devil's games are true, rather than imagined as is said, I believe you will no longer stubbornly oppose me.

Apistio: For now, my mind is not inclined to either of the two sides.

Dicaste: Tell me, have you ever seen a person rise from the dead?

Apistio: I've never seen such a miracle.

Dicaste: Do you believe that people can rise from the dead?

Fronimo: No, he won't deny it, since poets have often sung about it, and even philosophers, Plato especially, has written about it. They tell how the dead can come back to life and leave the underworld.

Apistio: I am not persuaded by these arguments. In such a serious matter I don't trust poets or philosophers, but rather the Gospels.

Dicaste: I will propose examples of other things, which are not mentioned in Sacred Scripture. Tell me: do you believe that ships left the ports of Cádiz, that is from those two islands that are at the end of Spain at the extreme west of where our land ends, dividing Europe from Africa, and also from Lisbon in Portugal? That they were carried by Zephyr breezes around twenty thousand leagues, more or less to a vast land—so large that its extent is still unknown—and that moved by this west wind across the Atlantic Ocean, they arrived at the Indian Ocean?[4]

Apistio: Yes, I believe it.

Dicaste: You believe it. But tell me, from whom do you believe it?

Apistio: From the many merchants who tell of having followed this route "over the broad back of the Sea."[5]

Dicaste: Have you ever spoken with one of them?

Apistio: Not personally, but I have spoken with people who have heard about this curious thing with their own ears from those who claim to have navigated to those places, confirming what they were like.

Dicaste: And tell me, Apistio, couldn't those people have deceived you?

Apistio: Ah, but who would doubt them? Why would such serious and trustworthy men delight in fairy tales and lies?

Dicaste: If I then brought forward no less a number of witnesses, just as serious and trustworthy as yours, who have confirmed under oath how female and male witches are transported to the gathering where demons disguised as women give sexual pleasure to men, and disguised as men they do the same to women? And if they have heard this from the mouths of these same male and female witches, swearing on the Sacrament, what would you say? Would you then be satisfied?

Fronimo: Any man who was not satisfied by that, could truly be called either foolish, crazy, or stubborn.

Apistio: And, by your faith, tell me for what reason?

Fronimo: Because when many people speak with the same voice, it is not seemly to deny it, unless you are driven by a good argument, one that is strong enough to demolish the opinion confirmed by so many men. I don't believe you have such an argument.

Apistio: Your reasoning is weak as regards things that appear supernatural, but applies to things that derive from human experience. This is why I have no difficulty believing in the voyages of those Spanish ships to India and to that new land and other places, but I find it hard to believe in those Games of Diana.[6]

Fronimo: There is much more to object to in the accounts of voyages to India than to those who tell of the nocturnal games of Hecate, that is, Diana. Inasmuch as the said voyage was completely unknown in antiquity: only a very few indications were found, on the basis of which some ships were said to have arrived from India to the Spanish shore. But now one navigates from Europe by way of the Ethiopian Sea to India, with maps depicting the shorelines and ports. At present, islands of marvelous size, never known to the ancients, have been discovered. And neither were these great, marvelous lands ever recorded by or commented on by philosophers, who if they had imagined the existence of more worlds in the natural order, perhaps would have even more definitively have proved their madness. Of such things discovered recently through such efforts, Strabo and Ptolemy made not a single mention, nor any others who are reputed to be even greater fabulists then they.[7] And yet witches are clearly mentioned not only in ancient, but in modern texts.

Apistio: I feel that little by little, though I know not how, my mind is moved to agree with what you say, but I would like to hear the evidence that Dicaste has promised to show us.

Notes

1 Herzig 59. Published in 1486, the *Malleus maleficarum* (*Hammer of Witches*) was a manual on witchcraft by German Dominican inquisitor Heinrich Kramer.
2 Philosophers and physicians had long made use of astrological magic, moreover, contemporaries made the distinction between "natural magic" or "white magic"—an ancient art believed to do good, heal illness etc.—and *maleficium* or "black magic"—practiced with the aid of the devil, which caused harm.
3 According to the Doctrine of Transubstantiation, Christ is actually present in the Eucharist, and "change of substance" occurred at the moment during the Mass when the priest elevated the Host, changing the wafer into flesh and the wine into blood. This doctrine, contradicted by the empirical evidence of the senses, had been arrived at by medieval theologians who employed philosophical distinctions of "essence" and "substance" derived from Aristotle. Hence, to desecrate the Host was a crime involving harm to the actual body of Christ, demonstrated by the blood claimed to issue from the wafer when struck.
4 Vasco de Gama left from Lisbon and circumnavigated Africa in 1497–9, arriving at the Indian Ocean. Magellan left Cádiz in 1519, reached Brazil and Argentina, then circumnavigated South America and arrived in the Philippines.
5 Homer, *Odyssey* 3:142.
6 Diana, the pagan Roman goddess of the hunt, was associated with the Moon and nighttime and sometimes identified as Hecate, the goddess of the underworld and magic. Often the witches' Sabbath was known as the "Games of Diana."
7 See Vespucci #75.

Sources

Gianfrancesco Pico della Mirandola, *The Witch* in *Libro detto Strega: o della illusioni del demonio del Giovanfrancesco Pico dall Mirandola*; nel volgarizzamento di Leandro Alberti; ed. Albano Biondi, Marsilio, 1989; and *La Strega (Strix) di Gianfrancesco Pico*; Italian trans. and ed. Lucia Pappalardo. Città nuova, 2017, trans. Kaborycha.

References

Burke, Peter. "Witchcraft and Magic in Renaissance Italy: Gianfrancesco Pico and His *Strix*," in *The Damned Art: Essays in the Literature of Witchcraft*, ed. Sydney Anglo, Routledge & K. Paul, 1977, pp. 32–52.

Copenhaver, Brian. *Magic in Western Culture: From Antiquity to the Enlightenment*, Cambridge UP, 2015.

Duni, Matteo, ed. *Under the Devil's Spell: Witches, Sorcerers, and the Inquisition in Renaissance Italy*, Syracuse University in Florence, 2007.

Herzig, Tamar. "The Demons' Reaction to Sodomy: Witchcraft and Homosexuality in Gianfrancesco Pico della Mirandola's *Strix*," *The Sixteenth Century Journal*, Vol. 34, No. 1 (Spring 2003), pp. 53–72.

Maggi, Armando. "To Read the Body of a Monster: Exegesis and Witchcraft in *Strix* by Giovan Francesco Pico della Mirandola," Chapter One in *In the Company of Demons: Unnatural Beings, Love, and Identity in the Italian Renaissance*, U Chicago P, 2006.

Stephens, Walter. "The Witch-hunting Humanist: Gianfrancesco Pico della Mirandola's *Strix*," in *The Science of Demons: Early Modern Authors Facing Witchcraft and the Devil*, ed. Jan Machielsen, Routledge Taylor & Francis, 2020, pp. 83–98.

78 The marvelous city of Fez described

Giovanni Leone Africano (al-Hasan ibn Muhammad al-Wazzan), *The Cosmography and Geography of Africa*, 1526

Giovanni Leone Africano was born around 1486–8 in Granada and given the Arabic name al-Hasan ibn Muhammad al-Wazzan. When in 1492 the final phase of the Christian Reconquista was accomplished with the fall of Granada—the last Muslim stronghold on the Iberian Peninsula—al-Wazzan's family was faced with the choice of conversion or exile. Rather than abandon their Islamic faith, they emigrated to Fez where the boy was educated, attended an Islamic university, and became a diplomat. It was while on a diplomatic mission that al-Wazzan was captured by Christian pirates in 1518 and taken to Rome. There he was confined for more than a year in the Castel Sant'Angelo, given instruction in Christianity, and allowed to borrow Arabic manuscripts from the Vatican Library. He was subsequently presented to Pope Leo X (Giovanni de' Medici, #27), who took the Arab scholar under his wing. Al-Wazzan allowed himself to be baptized by the pope, taking the Christian name Johannes Leo—Latin for Giovanni Leone—after his mentor. In addition to the pope, Giovanni Leone had other important patrons within the Roman curia, including the humanist theologian Cardinal Egidio da Viterbo (1469–1532), whom he tutored in Arabic while also making revisions and commentary on a copy of the Qur'an that was in the cardinal's possession. The Moroccan man of letters spent a total of nine years in Italy, immersed in various literary projects: he transcribed an Arabic translation of the Epistles of St. Paul; he authored a number of books, including *Illustrious Men among the Arabs and the Jews*; and he collaborated on a dictionary of Arabic, Hebrew, and Latin. However, the work for which he is famous is his *Cosmography and Geography of Africa* (*Cosmographia et geographia de Affrica*). Written in 1526, it was later revised by a Venetian editor, published in 1550 as *Description of Africa*, and went on to become a bestseller as the first detailed account of much of Sub-Saharan Africa available to Europeans. Furthermore, it is an unusual work in the way it displays at the same time the author's intimate familiarity with the life and sensibilities of Christians in the world around him, along with a desire to accurately portray his North African homeland without offending either culture. Forced to live "between worlds," according to historian Natalie Zemon Davis, Giovanni Leone Africano wrote "taking care to placate the Christians while not defaming

DOI: 10.4324/9781003284284-86

Islam."[1] He returned to North Africa after the 1527 Sack of Rome and settled in Tunis; little else is known for certain about the remainder of the life of al-Hasan ibn Muhammad al-Wazzan.

Giovanni Leone Africano, *The Cosmography and Geography of Africa*, 1526

Detailed description of Fez

Fez is certainly an enormous city,[2] encircled all around with high, beautiful walls; it is almost entirely situated on hills and mountains, and only half the city is flat, but on all four sides there are mountains. Water enters the city in two places, as the river splits in two, one passing through the newer part of Fez and the other through the [old] city; that is, the part of the city that faces south, and the other to the west. And when this water enters the city, it is divided into many canals and most of them go past homes of citizens, courtiers, and others. And similarly, every temple and place of prayer has access [to water], as well as inns, hospitals, and colleges, especially those near the temples . . . and the houses in this land are well-constructed from bricks and stones, and most of them are very lovely, adorned with beautiful mosaics and tiled on the outside and in the porticos with certain glazed bricks of diverse colors. They are similar to maiolica vases, painted all over with delicate brushwork and decorated with precious colors such as gold and azure. And the roofs of their houses are made with flat tiles to be able to easily hang laundry or to sleep on in the summer. . . . And everywhere there are charming, low fountains, made of the colored glass bricks previously mentioned, although sometimes there is a round marble basin as in European fountains. . . . And [the water] keeps the city always clean and fresh, especially when used in the summertime; within the household, the whole family bathes in it—men, women, and the little ones. It is the custom to construct certain rooms in the house in the form of a tower, and inside there are certain little ornately decorated rooms where the women like to go when they are tired from work, because from those towers one has a view of almost the entire surrounding countryside. Furthermore, in this city there are around 700 temples and mosques, that is, small oratories, of which fifty are large, well-built, and adorned with marble columns and other ornaments. In each of these, made from exquisite marbles and from other stones unknown in Italy, there are gracious fountains under galleries worked in mosaics and with inlaid tiles. And all the roofs of these temples are made like the temples of Europe. . . . There are two chief temples in this city: one is called the al-Qarawiyyin Mosque, an immense temple that is a mile and a half around, with thirty-one very wide, high doors. . . . All around this temple are many pergolas, that is along the inner walls where every morning certain learned doctors read aloud to the people from various sacred texts. . . . And in this city there are eleven colleges [madrasas] for scholars, well-constructed . . . each has many rooms, the large colleges have around one hundred, some more, some less. . . . The largest was built by King Abū 'Inān, a marvel of size, beauty, and ornament . . . its doors are all made of bronze, beautifully wrought, and in the great hall, where prayers are said, there is a raised covered platform surrounded by nine staircases, all made of ivory and ebony, truly a wonderful sight to see. It is said that after listening to many of his teachers, as they had listened to teachers before them, King Abū 'Inān asked to see the account book. After briefly turning over the pages of one of the books, he found that he had spent around 40,000 ducats. Marveling at the expense, he tore up all the account books and threw them in the brook that passed though the college, and cited a verse of the Arab sages: "A costly thing, if it is beautiful, is not costly; anything pleasing to the heart is priceless."

[. . .]

Hospitals and baths

In Fez there are many hospitals, which in beauty are not inferior to its colleges, and it was the custom to give foreign pilgrims three days' lodging there. . . . The hospital has its professional staff, namely, notaries, managers, guardians, cooks, and others to take care of the sick, and each receives a decent salary. When I was young, I worked there for two years as a notary, as young students are in the habit of doing, earning a salary of three ducats every three months. . . .

When a man wants to go to one of the baths, after entering by the front door, he passes into a room, which is cold, from the fountain they keep there to freshen the water when it is too hot. From there he goes by a door into the second room, which is somewhat warmer, and the attendants wash him, applying perfumes, and cleaning his body. Then he passes into the third room, which is very hot, and he sweats for a certain amount of time. That is where the heater is located that heats the water, which they carefully draw out with wooden pails, giving each man two of them. And if someone wants more, or requests to be washed, he is required to give the attendant two pennies, or one at least. The proprietor is only paid two quattrini. The water is heated with animal manure, so the owners of the baths need to employ many houseboys and lackeys who run about the city collecting manure from stables, making a little mountain of it, letting it dry two or three months in the sun, later burning it instead of wood to heat the bathwater. The women have their own baths, separate from the men, although some serve both men and women, but at different times of the day. . . . Thus as a signal, when a curtain is hung at the entrance to the bath no man can go in there. And if it happens that a man wants to speak with his wife, he cannot go in, instead he must have a female servant carry his message. Both men and women of the city equally like to go out to dine in the baths and to sing loudly. The young men all enter the baths naked as they were born, looking at one another without feeling shame, but men of higher rank go in wrapped in a towel. They sit in the common area, but then stretch out to rest in certain small chambers that are always well-appointed and decorated for men of high standing. . . .

The hotels in this city

In the aforesaid city there are around 200 hotels; they are well-constructed and some are very large, especially those that are near the main mosque. Built on three floors, some have as many as 120 bedrooms, some more, some less. And all have fountains and lavatories with running water, which do not exist in Italy, except in the Collegio di Spagna in Bologna, even though the Palazzo [del Cardinal di] San Giorgio in Rome resembles them somewhat, and in those inns all the doors to the bedrooms open onto a corridor. In addition to the most beautiful lodgings, there are bad ones, without beds or bedding and the innkeeper gives each guest a pot and a slave girl and the guest buys things for the innkeeper to cook. And not only foreigners lodge in these hostelries, but all single men without home or family; one or more of them share a room, providing themselves with beds and doing the cooking. Even worse than these are the evil lodgings with hostelers who are a kind of men known as *elcheva*;[3] they go around dressed like women, adorn themselves like women, shave their beards, speak like women and spin. And each of these accursed hostelers keeps a man in the manner of a husband and it is also said that they are used as whores in European brothels. And these innkeepers are authorized to have wine in their hostelries and they sell it without being bothered at all by the court. For that reason, all disreputable men frequent such hostelries because they can get drunk, be with prostitutes, or worse, and be safe from the court.

Notes

1 Davis *Trickster* 266.
2 "Rome was a little more than half the size of Fez in population." Davis *Trickster* 65.
3 al-Wazzan was "transliterating either *alhhiwa*, an Andalusian word for 'sodomites' or *al-khanith*, mukhannath, 'effeminate men.'" Davis *Trickster* 201.

Source

Giovanni Leone Africano, *Cosmographia de l'Affrica*: Ms. V.E. 953, Biblioteca Nazionale Centrale di Roma, 1526, ed. Gabriele Amadori, pp. 271–80, trans. Kaborycha.

References

Johannes Leo Africanus. *The Cosmography and Geography of Africa*, trans. Anthony Ossa-Richardson and Richard Oosterhoff, Penguin, 2023.

Piera, Montserrat. "Vulnerable Medieval Iberian Travellers: Benjamin of Tudela's *Sefer ha-massa'ot*, Pero Tafur's *Andaàs e viajes*, and Ahmad al-Wazzan's *Libro de la cosmogrophia et geographia de Africa*," in *Remapping Travel Narratives (1000–1700): To the East and Back Again*, Arc Humanities Press, 2018, pp. 61–85.

Zemon-Davis, Natalie. "'Leo Africanus' Presents Africa to Europeans," in *Revealing the African Presence in Renaissance Europe*, ed. Joaneath Spicer, Walters Art Museum, 2012, pp. 61–74.

Zemon-Davis, Natalie. *Trickster Travels: A Sixteenth-Century Muslim Between Worlds*, Hill and Wang, 2006.

Zhiri, Oumelbanine. "Leo Africanus, Translated and Betrayed," in *The Politics of Translation in the Middle Ages and the Renaissance*, ed. Renate Blumenfeld-Kosinski, Luise von Flotow and Daniel Russell, U Ottawa P, 2001, pp. 161–74.

79 A strange and wonderful museum

Ulisse Aldrovandi, *Discourse on Nature*, 1572–3

Ulisse Aldrovandi, *Letter to Francesco I*, 1578

Figure 8.5 Anonymous illustrator, *Bolognese Dragon*, 1572, Biblioteca Universitaria di Bologna, Aldovrandi "Tavole di animali," Vol. 4:130. The naturalist Aldrovandi commissioned this image of the dragon after its alleged discovery in the Bolognese countryside.[1]

On the first page of Aldrovandi's multivolume work *Ornithology*, under the author's portrait is a Latin inscription that, when translated, reads, "This is not your likeness Aristotle, but that of Ulysses. The faces are different, yet the mind [*ingenium*] is the same." Born in Bologna, Ulisse

DOI: 10.4324/9781003284284-87

Aldrovandi (1522–1605) was named after the adventurous hero of Homer's epic. He was known to contemporaries as the "Bolognese Aristotle" for his boundless curiosity to discover the secrets of the natural world. The most renowned naturalist of his day started out as a law student at the University of Bologna, and he qualified to practice as a notary. Then he went on to study philosophy, mathematics, and medicine at the University of Padua, later receiving his doctoral degree in philosophy and medicine at the University of Bologna. There Aldrovandi joined a circle of religious reformers, and in 1549, they were all arrested on charges of heresy and taken to Rome to be tried by the Inquisition. Released several months later due to the death of the pope, Aldrovandi returned to Bologna where he taught natural philosophy at the university and was appointed director of its botanical garden.

Over the course of his life, Aldrovandi wrote thousands of manuscript pages and published scholarly tomes on subjects ranging from the natural sciences of botany, dendrology, toxicology, geology, minerology, paleontology, anatomy, embryology, zoology, entomology, ichthyology, and especially ornithology, to broader fields of the humanities such as art history, museology, pedagogy, philosophy, and theology. In his *Discourse on Nature* (*Discorso naturale*), Aldrovandi describes his scientific methodology and explicitly compares himself with Aristotle. He also viewed himself as a kind of Columbus with his discoveries of new and previously unheard of natural phenomena.[2] Aldrovandi wrote a work on abnormalities produced by Nature titled the *Monstrorum historia* (*The History of Monsters*, published posthumously in 1642). Evidence of contemporary fascination with all aspects of nature, but especially the strange and wonderful, is shown in the widespread custom at this time of collecting objects in a cabinet of curiosities (in German often called *Wunderkammer*, or a "wonder-room"). Aldrovandi's cabinet of curiosities was vast, with more than 18,000 specimens, and it was supplemented by a "paper museum" or "theater of nature," as he called it. These were illustrations created by a team of first-rate artists—notably including Jacopo Ligozzi (1547–1627), a favorite of the Medici— of rare plants and animals, many from the New World.[3] Whenever some unusual specimen was found, everyone knew Aldrovandi would want to have it. When on May 13, 1572, a peasant found and killed a terrifying two-footed "dragon" in the countryside near Bologna, he brought it to the naturalist. Natural wonders were often considered prophecies, and it happened that the dragon was discovered the same day Ugo Buoncompagni was elected Pope Gregory XIII. A dragon also figured in the pope's family crest, so his enemies were quick to see this as a bad, even demonic omen. As a central part of the Papal States (**#59**), Bologna was a city dominated by papal politics, so news of the creature spread quickly. Aldrovandi—who was incidentally a relative of Buoncompagni—demonstrated that rather than a satanic portent, the animal was a marvelous natural prodigy, and he exhibited it in his museum. He promptly published a study on dragons titled *Dracologia* and dedicated it to Cardinal Filippo Buoncompagni, nephew to the new pope, attracting the attention of wealthy and powerful patrons in Rome and beyond. Among the admirers of the Bolognese naturalist was Grand Duke Francesco I de' Medici, (r.1574–87). A practitioner of alchemy and an avid collector of natural substances, chemical compounds, as well as plants and animals, Francesco maintained a cordial friendship with Aldrovandi. Over the years the two exchanged many letters filled with scientific information, often accompanied by natural specimens. In a 1578 letter, Aldrovandi describes the "Bolognese dragon." Though it may appear implausible to readers today, it was less so to humanists steeped in Pliny the Elder's (23–79 BCE) descriptions of strange creatures in his *Natural History*, not to mention the many unusual animals being discovered in the New World.

Ulisse Aldrovandi, *Discourse on Nature*, 1572–3

I started considering the nature and differences, both outer and inner, of each natural thing, realizing that the true philosophy was to know openly generation, temperature, nature and faculty of each thing by means of experience. I was aware by Aristotle's witness in the second book of *Posteriora*, that experience originates memories, and memories give rise to universals, which are principles of the Arts and Sciences. True universals are based on the first matters devoid of which the universals are illusion of the bare intellect. Everyone knows that no thing reaches our intellect unless through our outer senses in the process of induction (as witnessed by our Philosopher [Aristotle]). . . . Clearly this natural philosophy of inanimate objects such as earths, stones, gems, marbles, metals, pebbles, and other mixed things, which are found in the bowels of the Earth and at its surface, cannot be known unless by diverse wandering . . . with great personal expenses and bodily exertion I had to see with my own eyes not only all of Italy, but also all of France and Spain and part of the German land with the only aim to have knowledge of these major mysteries of nature which shine in plants, animals and other subterraneous things. . . .

My *Natural History* was truthfully written, not having ever described any thing not previously seen with my own eyes and touched with my own hands, examining the anatomy of both external and internal parts: and preserving each, one by one, in my little natural world, so that everyone at any time can observe and contemplate, all [things] being stored as paintings and samples in our Museum, collected not only while I was a student but principally after my Doctorate in various trips for the benefit of scholars.

[. . .]

It seems to me I have observed many more animals and plants than the Philosopher [Aristotle]; I could observe and collect together ideas and samples of the species produced by the great God for our usefulness out of twelve thousand different things, in spite of not having obtained any assistance as he had from such a great king [Alexander the Great] . . . it takes a lot of labor, expenses and danger for life to acquire knowledge in this science, because to learn it well and perform the true anatomy one needs to be present in the mines and furnaces, otherwise one cannot learn it. I have gone deliberately inside them for checking so many beautiful speculations I had recorded in my *Natural History*. . . .

[*He discusses the role of public teaching in spreading scientific knowledge.*]

We consider in fact that such a public lecture, introduced in the Studios (universities) in our times, will bring innumerable benefits. Students coming from various parts of Europe to listen to this and other disciplines will maintain and expand it continuously because each of them having learned this knowledge will find new things once back home, and so the discipline will augment. I can witness it because many of my own students have sent to me new things I never saw before. The species of natural objects as to our knowledge are infinite for the man who cannot go everywhere. Additionally, the individual man cannot be perfect. However, many can find out different things, which the sciences together will then make perfect. This is the usefulness deriving from this public lecture.

Ulisse Aldrovandi, *Letter to Grand Duke Francesco I*, Sept. 6, 1578

To His Most Serene Highness the Grand Duke of Tuscany, my most revered lord and patron,

Among the four animals painted from life that I am sending Your Most Serene Highness, the first is an Indian fish called *guaicano* or *riverso* by the Indians. This fish is truly strange and marvelous for its behavior and its shape. It resembles the eel and the moray, but its head is much larger and it has there a kind of skin that is like a pouch that the Indian fishermen use for catching fish, just as hunters use quadruped animals like dogs to catch hare, wild boar, and other beasts.

[. . .]

Of the monstrous dragon with two feet

Last year I promised Your Highness that I would send you an image of that terrestrial dragon with two feet, which was killed by a peasant on the very same day that Gregory XIII was elected pontiff [May 13, 1572]. Within two months I had written a Latin treatise in seven books titled *Draconology*, in which I discuss the nature of dragons and their various species, and whether this animal can be termed a dragon, having no wings, and if it can be generated through the coitus of various serpents or the lizard, and of diverse species of snakes. In short, in that work I conclude that this wingless two-legged dragon (let us call it that to distinguish it from the Ethiopian winged dragon with two legs) is a monstrous serpent. And in order to provide Your Highness with a brief outline, I will add a description of it.

The length of this monstrous serpent from the head to the end of its tail was two braccia.[4] The head was similar to that of a viper, and the uppermost part of its head was blackish, the scales of its neck ashen in color, the extremities silvery. The opening of its mouth was the width of two fingers. The tongue was slender, long, and forked like that of other serpents. The teeth of both jaws were fine and tightly meshed fitting together like a saw. In the front part it had no teeth, unlike the viper, however. I believe that it did not contain poison there, which the viper does in concave teeth at the end of which is a tiny venom sac holding toxic rot, which when it bites, is sent forth into the wound. Since our monstrous dragon serpent did not have such teeth, it is unlikely that it had venom there, possessing only teeth on the sides for eating. This is similar to the viper, which has thirty-six teeth on both sides that it uses for mastication, not described by any other writer, but which I have diligently observed through anatomical study. It had rather large eyes in comparison with its body; they were golden-colored and very bright. The holes for its ears were like those of other snakes. Directly beneath the head was a white band that resembled the collar of the banded water snake named for the marking on its neck like certain birds that are called banded ducks or the collared thrush. And it was a beautiful thing to see in this dragon: that collar was perfect, encircling the entire neck, which was two-fingers' wide and its entire shape similar to a viper. Then came its body, its belly, with its back raised like the shell of a tortoise, almost in an arched shape, and at the point where it begins to widen can be seen on each side the two feet, like those of a lizard, though divided into four, rather than five toes. It had rather small nails, indicating that it was a young specimen.

It ought to be noted that from the mouth to the beginning of the wide part of the body was the length of a span, and from that part to the tail another span, and from there to the end of the tail another cubit, so that the entire length was two cubits. And its scales, which covered the entirety of its back, were part green, part rust-colored, part black, their extremities silvery, and in all that part unlike the viper. The tail was very similar to that of the viper, both in color and shape, however, it must be noted that at the end of the tail it was armed with a black pierced stinger, like that of the scorpion. And at the base of that stinger was small sac full of venom that it used, in my judgment, to poison, by striking with that stinger as a scorpion does. Aelian (Book 2, Chapter 26) writes about this same stinger, with which the dragon is armed to defend itself against other animals.[5] This is basically what I have to tell you in particular description of this monstrous serpent.

On the plant called tiger flower

This plant is the tiger flower, also known as *flos tigridis*. It does not originate in Europe, but in America. Its leaves are long and narrow like our iris that is called a lily; its flower is mostly yellow with some red spots. [. . .]

Notes

1 Ruffini writes that "the account was a hoax. The Bolognese naturalist manufactured the supposed dragon in his museum/laboratory by inflating the abdomen of a large serpent and attaching to it the feet of a bird and the head of a fish." 86.

2 "Like many Renaissance naturalists, Aldrovandi avidly read all the literature on the voyages of exploration. He owned two copies of Columbus's letters, and the Italian translations of Oviedo's and Acosta's natural histories of the Indies. . . . 'It is already ten years since I conceived of this fantasy of going to the newly discovered Indies,' he wrote in his *Natural Discourse* in 1572–1573. 'And disregarding every difficulty, I would find a way to make this voyage in the guise of Christopher Columbus.'" Findlen *Possessing Nature* 314.

3 "By about 1595 Aldrovandi's museum contained approximately 8,000 tempera illustrations and fourteen cupboards containing the wood blocks which were used to illustrate his printed works from 1599 onwards. These were in addition to his 11,000 animals, fruits and minerals and 7,000 plants 'dried and pasted' into fifteen volumes. His programme can be viewed as an attempt to transfer the entire world of nature from the often inaccessible outdoors to the restricted interior of a museum." Olmi "Science—Honour—Metaphor" 4.

4 The *braccio* was a form of measurement that equaled .58 of a meter; thus, the dragon would have been 1.16 meters long.

5 Claudius Aelianus (*c.*175–235 CE) Roman author of *On the Characteristics of Animals*, written in Greek.

Sources

Aldrovandi, *Discourse on Nature* in Gian Battista Vai and William Cavazza, "Ulisse Aldrovandi and the Origin of Geology and Science," in *Geological Society of America Special Paper 411*, 2006, 43–63, pp. 48–50.

Aldrovandi, *Letter* in Alessandro Tosi, ed. *Ulisse Aldrovandi e la Toscana: carteggio e testimonianze documentarie*, Olschki, 1989, pp. 254–60, trans. Kaborycha.

References

Bentz, Katherine M. "Ulisse Aldrovandi, Antiquities, and the Roman Inquisition," in *The Sixteenth Century Journal*, Vol. 43, No. 4 (Winter 2012), pp. 963–88.

Daston, Lorraine and Katharine Park. *Wonders and the Order of Nature, 1150–1750*, MIT Press, 1998, Chapter Six "Strange Facts" pp. 215–53.

Findlen, Paula. "The Formation of a Scientific Community: Natural History in Sixteenth-Century Italy," in *Natural Particulars: Nature and the Disciplines in Renaissance Europe*, ed. Anthony Grafton and Nancy Siraisi, MIT Press, 1999, pp. 369–400.

Findlen, Paula. *Possessing Nature: Museums, Collecting, and Scientific Culture in Early Modern Italy*, U California P, 1995.

Groom, Angelica. "Early Modern Science as an Agent for Change in Naturalist Paintings: Jacopo Ligozzi's Zoological Illustrations as a Case Study," in *Knowing Nature in Early Modern Europe*, ed. David Beck, Pickering & Chatto, 2015.

Olmi, Giuseppe. "Science – Honour – Metaphor: Italian Cabinets of the Sixteenth and Seventeenth Centuries," in *The Origins of Museums: The Cabinet of Curiosities in Sixteenth- and Seventeenth-century Europe*, ed. Oliver Impey and Arthur MacGregor, Ashmolean Museum, University of Oxford, 2017.

Ruffini, Marco. "A Dragon for the Pope: Politics and Emblematics at the Court of Gregory XIII," *Memoirs of the American Academy in Rome*, Vol. 54 (2009), pp. 83–105.

Senter, P., L.R.C. Hill and B.J. Moton. "Solution to a 440-Year-Old Zoological Mystery: The Case of Aldrovandi's Dragon," *Annals of Science*, Vol. 70, No. 4 (2013), pp. 531–7.

80 Discovery of an ideal, "nowhere" city

Tommaso Campanella, *The City of the Sun*, 1602

Englishman Thomas More (1478–1535) titled his 1516 book *Utopia*, a name he coined from the Greek words for "not" and "place," meaning "nowhere." Inspired by Plato's *Republic*, it is set on an imaginary island somewhere in the New World, and the tale is told by a fictional Portuguese sailor said to have accompanied Amerigo Vespucci on his voyages. More's *Utopia*, written in Latin, in turn inspired many similar works, specifically in Italy, where it was first translated into Italian in 1548. Before this, there had been thinkers such as the medieval mystic Joachim of Fiore (1135–1202) who envisioned ideal societies based on brotherly love and enlightened principles of freedom and equality. Later, beginning in the sixteenth century, a great number of literary utopias inspired by More began to appear, including Anton Francesco Doni's *Wise and Crazy World* (1552–3), Francesco Patrizi's *Happy City* (1553), and Lodovico Zuccolo's *Republic of Evandria* (1625).[1] The most well-known of these is *The City of the Sun* (written in Italian in 1602, translated into Latin, and published in 1623) by the Dominican friar Tommaso Campanella (1568–1639). Many parallels can be drawn between Campanella's utopian fantasy and More's: both authors envision their ideal societies as following Christ's principles, but unencumbered by religious dogma; they advocate elimination of capital punishment, promote free education, and greater equality for women. The two authors eliminate private property and advocate reducing the hours of the workday—More proposes a six-hour workday, Campanella, four. One significant difference is that More accepts the institution of slavery, while Campanella rejects it. In their City of the Sun, the citizens, known as Solarians, are ruled by a learned philosopher, known as Sun, who is both a spiritual and temporal leader, and under him are three magistrates: Power, Wisdom, and Love. Power is responsible for military affairs, while Wisdom directs scientific projects, and Love, in addition to education, medicine, and agriculture, "has charge of breeding and sees to the coupling of males and females who will produce healthy offspring."[2]

Giovanni Domenico Campanella was born in Calabria, the son of an illiterate cobbler. When he was fourteen years old, the boy joined the Dominican order, where his exceptional memory and quick intelligence thrived; he

DOI: 10.4324/9781003284284-88

took the monastic name Tommaso, after the great Dominican theologian and logician Thomas Aquinas. Reading widely, his unconventional beliefs were judged contrary to Catholic doctrine and repeatedly brought him before the Inquisition. In 1599, Campanella was arrested for having inspired a popular uprising through his prophetic preaching; many of those ideas are expressed in *The City of the Sun*, composed two years later while he was imprisoned in Castel Nuovo.[3] Charged with heresy and conspiracy, Campanella was confined in dungeons, interrogated, and tortured. He would eventually spend twenty-seven years in prison. It was there, in addition to *The City of the Sun*, that he wrote books on topics including astrology, medicine, poetics, rhetoric, politics, theology, metaphysics, and natural philosophy. His thoughts on the latter topic were strongly influenced by the writings of Bernardino Telesio (1509–1588) and Giordano Bruno (#9). Like those philosophers, Campanella explored astrology, magic, Kabbalah, and panpsychism. Campanella especially admired Galileo, whom he had met in 1592. When attacks on Galileo's Copernicanism began, in 1616 Campanella wrote *Apologia pro Galileo* (*Defense of Galileo*, published in Frankfurt in 1622). Though Campanella did not accept heliocentric theory, he was enthusiastic about Galileo's observations of the heavens and supported his right to freedom of expression. After reading Galileo's *Dialogue on the Two World Systems* in 1632, Campanella wrote: "these innovations (*novità*) according to ancient truth, of new worlds, new stars, new systems, new peoples etc. are the beginning of a new age."[4] His prediction proved overly optimistic; the following year, Galileo was brought to trial by the Inquisition and forced to renounce Copernicanism. Both Thomas More and Tommaso Campanella had high hopes for this new age, an age of explorations and discoveries, though neither Campanella, who spent half his adult life imprisoned by the Catholic Church, nor More, who was executed by a Protestant king,[5] was able to enjoy the freedoms they had dreamed of in their imaginary ideal societies.

Tommaso Campanella, *The City of the Sun*, 1602

A Poetical Dialogue between a Grandmaster of the Knights Hospitallers[6] and a Genoese Sea-Captain, his guest

G.M. Prithee, now, tell me what happened to you during that voyage?

Capt. I have already told you how I wandered over the whole Earth. In the course of my journeying I came to Taprobane, and was compelled to go ashore at a place, where through fear of the inhabitants I remained in a wood. When I stepped out of this I found myself on a large plain immediately under the equator.[7]

G.M. And what befell you here?

Capt. I came upon a large crowd of men and armed women, many of whom did not understand our language, and they conducted me forthwith to the City of the Sun.

G.M. Tell me after what plan this city is built and how it is governed?

[*There follows an extended description of the landscape within which the city is situated, the layout of its streets, architectural features, public art, scientific exhibits, etc.*]

G.M. Tell me, please, of the magistrates, their services and duties, of the education and mode of living, whether the government is a monarchy, a republic, or an aristocracy.

Capt. This race of men came there from India, flying from the sword of the Magi, a race of plunderers and tyrants who laid waste their country, and they determined to lead a philosophic life in fellowship with one another. Although the community of wives is not instituted among the other inhabitants of their province, among them it is in use after this manner: All things are common with them, and their dispensation is by the authority of the magistrates. Arts and honors and pleasures are common, and are held in such a manner that no one can appropriate anything to himself.

They say that all private property is acquired and improved for the reason that each one of us by himself has his own home and wife and children. From this, self-love springs. For when we raise a son to riches and dignities, and leave an heir much wealth, we become either ready to grasp at the property of the State—if in any case fear should be removed from the power which belongs to riches and rank—or avaricious, crafty, and hypocritical, if any one is of slender purse, little strength, and mean ancestry. But when we have taken away self-love, there remains only love for the State.

G.M. Under such circumstances no one will be willing to labor, while he expects others to work, on the fruit of whose labors he can live, as Aristotle argues against Plato.[8]

Capt. I do not know how to deal with that argument, but I declare to you that they burn with so great a love for their fatherland, as I could scarcely have believed possible; and indeed with much more than the histories tell us belonged to the Romans, who fell willingly for their country, inasmuch as they have to a greater extent surrendered their private property. I think truly that the friars and monks and clergy of our country, if they were not weakened by love for their kindred and friends, or by the ambition to rise to higher dignities, would be less fond of property, and more imbued with a spirit of charity toward all, as it was in the time of the Apostles, and is now in a great many cases.

G.M. St. Augustine may say that, but I say that among this race of men, friendship is worth nothing; since they have not the chance of conferring mutual benefits on one another.

Capt. Nay, indeed. For it is worth the trouble to see that no one can receive gifts from another. Whatever is necessary they have, they receive it from the community, and the magistrate takes care that no one receives more than he deserves. Yet nothing necessary is denied to anyone. Friendship is recognized among them in war, in infirmity, in the art contests, by which means they aid one another mutually by teaching. Sometimes they improve themselves mutually with praises, with conversation, with actions, and out of the things they need. All those of the same age call one another brothers. They call all over twenty-two years of age, fathers; those who are less than twenty-two are named sons. Moreover, the magistrates govern well, so that no one in the fraternity can do injury to another.

[. . .]

G.M. Tell me the manner in which the magistrates are chosen.

Capt. You would not rightly understand this, unless you first learned their manner of living. That you may know, then, men and women wear the same kind of garment, suited for war. The women wear the toga below the knee, but the men above; and both sexes are instructed in all the arts together. When this has been done as a start, and before their third year, the children[9] learn the language and the alphabet on the walls by walking round them. They have four leaders, and four elders, the first to direct them, the second to teach them, and these are men approved beyond all others. After some time they exercise themselves with gymnastics, running, quoits, and other games, by means of which all their muscles are strengthened alike. Their feet are always bare, and so are their heads as far as the seventh ring. Afterward they lead them to the offices of the trades, such as shoemaking, cooking, metal-working, carpentry, painting, etc. In order to find out the bent of the genius of each one, after their seventh year, when they have already gone through the mathematics on the walls, they take them to the readings of all the sciences.

[. . .]

G.M. I really wish that you would recount all their public duties, and would distinguish between them, and also that you would tell clearly how they are all taught in common.

Capt. They have dwellings in common and dormitories, and couches and other necessaries. But at the end of every six months they are separated by the masters. Some shall sleep in this ring, some in another; some in the first apartment, and some in the second; and these apartments are marked by means of the alphabet on the lintel. There are occupations, mechanical and theoretical, common to both men and women, with this difference, that the occupations which require more hard work, and walking a long distance, are practiced by men, such as plowing, sowing, gathering the fruits, working at the threshing-floor, and perchance at the vintage. But it is customary to choose women for milking the cows, and for making cheese. In like manner, they go to the gardens near to the outskirts of the city both for collecting the plants and for cultivating them. In fact, all sedentary and stationary pursuits are practiced by the women, such as weaving, spinning, sewing, cutting the hair, shaving, dispensing medicines, and making all kinds of garments. They are, however, excluded from working in wood and the manufacture of arms. If a woman is fit to paint, she is not prevented from doing so; nevertheless, music is given over to the women alone, because they please the more, and of a truth to boys also. But the women have not the practice of the drum and the horn. And they prepare their feasts and arrange the tables in the following manner. It is the peculiar work of the boys and girls under twenty to wait at the tables.

[. . .]

G.M. Tell me, I pray you, is there no jealousy among them or disappointment to that one who has not been elected to a magistracy, or to any other dignity to which he aspires?

Capt. Certainly not. For no one wants either necessaries or luxuries. Moreover, the race is managed for the good of the commonwealth and not of private individuals, and the magistrates must be obeyed. . . . Pride they consider the most execrable vice, and one who acts proudly is chastised with the most ruthless correction. Wherefore no one thinks it lowering to wait at table or to work in the kitchen or fields. All work they call discipline, and thus they say that it is honorable to go on foot, to do any act of nature, to see with the eye, and to speak with the tongue; and when there is need, they distinguish philosophically between tears and spittle.

Every man who, when he is told [to go] off to work, does his duty, is considered very honorable. It is not the custom to keep slaves. For they are enough, and more than enough, for themselves. But with us, alas! it is not so. In Naples there exist seventy thousand souls, and out of these scarcely ten or fifteen thousand do any work, and they are always lean from overwork and are getting weaker every day. The rest become a prey to idleness, avarice, ill-health, lasciviousness, usury, and other vices, and contaminate and corrupt very many families by holding them in servitude for their own use, by keeping them in poverty and slavishness, and by imparting to them their own vices. Therefore public slavery ruins them; useful works, in the field, in military service, and in arts, except those which are debasing, are not cultivated, the few who do practice them doing so with much aversion.

But in the City of the Sun, while duty and work is distributed among all, it only falls to each one to work for about four hours every day. The remaining hours are spent in learning joyously, in debating, in reading, in reciting, in writing, in walking, in exercising the mind and body, and with play. They allow no game which is played while sitting, neither the single die nor dice, nor chess, nor others like these. But they play with the ball, with the sack, with the hoop, with wrestling, with hurling at the stake. They say, moreover, that grinding poverty renders men worthless, cunning, sulky, thievish, insidious, vagabonds, liars, false witnesses, etc.; and that wealth makes them insolent, proud, ignorant, traitors, assumers of what they know not, deceivers, boasters, wanting in affection, slanderers, etc. But with them all the rich and poor together make up the community. They are rich because they want nothing, poor because they possess nothing; and consequently they are not slaves to circumstances, but circumstances serve them. And on this point they strongly recommend the religion of the Christians, and especially the life of the Apostles.

Notes

1 These works and others are discussed by Donato.
2 Donno 37.
3 "Many of the statements made by the conspirators during their trial sound almost exactly like passages from the *Città del sole*, which Campanella wrote down two years later in prison." Firpo 167.
4 Headley 342.
5 More was convicted of treason for refusing to sign Henry VIII's 1534 Oath of Succession that gave the king, not the pope, supreme authority.
6 "A knight of Malta or, more fully, a knight of the Order of Hospitallers of St. John in Jerusalem." (DD)
7 "Though some Renaissance maps of Asia situate Taprobana (or Taprobane) below the equator on the island of Sumatra—and this may be the location Campanella has in mind—earlier tradition identifies it with Ceylon." (DD)
8 "In refuting Plato's argument for common ownership of property (*Republic* 462c), Aristotle remarks that such property receives the least attention since men have the greatest concern for what they own privately (*Politics* 1261b)." (DD)
9 The Italian original reads "*fanciulli*," which refers to both boys and girls. Henry Morley translated this word in 1890 as "boys." Here I have substituted the gender neutral "children," following the translation by Donno, p. 41.

Source

Campanella, *The City of the Sun*, in Henry Morley, *Ideal Commonwealths*, Routledge, 1890, ed. Kaborycha.

References

Campanella, Tommaso. *A Defense of Galileo the Mathematician from Florence*, ed. R.J. Blackwell, U Notre Dame P, 1994.

Campanella, Tommaso. *La città del sole: dialogo poetico = The City of the Sun: A Poetical Dialogue*, trans. with introd. and notes by Daniel J. Donno, UC Press, 1981.

Donato, Antonio. *Italian Renaissance Utopias*, Palgrave Macmillan, 2019.

Ernst, Germana. *Tommaso Campanella: The Book and the Body of Nature*, trans. David L. Marshall, Springer, 2010.

Firpo, Luigi. "Renaissance Utopianism," in *The Late Italian Renaissance: 1525–1630*, ed. Eric Cochrane, Macmillan, 1970, pp. 149–67.

Fokkema, Douwe. *Perfect Worlds: Utopian Fiction in China and the West*, Amsterdam UP, 2011.

Headley, John M. *Tommaso Campanella and the Transformation of the World*, Princeton UP, 1997.

Index